Reconciliation and Resistance in Early Modern Spain

Reconciliation and Resistance in Early Modern Spain

Hernando de Baeza and the Catholic Monarchs

Teresa Tinsley

BLOOMSBURY ACADEMIC
LONDON • NEW YORK • OXFORD • NEW DELHI • SYDNEY

BLOOMSBURY ACADEMIC
Bloomsbury Publishing Plc
50 Bedford Square, London, WC1B 3DP, UK
1385 Broadway, New York, NY 10018, USA
29 Earlsfort Terrace, Dublin 2, Ireland

BLOOMSBURY, BLOOMSBURY ACADEMIC and the Diana logo are
trademarks of Bloomsbury Publishing Plc

First published in Great Britain 2022
Paperback edition first published 2024

Copyright © Teresa Tinsley, 2022

Teresa Tinsley has asserted her right under the Copyright,
Designs and Patents Act, 1988, to be identified as Author of this work.

Cover image: Portrait of Tommaso Raimondi 1500 by Amico Aspertini (1474–1552)
Italy (© Peter Horree / Alamy Stock Photo)

All rights reserved. No part of this publication may be reproduced or
transmitted in any form or by any means, electronic or mechanical,
including photocopying, recording, or any information storage or
retrieval system, without prior permission in writing from the publishers.

Bloomsbury Publishing Plc does not have any control over, or responsibility for,
any third-party websites referred to or in this book. All internet addresses given
in this book were correct at the time of going to press. The author and publisher
regret any inconvenience caused if addresses have changed or sites have ceased
to exist, but can accept no responsibility for any such changes.

A catalogue record for this book is available from the British Library.

A catalog record for this book is available from the Library of Congress.

ISBN: HB: 978-1-3502-3277-8
PB: 978-1-3502-3276-1
ePDF: 978-1-3502-3278-5
eBook: 978-1-3502-3280-8

Typeset by Integra Software Services Pvt. Ltd.

To find out more about our authors and books visit www.bloomsbury.com
and sign up for our newsletters.

Porque en poco menos de cincuenta años que he estado en España ninguna cosa más deseé, de ninguna tuve mayor cuidado e ninguna trabajé más continuamente, con más placer mío, que en buscar con mucha diligencia y ver con mis propios ojos todas las cosas grandes y memorables de España.

Lucio Marineo Sículo, c. 1533[1]

Contents

List of illustrations	ix
Foreword by John Edwards	x
Acknowledgements	xiv
List of abbreviations	xvi
Glossary of foreign words	xvii
Maps	xx

	Introduction	1
	Reconciliation	4
	Managing dissidence	5
	Approach and sources	6
1	**Cordoba, the frontier and the Inquisition, 1450–87**	9
	Competing visions for Christianizing Iberia	9
	Cordoban *conversos*	12
	Civil war in Castile, 1465–8	14
	Anti-converso riots, 1473	16
	The Inquisition comes to Cordoba	19
	The frontier with Granada – cross-cultural contacts and values	22
2	**The conquest of Granada**	25
	The first phase of the war, 1482–8	25
	Changing alliances	28
	Ambassadors, spies and mediators	32
	The bias of surviving historical record	35
	The terms of surrender	38
	Celebrations of the conquest	42
	From propaganda to historiography	43
3	**Among the Andalusian élite**	47
	Reconciliation	47
	Rehabilitation	48
	Matrimonial strategies	49
	The new Marquisate of Priego	51
	Servants and masters	52

	The intellectual world surrounding Hernando de Baeza	55
	Gonzalo Fernández de Córdoba	56
	Vatican intermediary	57
	Conclusion	59
4	**The Spanish in Italy**	**61**
	The conquest of Naples	61
	The papal conclaves of 1503	64
	The capture of Cesare Borgia	68
	The schismatic Cardinal Carvajal	71
	Diplomacy in the succession crisis	72
	The conflict between the *Gran Capitán* and Fernando of Aragon	76
	Fernando in Naples	79
	Conclusion	81
5	**Reconciliation and resistance to Fernando as governor of Castile**	**83**
	Lucero and the intensification of Inquisition activity	83
	The campaign against Lucero	86
	The pursuit of ecclesiastical benefices	90
	The 'rebellion' of the Marquis of Priego	93
	Hernando de Baeza and the wider ideological struggle	96
6	**Genesis of the memoir**	**99**
	Baeza's Granada	99
	Date of writing	100
	The manuscripts	102
	Baeza and Pulgar	104
	Baeza's connection with other chroniclers	106
	Baeza's work in its historiographical context	109
7	**Castile in the mirror: A resistance narrative of the conquest of Granada**	**113**
	Representations of the Catholic Monarchs	113
	Moors and Christians	116
	Conversos 'under erasure'	120
	Conclusion	123

Hernando de Baeza's history of Granada (translation)	125
Notes	147
Selected bibliography	191
Index	200

Illustrations

1	Iberia c. 1480	xx
2	Andalusia – main locations cited	xxi
3	*La Fuente de la Gracia* by Jan van Eyck	11
4	The family of Hernando de Baeza – genealogical chart	12
5	Statue of Boabdil by Salvador Amaya	26
6	Addendum to Hernando de Baeza's letter to the Marquis of Priego, 1504	53
7	The *Gran Capitán* in Naples from *Cronaca della Napoli aragonese*, c. 1498	62
8	Italy – main locations cited	64
9	Sixteenth-century ceramic tile with the Count of Cabra's coat of arms	91
10	Initial page of the El Escorial manuscript	103
11	*The Catholic Monarchs with Saint Helena and Saint Barbara*, Maestro de Manzanillo (detail)	114

Foreword

Sometimes, a historical figure manages to be everywhere, and do anything, without being noticed by most people, either during their lifetime or subsequently, and such is the case of the subject of Teresa Tinsley's new study.

Hernando de Baeza, of Jewish origin but himself a Catholic Christian, was born in the 1450s, in the Andalusian city of Cordoba. Since at least the 1420s, his relatives, who were of middling social rank and wealth, had devoted themselves to public service in their home city and they would continue on this path for many years thereafter. Hernando de Baeza became a servant and close associate of the leading members of the main branch of the Fernández de Córdoba family who often fought each other for control of both that city and its surrounding region, in the late fifteenth and early sixteenth centuries. Hernando began by working for the head of the family, Don Alonso de Aguilar, who, as well as being lord of numerous estates in the area, was chief magistrate (*alcalde mayor*) of Cordoba, and then moving on to serve Don Alonso's brother, Gonzalo Fernández de Córdoba, later known as the Great Captain (*Gran Capitán*) for his military exploits in the Christian conquest of Granada and later in Italy. Later, Hernando went on to serve Don Alonso's son and heir, Don Pedro Fernández de Córdoba, who received the title of Marquis of Priego. As Teresa Tinsley points out, being designated as a *criado* (literally a servant) of that family, Hernando de Baeza was far more than a menial functionary, and rather a confidant of his lord at the time, which meant that, during his varied and eventful career, he came into personal contact with many leading figures of the age, in Spain and also Italy.

By the time that he died, probably in about 1511 as this study indicates, Hernando had lived through an often bewildering, and sometimes almost overwhelming, sequence of events, in his native city of Cordoba, in the wider region of Andalusia, in Spain as a whole, in the rest of Europe, especially Rome and the kingdom of Naples, and even, to some extent, the rest of the world, including the Spanish 'discovery' of Caribbean islands and the coasts of the American mainland, and Portuguese voyages to India and East Asia.

Hernando de Baeza's family, like thousands of other formerly Jewish families in Spain, for ever after had hanging over them the terrible attacks on the established Jewish inhabitants of most of Spain's main cities, including Cordoba, in the summer of 1391. These had been precipitated by the violently anti-Jewish preaching of the then Archdeacon of Écija and current administrator of the vacant archdiocesan see of Seville, Ferrán Martínez. In Cordoba, as elsewhere in the various kingdoms of Castile and Aragon, Jews of all ages had their property attacked and often destroyed, and in dozens of cases lost their lives. Also, with long-term consequences for Spain and anywhere Spaniards travelled and settled thereafter, large numbers of Jews were baptized as Catholic Christians, with the consent of the Church, which allowed the perceived intrinsic power of that sacrament to prevail over any notion, in most cases, of personal consent and commitment to the Christian faith.

Teresa Tinsley, who is deeply aware of the historical, and indeed the moral, dimensions of the Baeza family history, follows its successive generations from the consequences of the violence of 1391, through the conversion of the family to Christianity, to the campaign to discredit the 'new' Christians, which got under way around 1450, and finally to the establishment, from 1478 onwards, by Pope Sixtus IV but at the request of Isabel and Fernando of Castile and Aragon, of a new foundation of the Holy Inquisition. A tribunal was set up in Cordoba in 1480 and started work two years later, with immediate and drastic consequences for the city's Christians of Jewish origin, even though their conversion had taken place several generations back. These people were commonly known as *Cristianos nuevos* or *conversos* (converts), even if they had never themselves been Jews. It became clear, right from the start of the inquisitors' campaign, that there were social and economic, as well as the obvious religious, aspects to this often violent offensive, which led to loss of property and all too often of lives. As Tinsley shows, Hernando de Baeza's family was an obvious target for this assault, given its deep involvement both in the municipal government and in its service to the city and region's leading nobles. Although Hernando himself escaped with his life at this time, some of his closest relatives were less fortunate. Thus, his family had its own existential struggle, in addition to being caught inevitably in the complex factional politics of the city of Cordoba itself, consisting of conflict between the leading noble families and their attempts to keep the authority of the Crown at bay. But there were yet more dimensions to Hernando de Baeza's life.

Like other large fifteenth- and early sixteenth-century towns, the municipal council (*cabildo*) of Cordoba administered a scattering of surrounding smaller towns and villages, together with agricultural lands and other resources, on behalf of the Crown, and this situation inevitably produced spasmodic conflict between the municipality and neighbouring lords (*señores*). These included Don Alonso de Aguilar and his son and heir the Marquis of Priego, whom Hernando served successively, and who both also had a substantial social and political presence in the city itself. In addition, looming over the whole region during Hernando de Baeza's lifetime, was the centuries-old conflict, often in stalemate but sometimes warlike, between the Christian 'Crown' of Castile and the Muslim Nasrid Emirate of Granada, which became a main focus of Hernando's life and forms the core of this book. Teresa Tinsley here provides the first English translation of his own 'Memoir' of the last days of Nasrid Granada, based on her careful collation of the surviving, and varying, manuscript versions of the text. This unusual work, which has often been cited previously but never before fully studied, is based on Hernando's experience as an Arabic-speaking Castilian envoy to the last Emirs. It demonstrates, as the present author points out, an extraordinary breadth of comprehension of, and sympathy for, Muslim political and religious life, as acted out in the period up to the formal surrender of Granada to Queen Isabel of Castile and King Fernando of Aragon, at the beginning of January 1492. In her acute and detailed analysis of Hernando's text, Tinsley rightly focuses on the author's sometimes more than implicit criticism of the generally intolerant attitudes of Christian Spaniards, including secular rulers and senior churchmen, towards Muslims in Spain, and Islam as a religion. Hernando's rare and fascinating approach to these matters focuses in particular on the question of what would happen, after the Christian victory and conquest, to the former Christians, known as *elches*, who had been living under Nasrid rule up to that point. Some of these may in fact have chosen to become Muslims, having fled, for whatever reason, from Christian territory, but Hernando, unlike many of his Castilian compatriots, was evidently aware that Christian captives were commonly forced to become Muslims, whatever their personal views. This was a problem which would continue to haunt Spaniards well into the modern period, in the context of North African piracy, in both the Atlantic and the Mediterranean. The most remarkable feature of Hernando de Baeza's memoir is, however, his ability to go beyond these obvious circumstances and recognize that some Christians may actually have *wanted* to become Muslims out of a positive attachment to that religion, as represented by pre-1492 Granada as a uniquely Islamic territory in the Iberian Peninsula. Tinsley rightly places this phenomenon in the context of the attempts by the first Catholic Archbishop of Granada after the 1492 conquest, Friar Hernando de Talavera, to win Muslims over to Christianity by persuasion, rather than the brute force that would be applied after 1500.

Hernando's memoir is of course the centre and heart of this study, but it is by no means the only fascinating aspect of his life which Teresa Tinsley is able to highlight, by means of painstaking documentary research. Before the final Christian victory in Granada, Hernando de Baeza had entered the service of Don Alonso's brother Gonzalo, who was later known as the 'Great Captain' for his military exploits in Italy as well as Spain. Having acquired high-level diplomatic experience in the last days of the Granadan Emirate, Hernando proceeded to apply his skills and insights in the midst of the complex Italian politics of the period, thus meeting Popes and Cardinals, and participating in diplomacy on an international scale. This meant that, in the last decade of his life, he played a quite prominent role in the equally difficult politics of Spain, after the death of Queen Isabel 'the Catholic' in November 1504. Returning to his homeland, he found himself back in still-fractious political and social affairs of his native city and country, including the controversy that surrounded his family's old enemy, the Inquisition.

Only recently have scholars begun to question the traditional narrative of Spanish history between 1504 and January 1516, when Isabel and Fernando's eldest grandchild, Charles, became King of both Castile and Aragon. Hernando de Baeza's home town of Cordoba was prominent in the conflict over the Castilian succession, in which Fernando tried, contrary to the provisions of his late wife's will, to retain power in Spain, using the excuse that his daughter and successor, there, Juana, was supposedly mentally unfit to govern. Between November 1504 and September 1506, Juana reigned with her Habsburg husband Philip, but after he died unexpectedly, conflict broke out again, and would outlast Hernando de Baeza's death. In the meantime, not only did the Cordoban's family continue to be enmeshed with the controversy of the Inquisition, in which its tribunal in that city played a crucial role, but Hernando and his surviving family were inevitably affected by the ensuing bitter conflict between Fernando and the senior line of the Fernández de Córdoba family, in the persons of the Marquis of Priego and the Great Captain. On top of all this, Hernando managed to find time to revisit Granada, witness the beginnings of the city and kingdom's 'Christianization' and draw up the memoir which prompted this fascinating and commendable study of the life and times of an equally interesting Spaniard. As Teresa Tinsley rightly says, Hernando de Baeza, whose traditional loyalties combined with his serious questioning of the traditional religious certainties of his age, beautifully focuses the tensions that were affecting all of European society in the years up to and after 1500.

JOHN EDWARDS
University of Oxford, UK

Acknowledgements

This book is dedicated to the memory of Professor Simon Barton, whom I tracked down at a very early stage in my interest in undertaking historical research as one of the few British historians who would be able to supervise a PhD thesis on interfaith relations emerging from medieval Spain. I could not have hit upon a more supportive and inspirational person than Simon. I count myself truly fortunate in finding someone who was able to understand my motivation and channel it gently and productively. He shared my excitement at each discovery I made and was able to combine a delight in small details with an immediate understanding of how things might fit into a bigger picture. His untimely death as I was entering the final stages of completing my research was a sad and shocking blow and continues to be felt very keenly. I am extremely grateful to Professor Maria Fusaro who, in such difficult circumstances, took on the role of supervisor, and has been constantly supportive. My thesis buddy Stephen Lynam continues to be an unfailing source of wisdom and encouragement and must also receive my heartfelt thanks.

I was delighted when Dr John Edwards agreed to write the foreword to this book, since in searching for secondary sources to enlighten my work I found myself consulting his own extensive research on so many occasions. The ideas contained therein invariably chimed with my own unformed findings and deepened my understanding of my subject and his milieu. I am therefore sincerely grateful to him not only for his contribution here but also for an exceptionally rich and thought-provoking body of work on which I have been able to build.

The research which underpins this book has been made possible by the dedication and expertise of those who have patiently attended to me in the many archives I have visited. Among these, the following have been outstanding for the help they have provided: Amalia García Pedraza (Archivo de Protocolos Notariales de Granada), Patxi Guerrero (Archivo Ducal de Medinaceli), Antonio Luis Jiménez Barranco (Archivo de Protocolos Notariales de Montilla). I am also extremely grateful to Professor Miguel Angel Ladero for his advice and access to documents at the Real Academia de la Historia.

I would also like to thank Angel Ruiz Gálvez, Enrique Soria Mesa and the late Joaquín Zejalbo, for sharing genealogical sources; Antonio Díaz Rodríguez, José Rodríguez Molina and Hugo Vázquez for help with palaeographical conundrums; and Mercedes Delgado, Alvaro Fernández de Córdova Miralles, José Antonio Ollero and José María Ruiz Povedano for sharing work in progress. Wholehearted thanks also go to the following whose wisdom and kind responses to my queries have fed into this book: Amparo López Arandia, Roger Boase, Simon Doubleday, Soledad Gómez Navarro, Javier López Rider, Levi Roach, Juan Pablo Rodríguez Argente del Castillo, Manuel Vaquero Piñeiro, Ramón Vega Pinella, Francisco Vidal, Rosa Vidal, Alun

Williams, Teresa Witcombe, Josef Ženka and the anonymous reviewers at Bloomsbury. I must also mention the sculptor Salvador Amaya for his kindness in providing me with photographs of his work.

Finally, huge thanks must go to my husband, Keith Colley, for his unfailing support and patience, his good-natured company on so many research trips and his willingness to share our marriage for so many years with Hernando de Baeza.

Abbreviations

ACS	Archivo de la Catedral de Sevilla
ADM	Archivo Ducal de Medinaceli
AGA	Archivo General de Andalucía
AGS	Archivo General de Simancas
AHMA	Archivo Histórico Municipal de Antequera
AHN	Archivo Histórico Nacional
AHNOB	Archivo Histórico de la Nobleza
AHPC	Archivo Histórico Provincial de Córdoba
AHPS	Archivo Histórico Provincial de Sevilla
AMC	Archivo Municipal de Córdoba
APNG	Archivo de Protocolos Notariales de Granada
APNM	Archivo de Protocolos Notariales de Montilla
ASV	Archivio Segreto Vaticano
AZ	Archivo y Biblioteca Francisco Zabálburu
BRAC	Boletín de la Real Academia de Córdoba
BRAH	Boletín de la Real Academia de Historia
CEHGR	(Revista del) Centro de Estudios Históricos de Granada y su Reino
CODOIN	Colección de Documentos Inéditos para la Historia de España (series of 113 volumes published between 1842 and 1895)
DBE	Diccionario Biográfico Electrónico (published by the Real Academia de la Historia)
HEMP	Historia de España de Menéndez Pelayo
HID	Historia, Instituciones, Documentos (Journal)
IVDJ	Instituto de Valencia Don Juan
LEG (Leg.)	Legajo = file of documents[2]
MEAH	Miscelánea de Estudios Arabes y Hebréos (Journal)
RAH	Real Academia de la Historia
RB	Real Biblioteca de Madrid
RBME	Real Biblioteca del Monasterio de El Escorial
RGS	Registro General del Sello

Glossary of foreign words

alcaide	commander, usually of a fortress
Alcaide de los Donceles	a position in the Castilian royal court, largely honorary in the period under consideration, held by a branch of the Fernández de Córdoba family
alcalde, alcalde mayor	magistrate, chief justice
alcázar	castle, fortress
alfaqui (mayor)	(chief) professional theologian, expert in Islamic law
alguazil (mayor)	(chief) constable
alhaqueque (mayor)	(chief) person responsible for arranging the ransom of captives across borders
Almirante de Castilla	senior position in the Castilian royal court, largely honorary in the period under consideration, held by the Enríquez family
almojarifazgo	import duty
auto de fe	public ceremony penancing condemned heretics
caballero	high-ranking person, lit. one who rides a horse
capitulaciones	(clauses of) a treaty or legal agreement
chantre, chantría	precentor (church dignitary), precentorship
comunero	member of the rebel movement which rose up against Charles V in 1520
condottiero	(Italian) a captain in charge of a mercenary fighting unit
contador	accountant, financial administrator
converso	convert to Christianity, a Christian of non-Christian heritage
convivencia	Lit. living together, co-existence
corregidor	chief magistrate appointed by the Crown
criado	servant, retainer
Curia	papal court/governing council

ducado	unit of currency equivalent to 375 *maravedís*
elche	Christian convert to Islam
encomienda	system of parcelling out access to the labour and taxes of native peoples of the New World
escribano, escribano mayor	notary, Town Clerk, notaryship
gonfalonier	captain of the papal army
Gran Capitán	Lit. 'great captain', honorary title given to Gonzalo Fernández de Córdoba
hidalgo	untitled person with some claim to noble blood
infante	Prince
judeoconverso	Christian of Jewish origin
jurado	parish representative on town council
letrado	lawyer, person with a university degree
Licenciado	person with a higher-level degree
limpieza de sangre	the concept of blood purity – that is, not of Jewish or Moorish descent, or having had ancestors condemned for heresy
maravedí	unit of currency
mayordomo	steward, administrator (esp. of property)
mayordomo de los propios	official position with responsibility for managing a town council's assets
mizwar	(Arabic) chief justice, bodyguard (according to Baeza)
morería	Muslim district of a town or city
morisco	Christian of Muslim descent
moro	'Moor' – see discussion in text pp. 117–18
mudéjar	Muslim living in Christian territory
nuncio	papal ambassador
reconciliado	repentant heretic received back into the Catholic Church
Reconquista	the ideology based on the idea of Iberian medieval history as the progressive recovery of lands occupied by Muslim invaders
sefardí	Iberian Jewry

trujumán	person working across different languages as a mediator or interpreter
umma	the whole community of Muslims
vega	the rich agricultural plain outside Granada
veinticuatro	alderman, member of city/town council

Maps

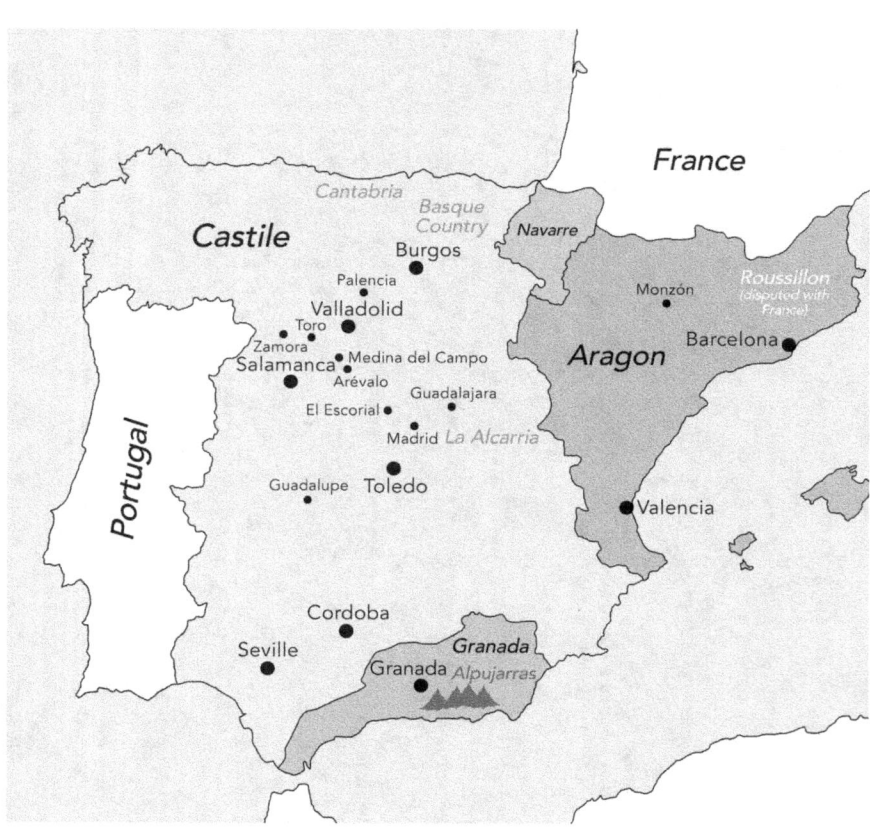

Image 1 Iberia c. 1480. © Teresa Tinsley.

Maps xxi

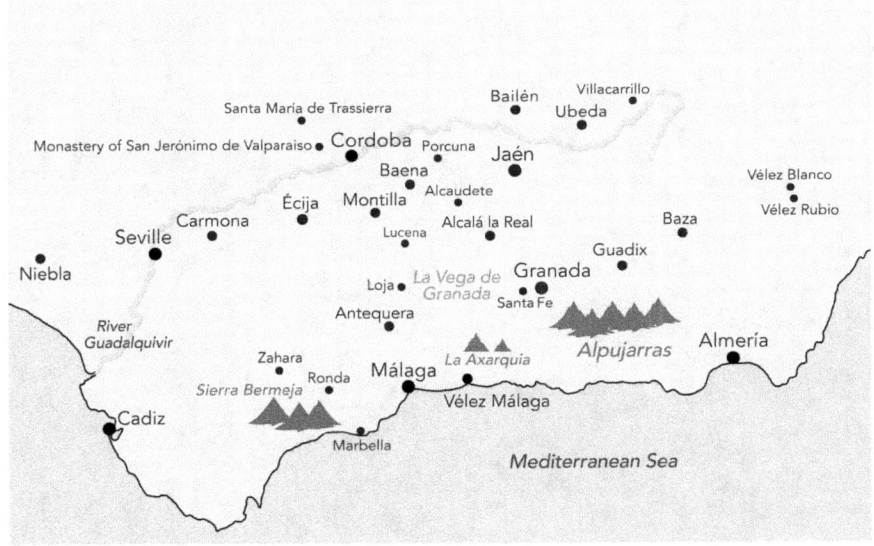

Image 2 Andalusia – main locations cited. © Teresa Tinsley.

Introduction

Granada, November 1491. The forces of Isabel of Castile and Fernando of Aragon are camped outside the city walls. Neither side wants to endure a winter of siege. Both understand that they are on the verge of a transcendental moment in history, when what is left of the last Muslim kingdom of medieval Iberia will fall to the Christians. Surrender negotiations have been going on for some time, with messengers and envoys on both sides making their way across enemy lines to discuss terms. Inside the Alhambra, one of the intermediaries welcomes two senior negotiators from the Christian side into the presence of the emir, Abū ʿAbd Allāh Muhammad – the man known to European history as 'Boabdil'.[1] Only two final details remained to be resolved. One is about what part Boabdil will play in the surrender ceremony that has been planned. He is determined not to be humiliated by making a public act of obeisance to the monarchs. That is easily resolved. The other is about more than symbolism. It concerns the status of former Christians living in Granada who have become Islamicized. Should they be forced to return to Christianity? Recalling the scene some twenty years later, our intermediary, Hernando de Baeza, wrote: 'it seemed to me, although I was nothing there, that [this] should not rightfully be done'.[2]

With this laconic comment, Baeza opens a window on the imposition of Christianity on multi-faith Iberia and a controversy which would soon be extended to the indigenous populations of the New World. At that stage in the negotiations for Granada, the monarchs had already agreed that Muslims should be allowed to continue to practise their religion, along with the legal and cultural norms associated with it. This was in line with the surrender treaties of other towns during the Granada War and longstanding practice during the conquest of al-Ándalus, by which Muslim subjects were incorporated into Christian society as *mudéjars*.[3] However, by the time Baeza was writing, in around 1510, Granadan Muslims had already lost those rights, having been forced to emigrate or accept baptism at around the turn of the half millennium.[4] The group whose rights were being disputed was the *elches* – baptized Christians living in Granada who had adopted Islam, often as a result of having been brought there in childhood as captives. Having been baptized as infants they were, in the eyes of the Catholic Church, apostates, but from the point of view of the Muslims they were irrevocably part of the *umma*, deserving of the same rights and respect as all members of the Islamic community. Conscious of his own vulnerability in revealing his partisanship, Baeza understands both sides and, as a way of reconciling the competing positions of the Catholic hierarchy and Islamic law, advocates the pragmatic solution which had governed frontier practice for centuries: respect for the free will of the individual.[5]

In speaking out against coercion in the definition of religious identity, Baeza enters a live polemic, implicitly recalling the experience of Spain's Jews, the majority of whom had been forcibly converted a century before, only for their descendants to suffer persecution at the hands of the Inquisition, established by the monarchs in 1480–2.[6] Baeza's statement is a clear assertion of alignment with the idealists in this polemic, who valued inner conviction over the idea that souls could be saved through the rigorous application of canon law and hoped that universal Christianity would come through people of other faiths turning to Christ through their own volition. It is a position which reflects a new current of spirituality developed and disseminated by Castilian humanist thinkers in the second half of the fifteenth century, predating that associated with Erasmus of Rotterdam.[7]

Baeza's declaration in favour of religious self-determination is full of significance for other reasons too. It is testament to the diversity and fluidity of religious adherenc on the Granadan frontier – rather than an irresistible onward march of Christianity there was 'conversion' and 'reconversion' in multiple directions in a population possessed of a complex array of faith identities. As the monarchs approached the negotiations with the Granadan emir and his ministers, and considered the sort of society they were about to create, there were different options on the table and different pathways to Christianization open to them. Baeza's cautious statement illustrates the circumspection with which supporters of more lenient positions were approaching issues of religious coercion. He claims that he was 'nothing there', but there is defiance as well as deference for traditional hierarchies in his act of assertion. It exposes a tension between consciousness of his own social inferiority and the deliberate espousal of the cause of a new social group, between reticence and self-affirmation, between humility and boldness. This tension seems to be a useful way in to understanding the options and struggles of that turbulent period of transition, and how individuals managed the expression of opposition, even dissent, in the Spain of the Catholic Monarchs, and perhaps in early modern Europe more widely.[8]

Baeza's short work – published here for the first time in English – is in no way presented as a polemic, but rather as a history of the decline and fall of the Muslim kingdom of Granada, written to recount – in his own words – 'the things that happened', in the manner of a royal chronicle. It is an integrated history, alternating between the 'Moorish' and Christian perspective in describing battles, drawing attention to the failings of the last Nasrid emirs, and seeking parallels between the two sides rather than highlighting difference. As he put pen to paper, a new, exclusively Christian society was under construction. How the conquest of Granada was conceptualized and exploited in that process would impact on questions of religious toleration, national identity and human rights which are still fundamental issues for us in the twenty-first century.

As is well known, the surrender of Granada was followed, just a few weeks later, by the Edict of Expulsion which forced all Jews remaining in Castile and Aragon to convert or go into exile. But the construction of Catholic Spain and the suppression of non-Christian religious practices went hand in hand with many other changes during

Isabel and Fernando's reign in that extraordinary period of discoveries, divergence and religious idealism straddling the fifteenth and sixteenth centuries. It was a time of increased trade and urbanization and of printing, learning and creativity which disrupted the ascendency of the aristocracy and brought their values into question. New thinking and new possibilities not only fed the ambitions of monarchs and popes, but also gave rise to critical analyses of their growing power and of established dogma. Across Europe, monarchs sought to expand their territories, increase their power and amplify their influence through alliance-making, war-making and the projection of idealized representations of themselves. Their ambassadors and envoys in Rome and in the courts of their rivals were active in managing these representations and in the ongoing construction of their sovereign's 'nations'.[9] Across Castile, after the chaotic years of the mid-fifteenth century, the idea of a strong monarchy had enjoyed widespread support; however, the authoritarian, absolutizing version of it – especially as adopted by Fernando of Aragon after Isabel's death in 1504 – gave rise to resistance. Members of the nobility in particular were aggrieved on account of privileges lost as the monarchs drew power to themselves.[10] It was in Andalusia, conditioned by its position on the frontier with Islam and already identified as a separate region within Castile, where these grievances were felt most bitterly and where resistance to Fernando's governorship after the death of Isabel was strongest. And it was in Cordoba where that resistance reached its apogee in a conflict closely linked to the issue of faith identity and the treatment of people whose families had descended from Jews.

Hernando de Baeza was an active player in all this. A high status *judeoconverso* from Cordoba, Baeza grew up under the protection of the Fernández de Córdoba family, lords of Aguilar, whose vast estates adjoined the kingdom of Granada.[11] His father, uncles and cousins were all condemned to death in the early years of the Inquisition for 'following the Law of Moses' but, despite the ignominy attaching to his family, he went on to enjoy a distinguished career in the service of Gonzalo Fernández de Córdoba, dubbed the *Gran Capitán*, second son of the lordly family, who conquered the kingdom of Naples and became its Viceroy under Fernando. Baeza intervened in various key episodes of international politics as his secretary and representative and was able to observe parallels and disparities between the conquest of Naples and that of Granada twelve years earlier. It was after this Italian interlude that Baeza wrote his short personal account of the final years of the Islamic regime, including his own experiences as an intermediary between Boabdil and the Spanish monarchs. His version of events eschews the *Reconquista* ideology and glorification of Isabel and Fernando which pervade other contemporary accounts of the Christian conquest of Granada. It also resists the ascendant *limpieza de sangre* doctrine which came to dominate and distort Spanish society in its Golden Age – and led to the expulsion of the *moriscos* in 1609–14. It must be read as intentional contribution to ongoing debates surrounding the construction of Catholic Spain and as an expression of discreet criticism of the surviving monarch.

Baeza's life and work therefore provide an exceptionally useful lens for taking a fresh look at some of the most significant events of the period and exploring the opposing qualities of reconciliation and resistance in an age which begged reform yet demanded increasing conformity.

Reconciliation

I have already used the word 'reconciliation' in its general sense of establishing compatibility between opposed positions; it can mean either compromise by both parties or, more frequently in the period under consideration, submission by the weaker party to the stronger one. In this book it also has a specific meaning in relation to the workings of the Spanish Inquisition. In the elaborate, terrifying ritual of the *auto de fe*, not all prisoners were condemned to public burning. Those whose sins were deemed to be minor or insufficiently proven were 'reconciled' and admitted back into the Catholic Church. The public degradation of these individuals as redeemed sinners added to the macabre drama of ceremony, shot through with allusions to the Last Judgement.[12] *Reconciliados* were banned from wearing gold or jewels, carrying arms or occupying public offices and they were kept under ongoing scrutiny to ensure they fulfilled the conditions of their penances and lived unblemished Christian lives. Any deviation from the terms of their reconciliation meant they were treated as relapsed heretics and forced to submit to the 'correction and severity of the sacred canons'.[13]

The Inquisition has come to symbolize the violent, exclusionary brand of Christianity associated with the 'Black Legend' of Spain as told by Protestant historians. It was established by the Catholic Monarchs as a response to violence and resentment against *conversos* and the fear that individuals were returning to Jewish beliefs and practices, representing a grievous danger to Christian society. The institution broke new ground in extending the limits of monarchical power, since the Inquisitors were appointed by the crown, rather than by the Pope, and the property they confiscated from those accused was received into the royal exchequer.[14] So behind the awe-inspiring pageant of the *auto de fe* there lurked the spectre of royal power and an uncertain distinction between temporal and religious authority. While religious transgressions such as schism, heresy and sacrilege could be framed as crimes against the state, political dissent could be presented as heresy.[15]

But hindsight can impose a spurious logic. The creation of an Inquisition did not in itself necessitate an extreme persecuting ideology, nor did the Catholic Monarchs always adopt one. There were other paths and other possibilities open to them – and actively propounded by those close to them. The expulsion of the Jews, forced baptism of Muslims and persecution of the descendants of converts on the basis of their genealogical origins may have all derived from the same ideological base, but they were not part of a pre-planned programme for the Christianization of their realms. Different positions competed for influence, as demonstrated powerfully in Baeza's account of the negotiations surrounding the conditions for the surrender of Granada. It behoves us to examine alternative paths and programmes which were 'on the table' in 'the Spains which might have been' – in order to explore how people were attempting to make sense of their world, and why certain ideas achieved supremacy while others did not prevail.[16] It is in the stories of failed influencers, dissenters and critics, who in their day hoped for a different future, that we can better understand the tensions, compromises and competing interests which underlay the construction of modern Spain.

Managing dissidence

How might an individual in Hernando de Baeza's position balance resistance with reconciliation? How he might handle his own non-conformity, even dissidence, while still managing to survive, lead a successful career and find space to make the case for a more compassionate use of power in the Spain of the Catholic Monarchs?

Baeza dedicates two pages at the beginning of his short work to exemplifying this dilemma.[17] He describes how a high-ranking servant of the emir Abū al-Ḥasan (Boabdil's father, reigned 1464–82) spoke out against his sovereign for having repudiated his queen of noble blood in favour of a Christian slave girl. Despite repeated warnings and inducements, the courtier declares valiantly that he would rather pluck out his own eye than imagine he could ever love or honour such a man. Baeza portrays him as an honourable objector, nobly defending his values; however, the consequences he describes contain a lesson on the futility of such reckless dissidence. 'Kill the unbeliever', Baeza has the emir saying as he orders the man's execution – words which would have had a powerful resonance for the author and his readers, especially as ballad which is thought to mention the same incident links it to asylum given in Granada to the 'Jews of Cordoba' around the time of the 1473 pogroms.[18] Baeza's tale is an invitation to reflect on the limits of unbending adherence to principle in the face of a monarch who wields the power of life and death. 'I know his Highness is here on earth in the place of God,' says the stubborn courtier, in a baleful echo of the messianic aura surrounding the Catholic Monarchs which blurred the difference between divine and temporal power.[19] There are other passages too where Baeza presents at some length the dilemmas of courtiers impelled to speak truth to power.[20]

Hernando de Baeza's life history is closely bound up with the multiple processes by which Catholic Spain took shape out of multi-faith Iberia: the evolution from an array of medieval kingdoms to the hub of an empire, the mass conversions of Jews and Muslims, the emergence of new conceptions of spirituality and political consciousness and the Inquisition's role in policing orthodoxy. But this is not the story of a redeemed *converso* climbing his way back up the social ladder. The stance that Baeza adopts in relation to the *elches* and the tyranny of Abū al-Ḥasan is not uniquely attributable to his *converso* condition, but to other varied experiences which shaped his world. It was powerfully conditioned by his role as an intimate protégé of the free-thinking and often rebellious House of Aguilar, the Fernández de Córdoba family, whose role was to defend and manage a frontier at the extreme end of the Christian world.[21] For the Fernández de Córdoba's, interchange with people of other faiths was an essential part of delivering justice, minimizing damage to people and property from raiding, enabling diplomatic relations and ransoming and exchanging captives. This put Baeza in the front line of contact with merchants, envoys, emigrés and multilingual mediators. He himself was an Arabic speaker and fulfilled this latter role in Boabdil's court. It was in the service of the Fernández de Córdobas that he gained the skills and dispositions that enabled him to be a credible go-between with the Catholic Monarchs and later to write about it in the way he did: knowledge of court protocol, political sensitivity, chivalric ideas and values, and access to humanist literature and learning. While in Italy and as Gonzalo

Fernández de Córdoba's representative, he came into contact with intellectuals and churchmen in the Roman Curia, patrons of art and literature, diplomats and envoys from across Europe, who further sharpened his political consciousness and exposed him to the new ideas and new thinking which were shaping this critical period of change and transition. Finally, he was also a father, a widower seeking to secure the status of his sons and daughters after his death.

The presence of *converso* élites in the court of Isabel of Castile is well known.[22] Baeza knew and worked with the chronicler Fernando del Pulgar, the royal secretary Hernando de Zafra and most probably also Hernando de Talavera, the first Archbishop of Granada. His work contains a highly significant quotation from Juan de Mena, the *converso* court poet from the time of Juan II.[23] Just as the nobility and high-ranking clergy imitated royalty by creating their own 'courts', so these figures would have been the role models that Baeza aspired to as a high-ranking servant of the Fernández de Córdobas. Like Fernando del Pulgar, Baeza rose from secretary to diplomat and chronicler – although unlike the royal chronicler he did not have the benefit of a background in Latin.[24] Like Bishop Arias Davila, Pedro de Aranda and other *conversos* under suspicion from the Inquisition in Castile, Baeza found that Italy, and proximity to the Vatican, offered protection and a more propitious climate for advancement: he can be documented there with Gonzalo Fernández de Córdoba in 1497 and again from 1503 to 1507.[25] Hernando de Baeza's trajectory is a close parallel with that of Baltasar del Río, another Andalusian ex patriate who also started his career as a secretary and shrugged off the stigma of his family's heresy under the protection of a noble family.[26] Del Río's satirical treatise on courtly life in Rome is exactly contemporaneous with the time Baeza spent there and later, as Bishop of Scalas and a canon in Seville, del Río became a close colleague of Baeza's son.[27] Baeza's life history therefore provides a window on the wider circles and networks he inhabited and the choices he faced with other members of these groups.

Approach and sources

The reign of the Catholic Monarchs has been told variously as a narrative about the growth of royal power, the rise of nations, the foundation of empire, the suppression of minorities or a backdrop for literary production and the emergence of the 'Golden Age'. The enormous transcendence of events such as the conquest of Granada, the expulsion of the Jews and Columbus's voyages of discovery can often overshadow discussion of the later years, especially the twelve years between the death of Isabel and that of Fernando, which sometimes appear as a mere epilogue.[28] However, during his solo monarchy, Fernando pursued a distinctive agenda in the Mediterranean and his governorship of Castile reaggravated old conflicts as well as sparking new grievances.[29] Hernando de Baeza's life story is a thread which links this later period with the earlier pivotal events of the joint reign, connecting the unfolding circumstances, controversies and preoccupations of the emerging Catholic Spain. Studies of Fernando tend towards admiration for their protagonist; mine perhaps errs in the opposite direction by presenting a more critical perspective as seen through the eyes of those at the sharp end of his policies.[30]

My interest in Hernando de Baeza was stimulated by his apparent position at the intersection of the so-called 'three cultures' of medieval Iberia as it became Catholic Spain.[31] My original aim was merely to find out who he was and why he wrote as he did. I did not expect to find such a rich source of insights into political agency in the age in which he lived, or that the focus of my research would move from Granada to the Rome of the High Renaissance and back to Andalusia and the Inquisition in the succession crisis following the deaths of Isabel and Felipe I. Hernando de Baeza was a man who was politically engaged and made history in both senses of the expression. In using his life and work as lens through which to view the tensions and compromises of his age, I have been unashamedly selective in focussing on episodes and influences and which I have judged relevant to understanding the reign of the Catholic Monarchs and the emergence of early modern Spain. The result is not a biography, nor the contextualization of the life of a literary figure in the manner of Stephen Gilman's excellent *Spain of Fernando de Rojas*, but a history using one man's life and short piece of writing to offer a deeper understanding of the multifaceted upheavals of the times in which he lived. [32] I have focussed on three key periods: before, during and after the experiences in the Granadan court about which Baeza writes, bringing together data on the man, his contacts and the wider social and political context during each of these periods. This in turn has allowed me to unpick the 'social logic' of his text, published for the first time in English as an appendix.

Baeza's activity as a historical personage is recorded by the Aragonese chronicler Jerónimo Zurita (1512–80) in his *Historia del Rey Don Fernando* (1580) and also in an anonymous history of the *Gran Capitán*'s exploits in Italy, written in the mid-1550s by a member of his household.[33] Baeza also receives mentions in various despatches of his time and in correspondence between King Fernando, Cardinal Bernardino López de Carvajal and the *Gran Capitán*. In addition to his one known piece of historical writing, I have been able to bring to light five personal letters Baeza wrote from Italy to his lordly masters in Montilla and, in establishing his genealogy and identity, I have drawn on the wills of members of his family preserved in notary archives. In all, I have been able to identify him in more than eighty documentary sources. However, it is one of the ironies of history that the reason why we are able to access so much sensitive information about a man, who was neither a member of the nobility nor 'a great man of history', is through attempts to erase and belittle him and his family on account of their ancestry. The vestiges of persecution contained in the records of Inquisition trials, *limpieza de sangre* proceedings and controversies over appointments recorded in cathedral chapter minutes have, with ironic justice, done most to enable his memorialization.

1

Cordoba, the frontier, and the Inquisition, 1450–87

'High-ranking people, good, God-fearing Christians'[1]

Competing visions for Christianizing Iberia

The process of Christianizing Iberia did not start or end with the Catholic Monarchs, but it was in their reign that the conquest of Granada and the expulsion of the Jews gave it increased momentum. Medieval Spain had had the largest population of Jews in Europe but, by the early fifteenth century, most had undergone baptism following a wave of violence against them. The pogroms had started in Holy Week 1391, in Seville where, incited by a hate preacher named Ferrán Martínez, the populace rose up against the Jewish community in a frenzy of slaughter and robbery which, two days later, was replicated in Cordoba and then spread to other towns and cities across Castile and Aragon.[2] A sixteenth-century account claimed that four thousand Jews perished in Seville alone and that, when King Enrique III later visited, 'almost all the Jews of that city had become Christian and in Cordoba and Toledo they did the same.'[3] The 'flood of baptisms', spurred on by an intense programme of proselytization led by Vincent Ferrer (1350–1419) and increasingly repressive measures against those who were unwilling to convert, sowed the seeds for the '*converso* problem' which emerged a generation later.[4] For the converts, becoming a 'new Christian' offered paths to social advancement which had previously been closed, but for existing Christians – now redefined as 'natural' or 'old' Christians – it meant having to share their privileges with a previously inferior social group whose conversion everyone knew had been coercive. These circumstances forced a reconsideration of the whole nature of Christian society from which, during the fifteenth century, two competing visions emerged. On the one hand, there arose an exclusionary ideology which sought to give old Christians precedence over the newly converted by limiting the latter's participation in civil society and, on the other, a theological position contending that the Christian church was a unity in which there were no distinctions between people of different races or origins and that Jewish people, as all others, were able to redeem themselves through baptism and divine grace.

As the rigid medieval distinctions between faiths became blurred, there was a turn to genealogy rather than confessional status as a way of expressing identity and difference.[5] During the reign of Enrique IV (1454–74), Alonso de Espina (1412–91) popularized the thinking of thirteenth-century theologian Duns Scotus, preaching and writing that Christian society had to be purified by rooting out the enemies of the faith, who he identified as Jews, Moors, demons and heretics.[6] Instead of being welcomed in, converted Jews were increasingly treated as suspect members of Christian society, if not as outright heretics. When, in the mid-fifteenth century, these ideas started to find expression in prejudice and violence against converts, leading *converso* intellectuals were motivated to develop the theological basis for the alternative, integrative position. Alonso de Cartagena's *Defensorium Unitatis Christianae* (1449–50) provided an arsenal of scriptural references to be drawn on later by those seeking to legitimize *converso* status within Catholic society and argue more widely for tolerance within the church. He drew particularly on the epistles of St Paul – a convert from Judaism *par excellence* – and argued not only that converted Jews could be as good Christians as old ones, but also that they had a primary role in God's plan for the redemption of the world. He contended that the sacrament of Baptism created a single Christian body and that any attempt to create division and distinction within it was therefore itself a heresy, bringing the extent of Christ's mercy into question.[7] In a similar vein to Cartagena, Alonso de Oropesa's *Lumen ad revelationem gentium* (begun in 1450, completed by 1465) reflected on the transformative role of Jewish *conversos* in creating spiritual unity within the church.[8] Oropesa argued that the union of former Jews with old Christians had moved the church on from the servitude of the 'Old' Law to the liberty of the 'New', one in which all its members were linked by their faith and through the spiritual power of the Eucharist in a single body in a perfect state of grace. Judaism and Christianity were not seen as opposed, but rather the former was a precondition for the latter, which was a 'perfection' of it. Oropesa, who was a Jeronymite monk and head of the Order from 1457, made a strong point about the dangers for humankind of neglecting to cultivate friendship and fellowship, stressing the importance of Christians living in peace and harmony with each other and citing St Paul on the prime virtue of charity above faith and hope.[9] These men are seen as the precursors of Erasmianism in Spain and an inspiration for the more compassionate positions in relation to the treatment of the native inhabitants of the New World as well as later spiritual movements arising in sixteenth-century Spain.[10] Juan de Torquemada (1388–1468), writing in response to the same events, made the Eucharist even more significant in forging unity between Christians and former Jews, arguing that Christians of all origins consume Jewish flesh and blood through the transubstantiation of the bread and wine, since Jesus was Jewish.[11] These egalitarian principles and the idea that virtue and nobility are independent of lineage were taken up and widely disseminated in humanist literature and poetry.[12]

Image 3 *La Fuente de la Gracia* by Jan van Eyck. This painting is believed to have been commissioned by Alonso de Cartagena in the mid-1440s to illustrate the arguments he makes in his *Defensorium Unitatis Christianae*: the importance of the peaceful conversion of Jews in the salvation story and the extension of God's grace to all.[13] © Museo Nacional del Prado.

Cordoban *conversos*

It is most likely that members of Hernando de Baeza's family were among those Jews who converted in the aftermath of the pogroms of 1391 since his father and, as far as we can tell, his grandfather were, at least nominally, Christian. The label 'converso' might suggest a recent, individual decision to adopt Christianity; in fact, it would have been several generations since members of Hernando de Baeza's family had been living as Jews. By the time he was born – probably around 1455 – his family had become deeply embedded in the political and economic life of Cordoba – the second city in Christian Andalusia after Seville. It was an industrious city with well-regulated trades such as leather, metalworking and textiles.[14] A huge variety of foods and primary materials such as dyestuffs and seeds arrived in the city via the Guadalquivir River or by land at one of its four gates. One of Hernando's uncles, Pedro Ramírez de Baeza, held the tenancy of the *Casa de la Aduana* or Customs House; another uncle was the Town Clerk (*escribano mayor*) and his father, Juan de Baeza, was the council's financial administrator (*mayordomo de los propios*).[15]

His family's circumstances are a close fit with the remarkably consistent descriptions of contemporary chroniclers of the rise of the *conversos* in the urban centres of Andalusia during this time. Writing post-hoc, to explain the need for the Inquisition, chroniclers describe them 'enriching themselves by dubious means', using public positions for their own benefit, obtaining royal favours, and intermingling with the nobility.[16] A witness in a later *limpieza de sangre* hearing remembered the Baezas as: 'high ranking people, good God-fearing Christians who were highly regarded by the Lords of Aguilar, in the best positions and related to the most high-ranking and richest people in Cordoba'.[17] As a witness nominated by the individual under scrutiny she

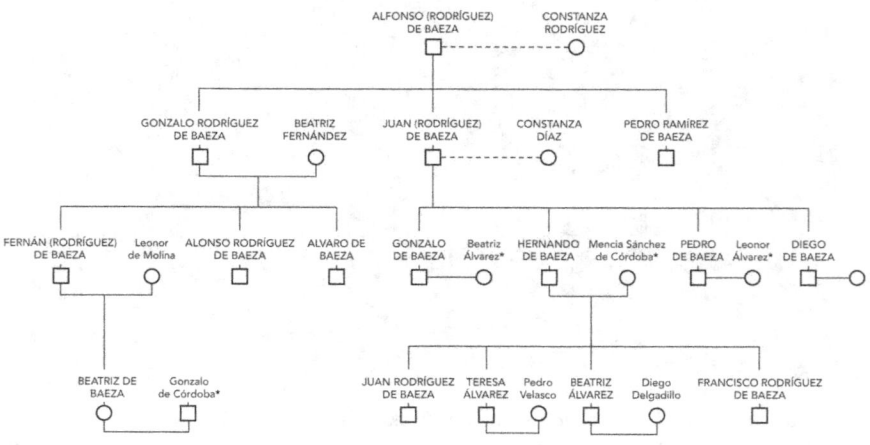

Image 4 The family of Hernando de Baeza – genealogical chart. © Teresa Tinsley.

would have certainly understood the importance of her testimony but, nonetheless, the evidence largely supports her assertion.

Hernando's father, Juan de Baeza and uncle Pedro are described in archive documents as *criados* of the powerful Fernández de Córdoba family – Lords of Aguilar – which dominated Cordoba during this period. Although the word literally meant someone living and brought up in a noble household, by the period under consideration, the term was used more generally to cover a very wide range of circumstances, from menial domestic service to roles which required a high level of responsibility and skill, such as the command of a fortress.[18] At what we might call the 'top end', the *criados* of great nobles such as the House of Aguilar were often high-ranking individuals themselves acting on behalf of their masters and it is in these roles that we find the Baezas, collecting rents, witnessing official transactions and acting as their legal representatives.[19] *Converso* families, such as the Baezas, acted as a buffer between the local nobility and the populace – the visible face of power, collecting taxes, managing finances and defending vested interests in their roles as members of the town council.[20] The word 'criado' is usually rendered in English as 'servant', which could imply dependency, exclusivity and unidirectional power influence. In fact, the Baezas' multifaceted relationship with their lords pulled in both directions and they were not simply followers but influencers too, especially during the minorities of their noble masters.

Hernando's father Juan de Baeza seems to have held his position as *mayordomo de los propios* from the mid-1440s, while Gonzalo Rodríguez de Baeza was Town Clerk from even earlier and his son Fernán – who has sometimes been confused with my subject, his cousin Hernando – was a *jurado* (parish representative) from 1449 or earlier.[21] These dates are significant because it was in 1449 that an infamous seminal attempt was made in Toledo to discriminate against new Christians by denying them access to public offices such as those held by the Baezas in Cordoba.[22] Fourteen *judeoconverso* members of Toledo town council were excluded on the grounds that the religion of their ancestors made their allegiance suspect. The rationale for this was the supposed enmity of both Jews and Muslims towards Christian society and the allegation that Jews had been betraying the people of Toledo ever since the Muslim invasion (i.e., since the year 711). Although the decree was part of a wider political rebellion which was quickly quashed, it marked the first attempt to institutionalize long-standing anti-Jewish sentiment against the *conversos*, a move that, in the following century, was to become embedded throughout public life in Spain through *limpieza de sangre* statutes.[23]

In the same year of 1449, there were anti-*converso* riots in Guadalupe, site of a venerated image of the Virgin around which the Jeronymite Order had established its lead monastery. The Order had attracted a large number of former Jews and was in the vanguard of developing a new, inner spirituality which was not a retreat from the world but rather one which harmonized with astute management of worldly resources.[24] Like Cordoba, where it seems there were also similar disturbances, there were a large number of *conversos* living in the village which had grown up around the monastery.[25] It was these expressions of prejudice and violence which motivated Cartagena and Oropesa to develop their defence of converts within the Christian Church. Baeza would later reveal his own inclination towards the Jeronymite Order and write about the power of the Eucharist to unite the Christian forces fighting against the 'Moors', aligning himself with the new theology of these writers.[26]

The affinity with the Jeronymites expressed in Baeza's text is supported by evidence that members of his family – and their noble masters – were already sympathetic towards the Order by the mid-fifteenth century. Fernán Rodríguez de Baeza, Hernando's older cousin, had been a page to Pedro Fernández de Córdoba, Lord of Aguilar from 1441.[27] In 1455, aged only 31, Don Pedro died, leaving Fernán two horses in a will made on his deathbed.[28] The following year, Fernán made a donation of two mills to the local Jeronymite monastery of Valparaíso which adjoined his own family's property just outside Cordoba, with a behest for the monks to pray for his master's soul.[29] The connection with the monastery spread over several generations: Hernando's daughter, Teresa Álvarez, was buried there and his grandson, Captain Gaspar de Velasco, asked to be buried alongside her.[30] Fernán's 1456 donation was a public assertion of his Christian identity and, given the mid-century hardening of attitudes towards *conversos*, suggests that he may have started to feel under suspicion. Coinciding with the development of Alonso de Oropesa's integrationist arguments concerning the role of *conversos* within Christianity, it was an affirmation of his own social and religious status and highlights the importance of Hernando's own deliberate expression of affinity with the Jeronymite Order. Gonzalo Fernández de Córdoba, the man in whose service Hernando would make his greatest contributions to history, is well known for his attachment to the Jeronymite Order and as a teenager is credited with having presented himself at the gates of this same monastery, seeking to become a monk.[31]

Civil war in Castile, 1465–8

Mid-fifteenth century Cordoba was a dangerous and unstable place.[32] Contemporary chroniclers and later historians alike tended to exaggerate the 'anarchy' in the period leading up to the accession of Isabel I (1474–1504) in order to stress the virtues and legitimacy of the Catholic Monarchs but, even so, there is plenty of evidence of violence and disorder. Unruly competition between members of the nobility for power, land and titles became entangled with court politics and ethnically charged unrest.[33] In Cordoba, warring branches of the Fernández de Córdoba family fought for control of the city – on one side, the Baezas' young lord and patron, Don Alonso de Aguilar (1447–1501) and, on the other, the Count of Cabra (1410–81), whose seat was in nearby Baena. Each had their own band of followers within the city council, for whom an increasing number of official positions were created, including some of those occupied by the Baezas.[34]

The devices of nobles struggling for power, in particular the brothers Juan Pacheco and Pedro Girón, who formed a power block against the King Enrique IV, are blamed for the Civil War which played out in Castile between 1465 and 1468. Pacheco, Girón and their faction revolted against Enrique, setting up the future Isabel I's young brother Alfonso as King. In Cordoba, the conflict was played out between two opposing factions of the Fernández de Córdoba family with Aguilar, under the influence of Pacheco – he later married one of his daughters – supporting the rebels, while Cabra was loyal to Enrique IV. The young pretender to the throne told Aguilar to keep control of Cordoba at all costs – a *carte blanche* for the teenage lord to abuse his position.[35] He is reported to have done so by expelling Enrique's representatives, making arrests and slapping taxes on church and laity with impunity. His charge sheet included having 'arrested six canons from the cathedral and kept them prisoners for more than six months' and having 'sacked and burnt the Bishop's house'.[36] Even allowing for the bias of the chroniclers and the values of his times, it seems certain that the young Lord and his followers contributed to the prevailing anarchy and lawlessness and that codes of conduct were broken in the violation of both church and personal property.

It seems likely that the Baezas were able to exert a strong influence in their roles as advisers and stewards during Alonso de Aguilar's minority, and that they were active players in forming the attitudes and dispositions associated with civil unrest and the frontier with Granada during this time.[37] When the Bishop of Cordoba, Don Pedro Solier, lent his weight to the loyalists by handing down excommunications on Alonso de Aguilar and his men, this punishment would have much more dire consequences for the *conversos* than for their noble lord. One source shows that Hernando's father Juan was excommunicated at some point before May 1467 (when his absolution was requested) for his role in attacking property.[38] Another excommunication was issued on Alonso de Aguilar and his supporters in July 1472, listing eleven reasons including, again, the issue of taxation and the charge that Alonso de Aguilar had given arms and horses to the Muslims. Several members of the Baeza family including Hernando's father, uncle and two cousins were explicitly excommunicated for their role in imposing the tax.[39] In 1474, two more members of the Baeza family network, Pedro (Ramírez) de Baeza and Sancho Sánchez, were excommunicated, again for reasons relating to taxation, accused of having appropriated the proceeds.[40]

It appears then that members of the Baeza family were excluded from the Christian sacraments for as long as six or seven years during what would have been Hernando's formative years. In the earliest days of the establishment of the Inquisition, Fernando and Isabel explicitly identified the issue of the excommunication of *conversos* as hastening a departure from Christian practices and the risk that *converso* children were not receiving appropriate instruction. Their rather convoluted reasoning claimed that such *conversos* had departed from the Christian faith (or had been insincere in the first place), and that this had led them into unholy practices which had resulted in them being excommunicated, and now this represented a real danger since it meant that not only were they able to continue with their own heretical practices, but their children were also being 'infected'.[41] This tends to suggest that excommunication which, in the case of the Baezas at least, was clearly a measure which had more to do with politics and power than with articles of faith, had perhaps had a knock-on effect on *converso* beliefs and behaviours and certainly on the way that they were perceived by others.

Tax- and rent-collecting was a widespread source of resentment against Jews and *conversos* and again the Baezas conform to stereotype.[42] Alfonso Rodríguez de Baeza, identified in a later *limpieza de sangre* investigation as Hernando de Baeza's grandfather, is described as 'paymaster' of Alcalá la Real and may be the same individual who was responsible for payments to members of Enrique IV's Moorish guard.[43] Hernando's father Juan and his two uncles, Pedro Ramírez de Baeza and Gonzalo Rodríguez de Baeza, together with another close relative, Sancho Sánchez de Córdoba, were all variously involved in collecting the *almojarifazgo* – the duty on goods arriving in Cordoba – from at least 1455 up to 1483.[44] In at least one tax-collecting period, 1467–71, they worked in concert with a man named as Rabí Zag (possibly Isaac), described as a Jew from Arévalo.[45] The system which operated in Castile meant that they were responsible not only for the tax collection, but also for the distribution of the income to beneficiaries, for example, payments for the upkeep of frontier fortresses such as Alcalá la Real.[46] This, in conjunction with occupation of influential local government positions, gave control over a significant part of the local economy and enabled them and their noble masters to raise and spend money virtually in their own interests.

During the period of the Civil War, Gonzalo Fernández de Córdoba (1453–1515), the younger brother of Alonso de Aguilar, was sent as a page into the service of the young pretender, the *Infante* Alfonso. His biographer José Enrique Ruiz Domènec sees the experience of growing up in a civil war as leading to his later rejection of factionalism, unthinking reaction and gratuitous violence.[47] It is possible, given the later closeness and rapport between the future *Gran Capitán* and Hernando de Baeza, that Hernando accompanied him as a servant and underwent the same formative experience. The interrelation between these two men is crucial to understanding the later conflicts and tensions which emerged with the surviving Catholic Monarch after Isabel's death.

In 1468 the *Infante* Alfonso died unexpectedly, and with the Treaty of Guisando (19 September 1468) signed between his sister Isabel (later Isabel I) and her half-brother Enrique IV, a settlement was agreed whereby Enrique would remain in power until his death, but Isabel would succeed him. Enrique then travelled to Cordoba to order a reconciliation between the opposing factions there. On 30 May 1469, we find the Baeza elders Juan and Fernán de Baeza, Alfon(so) Rodríguez de Baeza (standing in as town clerk), Pedro Ramírez and Sancho de Córdoba swearing allegiance to Enrique IV, along with Alonso de Aguilar and the other members of Cordoba town council.[48] However, rivalry between the opposing Fernández de Córdoba factions proved stronger than reconciliation, and conflict between them continued unabated.

Anti-converso riots, 1473

In 1473, Cordoba witnessed a horrific bloodbath that demonstrated the rising tide of anti-*converso* feeling and is seen as one of the key events leading up to the establishment of the Inquisition.[49] Three days of brutal violence and looting saw *conversos* robbed, murdered, raped, and forced out of their homes. Alonso de Aguilar was unable to quell the rioting and was forced to take shelter within the old fortress, along with some of his *converso* followers: I surmise that these included the Baezas.[50] Afterwards, the young lord had to agree to expel the remaining *conversos* from Cordoba and to ban them from taking up public offices again. Hernando's father Juan and his uncle Gonzalo

Rodríguez de Baeza were among many who lost their positions within the town council, and it is likely that they took shelter in nearby Montilla, site of the Fernández de Córdobas' family seat, which boasted one of the most magnificent castles in Andalusia.[51] Hernando and his wife Mencia Sánchez de Córdoba were both born in Cordoba but their children are described as having been born in Montilla.[52] It seems likely that this was the moment at which the family moved their base there, allowing Alonso de Aguilar to receive credit later for having 'repopulated' the town.[53]

Alonso de Aguilar's perceived betrayal of the *conversos* in the face of popular pressure came under harsh criticism, a fact which sits oddly with his reputation elsewhere as their 'protector'.[54] Antón de Montoro's contemporaneous poem about the events has been taken as a reproach to Alonso de Aguilar for his actions in failing to defend the interests of people who had served him loyally.[55] Alonso de Aguilar is reported to have made a particularly grim comment when challenged about having buckled under pressure from the mob: 'Let me take these beehives', he is supposed to have said, 'when I have taken all the honey from them I will help to burn them myself'.[56] The comment is probably apocryphal, written post hoc to appear prophetic of the Inquisition fires. In contrast to accounts which paint the Fernández de Córdobas as having betrayed the *conversos*, others have read the incident as a supreme example of their protection of them.[57] In the case of the Baeza family, this certainly seems to have been the case. It seems to have drawn them closer into the family's protection through their move to Montilla and may perhaps have acted as a bonding mechanism between the noble family and the four Baeza brothers Gonzalo, Hernando, Pedro and Diego, all of whom worked for them in some capacity at a later stage, and whom Gonzalo Fernández de Córdoba, the future *Gran Capitán*, described as his friends (see genealogical chart p. 12).[58] There is plenty of evidence from records of property later confiscated by the Inquisition that *conversos*, including the Baezas, continued to own and inhabit property in Cordoba into the 1480s and beyond, so the idea that they were permanently expelled *en masse* is unsustainable. In fact, despite the cataclysmic events, they continued to operate in some of the same roles. In 1475 the cathedral notary issued a document certifying that Juan de Baeza, cited as a *veinticuatro* (alderman) of Cordoba, had been appointed to collect the tithes on wine and oil due from the village of Cañete.[59] These were in fact the very taxes on account of which the Bishop had previously excommunicated him.[60]

The many references to the 1473 riots in documentation from the years that followed bear witness to the traumatic impact they had on all concerned.[61] Some fourteen years later, when the Count of Cabra made his will, he revealed that what he called the 'robbery of the *conversos*' had been preying on his conscience.[62] He said that he had taken bribes in relation to the incident, and that 'Juan de Baeza' (I take this to be Hernando's father) knew from whom. He asked that his executors should look into the matter and establish whether he ought to have accepted the money in good conscience and if not, it was to be returned. Also on Cabra's conscience was the fact that he had taken money from *conversos* who passed through his territory as they fled to Granada to escape the violence, and he asked his executors to look into this too.[63] These matters of conscience are particularly interesting given that Baeza depicts the Count of Cabra as 'saintly' and says in his account that he was close to the Jeronymite friar who was the Count's confessor (named in the will as Fray Fernando, vicar of Doña Mencia).[64] He appears to have gained insights into the Count's actions and motivations through this connection.

On the death of her half-brother in 1474, Isabel immediately claimed the throne and launched into a war of succession against supporters of Enrique's daughter Juana, whom Isabel and her followers claimed was not his daughter at all, but the result of the queen's affair with one of his courtiers. While they were still engaged in this struggle, Gonzalo Fernández de Córdoba left Andalusia to go into the service of the young monarchs in support of what was seen as a modernizing, reformist agenda.[65] Once again, we have no evidence concerning Hernando's whereabouts. He may well have accompanied Gonzalo to court, learning the manners and protocols which he so clearly exhibits in his later life.

Once Isabel and Fernando had secured their position, they turned their attention to imposing their authority on towns such as Cordoba. This meant taking control of military installations and appointing their own *corregidor* (royal representative as leader of the council). They sought to put an end to the clientelism that had allowed nobles to dominate urban life but had to balance bringing the local nobility and their influential *converso* followers to heel with ensuring their loyalty as part of the new settlement.[66] They issued a long list of restitutions, re-appointing individuals to positions they had lost during the troubles of 1473.[67] These included Hernando's father and other members of the Baeza family, though he and Gonzalo Rodríguez de Baeza, reinstated as town clerk, also required a letter of safety giving them royal protection from 'certain persons' whom they feared would injure or wound them or their families, or seize their possessions.[68] On the one hand, they must have welcomed a firm hand of government which appeared to protect them from discrimination and physical danger – favours direct from the crown were as much of interest to them as those obtained through their noble lords; in the anarchic years of Juan II's reign, *conversos* such as Alonso de Cartagena and the court poet Juan de Mena had placed their hopes in a strong monarchy. However, at the same time, disruption to the power network they shared with their patrons must have left them uneasy, and there were signs that royal prerogative was not always going to work in their favour. When the town clerk died soon afterwards – we do not know the circumstances – his successor's letter of appointment specifically excluded anyone nominated by the previous incumbent.[69] This was a move by the Crown against the power of lineages such as the Baezas to maintain control of key roles from one generation to the next – Rodríguez de Baeza's son Alonso had already been acting in that role.[70] Hernando would have been directly affected by the policy, since the letters and the documents he issued indicate that he had acquired his technical and semi-legal skills through notary training, presumably in order to occupy just such a position.[71]

In 1481, probably as a result of a food shortage and a contracting economy, Juan de Baeza found himself unable to meet his obligations in relation to tax collecting. He was forced to mortgage his house and winery in La Rambla to Alonso de Aguilar and to hand over a large estate, the *Cortijo de la Banda*, to pay the crown's treasurer.[72] Hernando's presence witnessing this document is the earliest mention of him in a public role – it seems he had come of age just as the monarchs were starting to exert their power.

The Inquisition comes to Cordoba

If the *conversos* hoped that Isabel and Fernando would be their arch-defenders, they were soon disabused of that notion. While the monarchs were in Seville in early 1478 issuing restitutions and safety notices for the Baezas, they were regaled with tales of Jewish rites, secret meetings and failures of Christian observance among the *conversos* of Andalusia. With a Dominican prior, Alonso de Hojeda, preaching fervently about the dangers posed by false converts, the monarchs are believed to have feared that anti-Semitic mobs would be stirred up to take matters into their own hands, as they had done in Cordoba in 1473 and across Castile and Aragon in 1391.[73] A spate of rioting and lynching was exactly what they did not want just at a time they were starting to impose order. In November that year (1478), they obtained a papal bull providing for the appointment of inquisitors by the crown; however, they took no action immediately. A more moderate way of combatting residual Judaism and backsliding by *conversos* was advocated by the Archbishop of Seville, Pedro González de Mendoza. He set in motion an extensive campaign of preaching against heresy, led by the queen's confessor, Fray Hernando de Talavera, and the Bishop of Cadiz, Alfonso de Solís. Already, the battle lines were being drawn up with this more moderate approach informed by Alonso de Oropesa's Jeronymite ideas of peaceful conversion opposed to the mendicant orders – Dominicans and Franciscans – calling for the establishment of an Inquisition.[74] It is significant that one of the earliest uses of Hernando de Baeza's text – one that credits him by name – was in a biography of the pro-instruction Archbishop (later elevated to Cardinal) written by a member of the Mendoza family around 1550.[75] However, despite these efforts, by 1480 the monarchs were persuaded to implement the power given them by the bull and appointed the first Inquisitors in Seville.

The new Inquisition's function as an instrument of social control in stemming resentment against wealthy and powerful *conversos* such as the Baezas was openly recognized by contemporary chroniclers, who make as much of this as of its direct purpose to root out heresy. The Baezas' unpopularity as tax collectors, combined with their reinstatement to public positions which had been held by others since 1473, must have made them a focus of exactly the sort of ill-feeling the monarchs hoped to quell, and the Inquisition's system of anonymous tip offs provided a conduit for grievances to be avenged.[76] The Cordoba tribunal, established in 1482, immediately started to pitch into the Baeza network. It was not a single blow but an ongoing process of attrition and its impact would continue to be felt on the family for well over a century, as later *limpieza de sangre* investigations show. By 10 October 1483, Juan de Baeza's business partner Sancho Sánchez de Córdoba had been condemned for 'iniquity, perversity, and corruption of customs' and his land seized and sold at public auction.[77] In February 1484, Pedro Fernández de Alcaudete, the Cathedral treasurer who had commissioned Juan de Baeza to collect the controversial church tithes in Cañete, was found guilty of being a covert Jew, stripped of his clerical status and burnt alive.[78] Gonzalo Rodríguez de Baeza had already died but, by October 1494, his widow, Beatriz Fernández, had had her property seized by the Inquisition and was being 'pursued by justice'. Her three sons, Fernán, Alonso and Alvaro, brought a legal case against the receiver, Bartolomé de Zafra, saying that the property belonged to them, not to their mother, and had therefore been illegally seized.[79] This suggests a certain confidence in their own immunity which turned out to be misplaced. Fernán de Baeza was soon required to present himself to the Inquisition tribunal and reconcile himself with the Catholic Church. Rather than doing so, he fled – perhaps across the border to Granada. He was found guilty in his absence and condemned to death, while the monarchs gifted his winery, vineyards and olive groves to one Diego de Velasco.[80] Several other members of the Baeza family also fled and their property was seized and redistributed in the same way.[81] Beatriz Fernández was publicly burnt and her late husband, the town clerk, condemned posthumously.[82]

The members of the family who survived were 'reconciled' to the Catholic Church, with fines and/or penances. However, it is less clear that they were forced to submit to the public humiliation of an *auto de fe*. In common with practice in other cities, the *conversos* of Cordoba negotiated a series of payments on behalf of the whole community who were authorized by the crown to be 'reconciled' collectively. This seems to reveal an underlying understanding by both sides that the Inquisition was targeting the whole *converso* social and ethnic group, not just ridding the community of wayward individuals suspected of not being true Christians. It is also revelatory of a certain cynicism on the part of the *converso* leaders who negotiated the deal – that they saw reconciliation not as an inner resolve to be a better Christian, but as a paid-for indulgence to be granted by the monarchs. There were in total six mass reconciliations in Cordoba up to 1491, each squeezing the *conversos* for more money.[83] Being reconciled meant the ongoing humiliation of not being able to bear arms, wear silk or jewels or hold public office, and being kept under ongoing scrutiny to ensure they did so.[84] Neither Hernando's father Juan nor his uncle Pedro seem to have accepted their reconciliation with the necessary contrition. By March 1488, the former *mayordomo* Juan de Baeza had been condemned and another of his country properties, the *Cortijo de Nublos*, granted by the Crown to someone else, while Pedro too had succumbed to the Inquisition.[85] It is not recorded whether either of them were publicly burnt.

These attacks on members of the Fernández de Córdoba household, and the gifts of their land and property to others, would have been felt as a manoeuvre against the noble family since they bolstered royal influence in the town at the expense of their own. Alonso de Aguilar and his successors contested the Inquisition's seizures over many years in an attempt to regain the Baezas' property. Soon after Juan and Pedro's demise, Alonso de Aguilar made a claim against the Inquisition's receiver, alleging that both men had owed him considerable sums of money from taxes and rents they had collected on his behalf.[86] His financial manager (*contador*), who would have provided the detailed evidence required to put this case together, was Alfonso de Córdoba, a man who had a close personal interest in the outcome, since three of his daughters were married to Juan de Baeza's sons (see genealogical chart p. 12). He was, in fact, Hernando de Baeza's father-in-law. In 1503, Alonso de Aguilar's successor Don Pedro, Marquis of Priego, obtained royal confirmation of his right to a mill near the village of Santaella which he claimed his father had bought from Gonzalo Rodríguez de Baeza, and houses in Cordoba belonging to Gonzalo de Córdoba, a tax-collector, *before* they were condemned as heretics.[87] Thirty years later, his successor the Marchioness was still being pressured over who they belonged to and when the sale had taken place.[88] It seems likely, therefore, that at least some of the Baezas' fortune was protected from the Inquisitors by the Fernández de Córdoba family, possibly through subterfuge as well as by legal challenge. This perhaps explains why, despite the Inquisition's fierce assault on his family's wealth, Hernando de Baeza was able to write home from Italy in 1504 describing himself as a rich man and boasting that he had already been rich before he arrived there.[89] It positions the noble family and their *converso* followers working in concert against the oppressive measures being taken forward by the Crown and the Inquisition – a position which was to develop further in the tense years after the death of Isabel.

The policy of 'reconciling' penitent *conversos* was designed to push them back down the social ladder and prevent them from regaining positions of power over old Christians. They were intended to suffer social degradation and to show public 'humility and contrition' in penitence for their previous 'arrogance'.[90] The evidence that Hernando's father was a key collaborator with Alonso de Aguilar in exacting taxes suggests a man with an uncompromising character, confrontational rather than collaborative, and certainly capable of using public offices for his own gain. Hernando's cousin Fernán first defied the Inquisition over his parents' property and then fled rather than submitting to humiliating reconciliation conditions, suggesting he had a proud, combative disposition. This is in stark contrast to the image that Hernando de Baeza presents of himself in his work: a man more inclined to influence by winning people over than by confrontation. It suggests that this conciliatory nature was either formed or deliberately adopted as a response to his family's degradation at the hands of the Inquisition and sheds light on the ambiguous stance of the author within the text who wants acclaim for his actions while at the same time appears not to want to draw too much attention to himself.[91]

The most recent biographer of Gonzalo Fernández de Córdoba, the *Gran Capitán*, has questioned why there were not more protests against the Inquisition in these early days by the Fernández de Córdoba family and like-minded courtiers such as Diego de Valera and Gonzalo Chacón.[92] Elsewhere, the royal chronicler Fernando del Pulgar, who did protest, is criticised for making his objections unduly mild.[93] In these early years of their reign, there was a weight of expectation upon the monarchs to provide justice and re-establish the royal authority that had broken down during the years of the Civil War: a strong monarchy was seen as a liberating rather than repressive force.[94] There were clearly at least some cases of *conversos* who had reembraced their former religion wholesale, and many more retaining some Jewish practices. As a result of these 'bad Christians', *conversos* in general were being blamed for social ills.[95] In this context it is possible to understand how a policy rooting them out might be seen to be of benefit to old and new Christians alike. The idea that lynchings and riots would be replaced by a legal process which would punish those guilty and prevent the mob taking matters into their own hands might have seemed a reasonable proposition, with the Inquisition working as an instrument of social control for both sides.[96] It would have been hard to make a case against such an argument, even for people who were not *converso* courtiers in the pay of the monarchs such as Pulgar. Pulgar's point, which has already been the subject of much scholarly analysis, was not *whether* the Inquisition should exist, but *how* it should operate.[97] The problem, as he put it in a public letter to

Cardinal Mendoza, was that the Inquisition had been set up in a discriminatory way which put all *judeoconversos* under suspicion on the basis of their lineage.[98] He also argued against harsh and inappropriate penalties for people, especially women, who had had no opportunity for in-depth instruction in the Christian faith – a plea for understanding which Baeza echoes in his own work. The meanings attached today to the Spanish Inquisition – persecution, prejudice and intransigence – were not fixed at the time it was first established, but still open to negotiation and influence. Rather than already symbolizing the extreme exclusionary tendency in Spanish society, the Inquisition was a scenario where the struggle between the integrationist and the exclusionary ideology was being acted out. The courtier, diplomat and cleric Juan de Lucena went further in publicly criticizing the Inquisition and the arguments he set out against forced conversion and its consequences were widely cited in later debates. He argued that excommunication was repressive and counterproductive, that burnings would not lead to true repentance or the saving of souls and that, since faith was a voluntary act, forced baptism was invalid – a similar position to that espoused by Baeza in his comment about the *elches*. However, Lucena was forced to retract publicly – in Cordoba, sometime between 1481 and 1492 – and only his status as a papal protonotary saved him from being put on trial.[99]

That the Baezas were tax collectors, allied to Jews, favoured members of their own network for marriage and business partnerships, and exerted what was seen as undue power through their relationship with the local nobility and occupation of public offices, provides ample socio-economic explanation for their being targeted by the Inquisition. But they were also excommunicants and deemed to be returning 'like vomit' to their old Jewish practices.[100] We have little evidence from this time of their religious beliefs or practices apart from Fernán's donation to the Jeronymite monastery, except for one other indication. Fernán did not flee permanently but returned to Cordoba to be tried by the Inquisition in 1490. In his genealogical declaration, he said that his wife had given birth to twins ('two children from the same belly') and that one, named Mencia, was 'baptised at her mother's feet' but died almost immediately.[101] Although the evidence was clearly given for the benefit of the Inquisitors, this rather sad and unusual detail has a ring of truth about it and I am inclined to picture at least some members of the Baeza family participating sincerely in the Christian rituals of their masters even if some beliefs or practices survived from their ancestral religion, or were revived during the time they were excommunicants.

The frontier with Granada – cross-cultural contacts and values

The Fernández de Córdoba family were reputed to have taken a light touch approach towards any evidence of Judaism on the part of their followers. Alonso de Aguilar apparently 'thought it was better to confirm them in our faith with gentleness than with punishment' – exactly the stance on religious orthodoxy which is reflected in Baeza's Granada memoir.[102] Hernando therefore grew up within an environment in which there was a certain amount of tolerance and friendship between members of different faith groups, as well as violence and prejudice towards cultural and religious difference.¹⁰³ This ambivalence applied not only in the case of *conversos*, but also in relation to Muslims and cross-border relations with the Kingdom of Granada.

The basis for the Fernández de Córdobas' occupation of the lands under their control – and their relative autonomy from central power – was defence of the frontier. The Lord of Aguilar traditionally fulfilled the role of *juez mayor entre moros y cristianos* – a magistrate with cross-border responsibilities for ensuring that the frontier did not provide a means for wrongdoers on either side to escape justice.¹⁰⁴ This institution, which has been identified as one of the defining features of the Granadan frontier, required the person undertaking the role to be recognized and respected on both sides.¹⁰⁵ In order to negotiate truces, keep the peace and to provide justice on matters which affected both sides such as trade disputes, raiding and the ransoming of captives, Pedro Fernández de Córdoba (1424–55) had maintained open channels of communication with contacts in the Muslim kingdom.¹⁰⁶ It was these activities which led to the long-standing association between the Fernández de Córdobas and the powerful Abencerraje family, whom Baeza depicts rebelling against the tyranny of their emirs.¹⁰⁷ As a result of the vicious persecution they suffered – described by Baeza in what seems to have been a mirror image of the oppression suffered by his own family – they were forced to flee to Castile where they lived as political exiles under the protection of the House of Aguilar for about twelve years, from mid-1470 to 1482, waiting for the political tide to turn.¹⁰⁸ It has been estimated that the exiled family group comprised more than seventy members, though the actual number including women, children and servants might have been significantly greater.¹⁰⁹ These circumstances explain Baeza's network of contacts, his knowledge of Arabic and understanding of aspects of Granadan culture and his positive portrayal of the Abencerrajes themselves. The friendships and contacts made became important during the Granada War as channels for intelligence and negotiation.

During the Civil War (1465–8), the conflict between the Cabras and the Aguilars became entwined with political unrest within Granada as events there mirrored those of Castile. The Count of Cabra and his faction had good diplomatic relations with Abū al-Ḥasan, the emir of Granada, whereas the Aguilars supported the rebel Abencerrajes.¹¹⁰ A lengthy and angry exchange of letters between Alonso de Aguilar and the Count's eldest son bears witness to the complex networks of alliances during this period before the Granada War.¹¹¹ It highlights the contradictions of frontier life in which Hernando de Baeza was immersed from a young age: on the one hand, the Granadan emir describes the Count of Cabra as 'our friend, the distinguished, renowned, perfect and noble knight, may God honour him' and receives from him an array of expensive gifts, while at the same time the two young Christian rivals compete to show who has done more damage to his subjects in cross-border raids.¹¹² Hernando de Baeza's memoir is an attempt to make sense of these contradictions as he looked back on his experiences from the perspective of a Spain which had become exclusively Christian.

The friendship between the Cabras and the Granadan emir made possible the many raids into territory held by the Aguilars and the Order of Calatrava which are described by Hernando de Baeza and which would have had a personal significance for him. One of these was on the town of Cañete – part of the Aguilar estate.¹¹³ Baeza also describes a Granadan attack on two villages in Calatrava territory – held by the Aguilars' ally Pedro Girón, as Master of the Order – noting that the raid set off from Alcalá la Real and Alcaudete, 'because the king [of Granada] had signed peace agreements with them' – that is with the Count of Cabra.[114] He describes the devastation wrought on these villages – Santiago and La Higuera – where 'all the people and livestock were snatched', 'many people killed in the farms and on the roads' and more than one thousand captives taken, who remained in Granada until the fall of the Nasrid regime – more than twenty years. The sympathy for these people he expresses in his work is therefore not just out of general humanity, but a specific concern for people his family would have regarded as allies. When Baeza was writing his account of the divisions and discord which were the ruin of the Nasrid regime, he must have been more than conscious of the earlier splits on the Christian side.

Traditional biographical portraits of Alonso de Aguilar tend to cast him as an inveterate crusader against Islam, but his long association with the Abencerrajes and the political asylum he offered them and others suggests a more complex picture.[115] His last recorded public act before his death at the hands of rebellious *mudéjars* in 1501 highlights a preference for dialogue and the avoidance of conflict rather than the repression of members of a minority religious group. In January that year, the Catholic Monarchs ordered him to join a military 'task force' in the Sierra Bermeja aimed at pacifying insubordination by Muslims who had been ordered to convert to Christianity or move to Muslim districts (*morerías*) in other parts of Castile outside Andalusia.[116] But local Christians were mistreating them and preventing them from being baptized, probably to encourage their exodus. Alonso de Aguilar wrote to the authorities in Marbella appealing to them to prevent locals giving the Muslims any further cause for discontent by stealing their property or standing in the way of their being baptized.[117] The letter highlights the tensions within Christian society between a disposition in favour of dialogue and integration, and a forceful current which regarded Muslims as fair game for plunder and sought to exclude them.

This is the cultural and political backdrop to the iconic year of 1492 and the events that followed it.

2

The conquest of Granada

'I was nothing there'[1]

The first phase of the war, 1482–8

While the Spanish monarchs were waging war on heresy inside their kingdoms, they were also engaged in an external conflict with Granada. The outbreak of hostilities is generally regarded as the Granadans' surprise attack on the town of Záhara, across their western border, while the Christian guards were celebrating Christmas in 1481. The Andalusian nobles whose job was to defend the frontier struck back in a daring attack which won them the town of Álhama, only sixty kilometres from Granada. The loss of a town so deep inside the Muslim kingdom was a blow to the emir Abū al-Ḥasan's credibility and an opportunity for the rebel Abencerrajes, in exile on the Aguilar estates, to unseat him and put his son Boabdil on the throne in his place.[2] Baeza credits his friend Abrahén de Mora – 'a good man and a clever strategist' with masterminding a successful plan to smuggle Boabdil out of the Alhambra by night and use the town of Guadix as a base from which to launch a coup d'état against his father.[3] Once installed as emir, Boabdil was persuaded to make an ill-judged incursion into the area round Lucena where, in a stunningly fortunate circumstance for the Christian side, he was captured by the frontier nobility. He was released later that summer, or possibly early autumn, having signed an alliance with Fernando and Isabel, and it was then that Baeza says he first met him, in the frontier town of Alcaudete.[4]

Baeza's account of the coup and his contacts with the rebel faction show that he was aware of the developments which put Boabdil on the throne from the Christian side of the border. The House of Aguilar seems to have acted as a pre-diplomatic conduit between the Granadan and Castilian courts: it is recorded that, in 1485, the Granadans sent a 'Jew' to Alonso de Aguilar to ask if he could obtain safe conducts from the monarchs for the official envoys.[5] It is possible that Baeza's role was to facilitate these sorts of contacts – and Alcaudete would have been an ideal base from which to do so. In the hands of the Fernández de Córdoba family from the end of the fourteenth century, the town had long acted as a thoroughfare between Granada and Cordoba for merchants, political exiles, religious asylum-seekers and spies. Under the purview of its lords, it had a reputation for tolerance of difference and deviance, a place where

Image 5 Statue of Boabdil by Salvador Amaya, Parque Histórico de San Sebastián, Navalcarnero. Photo: Salvador Amaya.

social norms were able to be challenged and disregarded.[6] Apart from being one of the major trading posts between Granada and Cordoba, where merchants of all three religions were allowed to trade and through which merchandise, ransomed captives and refugees passed, Alcaudete also had special status as one of only two places in Spain which had a royal licence (*privilegio real*) to give asylum to adulterous women fleeing their husbands, and it seems it was well known for this.[7] Although the licence was supposed to have been revoked in 1480, Alcaudete remained a place where couples cohabited, transgressors went unpunished and people lived without going to confession, until at least the early years of the sixteenth century.[8] Baeza's stay there may have influenced his attitudes towards unorthodoxy and hybridity, and he may even be signalling this to his readers by emphasizing his sojourn in the town.

Baeza's presence in Alcaudete coincides with the first *auto de fe* held in Cordoba in 1483 and with the Inquisition's first assaults on the Baeza family.[9] It is possible that he may have fled there to escape persecution; however, the town would not necessarily have provided a safe haven since, from 1484, *conversos* were specifically targeted there and in the surrounding areas.[10] Whether or not he was a fugitive from the Inquisition, it is likely that his main purpose for being in Alcaudete was to enable cross-border contacts and gather political and military intelligence on the situation in Granada.

One incident, which led to a later court case, provides another clue as to his possible role there.[11] In March 1483, the Christians had mounted a disastrous expedition in the mountainous country above Malaga known as La Axarquía in which perhaps as many as 1,500 of them had been taken captive. But, just a month later, the tables turned when the Boabdil and many of his troops were captured outside Lucena – among them a Granadan who came into the hands of the Lord of Alcaudete, Martín Alonso de Montemayor. It turned out that the captive Granadan was the brother of a man holding a prominent Cordoban alderman (*veinticuatro*) named Pedro de Aguayo, who had been taken to Malaga following the La Axarquía debacle. While in captivity, Pedro de Aguayo had written to Alonso de Aguilar telling him that the only way he could be released was in exchange for his captor's brother. On receiving this letter, Alonso de Aguilar and his wife had sent someone – presumably a trusted member of their household – to discuss an arrangement with Martín Alonso de Montemayor whereby he would be paid a very large sum of money – 600,000 *maravedís* – in exchange for releasing the Muslim prisoner, and gold necklaces belonging to Don Alonso's wife were given as surety. The court case was brought by Pedro de Aguayo, once he had been released, against Martín Alonso de Montemayor, contesting the excessively high ransom fee, and citing a law passed by Enrique IV in the Cortes de Toledo (1462) which put a cap on profit-making in relation to the rendition of captives.[12] The person who had negotiated the agreement had clearly driven a hard, albeit somewhat illegal, bargain with Pedro de Aguayo's relatives on behalf of the Lord of Alcaudete and the court reduced the total amount to 400,000 *maravedís*.

The timing makes it entirely possible that Hernando de Baeza in fact was the person sent by Alonso de Aguilar to Alcaudete to negotiate the deal. The interest Baeza expresses in captives, his evident skill in negotiating legal agreements, and not least his knowledge of Arabic, also suggest that at least part of the reason for his presence in Alcaudete might have been to support cross-border transactions of this sort. His friend, the clever strategist Abrahén de Mora, is known to have been involved in the ransoming of captives and is described as an *alhaqueque*.[13] These were cross-border intermediaries charged with the redemption of captives between Castile and Granada, generally bilingual themselves, but often supported by an interpreter ('lengua') and a notary or scribe whose role sometimes crossed over with that of the interpreter. Intelligence-gathering was an important part of their work, so much so that the institution was officially abolished on the Christian side in 1485, since it was considered a 'veiled form of espionage'.[14]

A core principle which underlay the work of these cross-cultural mediators was respect for the religious self-determination of those who had adopted a different religion during their captivity. This was institutionalized and accepted by the authorities on both sides, and by the families concerned.[15] Cross-border protocol allowed for a 'cooling off' period for redeemed captives before any decision was made as regards reconversion – an opportunity to reflect away from the pressure of family members, in order to ensure that all reconversions were genuine and from the heart.[16] This principle, that faith is a voluntary act, reflected the teaching of Thomas Aquinas (1225–74), and was underpinned in law by Alfonso X's *Siete Partidas* which, while advocating conversion to Christianity as the best ultimate outcome, called for both Muslims and Jews to be converted 'with kind words' rather than by force.[17]

There is a further twist to the story of Pedro de Aguayo's ransoming in that he had played a dubious role in the anti-*converso* riots of 1473.[18] He had apparently sheltered his *converso* neighbours in his house and invited them to deposit their valuables with him for safe keeping. When the rioters broke in and massacred them all, the rumour spread that he had tricked the *conversos* for his own gain.[19] If Baeza was responsible for negotiating his release and was aware of this story, it is not surprising that he sought to drive such a hard bargain.

Changing alliances

With wars come new opportunities for interconnection, circulation and interchange. During the Granada conflict Baeza and his close associates occupied a cross-cultural 'third space', with all the ambiguity and contradictions which that involved.[20] As the Christians gained ground during the course of the war and the physical frontier edged towards Granada, the positions of these frontier individuals became doubly ambiguous, as a result of shifting alliances.

In order to secure his release after being taken prisoner at Lucena, Boabdil became a vassal of the Spanish monarchs, achieving his freedom by pledging his allegiance to them in opposition to his father, who reassumed his position as emir.[21] In describing this agreement, Baeza frames the notion of Granadan emirs as vassals of Castile within a historical tradition going back to the days of Juan II (1406–54), signalling that this was nothing new or unusual.[22] Indeed, since the Treaty of Jaén in 1246, Nasrid emirs had often made acts of feudal submission to Castilian monarchs, and some claim that the Kingdom of Granada had been in a state of continuous vassaldom ever since.[23] It may well have been that making Granada a protectorate of Castile was Fernando's strategy at the beginning of the war, shared by Gonzalo Fernández de Córdoba, but this was dropped for a more ambitious plan as events turned in the Christians' favour.[24] The thinking in releasing Boabdil was to drive a wedge between Boabdil and his father to further divide and weaken the kingdom of Granada.[25] The terms required him, among other provisions, to hand over his infant son Ahmed as a hostage who, together with a small retinue, was placed in the custody of the commander of the frontier fortress at Porcuna, Martín de Alarcón – a man who is closely associated with Hernando de Baeza.[26] Further hostages were placed with other frontier nobles also associated with Baeza: Gonzalo Fernández de Córdoba took responsibility for the son of a man named Alhadramín, 'Hosmín' was in the custody of the Count of Tendilla (Íñigo López de Mendoza, who commanded the fortress at Alcalá la Real) and 'Aben Reduan' with the Count of Cabra.[27]

After his alliance with the Christians, religious leaders in Granada immediately issued a fatwa declaring Boabdil a pariah.[28] However, the deal struck gave him access to support from 'Andalusian grandees' whom Baeza says he met in Alcaudete to discuss what his next move should be.[29] There is no other record of this meeting and we do not know who these 'grandees' were – the term had not been institutionalized at the time Baeza was writing and the concept of *grandeza* is understood as referring rather loosely to political power deriving from the ownership of great estates.[30] It seems likely then that Baeza was referring to his master, Alonso de Aguilar, to the Count of Cabra, and perhaps also to the Duke of Medina Sidonia, whose lands Baeza mentions elsewhere in relation to the asylum given to the Abencerrajes.

Baeza says he was introduced to the young emir by his 'great friend', Boabdil's *mizwar* (chief justice) Alhaje, whom he hints was a black African, having said earlier that the position was normally occupied by a black freed slave 'because black people from Guinea normally do not have relatives they can talk to about the king's justice, and no-one to be hurt by it'.[31] After this encounter, and presumably by agreement with those who attended, Boabdil was accompanied to the east of his kingdom – Baeza says to the villages of Vélez Blanco and Vélez Rubio – where he was supported financially and in kind by the Spanish monarchs.[32] His whereabouts for the next two to three years are not known for certain. He is believed to have returned to Castile at some point, very probably to Cordoba, possibly even under the direct protection of the House of Aguilar.[33] Hernán Pérez del Pulgar, one of the Christian heroes of the Granada War, who later wrote an early biography of Gonzalo Fernández de Córdoba and who is mentioned by Baeza in his text, stresses the close relationship between Boabdil and Gonzalo Fernández de Córdoba during this time. He says that the latter 'loved to please and serve the young man' and that Boabdil remembered him later for 'the good works and services he had done him during his captivity in Cordoba and his son's in Porcuna'.[34] There seems to have been a continuing association between the two, to which Baeza seems also to have been party.

In March 1486, the Albaicín (the district of Granada on the hill opposite the Alhambra) rose up in Boabdil's favour and there was fighting between his faction and that of his uncle 'Zagal' (Muhammad XII) – now occupying the role of emir after the death of Abū al-Ḥasan.[35] In circumstances which are uncertain, Boabdil again found himself overpowered by Fernando's troops at the strategically situated town of Loja.[36] He reportedly called Gonzalo Fernández de Córdoba – once again, the frontier noble associated most closely with Baeza – into the stricken town to broker new terms.[37] As the border with Granada moved forward, Gonzalo and his closest colleagues – Pérez del Pulgar, Martín de Alarcón and Fernán Álvarez, occupied the front line formed by the newly captured fortresses of Salar, Íllora, Moclín and Colomera.[38] Fernán Álvarez, described as a *caballero* from Alcalá la Real, had been living with his wife in Montilla and is closely linked to the Fernández de Córdoba family.[39] His second surname is given variously as 'de Alcaraz', 'de Sotomayor' and 'de Gadea', as well as 'de Alcalá', and this imprecision, typical of those wishing to hide their background, together with the notoriously *converso* name Álvarez, suggests to me that he may have been of *converso* origin, possibly even related to the Baezas (Hernando's two daughters used this surname).[40]

The new post-Loja accord enabled Boabdil to go back to Granada, to the Albaicín, and here Gonzalo Fernández de Córdoba, in close association with Martín de Alarcón and Fernán Álvarez, actively supported his efforts to re-establish himself as emir.[41] It is thanks to the fourth man of this quartet, Hernán Pérez del Pulgar, that we learn that these men spearheaded this cross-border strand of military action, which is passed over by other chroniclers, including Baeza.[42] The perspective of these men, with whom Hernando de Baeza is so closely associated, was far more nuanced and subtle than that represented in the predominant 'Moors versus Christians' accounts of the war, as it was they who supported Boabdil in order to return him to the status of emir – albeit one who would be a vassal of Castile. Baeza's reference to the grandees' earlier support for Boabdil, thus emerges as justification for this semi-clandestine strand of action involving men of lower rank.

Despite the caginess of chroniclers, which suggests a degree of secrecy regarding the military strand of support for Boabdil, documents record the monarchs' support for him in the form of clothing, provisions and money to pay his troops.[43] According to Pérez del Pulgar, Gonzalo also provided Boabdil with political advice, and he puts into the future *Gran Capitán*'s mouth a long speech to the people of the Albaicín, urging them to support Boabdil as their rightful emir and setting out the benefits in terms of the protection and trading opportunities they would enjoy with the Castilians.[44]

Baeza claims that the fighting in the Albaicín between Zagal's supporters and those of Boabdil lasted for a year.[45] It was during this time, he says, that Boabdil invited him to act as his go-between with the Spanish monarchs:

> He sent heralds to declare peace all along the frontier and a *mudéjar caballero* called Bobadilla went to the town of Alcaudete to do this. Abrahén de Mora [...] gave him a letter for me on the orders of the king [=emir] to tell me some of the things that had happened and saying that, as he needed a person who would come to the Catholic King and Queen on his behalf, he would be pleased if I would be willing to do that.[46]

So, while Gonzalo Fernández de Córdoba and the new frontier commanders were supporting Boabdil militarily inside Granada, Baeza, in parallel, was being asked to act in a quasi-diplomatic role on his behalf. Gonzalo must, at the very least, have been aware that a member of his family household had been invited to perform this role and was, in my view, probably instrumental in arranging it. Hernán Pérez del Pulgar tells us that he had 'spies' in Granada who acted as 'terceros' or intermediaries.[47] However, Baeza is at pains to stress that the invitation came directly from Boabdil himself; most likely to protect the reputation of Gonzalo. Although his account does not mention the support that the frontier commanders were offering Boabdil, it does capture the information that the Spanish monarchs were now allied with him. It is significant that Baeza uses the verb 'come' ('que viniese á los rreyes Catholicos de su parte'), which one has to resist translating as 'go' because it perfectly captures Baeza's ambiguous position, with a foot in both camps.[48] It places Baeza the author almost within the Spanish royal court as he is writing.

Baeza did not accept the emir's invitation immediately but delayed going until Boabdil's position as emir was secure – probably after the fall of Malaga (1487), which he does not mention at all, and the signing of a new accord with the monarchs.[49] This treaty required Boabdil to hand over the city in exchange for being granted extensive lands in the east of the kingdom and in the Alpujarras mountains.[50]

Baeza says he was then in close contact with Boabdil for 'three or four years' which, working back from January 1492, suggests he entered the emir's service sometime in 1488.[51] It has been assumed that he actually lived in Granada during this time, but this cannot be derived from the text.[52] The fact that he describes his role as 'coming to the Catholic Monarchs on his behalf' suggests that he was coming and going across the border. Pulgar notes that the queen was sending Boabdil money 'every month for his own maintenance and that of those who were with him' and it may be that he was involved in this, along with Abrahén de Robledo, another man who makes an appearance in Baeza's memoir.[53] Other evidence also suggests that he was not permanently behind 'enemy' lines, at least, not initially, having been witness to a will made by Don Alonso in his castle at Aguilar on 6 August 1488.[54]

When Baeza agreed to act as an intermediary between Boabdil and the Spanish court, he would have been under the impression that this would be for a period of perhaps just a few months. In fact, the war drew out for nearly another four years. One of the reasons why the war took so long to be brought to a conclusion was the impossibility of sustaining long campaigns two years in a row. The long-drawn out siege of Malaga in 1487 and that of Baza, a town in the north east of the kingdom, in 1489, meant that the intervening years (1488 and 1490) were ones of little military activity.[55] It was the defeat of Zagal and his troops at Baza that thrust Boabdil into the role of last-ditch defender of Muslim Granada. Zagal handed over all the eastern part of the kingdom, together with the Alpujarras – all the lands that Boabdil was to have received in exchange for Granada – directly to Fernando, making it unattractive for Fernando to return them to Boabdil, even in return for such a sought-after prize. Baeza says that once Baza had surrendered, Fernando sent Gonzalo Fernández de Córdoba and Martín de Alarcón to Boabdil to give him the bad news that their agreement would not stand.[56] They presumably did this rather diplomatically, because the message Boabdil took from it, according to Baeza, was that there was now a new angle on what had been agreed. Boabdil therefore sent his own messengers to the court in Cordoba, who came back with an uncompromising response which made the emir 'very shocked and frightened' – Fernando was already preparing to occupy Granada.[57] This was a turning point. Baeza says that Boabdil wanted to go back on a war footing but was persuaded to send another delegation to the Christian side, now in Seville. This included a 'very honourable merchant' named Abrahén Alcaiçi (el Cayci) who Baeza says was a very great friend of his.[58] The emissaries returned 'very discontented' saying that Fernando was not willing to keep to an arrangement which had been agreed twice.

Boabdil reacted by siding with his citizens and religious leaders who wanted to see a fierce defence of their city and, as Baeza, says 'from this time on the Christians and the Moors were at war'.[59] This was not strictly correct as some supporters of Zagal, now living under Christian rule and identified as *mudéjars*, were fighting on behalf of Fernando and against Boabdil.[60] Nevertheless, it highlights the change Baeza must have experienced in his own position: his friends Gonzalo Fernández de Córdoba and Martín de Alarcón were now fighting against Boabdil and he was behind enemy lines. This, for him, was the beginning of the war.

Boabdil succeeded in retaking various strongholds around the city, but his last stand was ultimately hopeless.[61] The last months of the conflict have passed into legend: the building of the town of Santa Fe, the overblown heroics of skirmishing in the *Vega* (the rich agricultural plain outside Granada) and the desperate Boabdil within the Alhambra, under threat from his own people.[62] But there was no heavy artillery: the idea was to put pressure on negotiations, not take the city by force of arms.[63] The fighting was in some senses a self-conscious charade with players acting out the last scene of a drama which they already understood to have great historical importance. Boabdil's dilemma was that he owed his position to the Christians but that, as emir, his people now looked to him to defend their city against the aggressors. Hernando de Baeza was all too aware of the drama and tragedy of the situation and described a tearful scene in which Boabdil says farewell to his mother, wife, sister and small son before going out to fight one morning with his body washed and perfumed 'as the Moors do when they are going into mortal danger'.[64]

Ambassadors, spies and mediators

These circumstances placed Baeza in a uniquely precarious yet pivotal position as the war entered its final phase. Boabdil was in constant contact with the monarchs during the time that Baeza claims he was working for him: there is evidence of two embassies in the second half of 1487, letters and exchanges of gifts in 1488 and 1489, and more intense negotiations after the fall of Baza in early 1490.[65] There were also open lines of communication with the child hostages who had been kept on the Christian side of the border.[66] Other than his own testimony, there is no direct documentary evidence of Baeza's role, though he was closely connected with those known to have been involved in these exchanges on both sides.

Baeza mentions various individuals who undertook embassies from Boabdil to the Spanish monarchs after the fall of Baza, when the relationship started to get more fraught. He describes how Aben Comixa (Yusuf ibn Kumasha), in his role as chief constable of Granada (*alguacil mayor*), undertook the embassy to Seville with Baeza's friend Abrahén el Cayci.[67] Baeza also mentions 'Abul Caçin el Male' who undertook the embassy to Cordoba, returning with unwelcome news which led Boabdil to set himself on a war footing with his former allies.[68] This is Boabdil's vizier and former tutor, Abū al-Qāsim, a powerful individual who, along with Aben Comixa and an *alfaqui* known as El Pequeñí, became the main negotiators on Boabdil's side.[69] Baeza expresses a poor opinion of this man and says that his own role was to prevent him from double-crossing Boabdil 'as he had already tried to do on another occasion'.[70] In one manuscript he is even described as a 'Moorish dog'.[71]

Other men known to have undertaken embassies to the Spanish court at this time were also close to Baeza, although he does not mention them in this respect. Abrahén de Robledo, a young man from Guadalajara who, according to Baeza, had taken part in the original conspiracy to put Boabdil on the throne, had acted as an emissary for the emir from as early as 1484.[72] The Castilians entrusted him with money to take to Boabdil at the time when they were supporting him financially and militarily in the Albaicín.[73] As one of Boabdil's closest collaborators, Robledo, like Baeza, was bilingual and used his linguistic skills in his master's service.[74] The ambiguity of Robledo's position is highlighted by the chronicler Palencia who describes how, during the fighting in Loja, he was taunted for switching sides by the Christians who recognized him. Baeza perhaps alludes to this when he describes him as having famously taken part in single combat in the *Vega* with Hernán Pérez del Pulgar.[75] Another man involved in the negotiations, another bilingual who is found acting as an interpreter and in negotiations for the release of captives, was Yuça de Mora, nephew of Baeza's friend Abrahén de Mora.[76] He later made a successful career for himself in Christian Granada and remained a Muslim until the mass baptisms of 1499–1500 when he took the name of Francisco Jiménez, presumably after Francisco Jiménez de Cisneros, the Archbishop of Toledo who instigated them.[77]

On the Castilian side, although Gonzalo Fernández de Córdoba and Martín de Alarcón were sent as envoys immediately after the fall of Baza, it was the monarchs' secretary, Hernando de Zafra, who led the subsequent negotiations, corresponding closely with Abū al-Qāsim and Aben Comixa.[78] Martín de Alarcón's role was viewed with suspicion by Zafra, and Pérez del Pulgar claims that Gonzalo Fernández had to insist on remaining involved.[79] He describes his hero secretly crossing the front line by night, presenting it as an example of his extreme bravery and desire to serve the monarchs, who he claims tried to stop him because they believed it was dangerous and the guide untrustworthy. He says that the future *Gran Capitán* had many opportunities to communicate with Boabdil during the siege of Granada and reassured the emir that he was 'as eager to serve him as when he had been commanded by his sovereigns to do so'.[80] This suggests a different, clandestine relationship, no longer sanctioned by the crown and no doubt facilitated by Baeza. Also on the Castilian side, Fernando sent a man named Juan de Baeza, his *escribano*, with a letter to Boabdil, but I have not been able to link this man to Hernando's family.[81]

The monarchs were certainly aware of Hernando's continuing presence in Boabdil's court. Baeza tells us that they sent him a secret message explaining who should have access to the Alhambra in order to carry out the final negotiation. They stressed how important it was to them that Granada should be surrendered promptly because of the cost of the campaign and the fact that winter was coming.[82] This evidence has led to suggestions that Baeza acted as a 'double agent' while in Boabdil's court, feeding back information to the Christian side.[83] Certainly, the frontier commanders, and especially Gonzalo Fernández de Córdoba and the Count of Tendilla, made great use of what are called 'espías' (spies) in Granada at different phrases during the war.[84] But terms like 'double agent' or 'spy', with today's cold-war connotations of aggression and betrayal, are not the right fit for this situation. Given the support that Boabdil had received from the frontier commanders, and the ongoing position of the prince and other young notables as hostages in their care, it is not surprising that they maintained close contact with him. Men such as Baeza enabled the contacts and negotiations which would bring the conflict to an end. Far from betraying one side or the other, these 'spies' were instrumental in bringing the two sides together – 'mediator' would be a better term.[85] Francisco de Medina y Mendoza, who drew directly on Baeza's account, describes him as an interpreter and his work as 'tercería' – matchmaking.[86] As the negotiations were being concluded, Abū al-Qāsim sent to Zafra a long list of Boabdil's collaborators and supporters who were to be given safe conducts.[87] Hernando de Baeza was not included in this list – perhaps it was clear to Boabdil and his circle that Hernando did not need a safe conduct: they were aware that the monarchs knew him and knew that he was there.

One activity in which Baeza says he was involved might at first reading lend weight to the thesis that he was an undercover agent secretly supporting the Christian cause. He says that he helped two Christians, who had been taken as captives to Granada many years previously and had converted to Islam, to escape back to their homes in Villacarrillo and Cieza.[88] The queen's treasurer records that in 1490, Teresa de Baeza and Beatriz de Molina escaped from Granada and were provided with charity by Isabel. These may have been the two *elches* rescued by Baeza, and the coincidence of the surnames raises the intriguing possibility that they may even have been relatives of his, since the Baezas were related to the Molinas, a powerful *converso* family in Úbeda, which is close to Villacarrillo.[89] Baeza also mentions that he released another former prisoner who had been living in Marbella.[90] Can this activity be read as an act of non-aggressive resistance to Boabdil, a betrayal of his position as a member of Boabdil's household? The fact that he says he did this 'secretly' might suggest so. But there is more than a little spin in Baeza's portrayal of them as 'captives' since, having converted to Islam, they would have escaped their enslavement and would have been living as free members of society – as Baeza's description of one of them as a 'resident' of Marbella lets slip. Baeza adds powerfully to his credibility vis-à-vis his readers by describing himself supposedly liberating captives in the same way that Pérez del Pulgar contributed to the legends being spun around the *Gran Capitán* in describing his glorious but failed attempt to release a much larger number of Christian captives in Granada from the notorious *corral* (pen) where they were kept.[91] Liberating Christian captives was one of the seven acts of mercy, an activity which was regarded at the time as the epitome of Christian virtue, as well as weighing in favour on the Day of Judgement. It was commonplace both before and after the conquest of Granada for testators to leave money in their wills for the release of Christian captives 'in the lands of the Moors'.[92] The liberation of Christian captives forms an important element in many Christian narratives of the Granada War, legitimizing the conquest and emphasizing the moral leadership of Isabel and Fernando within the Christian world.[93] The liberations themselves were staged as public spectacles which represented the monarchs in the role of redeemers of Christian Spain from the chains of Islam.[94] This same idea of the whole kingdom released from under the Muslim yoke in fulfilment of Old Testament prophecies is also expressed in the mass written by Archbishop Talavera to celebrate the victory.⁹⁵ However, Baeza's 'captives' were free men and women aware that Granada was about to fall and that in Christian society they would be regarded as apostates. Baeza engineered their escape not from the chains of Islam, but from retribution from the Christian side for having abandoned the faith in which they had been baptized, framing them as victims of war and stressing that they were 'as innocent as babes' and 'wanted to be Christians if they could'.⁹⁶

An activity that Baeza does not cover in his account, which ends with the signing of the surrender agreement, is his involvement in liberating captives from the other side. Immediately after they had taken over the city, the Spanish monarchs put a great deal of effort into implementing the terms of the *Capitulaciones* by which all the residents of Granada and surrounding areas who had been taken captive during the war were to be liberated.⁹⁷ Documents published by Miguel Angel Ladero show that 334 captives were liberated while the monarchs and their troops were still encamped in the *Vega* outside Granada, and the whereabouts of a further 351 identified.⁹⁸ The crown had to compensate their captors with cash sums which varied depending on the age of the captives, and from the records of these payments, we can see that Gonzalo Fernández de Córdoba played a leading role in rounding them up and collecting payment. Thirteen of those liberated in the *Vega* had apparently spontaneously presented themselves to Gonzalo, and there were another thirteen from Íllora, the fortress he commanded. There were also twenty-seven presented by a man named 'Baeza' on behalf of Gonzalo Fernández de Córdoba, the greatest number presented by any individual and it seems very likely that this Baeza is our Hernando.⁹⁹ Fernández de Córdoba received a total of 184,000 *maravedís* for his prisoners, vastly more than any of the others named.¹⁰⁰ His brother Alonso de Aguilar, who is recorded as having 67 captives, received the substantial sum of 105,000 *maravedís* and immediately after his name is another reference to a '<Baeza>' (*sic*, in brackets) identified as having one.¹⁰¹ We have no way of knowing whether this Baeza is the same one who presented captives on behalf of Gonzalo, but his proximity to Don Alonso would suggest that it was either Hernando or one of his relatives.

The bias of surviving historical record

Hernando de Baeza's account of the events leading to the surrender of Granada has been accepted as authentic, if a little fuzzy on chronology.¹⁰² His statement about his own presence there is detailed and specific:

> At ten o'clock on the second night, while the king was alone with me between the two doors of the patio of the *Cuarto de Comares* and the other door which goes out into the patio where the large water trough is set on the ground, a Moorish gentleman came in bringing with him Gonzalo Fernández de Córdoba and Hernando de Zafra.¹⁰³

However, despite the credibility of his claim that he played an active role in the negotiations – and with one exception which I will discuss below – he is not mentioned in any of the rich documentation relating to the last years of the Granada

War, the extensive to-ing and fro-ing which resulted in the *Capitulaciones*, or in the diverse narrative sources, all of which have been the subject of detailed and repeated scrutiny.[104] The documentation relating to the creation of early Christian Granada and the distribution of property, offices and land to both longstanding and new supporters of the Christian monarchs has been very closely examined, and Hernando de Baeza is absent from these too.[105] This is surprising given that he evidently possessed intercultural and linguistic skills which would have been extremely useful in the delicate task of establishing Christian rule over the Muslim populace. Others, both Muslim converts to Christianity and old Christians, were richly rewarded for their role in the process; this begs the question why the author, who seems to have been so well connected, did not receive similar honours. This is anomalous given the enthusiasm with which his work has been acclaimed as an authentic source and widely exploited alongside documentation from the period, both Arabic and Castilian, in scholarly narratives of the capture of Granada.[106]

We may imagine that Baeza was a fugitive from the Inquisition, since the start of his role as an intermediary coincides almost exactly with his father's demise as a result of his condemnation by the Cordoba Tribunal. However, it would be wrong to attribute Baeza's absence from documentary and chronistic record solely to the idea that a man whose father had just been condemned as a heretic would be unmentionable. Neither does the explanation that he was too insignificant to mention hold water. He clearly did play at least as important a role as some others who are mentioned and, by his own account, the monarchs were aware of his presence and keen to exploit it – irrespective of any ignominy that might be attached to him. I see his comment that he was 'nothing there' not as an admission of his own insignificance but rather as an assertion that he was there, a presence almost 'under erasure' but nonetheless an actor in the drama.

There are two reasons why there is barely any corroboration of his presence external to his own piece of writing. First, is the concern for secrecy – not relating to the Inquisition but relating to the way the monarchs wanted to manage their public image. The Spanish monarchs had an interest in maintaining an overarching public narrative that they were engaged in a bitter war against religious enemies, and contemporary chroniclers handle the question of their alliance with Boabdil with some caution or not at all. It seems more than a coincidence that none of the three treaties between Boabdil and the monarchs have survived intact and likely that they may have been systematically destroyed.[107] The chronicler Andrés Bernáldez (1450–1513) – almost an exact contemporary of Baeza – says that the terms of the 1483 treaty after Boabdil was captured at Lucena were secret, but we can infer that this information was perhaps coming into the public domain when Baeza was writing in around 1510, since he says that he will not provide details of the accord because this information 'will be written elsewhere'.[108] Gonzalo Fernández de Córdoba's role providing support to Boabdil in the Albaicín with Martín de Alarcón was mostly omitted by chroniclers, or only mentioned extremely briefly, until Pérez del Pulgar published his account in 1527, and the *Gran Capitán*'s knowledge of Arabic was only made public after his death by Lucio Marineo Sículo.[109] The uncertainty around Boabdil's whereabouts in the period 1483–6 – which led one scholar to argue that he remained in Christian custody until this later date – is further evidence of the extreme caution on both sides as regards public discussion of contacts between them.[110] Hernando himself is very reticent about details and dates which could be sensitive, and avoids linking himself with Gonzalo Fernández de Córdoba to the extent that nineteenth- and twentieth-century scholars were misled into thinking that he was working for Martín de Alarcón.[111] Fernando del Pulgar, who cites him as a source in his late work on Granada and the Nasrid royal family, specifically tells us that Baeza was a paid employee of Boabdil, that is not working for anyone else, but not an unpaid supporter either, nor there under duress as a slave or captive.[112] Pulgar's assertion seems unnecessarily trenchant and may disguise a more complicated reality. The claim that Boabdil was paying Baeza is somewhat meaningless, since the unfortunate emir claimed that he 'did not have a drachma' except that which came from the monarchs.[113] There are therefore many layers of subterfuge to peel away, aided by the knowledge of Baeza's background in Cordoba and Montilla, in order to grasp his real position.

If the need for secrecy explains why Baeza is not mentioned in the chronicles, it is not sufficient to explain why he does not appear in correspondence and other documentation linked to the final stages of the Granada War. However, these sources are skewed towards evidence preserved by the monarchs' secretary Hernando de Zafra. I see Baeza and Fernández de Córdoba as maintaining a different, perhaps even conflicting, channel of communication directly with Boabdil. The plentiful documentation published by Gaspar Remiro and others at the turn of the nineteenth and twentieth centuries can lead us to believe that we have a very full picture of how the negotiations were conducted; in fact, almost all the documentation comes from Zafra's family archive. It is clear that the monarchs did appoint both Fernández de Córdoba and Zafra to carry out the treaty negotiations: Alonso de Palencia describes them both frequently coming and going from the Christian camp to the Alhambra.[114] But Zafra's agitation about Martín de Alarcón shows how jealously he guarded his role as the official negotiator. Zafra was highly motivated to preserve documentation recording his exchanges on behalf of the monarchs with Abū al-Qāsim and Aben Comixa rather than that of a potential parallel line of communication involving Gonzalo Fernández de Córdoba, Hernando and Boabdil himself. Baeza saw his role as protecting Boabdil from the 'treachery' of Abū al-Qāsim, Zafra's main interlocutor.[115] There therefore emerges a picture of Baeza and Gonzalo Fernández de Córdoba taking forward diplomatic relations through their own personal contacts and cutting across the monarchs' own representative. This scenario was to be repeated in Italy, as discussed in Chapter 4.

Between 1490 and the handover of Granada, the queen made gifts of sumptuous cloth to men and women on both sides whom she wished to reward or draw closer to her.[116] These not only included men involved in the Granada negotiations, such as Abū al-Qāsim, Aben Comixa and Yuça de Mora, but also an individual named 'Baeza' who is almost certainly Hernando. On 27 July 1491, 'Baeza' received six yards of purple Florence silk (*azeytuní morado de Florencia*), two and a half yards of purple Florence satin (*raso morado de Florencia*), five yards of burgundy London cloth (*grana de Londres*) and two and a half yards of crimson satin (*raso carmesí*).[117] From the record, made by the queen's treasurer, it appears that these were handed over to him actually at the Christian camp. The next week, on 5 August, he received a further four yards of crimson silk, this latter as a gift specifically for himself.[118] Ladero, who has published this evidence, also believes that the 'Baeza' concerned is probably Hernando de Baeza and says that these gifts were intended to oil the wheels of the ongoing negotiations.[119] One of the motives may also have been to create a more magnificent spectacle at the surrender ceremony. The use of his surname alone may be another indication of a desire for secrecy, or evidence of his lesser social status. The document shows that the queen was aware of Baeza's involvement and the value was quite considerable, though it is not possible to say if everything handed to Baeza was for him personally. For comparison, Baeza received cloth to the value of more than 30,000 *maravedís*, while Abū al-Qāsim's gift was worth 22,300 *maravedís*; in the same account book the chronicler Tristan de Silva, who was in the Christian camp at the time, was given cloth worth just under 15,000 *maravedís*. Baeza was clearly someone of some importance, despite his protestation that he was 'nothing' there. His presence in the Christian camp in the run up to the surrender agreement is confirmed in another source which shows him as witness to an arbitration agreement between Alonso de Aguilar and the Count of Cabra in relation to the estate of Albendín.[120]

Baeza's virtual absence from record is typical not only of the liminal figures who helped shape diplomatic contacts between Muslim and Christian Iberia, but also of interpreters in war in our own day: their intermediate status is disruptive of grand narratives of conflict.[121] The synecdoche inherent in the use of the word 'lengua', reducing the man to a disembodied 'tongue', provides a clue to understanding the tension inherent in Baeza's text between a desire to stress his own presence and role, and a need to draw back and keep his identity hidden. The testimony of interpreters required to keep a low profile in our own times and sometimes referred to as 'lips', provides a clear parallel which sheds light on Baeza's sense of being 'nothing there'.[122] It has been observed that translators and interpreters in situations of conflict have to both represent and resist the narratives which create the intellectual and moral environment for the conflict in the first place.[123] It is Baeza's efforts to do both that have made his account so complex and so interesting.

The terms of surrender

The terms for the surrender of Granada, the *Capitulaciones*, have been seen as reflecting an integrative rather than exclusionary approach towards the defeated residents of the city, with their very diverse faith identities.[124] Although clearly establishing the dominance of Christianity, the treaty provided many guarantees to the Granadans about the preservation of their religion, legal system and way of life which, as events unrolled, were in place for less than a decade. The text of the document has been the subject of considerable debate from different viewpoints and the good faith of the signatories on both sides questioned. While it has been suggested that the monarchs never intended for the agreement to stand in perpetuity, Arabic sources criticize Boabdil for collaborating in the demise of the Muslim state.[125] In his elegantly constructed appeal for asylum to the King of Fez, after surrendering Granada but before leaving Spain, Boabdil himself made the case that he saved Granada from a fate such as Bagdad (1258), perhaps implicitly also referencing Malaga, whose inhabitants suffered a much harsher fate and were all sold into slavery in 1487.[126] Baeza's evidence, which has only come to light recently with the discovery of new manuscripts of his work (see Chapter 7), provides fresh evidence of the options on the table as the terms were agreed.[127]

The initial wording drawn up in the Alhambra was subject to a detailed legal review on the Christian side and the final document includes some small but significant changes which take a harsher line than the original proposal.[128] Baeza says that long discussions were held between the two sides in the Christian camp and that Gonzalo Fernández de Córdoba and Hernando de Zafra were brought together to the Alhambra to thrash out the final points on which negotiations were in deadlock.[129] This coincides with Alonso de Palencia's contemporary account, but it is Baeza who recounts the points on which these discussions turned.[130]

The first was regarding the preservation of Boabdil's honour at the point of surrender. Baeza says the emir would rather have been cut into a thousand pieces than offer public obeisance to Fernando by getting off his horse and kissing his hand. Dismounting from his horse would not only symbolize submission but also physically put him in a position where he could be captured or killed. A similar situation had occurred in 1478 when Don Alonso de Aguilar first submitted to the authority of Fernando and Isabel outside Cordoba. In the pretence of having an injury, he strapped his feet to his stirrups with taffeta bandages in order not to have to dismount from his horse and to enable him to flee if the situation demanded it.[131] Baeza describes how he suggested a solution involving a charade whereby Boabdil would make to dismount, at which point Fernando would, with apparent magnanimity, indicate for him not to.[132] Chroniclers describe a similar encounter after Boabdil's capture at Lucena, when he was taken to meet the king and queen in Cordoba. Just before his knee touched the ground as he knelt to kiss the king's hand, Fernando made him get up.[133] Baeza may have drawn on his knowledge of these incidents in suggesting the solution which appears to have been adopted, saving face for Boabdil and allowing Fernando to appear magnanimous in victory. He presents the issue dismissively as 'a matter of vanity', but it is a critique of Fernando's vanity as much as it is of Boabdil's. Baeza understood that his role as an interpreter was not merely to carry out a superficial transfer from one language to another, but also to manage the projection of symbolic meanings during diplomatic encounters. Alonso de Palencia's account of the handover, written less than a week after it happened, describes the encounter between Boabdil and Fernando as taking place exactly according to Baeza's diplomatic solution.[134] However, more propagandistic narratives and depictions from the Christian side show Boabdil kissing Fernando's hand.[135]

It is the other point of contention, the one referred to in my introduction, which goes to the heart of the controversies concerning the Christianization of Fernando and Isabel's Spain:

[…] in relation to the apostates or *elches* who are Christians who become Moors, that they should not be forced to return to our holy Catholic faith against their will […] in the discussions about this it seemed to me, although I was nothing there, that [this] should not rightfully/legally ['de derecho'] be done.[136]

Behind this laconic observation lies a tangle of unspoken meanings and, I think, the reason why this section of Baeza's text has been lost to us for so long. Baeza wades into a polemic which was live at the time he was writing and became even more fiercely contended as the century wore on.[137] The specific case which Baeza comments on is about the *elches* and whether, having been baptized as Christians before arriving in Granada as captives, they should be treated as apostates for having adopted Islam. Baeza depicts them as being as 'innocent as babes': 'en la ynocencia del capillo' – a reference to the cloth headdress used at baptism and in penitential rites.[138] I understand that he is drawing attention to their baptism as infants, before they were able to have any understanding of Christian doctrine and is asking his readers to consider whether religious faith can have any meaning if it is not accompanied by the ability to be self-conscious. In his reference to 'rights' I understand he is referring to the thirteenth-century legal code, the *Siete Partidas* and the principle of religious self-determination which had underpinned practice on the frontier. This takes him into the wider issue which had occupied theologians and canonists throughout the Middle Ages: the extent to which coercion should be used in the service of Christianity.[139]

Baeza adopts a position similar to Pulgar's earlier plea against harsh treatment for those who had had no opportunity for detailed instruction in the Catholic faith, and to that of Talavera who had called for a minimum period of eight months' religious instruction before baptism. Amid concern about *converso* judaizers in Seville in the period immediately before the implementation of the Inquisition, the future Archbishop had written that 'what is done through fear or by force [...] cannot be long-lasting; what is done through charity and love lasts forever'.[140] At the time of the Granada negotiations, Baeza already had direct personal experience of the consequences of a doctrine that taught that violence could be employed in the service of faith and had seen in his own family how easily new Christians could be accused of insincerity and heresy. At the time he was writing, the Edict of Expulsion of 1492 and the mass baptisms of Muslims after the breakdown of the *Capitulaciones* provisions had created another generation of new Christians to be assimilated. The debate over forced baptisms was increasingly entwined with the discussion of what should be done with those who, having converted under duress, later relapsed.[141] Baeza is therefore aligning himself with critics of the hard-line approach taken by the Inquisition which accepted the validity of conversion to Christianity through 'threats and intimidation' as put forward by Duns Scotus.[142] This approach relied on canon law – legal pronouncements made by the Catholic Church going back centuries, in relation to the conversion of Jews – which took precedence over the principles enshrined in Alfonso X's civil code. Those who argued for this approach increasingly tried to justify and define the use of coercion, by distinguishing between 'absolute' and 'conditional' force.[143] A later inquiry into the validity of forced conversion deemed that all were valid since those who did not want to convert could have 'chosen' to die instead.[144] In stating his position, Baeza was clearly aware of the difference between canon and civil law, as he reveals in a reference to the Nasrid legal system.[145] His use of the word 'derecho' and his implicit alignment with such figures as Juan de Lucena, who argued against forced baptism, must therefore be seen as deliberate.[146]

The only copies of Baeza's manuscripts which were known until very recently – one which can be dated around 1562 and a later eighteenth-century copy of the same – are missing the end section which contains this account of the surrender negotiations.[147] By the mid-sixteenth century, both the *morisco* question and that of methods used in the Christianization of the New World had become extremely sensitive. Theologians were using the *morisco* precedent to argue against forced conversion in the New World, but they had to address the topic indirectly in order to do so.[148] It is likely therefore that Baeza's final pages, which take such a clear line on forced conversion and cite 'rights', were regarded as dangerous or subversive and omitted or destroyed.

Comparison of the original proposal with the final *Capitulaciones* document shows that the question of the *elches* had indeed been a point of disagreement.[149] Boabdil's original text proposed that no-one of either sex who had converted to Islam should be forced to return to Christianity. The final document reformulates this, giving some protection to *elche* women who had married Muslim men (*romías*) but watering down the general provision by merely saying that Islamized former Christians should be treated with respect. Baeza was writing after all remaining Muslims had been forced to convert to Christianity and the *elches* had become the first target of the Inquisition.[150] He homes in on the *elches* as a hybrid religious group emerging from the frontier context and claimed by both sides, precisely the group whose harsh treatment sparked the 1499–1500 rebellion which saw all Muslims lose the rights enshrined in the *Capitulaciones*. In remembering the theological discussions to which he had been party regarding the status of Christian converts to Islam in the new social order, he highlights the clash of two radically different views of the new, exclusively Christian, society. The stance he takes must be read not just as a concern for the *elches* but as a wider appeal for all those who had converted, or were descendants of converts, from Islam or from Judaism.

Hernán Pérez del Pulgar's depiction of Gonzalo Fernández urgently gate-crashing the negotiations is no doubt invented, but it perhaps contains a truth in that it expresses the strength of the future *Gran Capitán*'s determination to be involved.[151] It is possible that he wanted to influence the blueprint for the new post-Conquest social order and prevent Zafra from taking a hard line on behalf of the monarchs – or influencers in their court – in his negotiations with Abū al-Qāsim, a man whom Baeza regarded as untrustworthy. A less rose-tinted view might see his role as using his influence with Boabdil to strike a deal at all costs and persuade the emir that it would be safe to surrender – Ruiz Domènec has him wracked with guilt for having betrayed a man with whom he was sexually involved.[152] The idea of a past homosexual relationship between Boabdil and Fernández de Córdoba is a wonderfully symbolic depiction of doomed *convivencia*, but one which is sadly lacking in corroborative evidence. What Baeza's testimony provides is an insight into the options on the Christian side as they approached discussion of the treaty. The famous negotiations for the surrender of Granada therefore emerge as much as a tussle between two approaches on the Christian side as diplomatic bargaining between Boabdil and the Catholic Monarchs.

Celebrations of the conquest

After the conquest of Granada, meanings were immediately attached to it in the public sphere through the outpouring of celebrations, public events, learned speeches and sermons designed to commemorate it.[153] There is no doubt that the victory of Fernando and Isabel was an event of major international importance. However, the extravagant celebrations it provoked were far from spontaneous, but orchestrated to glorify the achievements of the monarchs by associating them with the divine will, and to consolidate their political power both within their kingdoms and internationally. Within both Castile and Aragon, instructions were sent to churches and town councils as to how the victory was to be celebrated publicly with processions, church services and other public events.[154] When the monarchs visited towns within their domains, the authorities were ordered to mark their entry with huge victory parades.[155] The fetters of Christian captives liberated from Granada were displayed on the walls of churches and monasteries, symbolizing the redemption of Christian Spain from the chains of Islam – some of which still remain today.[156]

In Granada, its first Archbishop, Hernando de Talavera, wrote a mass designed to be celebrated annually on the anniversary of the conquest.[157] To read Talavera's mass is to sink deeply into the post-conquest mentality Baeza must have been familiar with. It is a text for a performance designed to inspire profound awe and intense religious fervour. Even without the chanting, the responses, the incense and the emotion of a live audience, the mass impresses with its depiction of the supposed oppression of Muslim domination, the cruelty and iniquity of the evil enemies and the mystical significance of the victory as fulfilling Old Testament prophecies. The conquest of Granada is greeted as a liberation from diabolic tyranny and the end of wars. The mass presents the monarchs with the power and glory of biblical heroes and celebrates the mystic destiny of Isabel, the seventh woman to be a Spanish queen and the idea that all Muslims will be converted by the End of Days.

In Rome, the response to the news was even more politicized.[158] Influential supporters of the monarchs within the Curia, including most prominently Bernardino López de Carvajal, soon to become Cardinal of Santa Cruz, had already acted as fundraisers and advocates for the war by lobbying for papal support in the form of indulgences, the diverting of church funds to finance the war, and bulls declaring it a crusade. They reported back on the impact of this support by amplifying the newsworthiness of each victory – Ronda, Malaga, Baza and finally Granada itself – through sermons designed for publication and wider distribution.[159] As news of each victory reached Rome, Pope Innocent VIII, whose papacy from 1484 to 1492 coincided almost exactly with the Granada War, would order flares or beacons to be lit, church bells to be rung and masses to be held in thanksgiving.[160] Through their sermons and orations in Rome between 1485 and 1492, the Catalan intellectual Pere Boscà, the protonotary Antonio Geraldini, and Carvajal shaped and developed the narrative of the Spanish monarchs as glorious crusading leaders of Christendom with a divine mission to overcome the 'enemies of the faith' – a political project which would culminate in the election of the Valencian Rodrigo Borgia as Pope Alexander VI in August 1492 and, indeed, continue throughout his papacy and beyond.[161]

The extravagant, lavishly financed ways in which the conquest of Granada was celebrated in Rome reinforced these messages. No expense was spared in harnessing the full artistic and technological resources of Renaissance Italy to communicate the world-changing transcendence of the event.[162] Significant among these were performances and reconstructions such as the interactive representation staged by Carvajal in what is now the Piazza Navona, with a wooden structure representing Granada and prizes for the first to enter it. Tournaments merged into that year's carnival celebrations and completely overshadowed those organized locally.[163] On 21 April 1492 the pontifical secretary Carlo Verardi presented a dramatization of the final events of the Granada War, performed at the residence of Cardinal Raffaele Riario. In the Aragonese court at Naples, there were at least two performances celebrating the triumph by the poet Jacopo Sannazaro, a man who was later a habitué of the *Gran Capitán*'s court there.[164]

From propaganda to historiography

The triumphalist narratives of the Christian monarchs 'recovering' land unjustly held by infidel invaders fed into later historiography and were repurposed by Catholic nationalist historians in the nineteenth and twentieth centuries as the *Reconquista*.[165] But, although the conquest of Granada was widely disseminated and celebrated throughout the Christian world as a major historical breakthrough, its repercussions were by no means certain at the time Baeza was writing, nor could they have felt clear to those whose task it would be to convert the extraordinary amount of news and propaganda surrounding the event into a matter of historical record. With the exception of the work of Andrés Bernáldez, who was not an official chronicler but, as chaplain to the Inquisitor General Diego de Deza, the purveyor of an extreme Scotist position in dealing with heresy and conversion, there was what I have called a 'historiographical hiatus' with the conquest of Granada not emerging into mainstream or official historiography until the middle of the sixteenth century. [166]

It was in this hiatus – perhaps, indeed, as a response to it – that Hernando de Baeza wrote the version of his text which has been handed down in the extant manuscripts. In the interim, Granada underwent far-reaching social, religious and cultural change as the terms agreed in the *Capitulaciones* were replaced by a requirement for all to convert to Christianity. Some ascribe the change of approach to the declining influence of Isabel and her *converso* advisers after the death of Prince Juan, the heir to the thrones of Castile and Aragon, in 1497. In Castile, Isabel could be succeeded by a daughter, but in Aragon only male children could inherit. With the continuing unity of the two kingdoms in doubt, and Isabel's power in decline, Fernando started to impose his own line and appoint Aragonese supporters to key positions previously occupied by Isabel's *converso* courtiers.[167] Talavera, who had been Isabel's confessor until becoming Granada's first archbishop, found his softly-softly approach towards converting the Muslims of Granada fall out of favour as the Archbishop of Toledo, Francisco Jiménez de Cisneros, swept into the city with more aggressive methods designed to achieve more immediate results. Soon after Talavera's death, a legend was spun around his figure painting him as a tireless preacher imbued with charismatic qualities and the virtues of the early Christian martyrs. His memory was invoked not only to denote a milder approach but also to register discreet opposition to Fernando and criticism of the methods used by the Inquisition.[168] It would be easy to ascribe to Baeza the position of Talavera as opposed to the harder line taken by Cisneros, who presided over the forced baptisms of 1499–1500.[169] However, Baeza's line is at once more culturally aware and more politically sensitive than Talavera's, with his well-meaning but overbearing admonitions to the *moriscos* (new Christians converts from Islam), such as shaving and adopting a 'Christian' diet.[170]

The first indication that the terms of the *Capitulaciones* were to be scrapped was the separation of *mudéjar* and Christian districts in Granada in 1498, followed by the introduction of the Inquisition under the man who would later turn his attention to those members of the Baeza family who had survived its initial bout of devastation in Cordoba: Diego Rodríguez Lucero. Lucero's first investigations were directed not at *moriscos* but at the *elches*, whose plight Hernando de Baeza highlights in his memoir.[171] At the same time, Cisneros set about demanding that the *elches* should return to Christianity, locking them up if they refused to do so.[172] The Muslims read all this as a direct threat, foreseeing that the persecution of the *elches* would soon spread to them. In December 1499, there was an uprising in the Albaicín. Peace was restored by Talavera and the Count of Tendilla, now the city's military governor, who negotiated an amnesty for those involved – but only in exchange for wholesale conversion of the remaining population to Christianity. This brought the Muslims into line with the Jews, who had already been forced to convert or emigrate as a result of the Edict of Expulsion in 1492. It was hailed as yet another triumph for the monarchs as unifying the whole of Iberia in the Christian faith for the first time in nearly 800 years.

Baeza must have been all too aware of the disconnect between the rhetoric and the reality, for the settlement resulted not in uniform Christianity, but in a population whose faith status was more complex and nuanced than ever before – we might call it 'superdiverse'.[173] Faith groups and sub-groups now included not only *conversos* descended from Jews and alleged 'judaizers' who had fled to Granada to escape persecution, but new converts and reconverts – former Christians who had become Muslims, or reverted to Judaism, who returned to Christianity. Among these, some had converted through genuine belief, others for reasons of convenience, others because they were unable or unwilling to emigrate and had no alternative. Children of interfaith marriages where one partner had converted or reconverted added another layer of complexity to the mix. There was also an ethnic dimension, which Baeza alludes to in mentioning that the emir's *mizwars* were normally black Africans. The city, and the kingdom of Granada more generally, saw important demographic changes, as Muslims not wishing to convert emigrated to North Africa and new colonizers from across Spain arrived to take their place, with ensuing intercultural difficulties.[174]

In this situation, being able to establish some common ground and unity of purpose was fundamental, yet the prevailing narratives on the ground were told only from the Christian perspective and a triumphalist one at that. Baeza was aware of historiographical traditions which had created a shared sense of the past within Christian Spain. For centuries, narratives stressing 'national' unity and shared faith had been used to overcome factionalism and unite the Christian kingdoms of Iberia in a drive to expel the Muslims. These narratives had enabled the successful union of Castile and Aragon which had propelled Spain to world power status. But now that former Muslims – and, indeed, former Jews – had become part of the Christian polity, how was the history of Granada to be told in a way that would unify rather than divide? And how was a *judeoconverso* going to write an account which would do this while avoiding being cast as a subversive?

In writing up his memories of the negotiations of 1491, Baeza was aware that the dream of peaceful conversion had been superseded by a harsher reality. But the ideal of a generous and compassionate Christian society, united in faith, was still alive and, despite his own precarious position, he wove into his memoir a clear message of support for it. But if his brief and almost apologetic comment aligns him with the integrationist positions of Cartagena and Oropesa, it also associates him with an oppositional political stance at the time he was writing, about which I will have more to say in Chapter 5.

3

Among the Andalusian élite

'... *that House where I grew up*'¹

Reconciliation

After the surrender of Granada, when Baeza returned to the world of the victors, he was immediately confronted with the harsh reality of his own situation as the son of a man only recently condemned to death by the Inquisition. Despite the relative tolerance expressed in the *Capitulaciones*, the victory over the Muslims inspired a hardening of the monarchs' policy towards Jews and heretics. The edict expelling Jews who wished to continue practising their religion was issued from Granada on 31 March.² Less than a month after the surrender of Granada, on 24 January 1492, twenty-four men and seven women were burnt as heretics in Cordoba.³

In September that year, Hernando was to be found in Montilla, as witness to a document issued by Gonzalo Fernández de Córdoba empowering another servant, Gonzalo de Herrera, to collect money on his behalf.⁴ Two months later, in December 1492, the monarchs announced the arrival of the Inquisition in the town. They demanded that the Inquisitors be assisted and treated honourably. It was necessary to write the letter, they explained, because 'despite letters and formal requests made by the Inquisitors to be shown heretics' property belonging to the Exchequer, some people had been making excuses not to do so'.⁵ They therefore asked that when the Inquisitors arrived in the domains of Don Alonso de Aguilar, they were to be treated with the same courtesy as had been shown to them in other towns. No-one was to impede the arrest and punishment of heretics by giving them shelter in their houses or fortresses and if any of the heretics or apostates were away, the Inquisitors were to be shown their property so it could be sequestered. We must understand this instruction as implying Alonso de Aguilar's likely resistance to the Inquisition and the targeting of *conversos* such as the Baezas living under his protection.

The noble lord's response – at least in the case of the Baezas – was to appeal to the monarchs over the heads of the Inquisition, calling in the debt of gratitude he must have felt was due to him for his role in the war against Granada. The evidence for this comes from testimony given by Hernando's brother-in-law, Alonso de Aguilar's *contador* Gonzalo de Córdoba, at his 1533 Inquisition trial (see genealogical chart p. 12). When challenged to say whether members of his family had ever been condemned or reconciled by the Inquisition, he claimed that Don Alonso de Aguilar had obtained a royal prerogative for his sisters, Mencia Sánchez, 'wife of Fernando de Baeza', and Beatriz Álvarez, 'wife of Gonzalo de Baeza' (Hernando's brother) to be given 'secret penitence'. He said that this had happened when Don Alonso de Aguilar 'went to Barcelona during the lifetime of the Catholic King'. As a result of Gonzalo de Córdoba's statement, the Inquisitors examining his case searched the files but had been unable to find a record of the trials of either the women or their husbands. However, they did find evidence that a third sister, Aldonza Rodríguez, had been disinherited by her father for fleeing to Portugal with her husband. They therefore accepted Gonzalo's statement, that their reconciliations had been in secret, as true.[6]

We can date Alonso de Aguilar's visit to Barcelona to 1493, a year which the king spent almost entirely in that city, after being wounded in a knife attack which nearly cost him his life.[7] When Hernando's daughter Teresa was questioned by the Inquisition in 1514, she stated that neither of her parents had ever been reconciled or penanced for heresy.[8] If, as Gonzalo de Córdoba claimed, the reconciliation was a secret one, it is possible that she genuinely believed this to be so, or perhaps she knew she could lie with impunity because there would be no record in the Inquisition's files. Either way, her testimony lends support to the idea of a secret reconciliation.

Rehabilitation

The initial period of intensified persecution of people of Jewish origin post-1492 has been seen as giving way to a new phase in 1495–7 when 'reconciliation' gave way to 'rehabilitation' – a restoration of full rights to bear arms, wear silk, hold public offices and take up roles such as legal representatives and tax collectors.[9] A document dated 11 May 1496 lists 1,589 *conversos* who had paid what were supposed to be final amounts of money to the Cordoba Inquisition to gain 'rehabilitation' into society.[10] The document does not list any people of significant wealth or high social status: most are middle-ranking artisans and trades people.[11] One of the highest payments on the list (13,000 *maravedís*) comes from Alonso Álvarez, a man who was no doubt a close relative of Hernando, given his name and that he is described as having been in charge of the Customs House, a position awarded to Hernando's late uncle Pedro by Enrique IV.[12] According to the document, he was a resident of the parish of San Bartolomé and the grandson of a heretic who had been burned at the stake.

Once again, Hernando and his brothers were able to obtain more favourable conditions for themselves than those prevailing for the vast majority of *conversos*. This would have been a natural step if their initial reconciliation had been undertaken secretly, and on this occasion the dispensation came directly from Rome. The evidence we have of this is a minute of a meeting of Seville's cathedral chapter in 1517. In that year, Hernando's son Juan Rodríguez de Baeza, in support of his claim to a canonry, presented a certificate of rehabilitation purportedly issued by Pope Alexander VI in 1496 for the brothers Gonzalo, 'Fernando', Pedro and Diego de Baeza, of Cordoba.[13] The document absolved them 'from any infamy attaching to them from their grandparents or parents for the crime of heresy and apostacy'.[14] The recourse to Rome follows a pattern of direct appeals to the Pope established by high status *conversos* since the early days of the Inquisition.[15] Alexander VI was only too pleased to swell his coffers with the fees charged for dispensations such as this and the dating coincides with Gonzalo Fernández de Córdoba's first Italian campaign, where he was accompanied by Hernando de Baeza, as we shall discuss in the next chapter. However, the Catholic Monarchs protested that, by issuing such pardons, the Pope was undermining their authority and, within a year, obtained a reversal of this policy. All papal rehabilitations were to be regarded as invalid.[16] Nonetheless, Hernando does not appear to have been affected by this revocation in his dealings with members of the Andalusian aristocracy.

Documents such as the one obtained by Hernando were intended to provide a bridge to insider status, since a papal dispensation would override any local ruling. But in one sense they only served as a badge of infamy since their existence was proof that the bearer or his family had a history of heresy. As more institutions started to introduce purity of blood statutes during the course of the sixteenth century, this contradiction became even more evident.[17] This, in fact, was the way that the Baezas' dispensation was understood by Seville cathedral chapter in 1517 and, indeed, it is still providing such evidence five centuries on.[18]

Matrimonial strategies

Hernando de Baeza and other surviving members of his family continued to occupy roles as high-status servants and trusted intimates of the House of Aguilar throughout the 1490s and into the following century.[19] As in the earlier period, we find them acting as their legal representatives, managing property, carrying out business deals and facilitating communications both within the family and with other nobles.[20] From 1492 until Alonso de Aguilar's death in 1501, Hernando appears in the documentation as 'criado del Señor Don Alfonso' and afterwards as the secretary of Pedro Fernández de Córdoba, who succeeded as Lord of Aguilar and was soon elevated to Marquis of Priego. Baeza's letters from Italy – and requests for payment – make it very clear that his first allegiance was to the head of the household.[21] This contrasts with the later accounts and the *limpieza de sangre* files which refer to him in the more impressive position as secretary of the *Gran Capitán* (the title given to Gonzalo Fernández de Córdoba after his first Italian campaign (1495-6)). His closeness to the Marquis, as well as to the *Gran Capitán*, is important in understanding their involvement in the political turmoil which unfolded after the death of Isabel and Baeza's position as he wrote his Granada memoir.

After the surrender of Granada, Hernando de Baeza played an important role firstly in setting up – and later dismantling – the marriage agreements which formed part of Alonso de Aguilar's family strategy. The detail is worth recounting since it shows the high level of trust accorded to the *converso*, his mastery of *caballero* aspirations and manners, his ability as a negotiator, and the access he had to members of the aristocracy. Aguilar negotiated two double sets of matrimonial alliances with different noble families, involving four of his children: his heir Pedro and his daughter Elvira de Herrera were to marry into the prestigious Enríquez family, who were related to the king himself. The other arrangement was more local: with the Lord of Alcaudete (also called Don Alonso Fernández de Córdoba) for a double marriage between his second son, Francisco Pacheco, and Alcaudete's daughter, María Carrillo de Velasco, while his daughter María Portocarrero would marry Alcaudete's son Don Martín Fernández de Córdoba.[22] Soon after Alonso de Aguilar's death in 1501, three of these four marriages were scrapped, in what appears to be a change of strategy – or perhaps the dissatisfaction of his heirs with the arrangements made for them. Only Pedro's marriage to Elvira Enríquez survived. Instead of marrying Don Martín, María entered a monastery, Elvira de Herrera's marriage to the Sevillian nobleman Don Fadrique Enríquez was dissolved and Francisco Pacheco instead married the Count of Cabra's daughter María Fernández de Córdoba, although not until 1510.[23]

In 1494, we find Hernando de Baeza at the May fair in Medina del Campo, making arrangements for the two-way marriage with the Enríquez family.[24] The complex and multifaceted agreement was made in person by the influential Don Enríque Enríquez, the king's uncle, and Baeza himself, named as Aguilar's legal representative. Also present were the future *Gran Capitán*, Gonzalo Fernández de Córdoba, and Luis Portocarrero, a veteran of the Granada war, Lord of Palma del Río and Gonzalo's brother-in-law.[25] The record of the ritual which sealed this agreement powerfully illustrates Baeza's position vis-à-vis the courtly world of *caballería*. To give substance to the contract, the *caballeros* Enrique Enríquez and Gonzalo Fernández de Córdoba had to swear a *pleito homenaje* or formal vow. This involved making the sign of the cross across their bodies three times 'in the custom of Spain', and swearing by God, the Virgin Mary and the words of the Holy Evangelists into the hands of another *caballero*, in this case Luis Portocarrero. Baeza also took part in the ritual, but he swore only a *juramento* (oath) on Alonso de Aguilar's behalf, without plighting a vow in this way. His role was as a facilitator and an active administrator of *caballero* culture, but at the same time not fully of it.[26] The matrimonial agreement was extraordinarily significant politically as an alliance between the two aristocratic families and was witnessed by a member of the Royal Council, *Licenciado* Pedrosa. But despite Baeza's crucial role in clinching the details, he had no status as a *caballero* and was not expected to make the same sort of vow 'in the custom of Spain'.

As part of the Medina del Campo agreement, Alonso de Aguilar pledged for his daughter Elvira a handsome dowry worth six million *maravedís*, and in 1499 a promissory certificate was issued to the groom relating to part of this debt. Like the marriage agreement, this document is almost certainly written in Hernando de Baeza's hand.[27] When the marriage was dissolved, Baeza was given the delicate task of recovering the vast sum that had been paid.[28] The matter was made more complicated by the fact that, while a portion of it had been paid in cash, the sum had been made up with titles to lands in La Rambla and Santaella and with hereditary rights to income in Cordoba granted to her father by the Crown. There was also a trousseau and jewels worth more than 200,000 *maravedís*. Hernando had to not only collect the cash, jewels and other objects of her trousseau, but all the legal titles and privileges relating to the lands and income from Cordoba. He also had to negotiate with Don Fadrique (or his representatives) to discount the value of jewels and other items he had given to his bride, which were still in her possession. The task was accomplished to the satisfaction of both sides and a legal document was signed in Seville on 17 March 1502, in which Hernando acknowledged receipt of items returned to a value of five million eight hundred thousand *maravedís*, which he then presumably had to transport safely back to Montilla.[29] Doña Elvira entered a monastery in Écija and soon after made her will, although she did not leave anything to Hernando for his services.[30] Several years later, he was still waiting for the 30,000 *maravedís* he said he was owed for his time and costs negotiating the deal – about 0.5 per cent of its value.[31]

Hernando de Baeza's contact with the other party in the unsuccessful marriage, Don Fadrique Enríquez, is an interesting one as he represented the new generation of the nobility interested in the ideas, cultures and learning of the wider world, and he left a substantial library.[32] He would later undertake a pilgrimage to Jerusalem, via Rome, and write his own account of it.[33] On returning to Seville, he built the splendid *Casa de Pilatos*, an exercise in architectural hybridity which reinterpreted aesthetic and design elements of the Alhambra, such as stucco and tiling, in a manner in keeping with the contemporary appreciation of classical culture which is associated with the Italian Renaissance.[34]

In November 1501, Baeza travelled to Guadalupe with Don Pedro and his other sister Maria to clinch the financial arrangements for her to enter the monastery of Calabazanos, near Palencia. With them was their mother's chaplain, Fernán Gómez de Medina – a man Baeza would later refer to as his 'compadre'.[35] Guadalupe was a place full of resonances in the conflict between the exclusionary doctrine of *limpieza de sangre* and the inclusionary philosophy of Alonso de Oropesa and the Jeronymites. During the course of the fifteenth century, the Jeronymite monastery there had become a magnet for a large contingent of *conversos* both as monks and as residents of the surrounding settlement, the Puebla de Guadalupe. The religious practices of these former Jews had come under increasing suspicion and in 1485 there was intense Inquisition activity with fifty-two people including a monk burnt as heretics. Many others fled, the Monastery instituted one of the first *limpieza de sangre* statutes and, in a measure pre-figuring the 1492 Edict of Expulsion, all Jews were expelled from the village.[36] Guadalupe at that time was the most important pilgrimage destination in Spain. With the frequent residence of the monarchs there, and the association created between the shrine and the Virgin's support for their political agenda, Guadalupe is seen as symbolizing the reimagined Christian community, purified by the actions of the Inquisition.[37] The arrival of the Fernández de Cordoba party there in 1501 coincided with an order from the chief Inquisitor, Diego Deza, which took ethnic cleansing a step further by expelling all *conversos* from the town. Baeza's presence there, at this most symbolic of Spanish shrines, is therefore full of significance in understanding his delicately balanced position and the inclusive Christianity that is evidenced in his work.

The new Marquisate of Priego

Alonso de Aguilar's death in March 1501, putting down a Muslim rebellion in the Sierra Bermeja, near Malaga, passed into legend as the closing episode in the conquest and Christianization of Granada and the end of the era of chivalry.[38] Chroniclers relate how

Francisco Álvarez de Córdoba (another of Hernando's brothers-in-law) had been with Aguilar in his dying moments and saved his less warlike son, Don Pedro from a similar fate.[39] Whether or not this was true, the story was later elaborated by the family to include a dying wish from Aguilar for Francisco's brother, Gonzalo de Córdoba and his wife, Beatriz de Baeza, to adopt two illegitimate daughters of his.[40] This tale was used in a later *limpieza de sangre* hearing to prove not only that the girls' descendants were free from the taint of Jewish blood, but also that they were actually descended from nobility.[41] Although this story was surely invented, it demonstrates how important the Fernández de Córdobas were in the minds of the Baezas as their protectors and how later generations used the memory of this connection in the narratives they spun to disguise their Jewish origins.[42]

Although still only fifty-three when he died, Alonso de Aguilar had been a dominant force in Cordoba and its surroundings for the best part of half a century. Nothing symbolized better the change of times than the passing of the lordship of Aguilar to Pedro Fernández de Córdoba, a well-educated, cultured man who had been tutored by the Italian humanists Pedro Mártir de Anglería (in Italian, Pietro Martire d'Anghiera) and Lucio Marineo Sículo, both of whom made significant contributions to the historiography of the period.[43] The family of his wife, Elvira Enríquez, with whom Baeza had negotiated their marriage terms, were also patrons of learning; it was her cousin Fadrique Enríquez, *Almirante* of Castile, who brought Sículo to Spain and her father, Enrique Enríquez (with whom Baeza sealed the marriage agreement) is himself credited with having written a historical work, no longer extant.[44] In honour of his father's services to the crown, the monarchs gave Don Pedro a noble title: henceforth the Baezas would be servants of the Marquises of Priego.

Alonso de Aguilar died on 16 March 1501, and Hernando de Baeza was present at the formal opening of the will in Montilla, on 26 April.[45] On 21 June and 7 July, he issued certificates in the names of Don Pedro and Alonso de Aguilar's widow, Catalina Pacheco, awarding lifetime grants to a man who had recovered Aguilar's body from rebel-held territory, Luis de Nicuesa.[46] On 1 February the following year, there is a first description of Hernando de Baeza as 'secretario del muy magnífico señor Marqués de Priego'.[47] The role of secretary itself speaks of new times: it has been described as the 'preferred profession' of humanists, and its development linked to the growth of diplomacy in Renaissance Italy.[48] This description will become increasingly relevant to Hernando as we trace his experiences in Italy in the next chapter.

Servants and masters

The relationship between the young Marquis and his *converso* servant is crucial in understanding the bitter resistance to Fernando and the Inquisition which emerged after the death of Isabel. We are fortunate to be able to draw on four extended letters written from Naples by Hernando de Baeza to Don Pedro which illuminate this relationship. They show that he was no simple amanuensis but an active participant in literary exchange. The two had a close, familiar relationship within a network which included family members on both sides. Hernando kept him abreast of news from

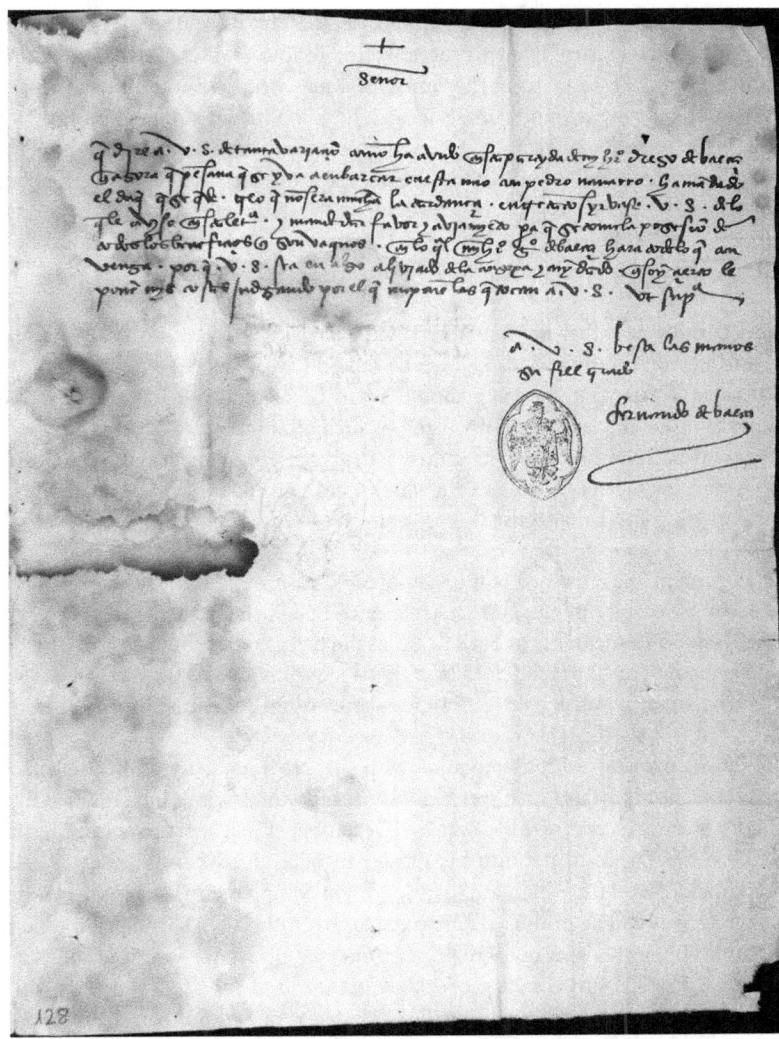

Image 6 Addendum to Hernando de Baeza's letter of 26 December 1504 to the Marquis of Priego, showing his signature. Archivo General de la Fundación Casa Ducal de Medinaceli, AH. Leg.199.23.

Italy and in turn gratefully received updates on the political mood in Spain.[49] There are shared confidences and unspoken references: 'remember what you told me one day about the Dean of Talanquera', Hernando wrote.[50] He provided his young master with advice bordering on instructions, for example:

> Your Lordship should do the same, so that if the matter were to become the subject of legal dispute you would be in a better position.[51]

Although it is tempting to visualize the noble head of the *Casa* at the apex of a pyramid, wielding top-down control over his servants and followers, these letters show that he might be better understood as at the centre of a network, responding to the interests and influence of those around him. Baeza's letters are full of supplications as from a social inferior, with much reference to kissing of hands and feet, but the tone of the letters reflects a generally comfortable, close, informal relationship, and the content bears witness to their shared interests.[52] In one of the letters, Baeza provides an explicit description of what he calls the 'law of virtue', in which the lord has a moral duty to protect his servant in exchange for loyalty and services:

> The length of time that my forefathers and I have served your Lordship's family means that you rightly and justly have, or should have, protection of my business, so it is right that your Lordship should act as he would do in his own, as God wishes. Not for me, as I am not worthy of such a boon, but to satisfy the law of virtue which is a contract of obligation which all generous people have signed, and the reward for services in this world which I have given, and will be able to give, your Lordship and your House.[53]

Baeza's argument that his lord is morally obliged to protect him because of services provided by his family in the past is a reference which the Marquis would no doubt have understood to mean his father's death at the hands of the Inquisition. The bonds of obligation and trust are seen not just as between individuals at a particular point in time, but between families over generations stretching from the past into the future and overseen by the Almighty.

The letters provide evidence that, as with the previous generation, the financial affairs of the Lords of Aguilar were closely intertwined with those of the Baezas, although not always without friction. In December 1504, from Naples, Hernando sent his brother Diego to petition his master in relation to 'certain matters relating to my financial situation which are justified'.[54] He complained that his good will and financial interests had been abused and asked for restitution.[55] An undated memo from the Medinaceli archive sets out what these financial grievances were.[56] The Marquis had not paid Baeza's agreed salary, of 20,000 *maravedís* a year, for two years while he had been in Italy; the Marquis's sister Elvira de Herrera had not paid him the 30,000 *maravedís* she owed him for his work recovering her dowry; his brother Pedro had lent the Marquis 139,500 *maravedís* before he died, and this money was now owing to the family. Hernando himself had paid for two hundred *ducados*' worth of 'shoes, harnesses, and caparisons' which the Marquis had ordered from Italy and had not been refunded.[57] Some rather terse notes in the margins of the document record the Marquis's responses and highlight the financial pressures he himself was under. He did not intend to pay Hernando for his services until he returned from Italy and he was unclear who was responsible, if anyone, for the payment in relation to negotiations for the return of Elvira de Herrera's dowry.

In 1506, with Hernando still in Italy, the bonds of loyalty became notably strained as the Marquis pressured Hernando to make payments on his behalf which his absent secretary was unwilling to front.[58] The Marquis's brother, Don Francisco Pacheco, also owed him money and Baeza asked his master to intervene to recover the debts, which related to rents that Hernando had been collecting for Don Francisco on his estate in Albendín.[59] The amounts of money involved in these financial exchanges are substantial and show that the Baezas were a source of credit for the Fernández de Córdobas. But they were hardly their bankers, or sources of major capital. Even the sum lent by Pedro de Baeza, equivalent to Hernando's salary for nearly seven years, pales into insignificance in comparison to the six million *maravedís* of Elvira de Herrera's dowry, or the 1.4 million *maravedís* worth of wheat the Marquis sold to Genoese merchants in 1509.[60]

The intellectual world surrounding Hernando de Baeza

Baeza's knowledge of courtly manners and protocol, evidenced by the fact that he was welcomed by Boabdil and his supporters as a valid intermediary with the Spanish monarchs, suggests that he gained a cultural education through the noble household of which he was a member. His early experiences there would have provided an education in the manners of the Andalusian nobility of the mid- to late fifteenth century.[61]

Don Pedro left a substantial library which was inventoried after his death in 1517, and whose contents provide an insight into the intellectual world surrounding Hernando de Baeza. It has been described as 'a library worthy of an *aficionado* of the Humanities in its widest sense, with all that implied for interest in a wide range of different fields and appreciation of classics as well as the fruits of the Italian Renaissance'.[62] Interchange between Italy and Spain has long been noted as an important feature of the rapid cultural and intellectual developments in this period and the Marquis's correspondence with Baeza shows that the latter acted as a physical conduit for this.[63] The Marquis had sent a friar to Italy with a list of books for Baeza to acquire for him. In September 1504, Baeza wrote to say that he was sending these with his brother Diego.[64] These books were of great interest to other nobles too. The Duke of Arcos, Don Rodrigo Ponce de León, wrote to the Marquis saying that he had heard via Gonzalo de Baeza – presumably Hernando's brother – that his people had sent him books from Naples and asked for details of their titles.[65]

It is not possible to say to what extent Baeza was a reader as well as a buyer of the exceptionally rich and diverse range of material contained in the Marquis's library. It was not inventoried until 1518, so later acquisitions would have been obtained after Baeza's death (see pp. 100–1). At the same time, it would not have been the only access he had to literature and ideas which might have influenced him. The Marquis's household and close contacts included some highly educated and erudite men. Among these were a certain Doctor Antonio de Morales, who was a beneficiary of Elvira Enriquez's will, and corresponded with the Marquis. He took the Marquis to Porcuna to see some – presumably ancient – marble statues which had been unearthed there.[66] Alonso del Toro, known as the Maestro del Toro, a man who would later provide evidence against the Inquisitor Lucero, was also a member of the household, corresponded with the Marquis and was an executor of his will.[67] Also close to the household was Doctor Gonzalo Velasco Romero, Dean of Talavera and *canónigo doctoral* (canon with responsibility for legal matters) in Cordoba from 1498. He was also an Inquisitor in Jaen 1502.[68] Hernando mentions him in two of his letters, indicating that he was a competitor for church benefices with his son.[69] The family also had a number of chaplains, among them Fernán Gómez de Medina who travelled to Guadalupe with Baeza in 1501. Another significant figure is the Cordoban lawyer *Licenciado* Diego Daza, who co-witnessed with Hernando de Baeza a number of documents issued on behalf of the family.[70] He was an executor of Alonso de Aguilar's will and attended its opening alongside Baeza.[71] And the Count of Cabra, whose father, the previous count, is depicted very favourably in Baeza's work, had a reputation as a 'lover of learning' and is understood to have collaborated with Pedro Martir d'Anglería on a translation of Sallust.[72] His brother Don Francisco de Mendoza, whom we will meet again later, was also a learned man and took over the post of *canónigo doctoral* from Velasco Romero in 1507.[73] Baeza therefore had many opportunities to absorb learning and ideas both second hand through conversation and discussion with his master and other members of the household, as well as through direct access to books.

The list of the library's 309 volumes includes Latin and Greek classical works, religious writings and works by Italian humanists as well as fourteenth- and fifteenth-century Spanish writers. The extent and diversity of the library makes it difficult to draw conclusions about which might have influenced Baeza. The works of St Jerome feature strongly, as do those of St Gregory and St Augustine. It would be tempting to conclude that he was influenced by the work of Josephus, whose *Jewish Wars* also features in the library, having been translated by Alonso de Palencia in the significant year of 1492.[74] Certainly, there is evidence that *conversos* were particularly interested in Josephus's work: another translation for a Juan Rodríguez de Baeza, *corregidor* of Medina del Campo in 1480 (not thought to be a relative of the Baezas of Cordoba/Montilla), appears in the British Library manuscript collection.[75] But we cannot necessarily assume that our author was especially interested in the work of Josephus or that of Herodotus, Boccaccio, Marsilio Ficino or Pico della Mirandola, all of which have a place in the Marquis's library and all of which it could be argued influenced him (the latter two in particular seem relevant in relation to Christian toleration and the harmony between Judaism, Christianity and Islam).[76] Juan de Mena's work, the *Trescientas*, which Baeza actually quotes from, is listed in the inventory, so the evidence here provides a clear trail of how he might have become acquainted with it.

Gonzalo Fernández de Córdoba

It is Gonzalo Fernández de Córdoba (1453–1515), whom we must regard as Baeza's almost exact contemporary, whose trajectory sheds most light on Baeza's education in values and in whose service he is most likely to have had access to court experience. One way in which Hernando and his brothers were able to rebuild their wealth was through association with Gonzalo Fernández de Córdoba's own glittering career as he leapfrogged over the status of his elder brother and became a Duke in his own right, obtaining extensive and lucrative estates in Italy to add to those in Andalusia acquired as a result of the conquest of Granada.⁷⁷ As trusted, able administrators, Hernando and his brothers benefited from these acquisitions too.⁷⁸

The future *Gran Capitán* spent two periods at court as a teenager and a young man. His biographer sees the second, in the early years of Fernando and Isabel's reign, as a time when his subject started to think for himself, rejecting the lawlessness and thoughtless violence of noble factionalism during the reign of Enrique IV and aligning himself with the monarchs' project of renewal and unification. He detects in Gonzalo Fernández de Córdoba the influence of two courtiers and authors who were influential during that period: the chronicler Diego de Valera, who in his book, *Doctrinal de Príncipes* (1475) called for renewed morality in the world of the *caballero* courtier – and Gonzalo Chacón, whose *Crónica de Alvaro de Luna* provides a model of loyalty to the crown and astute advice for ambitious courtiers.⁷⁹ He sees Gonzalo Fernández de Córdoba as being more closely aligned with Fernando than with Isabel, with whom he is legendarily associated at this time, leaning towards the king's shrewder, more analytical, and internationalist politics. It is likely that Hernando accompanied Gonzalo during at least some of this time at court, and that it was in these circumstances that he absorbed the lessons about courtly life and behaviours that he would apply in service to Boabdil and in Italy. It is likely too that it was under Gonzalo's influence that he developed elements of the value system which he displays in his writing, including loyalty, piety, discretion and the abhorrence of unnecessary violence.

Vatican intermediary

It was under Gonzalo Fernández de Córdoba that Baeza spent two periods in Italy, 1495–7 and 1503–7. There his portfolio of services to the Fernández de Córdoba family also included tasks related to their spiritual welfare. His son, Juan Rodríguez de Baeza, became a member of Pope Julius II's household, and Hernando's 'lord and protector' in Rome was one of the most powerful and influential Spaniards there, Bernardino López de Carvajal, the Cardinal of Santa Cruz (1456–1523).⁸⁰ Through these connections Hernando obtained an indulgence for the Marquis and his family:

> Diego de Baeza is bringing the indulgence ['confisional'] that my son wrote to your Lordship the other day that he was sending you. It covers my Lady the Marchioness and the children you have, God bless them, and those which it may please Him to give you in future.⁸¹

The document mentioned by Baeza is very likely to have been similar to one obtained by the Marquis of Tarifa in 1508, described as a 'confesional grande' which allowed him, among other indulgences, to have all his sins forgiven by a confessor of his choice and to be excused from fasting in Lent.⁸² This was a spiritual luxury, a high-status item seen to be endowed with special powers – although not so different from Hernando's certificate of rehabilitation in the sense that it had to be paid for. Among the Marquis of Priego's possessions valued in 1518 after his death, there is an item described as 'la yndulgençia de Roma', the least valuable item in his library, worth just

10 *maravedís*, which may well be the document Baeza's son obtained.[83] There were also other members of the Andalusian aristocracy, besides the Marquis of Tarifa, who were interested in the sorts of spiritual salves that could notoriously be obtained in Rome in this period immediately preceding the publication of Martin Luther's ninety-five theses (1517). Don Rodrigo Ponce de León wrote to The Marquis asking for details of an 'oraçión' (prayer) that Gonzalo de Baeza had told him about, which may have been this same document.[84]

In the same letter in which he referred to the indulgence, Hernando asked for his master's help to clinch the acquisition of church benefices for his son. He announced that the Pope, 'as a result of some justified causes which motivated him', had granted his son benefices to the value of 900 *ducados* (an absolute fortune compared to his own annual salary) and that he could take up the first benefices which became available in the Archbishopric of Seville.[85] Hernando said that he had named the Marquis as patron of the appointments, and now needed his help to take possession of them. There was fierce competition for church benefices, because of the economic security they provided not only for the incumbent but also for his extended family.[86] The regular income such benefices provided could be used as surety to raise capital, or they could be traded for other favours. Baeza found himself in competition with another of the Marquis's followers, the Dean of Talavera (Gonzalo Velasco Romero), over a canonry in Zamora. Baeza said that, although his son was known as 'Canon of Zamora' in Rome, Velasco was claiming that the position belonged to him.[87] Baeza graciously gave way, hoping that Velasco would arrange for his son to take possession of a canonry in Jaén and other benefices in the diocese including Alcalá and Alcaudete. He said that if Velasco couldn't do this, then Diego Fernández de Ulloa (a *veinticuatro* of Jaén) should act on his behalf, or any other person that the Marquis wanted to appoint, as long as they were gentry ('que ellos señores sean').[88] Baeza wrote:

> […] although I have a common desire for acquisition, that is no reason, God forbid, that it should be at the expense of someone close to me, especially when, like the Dean, they are servants of your Lordship's house where I grew up.[89]

Baeza's 'common desire for acquisition' repeats almost word for word an idea expressed by Fernando del Pulgar quoting from St Augustine in relation to the well-known *converso* courtier Fernán Álvarez de Toledo.[90] It reflects a comfortable acceptance of the idea of striving for material gain, which has also been identified as a feature of the Jeronymite Order during this period.[91] Baeza describes how he was lobbying and hustling in the Papal court 'with a dose of saliva' ('con una poca de saliva') – a graphic image of a man drawing on all his skills of persuasion to achieve his material aims.

His reference to Diego Fernández de Ulloa is interesting too. Ulloa served in the Granada war and, as a man who clearly knew the frontier well, was responsible for redistributing rents and property in Malaga, Vélez Malaga and Loja after they fell to the Christians.[92] He was made commander of Montejícar, south of Jaén, in an equivalent position to Gonzalo Fernández de Córdoba and his allies in Salar, Moclín and Colomera.[93] During the lull in the conflict between the sieges of Malaga and Baza, he had received a delegation of officials from Boabdil's court in his own house in Jaén, in order to agree accounts between Christian and Granadan *alhaqueques* responsible for the ransoming of captives from both sides. These had included Baeza's friend, Abrahén de Mora, described as Boabdil's secretary and *trujamán* and *alhaqueque mayor*, overseeing the settlement.[94]

Conclusion

Hernando's letters and other documentation discussed in this chapter reveal a close relation of loyalty and service between the *converso* and the noble family he served, covering a wide range of areas of experience. In the aftermath of the first wave of Inquisition activity, he and his brothers had opportunities under the protection of the Fernández de Córdobas both for learning and for profit, and they in turn contributed to the cultural, economic and, indeed, spiritual resources of their noble masters. The ties that bound the Baezas to the Fernández de Córdobas were not simply a pragmatic arrangement at a single point in time but a deep sense of obligation with its roots in past generations and stretching forward in time. Hernando de Baeza's world view – and certainly his access to learning – was as much conditioned by his status as a member of the Fernández de Córdoba household as by his experiences as a *converso*. This not only gave him access to élite networks and influence at the highest level but also brought him into situations of conflict. Both the Marquis and his uncle the *Gran Capitán* felt their values and interests under assault from Fernando's autocratic behaviour and both were involved in resisting it. However, as I shall discuss in the next two chapters, they became reconciled to it in different ways.

4

The Spanish in Italy

'I am dealing with it again from Rome through other people with a dose of saliva'[1]

The election of the Valencian Rodrigo Borgia to the papacy in August 1492 marks the beginning of 'the age of Spanish preponderance' in Italian history.[2] As Pope Alexander VI, Borgia, created nineteen new Spanish cardinals and the number of Spanish ex-patriates in Rome increased substantially as *conversos* and old Christians alike flocked there in search of ecclesiastical offices and the power and influence provided by proximity to the papal curia.[3] During the Borgia papacy, the city became a major site for the projection of the pre-eminence of the dual Spanish monarchy and its pretensions in the Mediterranean. It was Alexander VI who bestowed on them the title of 'Catholic Monarchs' as a much-coveted international seal of approval.[4] Central to these developments was the man who would become Hernando de Baeza's 'lord and protector' in Rome, Bernardino López de Carvajal, the Cardinal of Santa Cruz, who was a key point of contact between the monarchs and Rome during Alexander VI's papacy as well as a great patron of the arts and learning.

The conquest of Naples

The monarchs' interests in Italy – or, at least, Fernando's – went beyond Rome. Fernando himself was king of the island of Sicily – or Sicily *ultra farum* as it was known – which had been occupied by the Aragonese since 1282. However, Sicily *citra farum* – the kingdom of Naples, which stretched across the whole of the southern half of the Italian mainland, had been ruled by the House of Anjou until 1442, when it was conquered by Fernando's uncle, Alfonso V of Aragon. When he died in 1458 with no legitimate heirs, his brother (Fernando's father) succeeded as Juan II of Aragon and the throne of Naples went to Alfonso's illegitimate son Ferrante (reigned 1458–94) and then to Ferrante's son as Alfonso II of Naples (reigned 1494–5).[5]

Spain was not the only monarchy turning to Italy to boost its ascendancy. Charles VIII of France, with his hereditary title *Rex Christianissimus*, now claimed the throne of Naples on the basis of his Angevin ancestry. In the last months of 1494, accompanied by a huge army, Charles started his 'descent into Italy', marching down to Naples virtually unopposed. With Charles' army approaching, Alfonso II abdicated in favour of his own son, Ferrante II, and fled with the rest of his family to Sicily.[6] Fernando gathered a coalition against the French – the League of Venice – and, at the same time, sent Gonzalo Fernández de Córdoba to Sicily with a small force. His intentions at this stage may have been to protect his relatives, and certainly to defend his own interests in Sicily, but there was surely an element of opportunism in his response. Gonzalo arrived in Messina on 24 May 1495, where he found most of the Neapolitan royal family urging him to cross to the mainland in support of their resistance to the French and the French-supporting barons who were occupying strongholds across the vast kingdom. Leaving his supporters in charge, Charles made his way back to France but was engaged by Venice and Milan at Fornovo (July 1495). Although Charles claimed victory, he was left without booty or back up and after three months of stalemate, reached a settlement with Milan and returned to France. Meanwhile, Gonzalo was able to dislodge the French from their positions in the south, Naples was returned to the Aragonese monarchy, and he earned the title *Gran Capitán*.[7]

Charles VIII died in 1498 but his successor Louis XII continued with the same expansionist policy, occupying Milan in late 1499 and pressing the French claim to Naples. Meanwhile, Ferrante II had also died, naming his uncle Federigo as his successor. Fernando then pressed his own claim above that of Federigo and did a deal with Louis (the Treaty of Chambord/Granada, 1500) dividing the kingdom of Naples between Spain and France, whereupon Federigo surrendered his rights and

Image 7 The *Gran Capitán* in Naples from *Cronaca della Napoli aragonese*, c. 1498 f. 127r (detail) in Werner Rolevinck, 1425–1502, *Fasciculus temporum*. The pen and wash drawing shows Gonzalo Fernández de Córdoba and Cesare Borgia (as Cardinal) with the dowager queen Juana of Aragon after the expulsion of the French 1495–6. © The Morgan Library and Museum, New York. MS M.801.

was despatched to France.⁸ Meanwhile, Gonzalo was sent east into the Ionian sea to support of Venice in their war with the Ottomans.⁹ This fulfilled three objectives for Fernando – it reinforced his alliance with the Venetians, demonstrated his zeal in combatting the infidel and, perhaps most importantly, provided a pretext for a military presence in the area. Gonzalo's efforts enabled the Venetians to take possession of the island of Cephalonia and sealed his reputation as a brilliant commander on sea as well as on land. He then returned to Italy to take possession of the southern provinces of Naples allotted to Spain in the treaty with France. A few years later, Erasmus was to write sarcastically that 'at the present time, an agreement that starts a war is called a treaty' and this would be a good description of the Treaty of Chambord/Granada which had already served its purpose of dislodging Federigo.¹⁰ Boundary disputes soon degenerated into open warfare, in which Gonzalo gained the upper hand. In the last days of 1504, the French army was finally defeated, delivering the whole kingdom of Naples to Fernando, with Gonzalo as its first Viceroy.

Gonzalo's success owed much to the astute diplomacy and intelligence which underpinned his military tactics and it is here, rather than in the field of battle, where Hernando de Baeza intervened, though his activities have been obscured by tales of the valour of Gonzalo's captains and fighting men. The evidence that Hernando was supporting Gonzalo in both his Italian campaigns comes directly from King Fernando himself. Writing to the *Gran Capitán* in 1505, the King acknowledged 'Fernando de Baeza's services to us, both in the other war with King Charles and in this one which has happened now'.¹¹ Many years after his death, in 1588, Baeza's role as the *Gran Capitán*'s secretary was recalled by those who provided statements for his great-grandson's purity of blood investigation. Among them, *Licenciado* Luis de Bocanegra, a resident of Seville, claimed that he had been 'the most valiant man who had gone to Italy under his command [...] a highly-regarded person of some account'.¹² In 1505, the king wrote directly to Baeza thanking him for his services in giving the monarch's candidate, Alonso de Morales, precedence in relation to the *chantría* of Seville – one of the benefices Hernando was seeking to take possession of for his son.¹³ Baeza was clearly a figure known at court and someone also entrusted with authority. In late 1498, when issuing payments to Gonzalo Fernández de Córdoba's troops, the same royal treasurer Alonso de Morales specified that this should be carried out 'in the presence of Fernando de Baeza', as if this would be a guarantee of proper conduct for both sides.¹⁴

After the success of the first Italian campaign, Baeza reported to his master Don Alonso de Aguilar on 30 July 1497 that everyone was delighted to have received permission from the monarchs to return home, although they had first to travel to Calabria to ensure that fortresses under Gonzalo's command there were secure.¹⁵ However, it is the *Gran Capitán*'s second period in Italy, especially during his Viceroyship, which provides the most significant material for exploring Hernando de Baeza's position within the orbit of the Catholic Monarchs – and the way he handled growing resistance to Fernando of Aragon.

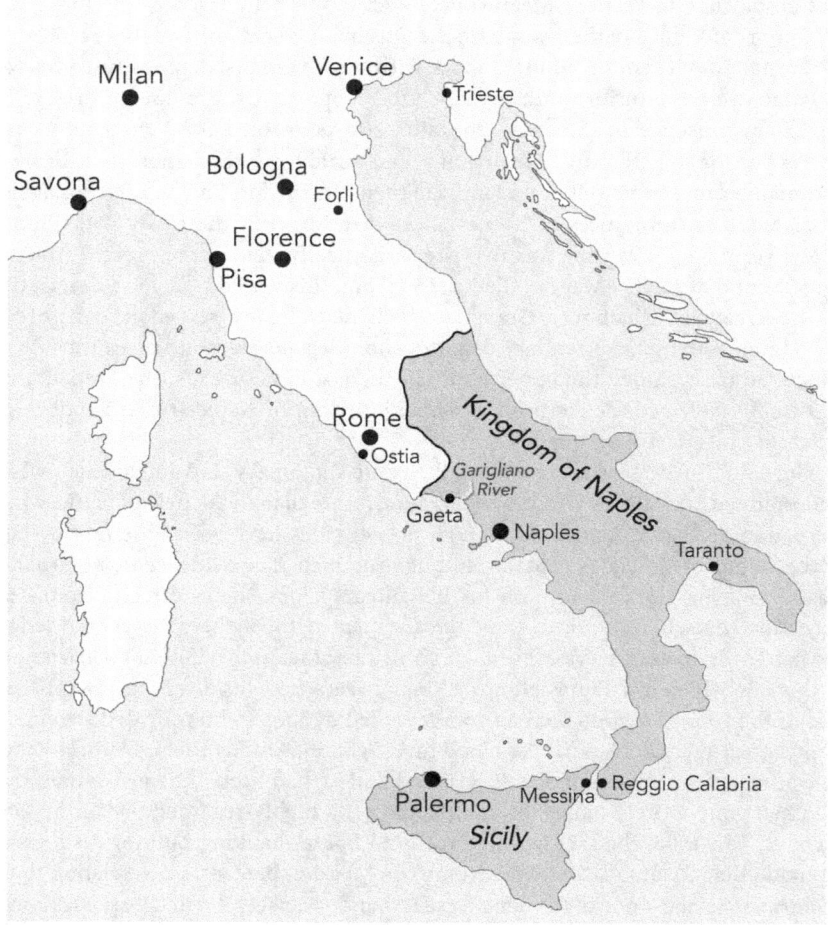

Image 8 Italy – main locations cited. © Teresa Tinsley.

The papal conclaves of 1503

In August 1503, with the fate of Naples still hanging in the balance, Pope Alexander VI died suddenly. His unexpected death was a huge threat to the Catholic Monarchs' growing supremacy in the Christian world. Under his papacy they had powerfully developed the potential of established diplomatic representation in Rome, generally working cooperatively with him on questions relating to the Inquisition, the approval of royal marriages, provision of ecclesiastical benefices, and, most especially, on their claims relating to newly discovered territories across the Atlantic.[16] Borgia and his son Cesare had been astute in balancing the rival claims of France and Spain on Naples and, although the Spanish monarchs did not trust them or approve of their notorious behaviour, the sudden demise of such a weighty figure created a very dangerous situation at a crucial moment in the war against France. The potential election of a pro-French pope was a threat to everything they had worked for, and especially Fernando's designs on the kingdom of Naples: Fernando believed that the future of Naples hung on the outcome of the conclave.[17]

When news of the pope's death arrived, the *Gran Capitán* and his army were besieging the port of Gaeta, having successfully taken the city of Naples from the French. Louis XII of France, furious at the *Gran Capitán*'s success, had gathered support against him from the Genoese, the Florentines, and the Bolognese and, on another front, was preparing to invade Roussillon and the Basque Country. Meanwhile, the Florentines had gathered an army and were threatening Pisa, and the Pisans were receiving help from Cesare Borgia who, with his father the pope, had been maintaining equidistance from both French and Spanish and looking to gain territory in Tuscany in the fall out.[18] In Rome, 'nothing reigned but jealousies and tumults'.[19] The death of the pope released a torrent of anti-Spanish feeling, with Spanish shops and houses set on fire. The whole city was on edge, caught between the two superpowers with armies encamped within eighteen miles of Rome.[20] Cesare Borgia was himself ill, but his power and that of the soldiers he commanded were no less feared for all that. There was ongoing rivalry between the Orsini and the Colonna barons, each with their own bands of soldiers and whose allegiance was contested.[21] It was into this chaotic and dangerous situation that Hernando de Baeza was sent on behalf of the *Gran Capitán*, as an anonymous chronicler reports:

> Then straightaway the *Gran Capitán* sent his secretary Hernando de Baeza to Rome to the Spanish cardinals and to Francisco de Rojas, the ambassador. He also sent accompanying his secretary a Neopolitan nobleman, a leading person in the house of Sanseverino, with a letter for the Italian cardinals.[22]

The conclave to elect Borgia's successor, which took place between 16 and 22 September 1503, was swiftly followed by another as Pius III, a stop gap choice due to his age and infirmity, also died.[23] The anonymous chronicler, thought to be a member of Gonzalo Fernández de Córdoba's household, described the role played by Baeza and the Neapolitan nobleman, Tommaso Regolano, in these delicate negotiations, collapsing both conclaves into one:

> When these two ambassadors arrived in Rome they worked so cleverly and so diligently that they influenced the Sacred College to make this Giuliano pope, and he was called Julius II.[24]

The representation of the two conclaves as one is not a bad reflection of reality, since the election of Pius III was only ever designed to provide a longer period of negotiation in which to break the stalemate between the French and Spanish factions. The lead candidate in the first conclave was the Cardinal of Rouen, a minister of Louis XII, whom the Spanish – cardinals, Ambassador and *Gran Capitán* alike – wished to block at all costs.[25] Because of appointments made by Alexander VI, eleven out of the thirty-eight voting cardinals were Spanish. The *Gran Capitán* clearly understood the importance of this voting bloc in sending Hernando to Rome. The Spanish cardinals, supposedly controlled by Cesare Borgia, did not favour any of the candidates supported by Ambassador Rojas or by the *Gran Capitán*, who were themselves at odds with each other. This meant that although the Spanish potentially had three levers of influence in the conclave (their ambassador, the Spanish cardinals and the *Gran Capitán*), there was no coherent strategy and they failed to act in concert. The *Gran Capitán* was disappointed with the election of Pius III; however, the Catholic Monarchs were reported to have been very pleased at this first outcome.[26]

Less than a month later, the death of Pius III provided a second opportunity to influence the result. Giuliano della Rovere, the future Julius II, had been vetoed by the Spanish monarchs in the first round because of his identification with the French faction and, as a long-standing enemy of the Borgias, he was also shunned by Cesare Borgia.[27] According to the dispatches of the Venetian ambassador, Antonio Giustinian, the Spanish cardinals were meeting nightly to discuss the conclave and by 27 October had still not made up their minds.[28] Niccolò Machiavelli, who arrived in Rome just as the conclave was about to start, charged with reporting back to the Florentine authorities, noted the way that della Rovere manoeuvred himself into the position of being the sole candidate by making lavish and unrealistic promises to anyone and everyone. He commented that at least someone was bound to be disappointed.[29] Della Rovere certainly made an approach to Gonzalo Fernández de Córdoba, giving him a blank certificate to write his own terms.[30] He also struck a deal with Cesare Borgia and, between the two and Hernando de Baeza's diplomacy, the Spanish cardinals at last made up their minds. According to Giustinian, the turning point came sometime in the evening of 29 October. A certain amount of bribery helped matters along: as one contemporary commentator observed, 'the Spanish cardinals did not intend to be poor when they came out of the conclave'.[31] A series of pre-election undertakings (*capitulaciones*) was also agreed, designed to limit the new pope's power and allow for more collegiate decision-making. Della Rovere agreed to take forward the war against the Turks, to convene a Church Council (*concilio*) within two years, not to declare war without the agreement of two thirds of the cardinals, and to consult the College of Cardinals regarding nomination of cardinals and other important matters.[32] Chief among the 'conciliarists' was Bernardino López de Carvajal, the Cardinal of Santa Cruz – a man close to both Baeza and Gonzalo Fernández de Córdoba. When, as with the Granada *Capitulaciones*, the agreement later proved to be little more than a device to achieve an immediate goal, the new pope's disdain for power-sharing with his cardinals led to Carvajal later becoming the lead rebel in the so-called Schism of Pisa (1511).[33]

The Spanish monarchs initially regarded the election of della Rovere as a disaster – perhaps in this they were influenced by their ambassador Rojas, whose preference for another candidate had been torpedoed by Hernando de Baeza's intervention.[34] However, despite the monarchs' early indignation at the result of the election, Julius II is regarded to have been one of Fernando's most effective allies and his election ultimately beneficial for Spain – or at least Aragon. In fact, his perceived pro-Spanish, anti-French position was one of the causes of the 1511 schism.[35] During his papacy he approved Fernando's investiture as King of Naples, allowed him to consolidate his image as 'Catholic King', and in the view of at least one commentator, he maintained a favourable political balance between the French and Spanish in north Italy.[36] He also issued crusade bulls in support of Fernando's north African campaigns which were worth very considerable sums of money.[37] Julius II also made a inestimable contribution to European cultural heritage in commissioning works from Michelangelo, Bramante and Raphael which are considered masterpieces of Renaissance art.[38] However, many of his actions compromised the papacy's spiritual authority and fed the desire for renewal which would eventually lead to the Reformation.[39] Pope Julius was severely criticized, by Erasmus, among others, for his frequent resort to the use of arms, and disappointment in his papacy made Carvajal one of his leading opponents.[40]

The nine hundred *ducados*' worth of church benefices which Baeza said he received from the pope (see previous chapter) suggests that he did indeed, as the chronicler suggests, play an important part. Less than two years later, Carvajal wrote in one of his letters to the *Gran Capitán* that 'his Highness and all of us owe Hernando de Baeza a great deal'.[41] It seems likely that he was referring to his role in this conclave and its exceptionally unanimous outcome from an unpromising and dangerous start. But what did Baeza actually do? Like Niccolò Machiavelli, he did not have the status of an official ambassador.[42] But while Machiavelli was charged with observing and reporting, Baeza's role was to influence the outcome. At what stage did Gonzalo Fernández de Córdoba decide to throw his weight behind della Rovere, a candidate whom Fernando and Isabel had previously vetoed? Was it on the basis of Baeza's astute observation of the situation in Rome between the two conclaves – and the inducements offered him by the future pope? Perhaps Baeza encouraged or facilitated the approach della Rovere made to his master or was involved in discussing the terms of his support: recognizing Spanish dominion in Naples. It is Gonzalo Fernández de Córdoba who has been credited with the creative judgement to support della Rovere, but it was Baeza's intervention that contributed to making this strategy a reality. His description of using 'a dose of saliva' in pursuit of his interests in the papal court provides a vivid depiction of him lubricating the levers of power, ingratiating himself with the prospective pope, negotiating favours for the Spanish cardinals and persuading them that it would be better to position themselves in the front line of support for the leading candidate rather than to be put in a position of grudging acceptance of the *fait accompli*.

If the election of Julius II was an important moment for the fortunes of the Spanish in Italy, the honours received by Hernando de Baeza were of no less significance for his own personal fortune. The anonymous chronicler notes that the new pope:

> [...] gave the Italian nobleman the archbishopric of Amalfi and gave Hernando de Baeza the *chantría* of Seville for his son and made him his chamberlain and gave him the benefices and church positions which his sons have today.[43]

Although the chronicler's wording is ambiguous, from other sources it is clear that it was Hernando's son who became Julius's II's chamberlain and whose sons (i.e. Hernando's grandsons) were occupying the benefices at the time he was writing – believed to be shortly after 1552.[44] In 1506, Hernando's son Juan Rodríguez de Baeza appears in Vatican records as a 'familiar' of the pope – a member of his personal household – and in 1508 as a 'scriptor' and apostolic notary.⁴⁵ Despite being an ordained priest, he had five children, at least one of whom was a cleric and it seems that he made use of a device of resigning in their favour so that they could inherit benefices he had occupied.⁴⁶

Baeza was conscious of his own reputation. In one of his letters, he refers to being fabled for having received a fantastical number of benefices for his son, although taking possession of them proved not to be straightforward, as I shall discuss in the next chapter.⁴⁷ Baeza's closeness to the pope was still remembered in 1588, as a witness in his great grandson's *limpieza de sangre* investigation of observed:

> The pope at the time [...] held him in high regard and treated him in a way that everything he asked and entrusted to him, Fernando Rodríguez de Baeza [sic] carried it out.⁴⁸

Hernando's contribution to the election of Julius II put both him and his son in a privileged position in the complex world of the traffic in benefices and the manoeuvring for intellectual and political supremacy which took place in the wake of the death of Isabel I. As in the negotiations for the surrender of Granada, he showed himself a master of compromise, a bridge-builder and an effective intermediary.

The capture of Cesare Borgia

Soon after the election of Julius II, Hernando de Baeza played an active role in the neutralization of Alexander VI's infamous son Cesare Borgia, who was at the epicentre of the international power struggles centred on Italy. Iconized by Machiavelli as a new-style prince of the Renaissance, the figure of Cesare Borgia has been a source of fascination, both in the popular imagination and for academic study.⁴⁹ He is remembered for his opulence and magnificence, and for the ruthlessness with which he transgressed established codes of conduct, overstepping the boundaries of acceptable behaviour and symbolizing the abandonment of medieval chivalric values. Made cardinal by his father in 1493, he left the church in 1498 after the suspicious murder of his brother Giovanni and, amid huge public scandal, took up a military role at the head of the pope's army. As *gonfalonier*, he captured lands, ostensibly for the church, in the region of Emilia-Romagna, ejecting the sitting barons. These lands were later legitimized as a seigneurial estate by the pope, which blurred the lines between the pope's public and private possessions and confirmed, in the eyes of many, the Borgias' dynastic ambitions. Chief among these possessions was the castle of Forlì, which Cesare regarded as the centre of his personal fiefdom and where he had amassed a large amount of captured loot, munitions and supplies.

When his father died, Cesare was ill himself but della Rovere promised to maintain his position as *gonfalonier* in return for his support for his candidacy. Cesare's willingness to trust a man who had been the Borgias' long-standing enemy is attributed to his weakened position: Machiavelli believed that it was the 'mala elezione' of Julius II that led to Cesare's downfall.⁵⁰ As a virtual prisoner of the new pope in the Vatican, Cesare promised to hand over his estates in the Romagna and was allowed to go to the port of Ostia, from where he could travel onwards by boat once his men had surrendered the fortresses they were holding for him. The man put in charge of overseeing this arrangement was none other than Hernando de Baeza's friend and protector in Rome, the Cardinal of Santa Cruz, Bernardino López de Carvajal. Carvajal was no less adept at political scheming than the pope or Cesare Borgia himself. In concert with the *Gran Capitán*, now installed as the Spanish monarchs' Viceroy in Naples, he arranged a safe conduct for Cesare to Naples, where the Borgia children had already been sent for safe-keeping, and allowed him to leave Ostia for Naples before the fortress of Forlì had been secured for the Pope. This naturally infuriated the pope, and the pope's fury enraged the Spanish monarchs when they heard about it. It jeopardized their budding relationship with him and the two pressing issues which Ambassador Rojas was entrusted with resolving for them: 'the English dispensation' (for their daughter Catherine of Aragon to marry the future Henry VIII) and 'the Naples investiture' (Fernando's own investiture as King of Naples).[51] They wrote to the *Gran Capitán* demanding that he should not only pressure Borgia to surrender Forlì, but that he should see that he left Italy completely. This left the *Gran Capitán* in a difficult position since he had given Borgia a guarantee of safety in Naples. When Borgia first arrived, he acted with courtesy towards him but, after winning his trust, he notoriously had him arrested and imprisoned in the fortress of Castel Nuovo.[52]

Contemporary commentators and later historians alike have found it difficult to explain the inconsistencies in the behaviour of Carvajal and the *Gran Capitán*. Rumours were rife at the time about their own ambitions and good faith. The dispatches of the Venetian ambassador, Antonio Giustinian, portray the sense of expectation in Rome and the attempts to make sense of a drama unfolding almost daily. He remarked that 'things to do with Cesare Borgia are more complicated than a labyrinth'.[53] Hernando de Baeza was deeply involved in the complex manoeuvring and delicate diplomacy which this tricky situation threw up. The Florentine ambassador in Naples, Francesco Pandolfino, reported on 27 April 1504 that the *Gran Capitán* had sent his secretary 'Ferrando di Baiza' to Rome on account of the fact that the pope was annoyed with Carvajal for freeing Borgia.[54] A few days later, he mentioned again that Baeza was in Rome to explain the situation to the pope and intercede on behalf of Carvajal.[55] Once again, Baeza appears as a mediator, bridging differences and difficulties through personal communication and contact. Carvajal had also written to the pope, and by 25 April he had reportedly been well received and had lunched with the pope and other cardinals and enjoyed a theatrical performance.[56]

Giustinian gives us to believe that Carvajal was uncomfortable with his task of supervising Borgia in Ostia, especially after it dragged on after the forty days' commission which had been agreed with the pope and the cardinals. He apparently justified his actions by saying that he thought it better to send Borgia to Naples for safe-keeping rather than allowing him to flee to France or anywhere else where he might cause trouble – a question of 'keeping your enemies close', perhaps. The *Gran Capitán*'s betrayal of the terms of the safe conduct he had given Borgia was remarked on at the time and his biographers have tended to excuse this perceived lapse of moral values by stressing Borgia's vices – Giovio describes him as 'pestilential' – and by explaining that the orders of the pope and his sovereigns had to take precedence.[57] He was certainly fulfilling the pope's orders, and Baeza's presence in Rome testifies to how important he considered the pope's good will to be. It has been argued that the *Gran Capitán* had a certain sympathy with Borgia and wanted to help him but gave in to the will of his sovereigns because he wanted to defy them over another matter: the question of the expulsion of the Jews from Naples.[58] The *Gran Capitán* certainly did not see eye to eye with Fernando over this issue. However, Borgia was arrested on 26 May and the monarchs' order to do so was issued on or around 20 May, hardly time for it to arrive.[59] On 17 May, the *Gran Capitán* had already written to Ambassador Rojas to say that he was minded to detain Borgia, and to send him to Spain for Fernando and Isabel to decide what to do with him.[60] This suggests that the *Gran Capitan* pre-empted his sovereigns' instructions and arrested Borgia on his own initiative. My reading of the documentary evidence is that Carvajal and the *Gran Capitán* had no clear plan when they arranged for Borgia to go to Naples, they simply recognized that having him in their power would give them a strategic advantage. In the month between Borgia's arrival in Naples and his arrest, the *Gran Capitán* was no doubt considering his options – and testing the water through Hernando de Baeza in Rome. In the end, he chose to go back on his word rather than oppose the pope.

Once Borgia was imprisoned, there was still the question of Forlì, the matter which had been exercising the pope all along. Here again, Hernando de Baeza was deeply involved. While Cesare was a prisoner, the *Gran Capitán* apparently refused to see him, but negotiated with him through 'third parties' which, of course, included Hernando de Baeza.[61] On 6 July 1504, Borgia was issued with a certificate, signed by Baeza, which clinched the handover of Forlì. Baeza's handwriting and signature are clearly recognizable on the copy which survives.[62]

It would seem that, thirteen years after his role in the *Capitulaciones* for the surrender of Granada, and under the direct orders of the *Gran Capitán*, he took an active role in drafting, developing and negotiating this document. In return for Borgia's surrender of the stronghold, the *Gran Capitán* promised to give him 15,000 ducats which were being held as surety by the pope, and all his (Borgia's) clothing – no doubt extremely valuable – artillery, ammunition and supplies that were in the castle. He was also promised all the silver and other goods previously captured from him by the Bolognese and the Florentines. Clearly these were promises that the *Gran Capitán* made on behalf of others and therefore impossible to guarantee. So there was also an escape clause: Borgia was to hand over the papers necessary for the surrender of Forlì, but if the *Gran Capitán* was unable to arrange for his side of the bargain to be fulfilled within ten days, these would be returned and the agreement would be void. He promised on his honour that this would be so. This was a clever and complex agreement, and despite its veneer of honour and good faith, it was in itself a betrayal, since it did not mention anywhere that Borgia would be freed, in order to be able to enjoy and exploit the resources which were to be returned to him. Baeza's negotiations paid off since, soon afterwards, the pope took possession of Forlì, and on 20 August Cesare Borgia left Italy for good, not to freedom, but as a prisoner of the Catholic Monarchs, dying in Spain in 1507.[63] His removal pleased almost everyone. Not only were the Catholic Monarchs and the pope delighted with the outcome, but Louis XII of France was relieved of an unwelcome obligation towards him (Cesare was married to his relative Carlotta d'Albret).[64] Borgia's removal at this point allowed free rein to negative propaganda against both him and his father which colours perceptions of the Borgias today. Once again, Hernando de Baeza had played a pivotal role which boosted the prestige of his master, strengthened the image of a powerful Spain, and provided another reason for Carvajal 'and everyone' to be grateful to him.

The schismatic Cardinal Carvajal

The evidence about Hernando de Baeza's role in Italy, not least his own letters, but also other correspondence and contemporary sources, consistently links him to one of the most colourful and energetic characters of the moment, Bernardino López de Carvajal, the Cardinal of Santa Cruz.[65] In his letter to the *Gran Capitán* stressing how much 'the king and everyone' owed to Baeza, Carvajal even referred to him affectionately as 'such a friend of mine', while Baeza called him his 'lord and protector in Rome'.[66]

Carvajal was an intellectual who began his career at the University of Salamanca as a star pupil of the free-thinking theologian Pedro Martínez de Osma, whose views on confession, indulgences and the primacy of the pope saw him condemned for heresy in 1479.[67] Distancing himself from the controversy, Carvajal remained in Salamanca and was its rector until 1482 when he settled in Rome as the representative of Cardinal Pedro González de Mendoza. His ambassadorial role developed as he represented Pope Innocent VIII as his *nuncio* in Spain (1484) and, from 1488, the Catholic Monarchs in Rome. Like Baeza, he was as an intermediary who faced in both directions. Closely associated with the growing influence of Spain in Rome during the papacy of Alexander VI, he amassed a rich portfolio of church positions and was an enthusiastic patron of the arts and architecture, literature and learning – especially that which promoted the image of Spain in Rome.[68] Carvajal is credited with having provided the ideological and theological basis for the monarchs' offensives against people of other faiths, legitimizing their conquest not only of Granada but of the New World.[69] Like Juan de Mena and Alonso de Cartagena before him, Carvajal was inspired by the idea of a strong Spanish monarchy. However, once this was achieved, he found himself in the position of resisting it. His rather puzzling trajectory from canny propagandist of the Catholic Monarchs to schismatic rebel against Fernando and Pope Julius II (1510–1) has not yet been adequately explained.[70] He has been cast variously as a cynical exploiter of the Vatican's systems, an ambitious wheeler-dealer – he narrowly missed being elected pope himself on a number of occasions – and an intellectual rebel led astray by extreme prophetic beliefs.[71]

Carvajal's house, where Hernando de Baeza lived while in Rome, was a place that attracted humanists, emigrés, translators, dramatists and poets at the cutting edge of intellectual thought as the world started to make sense of the role of Spain in the momentous global events of the period.[72] Paolo Cortesi used Carvajal as a model for his contemporary guide book on how cardinals should behave and exercise cultural power, highlighting libraries, public readings, lavish hospitality and literary gatherings as signs of magnificence. *De cardinalatu* (1510) describes the after-dinner debates staged by Carvajal in which erudite young men put forward opposing views on theological and intellectual issues of the day. Cortesi reports that the hardline arguments of Duns Scotus gave Carvajal nightmares.[73] Carvajal is also regarded as having led the development of Spanish theatre, through his patronage of men such as Bartolomé Torres Naharro and Juan del Encina.[74]

Carvajal was an enthusiastic advocate of universal Christianity and the special role of Spanish monarchs in delivering it. In his sermon on the conquest of Baza, given in the church of Santiago de los Españoles on 10 January 1490, he argued that Christ's coming had made all the world His and that unbelievers therefore had no right to their lands.[75] This harked back to the teaching of the thirteenth-century Italian canonist known as Hostiensis, and would later provide legal justification for Spanish sovereignty over the New World.[76] It is a different argument from that we have come to associate with *Reconquista* ideology, which stresses the recovery of lands previously occupied by Christians and the restoration of Visigothic Hispania.[77] Carvajal argued that, once the Spanish monarchs had conquered Granada, the papacy and all right-thinking Christians should support their onward march into Africa. In 1493, after Columbus's return from his first voyage of discovery, Carvajal obtained papal bulls giving the Spanish monarchs rights over the discovered territories and a duty to convert the native inhabitants.[78] His sense of the opening-up of the world and his hope for universal Christianity are given material expression in a map of the world, dated to 1502–6, showing both the New World and an earthly paradise located in Africa in which Carvajal's coat of arms hangs on a tree of knowledge.[79]

Carvajal's belief in the special destiny of a reunified Hispania was shaken when, in 1497, the heir to the thrones of Castile and Aragon, Prince Juan, died suddenly. The Roman heavyweight intervened to avert what he saw as a major political crisis threatening the future of the union by writing a public letter of condolence to the monarchs, with advice on the future direction.[80] Allow your daughters to inherit, he urged, and at all costs avoid splitting the kingdoms. The death of Prince Juan, swiftly followed by that of his unborn child, his elder sister Isabel, and her small son, is generally regarded as a turning point in balance of power within the dual monarchy, when the influence of Isabel and that of her circle of advisers started to wane and policy started to be skewed more towards the interests of Aragon. It was at this point too that Carvajal's relationship with the monarchs started to cool and, increasingly side lined by Fernando, he started leaning more towards the future Felipe I and his father, the Emperor Maximilian I of Hapsburg (1459–1519). With the birth of Felipe and Juana's son Charles in 1500, his hopes for a monarch who would usher in an age of universal Christianity started to transfer themselves to the young boy, grandson of both Maximilian and Fernando, who would unite Germany and Spain.[81]

Diplomacy in the succession crisis

The *Gran Capitán*'s *modus operandi* in Italy, as in Granada, was based on effective intelligence and exchange with other players through extensive use of envoys, informants and messengers. In Italy, he was in contact, among others, with the Venetians, with the Florentine *Signoria*, and with the Pisans and his counterparts in

Sicily as well as maintaining strong links in Rome.[82] His sphere of action also went beyond Italy, taking in the full sweep of European politics in contacts with Louis XII of France, the Emperor Maximilian, and his son, Philip of Hapsburg (later Felipe I of Castile 1505–6).[83] As Viceroy of Naples after the end of 1503, the *Gran Capitán* set about establishing new structures for government and justice, and what had been military intelligence-gathering became fully fledged international diplomacy, a phenomenon which was in rapid development at the time.[84] This irked the monarchs, and especially their ambassador in Rome, Francisco de Rojas, as it cut across their own channels of communication, policy-making and influence, subverting established chains of command. It was Hernando de Baeza's role at the centre of diplomatic activity in Rome that particularly irritated them, and which Fernando regarded with increased suspicion after the death of Isabel at the end of 1504, when his position in Castile was thrown into question. The first complaint seems to have come from Rojas, in relation to 'messengers' – note the disparaging description – sent by the *Gran Capitán* to negotiate the provision of ecclesiastical benefices: on 30 April 1504 the monarchs wrote to their ambassador, reassuring him that they had told the *Gran Capitán* to deal with this matter exclusively through him.[85]

On 15 May 1504, at the height of the Cesare Borgia crisis, Giustinian reported that a secretary of the *Gran Capitán* (who I am in no doubt was Hernando, given other evidence that he was in Rome at the time) had had an audience with the pope. He had told the pontiff that the *Gran Capitán* believed that he was inclining too much in favour of the French, and that he hoped he would not do anything to compromise his neutrality or give the Spanish monarchs any cause for complaint. This was presumably a very successful interview, as Giustinian reported that the pope replied 'affably and benevolently'.[86] This evidence is remarkable, given that Julius II notoriously had a rough and irascible character, given to unpredictable rages.[87] Hernando de Baeza and his 'saliva' appear to have had a soothing effect on even this most rough-tempered of pontiffs.

On 20 May, the same day as they wrote ordering the *Gran Capitán* to arrest Borgia, the Spanish monarchs wrote again to Rojas saying that they had told the *Gran Capitán* in the strongest possible terms to recall Baeza:

> We wrote to Gonzalo saying that if Fernando de Baeza has not left [...] he must write and tell him to go, and that from now on he is not to send messengers or do business of ours relating to Naples in Rome except directly through you or any other ambassador of ours living in Rome, and not through the Cardinal [of Santa Cruz] nor any other person.[88]

Apart from their fury over the Borgia affair and the ongoing struggle for influence over the provision of benefices, there was another sensitive diplomatic matter being managed by Baeza which had incurred their wrath. Baeza had apparently been arranging, via Cardinal Carvajal, for the *Gran Capitán* to send boats to pick up Maximilian I in Trieste and bring him to Rome to be crowned Holy Roman Emperor. This was an intervention in international politics which cut across Fernando's own delicately balanced negotiations and which he saw as aiding the French.[89]

The death of Isabel in late November 1504 only heightened Fernando's sensitivity and suspicion since he had no rights over the throne of Castile except as her consort. Isabel's heir, Juana, was married to Maximilian's son, Philip of Hapsburg – later Felipe I – and living in Flanders.[90] The queen had left instructions in her will for Fernando to be governor of Spain until such time as her daughter was able to come to Spain and take on her new role. The focus of attention for anyone wanting to influence the Crown of Castile had therefore moved to Flanders, and Fernando's position was much more fragile.[91] In this difficult and potentially dangerous situation Fernando, corresponding in code, wrote to the *Gran Capitán* begging him with increasing desperation to return to Spain to support him – or, more likely, to remove him from power in Naples where he might use his position in favour of Juana and her husband.[92] The transcriptions of these coded messages appear to be in Hernando de Baeza's hand, from which we can infer that he was a very close party to the delicate balancing act that his master now had to perform.[93]

Rojas complained again in March 1505 that the *Gran Capitán* was sending his own messengers to Rome who were dealing directly with Bernardino López de Carvajal and the pope over the provision of benefices – a key bone of contention between Fernando and Felipe.[94] The new situation following the death of Isabel gave the accusation a much more serious slant – one of deliberately sidestepping Fernando's authority.[95] The *Gran Capitán* had been in touch with the future Felipe I since the spring of 1503.[96] Felipe was being fêted as the new king of Castile by Castilian nobles disenchanted with Fernando who saw him as a monarch who would be more accommodating than Fernando regarding their feudal privileges. Pedro Martir d'Anglería commented in a letter how eager the nobles were to embrace Felipe and see the back of Fernando:

> The nobles, taking advantage of the situation, are roaring and sharpening their teeth like wild boars frothing at the mouth, desiring and expecting a profound change.[97]

Hernando's master, the Marquis of Priego, and the Count of Cabra, son of the Count he extols in his narrative of Granada, were among those welcoming a change of regime. One of the main foci of discontent, which I examine in detail in the next chapter, was the role of the Inquisition and the conduct of that most infamous of Inquisitors, Diego Rodríguez Lucero. Lucero's excesses came to symbolize Fernando's autocratic behaviour and provided a rallying point uniting *conversos* and *caballeros* against him and in favour of Felipe. Suffice it to say here that Hernando's family were among those who had been imprisoned at the hands of Lucero, and that there was a powerful lobby arguing for a suspension of the Inquisition and the mass burnings which Lucero had ordered.[98]

Isabel's death left the *Gran Capitán* in an ambiguous position.[99] He had conquered a kingdom, over which the Crown of Aragon had, arguably, a legitimate claim, on behalf of both Castile and Aragon, with an army paid for (or supposedly paid for – this itself was a bone of contention) by Castile. He had to reconcile loyalty to Fernando with respect for Felipe's position and the need to maintain the unity of the kingdoms which had been set out so eloquently by Carvajal on the death of Prince Juan. The stand-off between Felipe and Fernando became more pronounced as Felipe approached France for support against Fernando, but Fernando quickly wrong-footed him by himself entering into an agreement with France (the Treaty of Blois, 1505) by which he married Germaine de Foix, a 23-year-old relative of Louis XII.[100] This threatened Felipe's claim to Aragon and its possessions, including Naples and Sicily, since any son of the new marriage would be heir to these. The agreement also wrong-footed the *Gran Capitán*, who was required to return lands seized from French-supporting Neapolitan barons, which he had awarded to his own supporters in recognition of their services.[101] The conjuncture highlighted the frailty of Fernando and Isabel's unification of Aragon and Castile, a unity which Fernando appears willing to have sacrificed, had he fathered a son with Germaine.[102]

One of the most detailed accounts of Hernando de Baeza's diplomatic activity is precisely concerned with the status of the Felipe I at this uneasy time of dynastic transition.[103] This is in a note of a meeting which took place in June 1506, at a time when Felipe and Juana had arrived in Castile but had not yet met with Fernando. At this point, Felipe appeared to have the upper hand given the number of nobles who had flocked to meet them, and the perceived impunity with which some of them were already defying Fernando.[104] Among these was the Marquis of Priego who, in the absence of the *Corregidor* as a result of plague, had stepped in to take charge of Cordoba town council at a time of grave economic crisis.[105] It was at this juncture that Felipe's representatives in Rome, Philibert Naturel and Antonio de Acuña, sent envoys to the *Gran Capitán* to encourage him to delay his return to Spain, seeking also to probe his potential support for Felipe. Acuña (c. 1465–1526), who at the time was Archdeacon of Valpuesta and afterwards became Bishop of Zamora, later played a leading role in the *comunero* rebellion of 1520 in which he was described as 'another Martin Luther'.[106] Acuña had been acting as Felipe's representative in Rome since June 1505, with a brief to prevent any papal decisions concerning the provision of benefices or inquisitorial proceedings in Spain which might be against Hapsburg interests.[107] In this endeavour he had been working closely with Bernardino López de Carvajal, who had been corresponding in code with Felipe's key Castilian supporter and adviser, Juan Manuel.[108] This had enraged Fernando so much that in April 1505 he had ordered the *Gran Capitán* to arrest Acuña, but he had evaded capture.[109] His convenient escape is unlikely to have been an accident since, according to Naturel's notes from the meeting with Hernando and the *Gran Capitán*, the former had already been corresponding in code with Acuña and had acted as intermediary between the *Gran Capitán* and the representatives sent to Naples. Naturel reported that both Baeza and the *Gran Capitán* had acted courteously but guardedly towards them, careful not to commit themselves in an unpredictable and fast-moving situation in which news was still arriving from Spain on the progress of talks between the rival monarchs. They appeared to support Juana as Queen of Castile and were fearful of disobeying Fernando as their legitimate sovereign in Naples, but at the same time the *Gran Capitán* offered men and support to Felipe. The ambiguity of this dispatch echoes the ambiguity of the *Gran Capitán*'s position vis-à-vis Cesare Borgia, and indeed, his relationship with Boabdil: a caution born of the awareness that unexpected events could dramatically alter the political picture overnight, and that today's allies might become tomorrow's enemies. Just days after this meeting, the *Gran Capitán* issued a solemn protestation of loyalty to Fernando, possibly motivated by intelligence that the king, fearful of his Viceroy's loyalty, had hatched a plan to have him arrested.[110]

Here we see the *Gran Capitán* and Hernando de Baeza acting in concert in a precarious diplomatic situation in which the lives of people close to them were at risk, as I shall show in the next chapter. As in Granada, Baeza was involved in sensitive negotiations of significant international importance in which he was faced with having to maintain the trust of opposing sides. The Spanish monarchs' repeated insistence on his recall is a measure of the influence they perceived that he was able to command, and his designation as a 'messenger' an attempt to downplay his significance at a pivotal moment in Spanish history.

The conflict between the *Gran Capitán* and Fernando of Aragon

With his action at the Battle of Garigliano in the last days of 1503, and the capture of Gaeta, Gonzalo Fernández de Córdoba, the *Gran Capitán*, drove the French out of Naples and earned a growing reputation as one of the best military strategists since Julius Caesar.[111] On behalf of the Spanish sovereigns, he then set about establishing the rule of law and government functions in Naples which had broken down during the war years.[112] Rich contemporary documentation including Zurita's chronicle, published correspondence, and dispatches from ambassadors in Rome shows how complex the political situation was across Italy and how difficult it was for the *Gran Capitán* to juggle different considerations in a fast-moving situation in which orders were received from Fernando with weeks' or even months' delay.[113]

All the sources highlight the distancing and growing mutual distrust between Fernando and the *Gran Capitan* and the king's letters about Hernando de Baeza's role in Rome are symptomatic of this. The *Gran Capitán*'s links with Felipe I, and the fact that his nephew the Marquis of Priego was in open defiance of Fernando's authority in the period following Isabel's death, were obvious reasons for Fernando's mistrust of his viceroy, but there were more. Carlos Hernando Sánchez makes a case that the *Gran Capitán* was harbouring ambitions to set himself up as a prince in his own right, highlighting his celebrity status in Italy and the way in which he stage-managed his 'magnificent' image and coordinated his networks of agents across the peninsula.[114] Certainly, the contemporary Venetian diarist Marino Sanuto describes him as having 'a great reputation, like a king'.[115] There was also the suspicion that he might adapt to Italian ways and sell himself as a *condottiero* to others. Neapolitan nobles who had been ejected from their lands and others who resented the *Gran Capitán*'s rise to power in Italy accused him of enriching himself and his followers, allowing his troops to run wild and of failing to establish order and justice.[116] Another well-documented point of conflict was the question of the cost of the war and the accusation that the *Gran Capitán* had incurred excessive expenses and kept poor accounts of them.

The question of tolerance of religious minorities in Naples was also a crucial flash point, although the matter was clearly entwined with other issues, not least Hernando de Baeza's own role.[117] As early as 11 July 1503, with the war still not yet completed, the Catholic Monarchs had expressed their concern that *conversos* and those fleeing the Inquisition in Spain had been able to find asylum in the kingdom of Naples and announced that they would be sending Inquisitors to pursue them there. At the same time, they ordered the *Gran Capitán* to expel all Jews from the kingdom as soon as he could.[118] The order had to be repeated on 2 March 1504 and again, in Latin, on 20 April the same year.[119] The letter complaining about the role of Hernando de Baeza in Rome was written just a month later, suggesting that, among Baeza's business there, he might have been lobbying against the extension of inquisitorial jurisdiction. He may perhaps have influenced the change of direction taken by Julius II immediately after his election, reversing measures instituted by his predecessor in support of the Spanish Inquisition.[120] On 30 June 1504, another letter was issued by the monarchs advising Gonzalo that they had appointed the Inquisitor of Sicily, the Archbishop of Messina, to take charge of Inquisition activities in Naples, a decision which had been made in consultation with the Inquisitor General, Diego Deza.[121] This went against undertakings Gonzalo had given representatives of the city of Naples in May 1503, which he was keen to uphold.[122] In a letter to the monarchs dated 6 July, he set out his view that converts to Christianity should not be expelled or harried and that the very small number of actual Jews in the kingdom presented no threat.[123]

The *Gran Capitan*'s refusal to expel the Jews, and his friendly relations with the *sefardí* Abramavel family, exiled in Italy, have been seen as evidence of his 'tolerance' in contrast with Fernando's 'intransigence'.[124] Already during their first sojourn in Italy, he and Baeza had become aware of the international implications of the expulsions, migrations and forced conversions in a context where monarchs were competing to be the most 'catholic'.[125] In early 1497, Gonzalo drafted a letter to the king from Reggio-Calabria reporting the presence of 400 Jewish refugees there who had fled 'unrest' in Sicily, Spain and elsewhere, some of whom had been forcibly converted to Christianity by Charles VIII.[126] The *Gran Capitán* wanted to avoid blame for any unrest ('escándalo') which might ensue, explaining that due to the pressures of the war he had not had time to do anything about them. The scrap of the draft letter contains both Gonzalo's and his secretary's handwriting, but there is no record as to whether the letter was ever sent.

There was also another, less well-documented issue which the monarchs demanded Gonzalo clamp down upon. In their second letter ordering the expulsion of the Jews, their demand was prefaced by a much longer passage about the need to stamp out the 'abominable sin against nature' (sodomy) which they had heard was rife in the kingdom.[127] It is perhaps this dubious indication which has led one late twentieth-century writer to describe Gonzalo Fernández de Córdoba as a 'famous homosexual' and has possibly also stimulated the imagination of others in conceptualizing his relationship with Boabdil.[128] It can perhaps more plausibly be read as an indication of Gonzalo's relative tolerance of sexual behaviours. On another occasion, the monarchs demanded that he bring his wife to join him in Naples, perhaps in order to create a more 'refined' courtly presence there rather than appear as an undisciplined occupying army.[129]

On 20 July 1504, after receiving a bad-tempered letter from the monarchs complaining about his poor government, together with a reminder of their instructions regarding Cesare Borgia, the *Gran Capitán* wrote to the monarchs asking to be relieved of his post through ill health, and to be permitted to return to Spain. His motivation has not been entirely clear since, on 25 August, he wrote two further letters not mentioning this request but outlining some of the problems he faced as Viceroy.[130] Just two days' earlier, on 23 August, Hernando de Baeza wrote a letter to the Marquis of Priego which deals almost exclusively with the *Gran Capitán*'s state of mind and sheds new light on the tensions between him and Fernando at this juncture.[131]

Baeza said that his brother Diego had just arrived from Spain with some disturbing news from the Marquis which proved that 'blood boils without fire'. This would appear to have been about rumours circulating in the Spanish court which were detrimental to the *Gran Capitán*'s reputation. Baeza said that he was very pleased to be advised, and that the *Gran Capitán* would be very grateful for the tip off. He said that although the *Gran Capitán* had taken care to show that he was not resigning out of pique but purely through ill health, they were aware that rumours were rife about his intentions. He went on to express indignation about the way that the king had appointed two men, Luis Peixó and *Licenciado* Pedrosa, who were coming to Naples with orders that undermined the *Gran Capitán*'s authority. This, he said, would be seen as a very public attack on the *Gran Capitán*'s honour and reputation and any attempt to cover it up would be counterproductive because people would see through it.

From other sources, it is evident that Luis Peixó had been appointed *escribano de ración* – financial administrator – and *alcaide* of the central fortress, the Castel Nuovo, in place of the *Gran Capitán*'s man, Nuño de Ocampo and that Pedrosa had been appointed chief justice and 'master of royal property' in Naples.[132] Both appointments were aimed at constricting the *Gran Capitán*'s power as viceroy. Baeza was particularly outraged by the suggestion that the *Gran Capitán* would have to hand over a fortress which he had won at great personal danger and described how his master was nearly killed by a cannon and how two dozen French and Spanish soldiers had died at his feet. Baeza had been with the *Gran Capitán* at the time Castel Nuovo had been captured and had in fact written a short letter sending news of it to Ambassador Rojas.[133] The idea that these services to the crown should be forgotten ('no se hace memoria de el'), Baeza saw as a major injustice. The link he makes between 'memory' and 'justice' perhaps provides an insight into Baeza's own motivations in writing his history of Granada. However, he said he believed that justice would be done in the end because the part that the *Gran Capitán* had played was public knowledge in Italy and people were aware of the reasons behind the monarchs' suspicion of him. Pedrosa had very little impact, dying in September that year, but Peixó fulfilled both roles to which he had been appointed, and indeed produced 924 pages of figures on the *Gran Capitán*'s accounts.[134] Another bureaucrat, Alonso de Deza (nephew of the Inquisitor Diego) was dispatched during 1504 with a long list of the monarchs' demands establishing their authority and curtailing the role of their viceroy.[135]

Baeza said that the *Gran Capitán* was disposed to go to Spain and give an account of himself to the sovereigns, but there was a danger that if he did so the 'envious and aggrieved' French would step in and retake the kingdom of Naples for themselves.[136] He then went on to complain about the bad reputation the *Gran Capitán* and his followers, including himself, had acquired as 'famous thieves' as a result of 'people talking out of their own passions'. This not only references the dispossessed Neopolitan nobles and others who were spreading malicious reports about them, but was also quite clearly directed at Ambassador Rojas, with a jibe about how others who had started out with less money had enriched themselves while in Italy.[137] Again, it was the injustice of this situation which angered him, the sense of 'being judged without being heard'. However, in a section perhaps covering him for any indiscretion should the letter fall into the wrong hands, he was also prudent enough to acknowledge both sides of the story. He said that he believed that the Catholic Monarchs were well-intentioned, but they were a long way away and could only go on what they had heard. The strategy of presenting a critique of the Crown by claiming that the monarchs' intentions were good but that they had been wrongly advised mirrors that employed by Pulgar in relation to the establishment of the Inquisition – using exactly the same words.[138] The same device of not criticizing the sovereign's intentions but rather the impact of their actions was also used by the theologian Thomas Cajetan in his refutation of the Scotist doctrine which underpinned the harsher interpretations of the Inquisition's role, believed written sometime between 1507 and 1522.[139] We can infer, therefore, that in protesting that he can see both sides, Baeza is in fact delivering a harsh criticism of the monarchs; his interest in unpicking their point of view is in order to change it. He suggested that if the Marquis was able to, he should seek to put about the alternative view at court. He ended his letter by saying that the whole point of his 'sermon' – a nice example of his self-awareness – was service of the monarchs and that this was the 'cord we are all pulling' – a metaphor which suggests that this 'service' was understood as active influence.

Baeza's letter provides an insight into how important reputation and honour were seen to be in underpinning power and shows how aware both he and the *Gran Capitán* were of how it could be manipulated. The idea that pretence would lead to greater loss of face because people would see through it reveals a subtle and sophisticated understanding of human psychology and its impact on politics. The situation in August 1504 immediately following the *Gran Capitán*'s resignation was clearly very fraught. It provided a very fragile basis for overcoming the tensions of the dynastic crises which followed Isabel I's death that November, and the much less expected demise of Felipe I less than two years later.

Fernando in Naples

After Fernando had met with his rival Felipe I and signed the Concord of Villafáfila, recognizing Felipe's right to govern Castile and cutting Juana out of the picture, the widowed monarch left Castile and set sail for Italy to take possession of the new kingdom which the *Gran Capitán* had conquered.[140] He took with him a letter from the Marquis of Priego to Hernando de Baeza which he broke into and read on the way. Baeza later noted sarcastically that the king had compromised the 'virginity' with which the letter had left Spain.[141]

During his journey to Naples, Fernando received the news that Felipe I had died suddenly. This turned the tables in his favour since, if he could win over, or overpower, the nobles who sought to block his return, he could now have access to the crown of

Castile as regent for his daughter Juana. Her reputation as an able monarch in her own right had already been irreparably damaged by Felipe.[142] With the political wind now blowing in Fernando's favour, the *Gran Capitán* laid on a splendid entrance for him as he arrived in Naples in a great public demonstration of unity and loyalty.[143]

While Fernando was in Naples, the sources report a much-celebrated incident which demonstrates the political and literary sophistication of the *Gran Capitán*'s court, as well as his lofty disdain for the likes of Pedrosa and Peixó. Chroniclers report that one day, in response to the demands of the king's treasurers, the *Gran Capitán* presented a 'small book of accounts which imposed silence on the treasurers, greatly affronted the king, and gave everyone a good laugh'.[144] Line one of these accounts was 2,736 ducats 'spent on friars and priests and nuns [...] praying constantly to God and all the saints for his victory'; the second line was 7,494 ducats paid to spies whose information had allowed him to understand his enemies' designs – itself a wry affirmation of the *Gran Capitán*'s method of operating. The sources indicate that this book of accounts contained further items, but that Fernando quickly got the message and cut short what was clearly a staged piece of theatre, designed to poke fun at his bureaucrats. The *Tribunal de Cuentas* (the supreme government accounting agency in Madrid) holds a document, whose authenticity is disputed, which purports to summarize what the remaining items listed in this little book were. These include 10,000 ducats for 'perfumed gloves to preserve the troops from the stench of their enemies' corpses laid out on the battlefield', and 70,000 ducats for the replacement of church bells which had been worn out through continually ringing the *Gran Capitán*'s victories and end with 'one hundred million for my patience in listening yesterday to the king ask for accounts from someone who won him a kingdom'.[145] This charade which, from the evidence of the chronicles, surely has at least some basis in fact, has become one of the best-known anecdotes relating to the *Gran Capitán*, so much so that the expression 'las cuentas del Gran Capitán' has even entered into the language, meaning accounts which are 'exorbitant and arbitrary'.[146] It has been suggested that the incident struck a chord in the national psyche because the *Gran Capitán*'s hauteur and largesse in the face of pettifogging miserliness (*mezquindad*) was a reflection of the Spanish character – though I think this does not do justice to the subtlety and creativity of the act. In fact, Fernández de Córdoba kept very detailed accounts as a heavy tome in the Archivo General de Simancas bears witness.[147] The historian Juan Granados has written a novelized account of the life of the *Gran Capitán*, in which he makes Hernando de Baeza the main performer in the charade, his eyes widening as he reads out the script given to him.[148] I think it is likely that, as the *Gran Capitán*'s secretary and close confidante, Baeza was actually involved in designing the performance, and in drafting its satirical script, which takes the dullest of genres – an accountant's record of expenditure – fills it with absurd and exaggerated content, and then uses it as a script for a live comedy performance in front of the king. Although the augmented list of items no doubt contains some latter-day embellishment, the basic story reveals a highly developed sense of irony as a way of puncturing the self-importance of Fernando's officials. It targets not only Fernando's bureaucratizing state power, but also the all-pervasive religiosity which supported it. It shows open cynicism towards clerics and members of religious orders and the costs of maintaining them, and implicit criticism of the type of religious belief that hoped to change the world through prayer, a position not so far from that of Erasmus and, indeed, Martin Luther.[149] Such satire could hardly have been aimed directly at Fernando. I read it as an attempt to draw Fernando away from his bureaucrats back into *caballero* mentality that he and the *Gran Capitán* had shared in other times. But, from the accounts of chroniclers, it appears that the sovereign was not amused. The episode nonetheless highlights the intellectual creativity and risk-taking to which Hernando de Baeza was exposed as a close member of the *Gran Capitán*'s personal circle. This makes it difficult to read his narrative of Granada as a simple, naive collection of personal anecdotes. Baeza was politically engaged, alert to irony and certainly capable of the sort of sly humour that we can see in this episode.

Conclusion

The meanings attached to the conquest of Naples were very different from those surrounding that of Granada. There was no talk of 'restoration' or the completion of a divine mission, no sense that it heralded hope for the future of Christianity – rather the opposite in fact, since it laid bare the brutal reality of modernizing warfare between European monarchs battling for supremacy. Geopolitically, it was more significant because it brought the whole of southern Italy under the control of the Aragonese monarch and forced him to appoint as viceroy the man who had stood in his place at the head of his troops. Now acclaimed as a great leader in his own right, the *Gran Capitán* was one of the most powerful men on the Italian peninsula, setting him at odds with a king who had to protect his own status in Castile, while at the same time grappling with the institutional challenges of managing a multi-national monarchy.

The Italian context provided a new perspective on issues of reconciliation and resistance in relation to Fernando's power. It provided a vantage point from which Baeza and his associates were able to perceive more clearly the deceptions, betrayals and swift-changing alliances which underlay Fernando's manoeuvrings, and the discrepancies between the narratives being propounded and their own experiences. Fighting a war with a Christian enemy seems to have brought home to the *Gran Capitán* that Fernando's objectives in the Granada war were as much political as religious. In his resignation letter, he wrote that he had fought for the monarchs 'against Moors and Christians', a statement which casts both enemies as equal and emphasizes his role as a professional soldier, loyal to the crown.[150] This is in tune with Machiavelli's analysis, who wrote that Fernando used religion as a 'cloak' to 'assail Africa', 'come down on Italy' and 'attack France'.[151] While Fernando was held up as model by Machiavelli for his lack of scruples in increasing his power, the *Gran Capitán* seems to have been more troubled by the moral choices facing him as his king's policies diverged from his own. How was he to remain loyal to his king if the king himself broke *caballero* codes of magnanimity, loyalty and respect for noble deeds? How much was he to resist, how much to submit to his sovereign? He attempted to reconcile his position through argument but, with the Mediterranean Sea between them and the Ambassador Rojas taking a contrary position, his letters had little influence. He also tried appeasement – one example of this is his and Carvajal's reluctant agreement that Hernando de Baeza must cede the *chantría* of Seville to the king's preferred candidate. Then, when Fernando arrived in Naples, there was a public display of reconciliation and deference while, in a more private setting, those in the *Gran Capitán*'s close circle attempted to tease out Fernando's sense of fairness and proportionality with the *cuentas* charade. However, the situation that had developed in Castile in the wake of Felipe I's death meant that the gulf between autocracy and loyalty was too wide to bridge. The *Gran Capitán*'s nephew, the Marquis of Priego, together with Baeza's family in Montilla, were already giving more weight to resistance than reconciliation, as I shall discuss in the next chapter.

5

Reconciliation and resistance to Fernando as governor of Castile

'Blood boils without fire'[1]

Lucero and the intensification of Inquisition activity

While Hernando de Baeza and the *Gran Capitán* were performing a diplomatic balancing act in Italy, Cordoba became the site of intense resistance to Fernando in the uncertain period after the death of Isabel in November 1504. It revolved around one of the most notorious episodes in the history of the Inquisition and the infamous inquisitor Diego Rodríguez Lucero, who took over there in 1499. Urged on by Fernando after the death of the queen, Lucero extended the pursuit of heretics far beyond previous Inquisition practice. In a display of rigour which signalled Fernando's continuing control and power, 107 people were burnt at the stake in Cordoba on 22 December 1504.[2] A learned cleric known as the Maestro de Toro, a close ally of the Marquis of Priego, witnessed this *auto de fe* and was horrified to hear several of the dying victims cry out to Jesus and the Virgin and call for notaries to record that they had died as Christians.[3] Pedro Mártir de Anglería articulated widespread shock and disbelief when in Granada, the famously pious Archbishop, Hernando de Talavera, a man regarded as no less saintly in his lifestyle than St Jerome himself, was himself targeted as a judaizer.[4] This was the first time that an Archbishop had been accused of heresy and a special dispensation from Pope Julius II was required to arrest him, obtained via Fernando's ambassador Francisco de Rojas.[5] Talavera had always refused to allow the Inquisition to operate in Granada, in order to protect his new converts from Islam, and the Cordoba tribunal was not supposed to have jurisdiction there.

The excesses of Lucero and his co-inquisitors, Sancho de Castilla and Juan de la Fuente, provoked a huge public scandal which became closely embroiled in the political and ideological struggles which followed the death of Isabel, and these have been closely examined and discussed by scholars.[6] The number and profile of people accused of heresy provoked an outcry, since it went far beyond those known as *conversos* and impinged on reputable people believed to be old Christians with important positions within the church and town oligarchies. People were shocked by the brutal ways which the inquisitors used to extract confessions and force those accused to implicate yet more people, including the use of rape, torture and threats of the same. The most unlikely crimes were alleged, including houses supposedly used as 'synagogues' and marauding bands of 'prophetesses' sweeping through the countryside 'judaizing'. Inquisitors were later accused of planting evidence and benefiting personally from the cash, property and benefices seized.[7] There has also been a case made for their motivations being, at least in part, sexual.[8] The prevalence of messianic beliefs at this time does seem to have given rise to a genuine movement among some *conversos* to return to their old faith, which the inquisitors sought to halt and eradicate, but in doing so they allowed the situation to escalate massively in the troubled period after Isabel's death.[9] Whether moved by extreme religious zeal or by worldly impulses, Lucero and his team transgressed the rules and regulations governing inquisitorial action. Once this boundary had been crossed, they were unable to back-pedal without incriminating themselves or at least losing face. They knew that if they released or simply offered reconciliation to the prisoners, word would spread about the methods they had used to extract confessions: their only option was to burn them all. The fact that Inquisitors used gags and had prisoners beaten even as they were being burned suggests that they were desperate to avoid them testifying at the stake.[10] Through sermons, *autos de fe* and other public acts, they whipped up popular enthusiasm to see evil punished, and this in turn created demand for more. The Inquisitors' behaviour was so outrageous that it united the town council, the church, the nobility as well as a wide range of citizens in denouncing it. Their appeals for justice became a *cause celebre* in the backlash against Fernando post 1504, with the Marquis of Priego and the Count of Cabra at the forefront of a campaign which I shall discuss further presently.[11]

Hernando de Baeza's family were directly afflicted by this wave of brutality, and his own property was probably in danger. The Marquis had, by November 1506, moved some deeds and other documents relating to land owned by Hernando de Baeza to the house of the vicar of Montilla, for safekeeping.[12] The reason for this was no doubt to keep the property out of the clutches of the Inquisition. The vicar in question was a man named Rodrigo Blásquez, who in an undated letter written around this time, called on the Marquis of Priego to intervene because 'people want there to be a lot of heretics to see them arrested and burnt, so they are inventing cases which aren't true'.[13] He said that the inquisitors were encouraging witnesses to make statements beyond what they had actually heard and seen, and innocent people were suffering. Blásquez was evidently close to the Marquis and was present, in his role as vicar of Montilla, at the opening of his will in 1517.[14] He was also close to the Baeza family and, in 1513, witnessed a sale of their property involving the Marquis.[15]

In late 1506, after Felipe I's death, Hernando de Baeza and the Marquis had an exchange of correspondence about Lucero's activity which shows clearly how they were both affected by it, although the surviving letter avoids naming names or being too explicit.[16] The Marquis had apparently written to Baeza saying that his *contador* and the latter's children had denied the charges they were being accused of. I take this to be Baeza's father-in-law, Alfonso de Córdoba who had been the Fernández de Córdobas' financial administrator since 1469 and probably earlier.[17] From Hernando's reply, it is evident that he already knew about their arrest, since he said that at first just one of the sons had been arrested and, although the inquisitors had not been able to make the accusation stick, they had extracted a confession which had allowed them to arrest the whole family. Baeza told the Marquis that there could not be any truth in the allegations, especially given the 'abominations' which Lucero had been carrying out not only in Cordoba but also in areas outside his jurisdiction. This is a clear reference to Granada and contextualizes the concern shown in Baeza's narrative for the *elches*. In his letter, he said that he hoped that the Marquis would not take any notice of such a confession 'because lies cannot stand in for the truth' and that he hoped to God that his 'brother' would 'get out without punishment, just as he was taken in without cause'. Baeza calls Lucero 'Satanas', a sinister sobriquet which parallels Pedro Mártir d'Anglería's much-quoted 'Tenebrario'.[18]

From other sources, it is clear that Hernando was referring to his brother-in-law Gonzalo de Córdoba, who succeeded his father as the Marquis's *contador* and was arrested and imprisoned by Lucero at this time, along with his wife and other members of the family. Gonzalo de Córdoba underwent two Inquisition trials and although the original documents are no longer extant, they were referred to in an investigation into the genealogy of his great grandson, in 1626.[19] In the first trial, which was recorded on 30 July 1505, he was accused of 'observing the Law of Moses' but according to the note of that case, he was acquitted and his confiscated property was returned to him. Many years later, in 1533, he was arrested again and gave further details of what had happened back in 1505. He said that he and his wife Beatriz de Baeza, daughter of Fernando de Baeza, *veinticuatro* of Cordoba (i.e. Fernán, Hernando's cousin), had spent two years in prison during the time of Lucero. He said that they were released with all the other prisoners freed by 'the Marquis or the Count' (i.e. of Cabra) and that afterwards the Inquisitor Torquemada looked into his case and acquitted him and his wife. He also said that his mother, Teresa Álvarez, had been accused too, but had been ill and died before she could testify. The inquisitors had condemned her *post mortem* and ordered her property to be confiscated, but his father, the *Jurado* Alfonso de Córdoba, had given the Inquisition's receiver 10,000 *maravedís* for it instead. As a result of his mother's sentence, Gonzalo had been banned from acting as a *contador* and wearing silk, but he had obtained a royal letter rehabilitating him and restoring his reputation.[20]

The ties between Hernando de Baeza and the *contador*'s family were very close. Baeza was married to one of Gonzalo de Córdoba's sisters, while two other sisters had married Hernando's brothers Diego and Pedro (the latter now deceased) – see genealogical chart p. 12. The triple marriage had created a very strong extended family unit, working together for mutual benefit in uncertain times. Hernando's preoccupations during this time therefore included anxieties involving the life or death of close relatives. In June 1506, Lucero had intended to go ahead with another mass burning of his victims, which would surely have included Gonzalo de Córdoba and other members of Hernando's family, but this was narrowly avoided as a result of intervention by the nobility – discussed further below.[21] *Licenciado* Diego Daza, a man who acted as the family lawyer, and had worked alongside Baeza with both Don Alonso and the Marquis, was among others belonging to the Marquis's circle who were also arrested and charged.[22] Lucero's targeting of key members of the Marquis's household and the implication that he was harbouring 'judaizers' was an attack on the nobleman's integrity and his honour, and challenged his right to administer justice in his own domains. Some accounts even claim that the Marquis himself was summoned by Lucero to appear for trial.[23] The detention of his financial administrator and others who worked for him would also have had a practical impact on the smooth-running of his affairs.[24] In Granada, similar arrests were causing chaos for the Count of Tendilla in the administration of salaries and military preparations for a campaign in North Africa.[25]

The campaign against Lucero

The Lucero affair was important in exposing the use of the Inquisition as a political tool and this stimulated a more coherent critique of the ideology driving inquisitorial activity and the evolution of monarchical power.[26] The growing outcry against Lucero and the other inquisitors of the Cordoba tribunal turned into a full-blown campaign which was remarkable for constituting the first direct resistance to the Inquisition (as opposed to principled critique) since it had been established a quarter of a century previously.[27] It brought together a coalition of powerful players drawn from the nobility, church and town authorities in both Cordoba and Granada, who based their case on legal, political, economic and humanitarian challenges to the way the Inquisition was operating under Fernando.[28]

There is a great deal of evidence to suggest that Baeza was associated with the campaign at a number of levels. He had known about Lucero's reign of terror in Cordoba from an early stage. When in May 1505, Cardinal Carvajal wrote to the *Gran Capitán* about Hernando de Baeza, calling him his friend, he also mentioned that there was 'new activity' relating to the Inquisition in Cordoba, and no end in sight.[29] Carvajal was, of course, ideally positioned in the *curia* to pick up intelligence arriving in Rome. Baeza makes clear in his letter to the Marquis of late 1506 that he was receiving information on the situation via sources in Italy. He said, for example, that there were reports in Rome that Lucero had died suddenly.[30] Since, from the time it was first established, *converso* emigrés and intellectuals in Rome like Pedro Arias Davila and Juan de Lucena had been lobbying against the Inquisition, this was very likely one of the unspoken reasons why Fernando and Isabel had complained so bitterly about Hernando de Baeza.[31]

The campaign against Lucero was well-orchestrated, with lobbying in Rome and in Flanders as well as in Castile and throughout Andalusia, with Hernando's master the Marquis described as 'one of the greatest antagonists of the Inquisition in his time'.[32] The young monarchs, Felipe and Juana, were targeted at an early stage and the Marquis and his allies sent representatives to Flanders in 1505 to urge them to come to Spain as soon as possible.[33] On 30 September 1505, Felipe and Juana signed an order that all Inquisition activity should be suspended until their arrival in Castile. They also wrote to the Inquisitor General – Archbishop of Seville Diego de Deza – and other inquisitors calling into question the reasons why the prisoners were being detained and the conditions in which they were being held.[34] Deza was temporarily suspended and the young Prince Carlos's tutor, the Bishop of Catania, Diego Ramírez de Guzmán, appointed to take charge. As a result, the case files and, it is thought, many of the prisoners were transferred from Cordoba to Toro.³⁵ Fernando too received direct appeals, which he rebuffed, writing to his ambassador Rojas saying how he had refused *converso* 'bribes'.³⁶ Meanwhile, in Rome, with both kings vying for power, there was an 'active contest' between the representatives of Fernando and Felipe to influence the pope.³⁷ As Fernando pressed for papal bulls to be issued for the arrest of Archbishop Talavera, the Marquis of Priego sent the Bishop of Tagaste, Francisco de Mayorga, a resident of Baena (seat of the Count of Cabra), to protest on behalf of Lucero's victims in Cordoba.³⁸ Mayorga received an official appointment from the pope to investigate further, probably through the good offices of Cardinal Carvajal. The pope also sent the Bishop of Bertinoro, Juan Rufo, as his legate to investigate the case against Talavera. Pedro Mártir wrote that his mission was to uproot from hearts of the pope and cardinals the 'virus' sown there by Lucero.³⁹ As a man well connected with the curia, with Cordoba and with Felipe I's representatives in Rome, Hernando de Baeza emerges as a lynch-pin between Cordoba, Rome and Flanders. Just days after his meeting with Hernando, on 28 June 1506, Felipe's representative Philibert Naturel reported that he had urged the pope to take action in relation to the complaints received from Cordoba about the Inquisitors' activity.⁴⁰

Baeza's noble sponsors, the Marquis of Priego and the Count of Cabra, have been cast as rebellious aristocrats in taking direct action against Lucero, a continuation of the 'noble bellicosity' evidenced in the previous century, of which the Marquis's father Alonso de Aguilar was a prime example.⁴¹ Apologists for Lucero and the Inquisition have tried to pin the blame on the 'judaizers' themselves for sowing division between the Marquis and the Inquisition by testifying falsely against him and other notables.⁴² But I would argue that the conflict was one of values and opposed visions of the new Christian society which had emerged after 1492 as much as a power struggle between social groups. The Marquis was a very different man from his father and the situation in the early years of the sixteenth century very different from that of the 1460s and 1470s. Accounts which are more sympathetic to the Marquis highlight his 'prudence and authority' in maintaining public order in Cordoba in the period after the death of Felipe I.⁴³ The new generation of nobles behaved with caution and diplomacy and when they resorted to force of arms, they ensured they had legal backing for this. In June 1506, with drought, famine and plague threatening to plunge Cordoba into chaos and in the absence of its *Corregidor*, at the request of the council members, the Marquis and the Count of Cabra took control of the city. This lasted only until August, when a new *Corregidor* was appointed, but their assumption of authority is associated with the withdrawal of Lucero's plan for the mass burning that month.⁴⁴ The Count of Tendilla, who thought Lucero's plan wholly unjust and feared it would spark serious disorder, had written to the inquisitors reminding them that Felipe and Juana had ordered the suspension of all Inquisition activity until the wider questions of government had been settled.⁴⁵ He then wrote to Cabra and Priego, warning them of the impending *auto*, saying that Lucero's actions would cause a riot he would not be able to quash with his skirts. An institution which had been set up to quell public disorder had run out of control and was now doing the opposite.⁴⁶ At this point, Diego Fernández de Córdoba (1464–1518), a junior member of the noble family with the honorary title *Alcaide de los Donceles,* who was lord of the towns of Lucena, Espejo and Chillón, intervened on behalf of Fernando and the Inquisition.[47] A member of his household complained to Tendilla that Cabra and Priego had laid siege to the *Alcázar*, where Lucero's prisoners were being held, and were threatening the fortress of Castro del Río, which contained more of his victims.[48] Tendilla replied that he did not believe that there had been any disorder and that if they had 'opened some cages in order to let the birds fly away', they would have performed a useful service.[49] It is not clear whether the Count and the Marquis did actually free any detainees at this point, but they certainly were being lobbied by the relatives of the victims, urging them to take action.[50] In Baeza's letter to the Marquis of December 1506, in which he discusses the charges against Gonzalo de Córdoba, he gives the impression that the Marquis was uncertain of what to believe or how he should act. Baeza's aim was to convince him of his brother-in-law's innocence and encourage him to act to bring Lucero down. He said he hoped that the 'mud' the inquisitor was throwing – one feels he is resisting using a stronger word – would land on his own house and that the Cordoban nobility would not act like St Lazarus by not feeling their injuries. I take this to be a reference to leprosy, with which St Lazarus is associated, since one symptom of the disease is loss of feeling.[51] Baeza's letter, and the seventeenth-century report of Gonzalo de Córdoba's Inquisition trial referenced above, add to the rather patchy evidence relating to the Lucero affair: because of the extreme political sensitivity and the concern to protect reputations, neither side had an interest in preserving detailed records.

Baeza and his circle are also linked to other figures who took part in the campaign in Spain, particularly those who acted as mediators or negotiators. After Talavera's arrest, the Granada town council (*cabildo*) appealed to the pope in a letter written by an eminent Granadan lawyer named Jorge de Torres, who would later act as executor of the *Gran Capitán*'s will.[52] Torres strongly protested Talavera's innocence and called on Cardinal Carvajal, among others, to witness the injustices of the Inquisition. Another figure who took part in the lobbying, whom Baeza almost certainly knew, was Gonzalo de Ayora, a royal chronicler from Cordoba whose family had for generations been officials in the Customs House alongside Hernando's relatives.[53] In November 1506, Ayora was a member of a delegation to Queen Juana setting out the case against Lucero and Archbishop Deza's protection of him. A joint letter from the town and cathedral authorities bears witness to the extent of opposition to them, coming from 'the dean and cathedral chapter, and all other ecclesiastical persons, and the Council and *corregidor* and aldermen and parish representatives and all the nobles, *caballeros*, squires, good men and universally everyone from this town and bishopric.'[54] In July 1507, when Fernando returned to Spain, Ayora wrote to the king's secretary setting out the political and social damage which the Inquisition had caused.[55] He and representatives from Toledo and Granada had a meeting with Fernando in September that year, at which the king was given some shocking examples of the way the inquisitors had taken advantage of their victims both financially and sexually. He made the case that the king should intervene to avoid the threat of rebellion against the crown – and it is to be noted that this is a wider lesson that emerges strongly from Baeza's account of the experiences of the Granadan emirs.[56] Fernando said that *conversos* had always served him and his wife well but noted that since her death he had had reasons to find some of them disloyal.[57]

This seems to me to be an admission that his motives were indeed political and not, as has been claimed, evidence that Fernando was not prejudiced against *conversos* and did not use the Inquisition for political purposes.[58]

Priego and Cabra made a number of attempts to win over Lucero's 'line manager', Diego de Deza, the Archbishop of Seville. We must remember that it had been at Deza's urging that the monarchs had written to the *Gran Capitán* in relation to establishing an Inquisition tribunal in Naples.[59] Baeza mentions Deza in his letter of December 1506, complaining to the Marquis that the Archbishop was blocking his son's ecclesiastical appointments and refusing offers of compromise.[60] At first, the approach from Priego and Cabra appeared successful as, in the immediate aftermath of Felipe I's death, Deza joined the confederation of Andalusian nobles supporting Juana's claim to rule.[61] He also agreed to take part in a committee of enquiry to investigate Lucero's activity but soon withdrew, adopting a more hard-line position, probably on orders from Fernando.[62] Cabra and Priego then sent a delegation of high-ranking churchmen from Cordoba to appeal to Deza to have Lucero arrested and tried. These included the Count of Cabra's brother, Don Francisco de Mendoza, who was Archdeacon of Pedroche, and Don Pedro Ponce de León, a church dignitary in Cordoba and scion of the family of the Marquis of Cadiz, who was involved in helping Baeza's son to take possession of the church benefices the pope had ceded him.[63] However, Deza rejected their appeal and instead reassumed the role of Grand Inquisitor. He had the prisoners and case material brought back to Cordoba under the jurisdiction of his own appointee, Archdeacon Torquemada. This is the man who Gonzalo de Córdoba later said had exonerated him, although it is not clear whether this was a result of Priego's lobbying or direct action, since Deza's actions led to an uprising in Cordoba during which the prisoners were freed and Lucero reportedly fled on the back of a mule.[64] There are conflicting accounts of when this occurred (as early as October 1506 or as late as March 1507) and to what extent the Marquis and the Count were leaders of an armed rebellion, or trying to prevent further disorder by responding to popular demands for justice. Royalist accounts make more of the role of the two nobles and blame them for stirring up popular unrest.[65] However, others present it as a purely popular uprising.[66] On 9 November 1506, various high-ranking clerics and *caballeros*, including the Count's brother Don Francisco de Mendoza, entered the house of the Inquisition prosecutor, Juan de Arriola, and arrested him to prevent the Inquisition from functioning.[67] In a report to Queen Juana in December 1506, the civil and ecclesiastical authorities said that they had asked the Marquis and the Count to take control of the *Alcázar*, where 400 starving prisoners were being held, in order to protect both them and the evidence being held there, from Deza and Lucero.[68]

Hernando de Baeza said in his letter of December 1506 that he had received the Marquis's letter dated 20 November, at which time his brother-in-law was still under arrest.[69] The American historian Charles Henry Lea deduced that the prisoners were delivered back to Lucero as a result of a bull issued by Julius II in early 1507, which ordered them to be treated with the utmost severity. This would have been while the pope was in Bologna (presumably away from the influence of campaigners in Rome), and Lea believes that this then led to Priego and Cabra taking direct action to free them.[70] This analysis fits with Gonzalo de Córdoba's testimony that he spent two years in prison from 1505 onwards and that he was liberated by the Marquis or by the Count.[71]

In Granada, the Count of Tendilla was horrified at the inquisitors' behaviour. He wrote a series of letters to the king, to the royal treasurer Morales, and to the inquisitors themselves, complaining about the economic and political consequences.[72] Representatives of Granada who attended the *Cortes* held in Valladolid in July 1506 were instructed to report on the 'great damage' that the behaviour of the Inquisition had inflicted on Granada which had been the 'destruction' of the kingdom.[73] But although the activities of Lucero and his colleagues disturbed him, Tendilla remained strictly loyal to Fernando.[74] However, there was one member of the Andalusian aristocracy who fiercely upheld the hard line taken by the Inquisition and by Fernando in supporting it.[75] This was the Marquis of Priego's cousin, the *Alcaide de los Donceles*, who is seen as a lone defender of Fernando's interests among the Andalusian aristocracy, in direct opposition to Cabra and Priego. In a letter which Archbishop Deza wrote to Fernando while he was in Naples, he claimed that the Count and the Marquis were using the controversy surrounding the Inquisition to further their own power against the *Alcaide*.[76] As a more junior and less wealthy member of the Fernández de Córdoba family, the *Alcaide* sought royal favour by aligning himself with Fernando and supported his imperial campaigns in North Africa (and later in Navarre), which distanced him from his ancestral base in Andalusia.[77] As a teenager, the *Alcaide* had been involved in the capture of Boabdil after the Battle of Lucena, and Baeza cites him in a subtly insulting way in his memoir. He recounts how, in recognition of their role, the Count of Cabra and the *Alcaide de los Donceles* were both given the honour of bearing an image of the emir on their coat of arms:

> The Count, as the one who first captured the king, was given the upper half of the Moorish king's body to put on his coat of arms and, for his arms, the *Alcaide de los Donceles* was given the king's body from the waist down.[78]

This is indeed a bizarre image. I have not been able to find any heraldic representation of the bottom half of a human figure, let alone a Muslim, and it would be difficult to imagine how it might be portrayed in a way which reflected any glory on its bearer. I read it as an 'in joke' against a leading Fernandista, which demonstrates the same satirical humour as in the incident of the *Gran Capitán*'s cuentas. In fact, both men adopted a representation of Boabdil's head and shoulders, with a chain around his neck – see image 9.

The pursuit of ecclesiastical benefices

As the campaign against Lucero gathered force, Hernando de Baeza was simultaneously engaged in another personal struggle. It was one thing to have a healthy ecclesiastical income for his son granted by the pope, but quite another to bring it to fruition. The pope's favours could not have come at a worse time, with control over church appointments such a bone of contention in the succession crisis and Andalusia in

Image 9 Sixteenth-century ceramic tile with the Count of Cabra's coat of arms bearing an image of Boabdil with a chain around his neck and the twenty-two banners seized at the battle of Lucena. The motto is a quotation from John 1:3. Album/Alamy Stock Photo. Original: Instituto de Valencia Don Juan, Madrid.

turmoil. With many members of the Cordoban church hierarchy themselves under suspicion, there was heightened sensitivity towards 'infiltration' by people of Jewish origin. Prime positions within the church, though theoretically granted in Rome, proved difficult to realize on the ground in Spain.

The process had a promising start in the autumn of 1504, when Hernando first wrote to the Marquis about the 'reservation'.[79] He said it had been achieved through the good offices of his 'protector', Cardinal Carvajal, and that it was for the first high-ranking positions which came available (which was usually through the death of its occupier) in the dioceses of Cordoba and Jaén. The key to taking possession of such benefices was finding a reliable representative on the ground who could step in with the relevant papal papers at the moment one became free.[80] Baeza asked his master to act as his patron and suggested that a man named Martín Alonso de Córdoba should act as his son's representative, because 'he is a great friend of mine and my brothers, as his father was of ours'.[81] But in the troubled context Lucero had created in Cordoba, the Marquis vetoed this suggestion. Baeza later dubbed the man a 'Pharisee', which I take to mean that he had associated himself with the hard-liners against the Marquis.[82] Cruden's Concordance describes the Pharisees thus:

> They were formalists, very patriotic but bigoted in their patriotism as in their religion. [...] Jesus denounced the Pharisees for their hypocrisy, which was shown by their care for the minutest formalities imposed by the tradition of their elders, but not for the mind and heart.[83]

In using this analogy, Baeza associates himself and the Marquis with the earliest days of Christianity and the messages of Jesus's 'New Law'. He agreed that, although he had hoped that 'there would be birds in the nests of yester-year', Alonso would no longer be a suitable representative, though he had already commissioned him to take possession of a canonry in either Cordoba or Jaén. The change of plan highlights the speed of shifting alliances in the highly charged political context.

Baeza had been in contact with various legal representatives which by December 1506 he said had so far cost him a total of 120,000 *maravedís*. Don Pedro chided him for granting power of attorney to so many people, but Baeza's son still had not been able to take possession of a single benefice.[84] Seville cathedral records show that it was a man named Luis de Anaya who acted for Hernando's son in April 1505, enabling him to take possession of the much coveted *chantría*.[85] But this was superseded almost immediately after Fernando's intervention to demand that the position was handed over to his treasurer, Alonso de Morales. In the atmosphere of mistrust and tension, closely connected to disputes concerning the Inquisition, this blew up into a controversy involving both Carvajal and the *Gran Capitán* which went on throughout the summer. Baeza was accused of demanding compensation from Morales, and the *Gran Capitán* had to write a grovelling letter to Fernando assuring him that this was not so.[86] Fernando's demand for the post to be reassigned was not straightforward discrimination against a man of Jewish origin but, in the controversy surrounding Lucero and his opponents' support for Felipe I, Hernando's *converso* status was a key factor. In acceding to the king's wishes to allow Morales to take the *chantría*, Baeza used a legal device ('Regreso') which would allow his son to return to the position when it became vacant again.[87] But after Morales died in May 1506, Archbishop Deza, the Inquisitor General now deeply involved in the Lucero controversy, blocked Baeza from stepping in, as Baeza's letter clearly reveals.[88] Baeza told the Marquis that this was despite Cardinal Carvajal having offered Deza a third of the *chantría's* value in exchange for other benefices, but Fernando had told Carvajal to favour Deza's candidate, who Baeza describes as 'an intense man'.[89] This was most probably Deza's nephew, Juan Tavera (1472–1545) who succeeded Morales as *chantre* and, with the money he made in a brilliant career which included becoming a cardinal, president of the Royal Council, and Grand Inquisitor, founded an impressive hospital in Toledo.[90]

It is one of the ironies of history that this building now houses the Archivo Ducal de Medinaceli, which contains Baeza's letters.

Baeza said that the *Gran Capitán* was trying to block Deza's plans and that there were legal proceedings in Rome which he was sure would support his son's claim. He said that Deza must answer to his own conscience because he had also been blocking his son's appointments by placing his own secretary in a valuable benefice in La Alcarria. He also said that the Inquisition's prosecutor in Seville, Diego López de Cortegana, had leapfrogged over his son's prior claims to a canonry in Jaén and lucrative benefices in Carmona and Niebla.[91] Cortegana was a talented scholar and one of the first translators of Erasmus's work into Spanish.[92] His translation of the bawdy and irreverent work *Metamorphoses* by Apuleius (in Spanish: *El Asno de Oro*), appears in the Marquis's library collection.[93] He also produced an updated version of the chronicle of Fernando III, conqueror of Seville, which has been seen as displaying a more inclusive stance towards the city's *mudejar* and *morisco* population than the originals he worked from.[94] Cortegana later played a leading role in writing Seville cathedral's purity of blood statute but, despite this, seems to have represented a more compassionate tendency within the Inquisition. Years after Baeza's death (most probably in 1525), Cortegana's niece and heir married Baeza's grandson, also named Hernando de Baeza.[95]

These controversies highlight the flexibility and scope for persuasion that was seen to exist even as the Inquisition was taking on a more monolithic and intransigent aspect. In what was already a highly competitive situation, the controversy over Lucero and its link to the political crisis created very difficult conditions for *conversos* to take up important positions, even when supported by papal backing. In Baeza's case at least, this was not direct discrimination, but a consequence of the political scenario which positioned him in conflict with the hard-liners. In his quest for his son's integration into the ecclesiastical hierarchy, he employed every means at his disposal, drawing on the support of Cardinal Carvajal, the *Gran Capitán* and the Marquis, appealing to influencers and prominent figures in Spain, and spending large amounts of money on intermediaries, as well as on taking legal action through the Roman Rota to achieve his goals.[96]

The 'rebellion' of the Marquis of Priego

Between March and May 1507, with Fernando in Naples, there was a breakthrough for the campaigners against Lucero. It appears that a settlement which confirmed Fernando as regent for his daughter Juana involved him agreeing to replace Deza as Inquisitor General.[97] In April, Julius II cleared Talavera of any wrong-doing and in early June, the Archbishop of Toledo, Francisco Jiménez de Cisneros, who was made a cardinal in what appears to be part of the same deal, was confirmed as the new Inquisitor-in-Chief. Although Cisneros is portrayed as the hardliner in relation to the conversions of Muslims in Granada, he had been put forward by the campaigners as an honourable man capable of achieving a solution in Cordoba.[98] With Cisneros in charge, the campaigners finally saw justice done. A letter from the *Gran Capitán* to the Marquis provides a roll call of the influential churchmen and nobles lending their weight to the case against Lucero, and an insight into the network of resistance against Fernando.[99] These included the Bishops of Cordoba (Juan Daza), Badajoz (Alfonso Manrique de Lara, who had initially been incarcerated in Atienza by Fernando on his return), Catania (Diego Ramírez de Guzmán) and Osma (Alfonso Enríquez – an illegitimate scion of that noble family); the Admiral of Castile Don Fadrique Enríquez; the Constable of Castile, Bernardino de Velasco, and Don Francisco de Mendoza. The *Gran Capitán* said he was hopeful of a good outcome and indeed, Lucero was put on trial, found guilty of extorting false accusations, and dismissed from his post as inquisitor.[100]

But although the battle against Lucero was won, the political struggle with Fernando and the wider ideological conflict were far from over. Fernando continued to intervene to prevent confiscated property which had been donated to his supporters from being returned to its owners.[101] He sacked the Inquisition official Diego López de Cortegana for his soft line in relation to *Licenciado* Daza.[102] He also tried to remove Francisco de Simancas as Archdeacon of Cordoba for standing up for another of Lucero's victims.[103]

Fernando arrived back in Spain at the end of 1507, disembarking in Valencia, from where the Marquis received an account of his arrival from a well-wisher.[104] The Marquis travelled to Burgos with a huge, richly attired retinue to pay homage to him, but was rebuffed. The anonymous chronicler describes him as 'a spirited and free-thinking *caballero*, annoyed and unhappy with the king'.[105] The pro-Fernando chroniclers, Zurita and Bernáldez, report that the king wished to punish the Marquis for his disloyalty and pursuit of his own interests during the interregnum.[106] The latter's high-profile involvement with the campaign against Lucero identified him as a key target for Fernando's revenge. The fuse was lit by a clash between the Marquis and a representative of the *Alcaide de los Donceles* – Fernando's chief supporter in Andalusia – over the control of justice in Cordoba.[107] The Marquis humiliated his rival's man by smashing his official staff of office and placing the fragments on the public pillory.[108] This then led to Fernando, presumably responding to complaints from the *Alcaide*, sending in a judge to investigate. The Marquis unwisely arrested Fernando's man and had him imprisoned in the castle of Montilla. With Fernando threatening to take revenge, the Marquis had the man released and sent Doctor de la Torre, probably the same person who went to Rome to plead on behalf of Talavera, to explain the mishap.[109] But Fernando marched on Cordoba with a substantial army to take his revenge on the Marquis. The incident can be seen as Fernando counterbalancing his defeat over the Lucero case and, in the words of Pedro Mártir, 'grinding this bean on the Marquis's head' to establish his authority.[110] He was the price for the defeat of Lucero and, with the 'satanic' Inquisitor now in prison in Burgos, the Marquis too was arrested and held in Santa Maria de la Trassierra, outside Cordoba. He suffered the utter disgrace of having his castle demolished, being required to pay a huge fine, and being banished from Andalusia.[111]

Although narratives centre on the Marquis himself, the impact was felt across the city and many members of his household, as well as officials of Cordoba council, also received severe punishments.[112] Pedro de las Infantas, *alcalde* of Montilla, was condemned to having his hand and foot cut off and his house demolished; Fernando de Alarcón, a man who had acted as the Marquis's *contador* while Gonzalo de Córdoba was in the Inquisition's prison, was also to lose a foot.[113] Two prominent members of Cordoba council, Alonso de Cárcamo and Bernardino de Bocanegra, had their houses demolished and one account says that the king ordered an *escribano* to have his thumb cut off.[114] Some of Hernando's close associates and possible members of his family appear among those punished, fleeing from punishment or pardoned by Queen Juana for their role in the affair including Gonzalo de Baeza (very possibly his brother) and another Baeza who is rendered variously as Alonso and Alvaro.[115]

Although there is no evidence that Hernando de Baeza was directly involved either in the incident or in the subsequent punishments, the episode would have had a devastating effect on him. The way that Fernando dealt with the Marquis was regarded by contemporaries as exceptionally severe, and in particular the demolition of his castle was seen as a shocking reprisal not only for the Marquis but for the *Gran Capitán*, whose father's family seat it had been.[116] Chronicles refer to the beauty and strength of the castle and the immense manpower needed to raze it to the ground.[117] As an insufficient number of locals were able or willing to undertake the job, men had to be brought in from outside. When part of a wall collapsed killing several of them, the *Gran Capitán* is reported to have praised the castle for defending itself.[118] The bitterness inherent in this perhaps apocryphal comment and the personification of the iconic building highlights the significance of its demolition for the whole household. It was an immensely symbolic act against a place of memory for the Fernández de Córdoba family, which affected the *Gran Capitán* deeply.[119] For Baeza, it was symbolic of the power and protection the Fernández de Córdobas had given his family over the generations and would certainly have been another incident proving that 'blood boils without fire'.[120]

It is apparent that the Marquis suffered some sort of breakdown as a result of his arrest and sentence, since in recognition of his 'indisposition' and 'illness', Fernando allowed him to delay his departure from Andalusia until the beginning of 1509.[121] In January that year, as he passed through the town of Bailén towards Valencia where he spent his exile, he made a lengthy sworn statement setting out his position and the injustices he had received at the hands of the 'severísimo' King Fernando.[122] This document, which has not been given the attention it deserves, is important in that it sets out the Marquis's political philosophy at a time which coincides almost exactly with the point at which, as I shall discuss in the next chapter, Hernando de Baeza reworked his narrative. The Marquis explained that he had taken power in Cordoba legally on behalf of Felipe I and, on the latter's death, had continued to serve Juana as the rightful queen. He had done his best to govern Cordoba wisely and to keep public order during a period of considerable uncertainty. He had had no official communication informing him of Fernando's governorship and believed that if Juana was unable to fulfil her role as queen, any alternative should be established by consent of the nobility and the town authorities. He did not accept the validity of his trial, at which he had had no opportunity to defend himself and believed that the punishment was out of all proportion to the offence. In particular, he said that the demolition of his castle, his patrimony, which was at the heart of the institutional relationship between his family and the monarchy, was illegal. He had been ill while in prison, unable to mount a legal defence, and Fernando had instilled such terror by marching into Cordoba with his army that no-one had dared act as a witness or notary on his behalf.

The document is well-argued, rational and clearly expresses a profound sense of injustice, both in terms of Fernando's position in Castile, and at the way the Marquis was treated. Given Hernando de Baeza's personal involvement with the Lucero case, his attachment to Montilla, and the punishments meted out to members of his circle, it is reasonable to suppose that his sense of injustice was as deeply felt as that of the Marquis. This is significant for understanding Baeza's position as he wrote his Granada memoir, showing us why he highlighted the sort of tyrannical behaviour he found so offensive and divisive in Fernando.

Throughout the incident, the *Gran Capitán* tried to reconcile the Marquis with the king by acting as an intermediary. He had a long discussion with Cardinal Cisneros and appealed to his nephew to throw himself at the king's feet and hand over all his possessions.[123] He pleaded with Fernando to treat the offence as one of an inexperienced and over-heated young man and to be lenient in punishing him.[124] In particular, he appealed against the demolition of Montilla castle, asking for it to be saved as a personal favour in exchange for the many hundreds of castles he had won for Fernando in Italy. But the king refused to give ground and also withdrew from making the *Gran Capitán* Master of the Order of Santiago, an honour he had promised him while in Italy. Instead, he gave the *Gran Capitán* the Granadan town of Loja, a significant demotion for the man who had been Viceroy of Naples.[125] But however offensive these slights must have been to the *Gran Capitán*, he always avoided direct confrontation with Fernando and the appearance of disloyalty. He set up a magnificent court in Loja, rebuilt the houses and restored the property of those who had been punished with the Marquis in Cordoba and bided his time for another opportunity to contribute to the political scene.[126] It is possible to see, in the *Gran Capitán*'s prudent avoidance of confrontation and ability to maintain an ambiguous stance, an important model for Hernando de Baeza. The experiences of the Marquis and the *Gran Capitán* explain not only Baeza's heart-felt desire for a more just regime, but also his caution and reticence in expressing it. He saw that the overt defiance of the Marquis only led to his downfall, while the *Gran Capitán* lived to fight another day. Baeza's strategy as he wrote his account was to work with established power rather than setting himself up in opposition to it, and to avoid making himself a target for reprisal. His status as a *converso* would have made him particularly vulnerable in that respect, but not uniquely so.

Hernando de Baeza and the wider ideological struggle

The Lucero affair threw into perspective ideological differences which had been in play since the mid-fifteenth century and which came to a head in the struggle for ascendency between competing visions for the exclusively Christian, post-Isabelline Andalusia. The new, ultra-monarchist ideology identified the monarchs with Christianity and the divine will to such an extent that adherents of other religions became not only infidels but enemies of the state.[127] As we can see from his statement, the Marquis believed that

Fernando's autocratic vision of central power within his expanding domains should be counterbalanced by the traditional role of the nobility and town authorities, who were better informed on the ground to dispense justice. The Cordoban campaigners based their case on an assertion of the early Christian values of charity, sympathy for prisoners and avoidance of cruelty and unnecessary suffering: in the words of the Count of Tendilla, they did not believe in 'curing things with fire'.[128] They believed, rather, in a just society underpinned by the rule of law and the proper exercise of justice. Like Pulgar, their fundamental criticism was of the improper and politicized way in which the Inquisition was operating, not of its existence *per se*. Like Hernando de Baeza in his account, the Cordoba campaigners were at pains to present themselves as honourable citizens and devout Christians, rather than rebellious outsiders. They expressed a sense of close solidarity and a belief in the uniting power of Christianity, with clear echoes of the work of Alonso de Cartagena and Alonso de Oropesa: 'in this we were like in the early Church, almost as if we all had the same soul'.[129]

There is no doubt that the *Gran Capitán* shared his nephew's political philosophy, if not his approach to resisting autocracy. Hernán Pérez del Pulgar gives expression to this stance in his account of the advice given by the *Gran Capitán* to Boabdil when he was trying to win support during the street battles in the Albaicín.[130] 'It is easier to increase your estates by forgiving than by avenging', Pérez del Pulgar has the *Gran Capitán* saying. And especially when things are in doubt, there is a need for 'clemency and a loose rein' ('suelta') rather than 'rigorous government': a king gains more leadership through love than through fear. He quotes Sallust, an author favoured by the Count of Cabra, in support of this position, and urges the use of prudence and moderation to avoid shedding blood.[131] Elsewhere, he opposes 'rigour' to 'compassion' ('misericordia'), advocating the latter.[132] These sentiments were no doubt directed towards the new King Charles V at the time Pérez del Pulgar was writing (1527), but there is plenty of contemporary evidence to indicate that it was a good representation of the *Gran Capitán*'s political philosophy, which his twenty-first-century biographer presents as an early understanding of the concept of human rights.[133] On his return to Spain, the *Gran Capitán* was surrounded by an 'academy' of followers – soldiers, former captains under his command and noble relatives – who shared a sense of injustice at the side-lining of their hero and became a virtual political party opposed to Fernando.[134] These would have formed a core audience for Baeza's memoir.

In complaining about the excesses of Lucero, the Count of Tendilla remarked that so many people had been arrested there was no-one left to speak to.[135] I understand this as meaning that no-one would discuss or debate the unprecedentedly complex issues facing him, in particular, those relating to colonization: how to make a society cohere when a majority of its members had been forced to change their religion. We can see from his letters that Tendilla was an active, busy and practical person. His comment did not mean that he missed the niceties of abstract intellectual conversation, but rather that he was impatient with the intransigence of those who shut down debate rather trying to understand and analyse the problems he faced as a leader and discuss the pros and cons of different courses of action.[136] This tension has been characterized as a struggle between *'letrados'* and *'caballeros'* – the new upwardly mobile university graduates versus the aristocracy, a bipartite typology which perhaps tries too hard to make it a question of social position.[137] The struggle might more reliably be understood as between the 'absolutizers' and the 'relativists', with a spectrum of social groups represented on both sides.

The arrest of Talavera and members of his circle highlights the context of Granada as a particular battleground in this struggle. Both Tendilla in Granada and the *Gran Capitán* in Naples were concerned with the place which these newly conquered territories would occupy within the Spanish dominions, how they would relate to the crown, what institutions and justice systems they would have and above all, how to manage diversity. Baeza had observed at first hand the *Gran Capitán*'s efforts to establish authority and government in Naples, in a situation where he noted that there were 'seventy-two languages and seventy-two thousand minds, each with their own manner and opinion'.[138] In writing up his account of the divisions and injustices which led to the collapse of the Muslim kingdom of Granada, Baeza's preoccupation is with the political and moral struggles given urgency by the Lucero affair and Fernando's behaviour on his return to Castile.

6

Genesis of the memoir

'He is a reliable author who was party to those events and very well informed about things to do with the Moors'[1]

Baeza's Granada

Hernando de Baeza's descriptions of Granada are written from the point of view of someone returning after an absence to discover changes. His historical sensitivity is very strong, insisting on a number of occasions, on how the physical environment he knew *then* is different from the Granada that he and his readers could observe *now*. He tells us that the house where Abū al-Ḥasan installed his new wife is now part of the Monastery of Santa Isabel la Real.[2] In describing the great flood of the River Darro (1478), Baeza tells us that the water rose up over the bridge and down the street of the *Chancillería* (the High Court) right down to where the 'door of the city prison now is'.[3] He also tells us that Boabdil occupied houses in the *Alcazaba* (the old citadel) 'which now belong to the Marquis of Cenete' – here Baeza references Cardinal Mendoza's maverick son (Rodrigo Díaz de Vivar y Mendoza, 1466–1523), a friend of the *Gran Capitán* noted for his antagonism to Fernando.[4] His observations bear witness to the massive building programme which the city underwent in the first years after its conquest, with the construction or remodelling of religious and civic institutions, palaces and mansions for the new Christian élite, and a programme of street widening.[5] In a typically colourful passage, he describes a scrofulous old man who used to sell bathing products at the entrance to the women's baths 'which was knocked down to lay the foundations of the cathedral'. It was here that the *Capilla Real* (Royal Chapel) was being built (1506–17), to house the tombs of the Catholic Monarchs and celebrate the conquest of Granada and the mass baptisms of its Muslim inhabitants in its grand altarpiece.[6] The transformations Baeza records in the physical environment remind readers indirectly of the far-reaching social, political and religious, changes the city underwent in the twenty or so years after its conquest. They show that Baeza had been in Granada, and written his account – or at least the version of it that has survived – sometime after 1505. His last letter from Naples was written at the end of December 1506 and he was there during Fernando's visit (1506–7). In order to date the work more precisely, I have attempted to build a picture of Baeza's whereabouts in the years that followed.

After Fernando left Naples, he and the *Gran Capitán* travelled to Savona, near Genoa, where they held a meeting with Louis XII of France.[7] From the evidence of handwriting on a letter issued by the *Gran Capitán* while he was there, it appears that Hernando de Baeza was also present at this meeting, which took place between 28 June and 2 July 1507.[8] Afterwards, both the king and the *Gran Capitán* made their way back to Spain and we may presume that Baeza returned too, probably arriving in Valencia with the *Gran Capitán* at the end of July 1507.[9] Baeza's letters from Naples reveal that his daughters were living in Granada at the time, that he wanted to arrange for his eldest daughter to be married, and that he was looking to buy property for them either in Granada or in Antequera.[10] He had also asked the Marquis if he would be willing to sell him a house and vineyards he owned in Granada.[11]

During the winter of 1507–8, the king set up court in Burgos. The *Gran Capitán* went to meet him there, initially fêted as a returning hero but increasingly side-lined and, it is recounted, embittered, as it became evident that Fernando was not going to confirm his appointment as Master of the Order of Santiago.[12] The indignant Marquis was also there with a huge retinue. Two documents issued on his behalf while he was there, which may be written in Hernando de Baeza's hand, suggest that our author may have been at court too.[13] When the Marquis returned to Cordoba, the series of incidents unfolded which led to his downfall and humiliating punishment in September 1508 and Baeza does not appear to have been involved in this. Neither does he appear as a witness in the Marquis's sworn statement from Bailén on 23 January 1509.[14] After the Marquis was pardoned, two of Baeza's brothers-in-law were involved in supporting his return to Cordoba and reinstatement as *alcalde mayor*, but there is no mention of Hernando in the surviving documentation.[15] The *Gran Capitán*'s letters from the time he returned to Spain are either written by another secretary or in his own hand.[16] From what it is possible to piece together, it seems likely that Baeza returned from Italy with the *Gran Capitán*, briefly renewed his relationship with the Marquis of Priego but managed to avoid becoming associated with his 'rebellion'. To judge from a letter written by Baeza's younger son, Francisco Rodríguez de Baeza, in November 1508, he had already left, or was about to leave the service of the *Gran Capitán*, since the younger man writes that 'his lordship has offered me my father's position'.[17] Two notarial documents naming an Hernando de Baeza – from November 1508 and April 1510, respectively – indicate that he may then have gone to Granada to settle his daughters' affairs, though I have not been able to identify him with any certainty.[18]

Date of writing

Baeza's observations about the transformation of the physical environment in Granada have been used to date the work as having been written after 1505 (the establishment of the *Chancillería*) and the usual approximation given is 1510, although no explicit reason is given.[19] In Lafuente y Alcantara's published version, a respectful formula is used after a mention of the Catholic Queen to denote she has died.[20] However, the manuscript versions all give the rather awkward formulation: '[Zagal] entregó al Rey y a la Reyna Cathólicos, de gloriosa memoria, a Baça'.[21] The pluralization of 'cathólicos', rendered as singular in Lafuente's transcription, could imply that both monarchs had died and would therefore give a production date after Fernando's death in 1516. However, Lafuente's transcription error may reflect an interpretation that seems more probable – that the adjective 'cathólicos' refers to both monarchs, but the respectful formula only refers to the noun immediately preceding it – 'la Reyna'. All the extant manuscripts were copied after the death of both monarchs, so the respectful formula and/or the pluralization of 'cathólicos' might have been added by the copyists – which might explain the rather clumsy phraseology. Although this is the first reference in the text to Queen Isabel, Baeza has already introduced the Catholic King, without any indication that he has died.[22] What we do know, from the testimony Hernando's daughter gave to the Cordoba Inquisition tribunal in January 1514, is that Baeza was already dead by then and, on this basis, I would uphold the standard dating of around 1510.[23] There is no indication that it was a recent death and I would furthermore deduce that he died before May 1512, when the Marquis issued a will leaving money to Baeza's daughters but without mentioning their father.[24] In 1588, *Licenciado* Alonso Álvarez de Córdoba declared in his *limpieza de sangre* investigation that his great grandfather Hernando de Baeza, secretary of the *Gran Capitán*, had died in Rome, evidence which was corroborated by several witnesses.[25] He declared that his forebear had been buried 'in a stone tomb' in the church of St Jerome in Rome. This church, now known as San Girolamo della Carità, was consecrated in 1508 and was later given over to a prestigious charitable foundation, the *Archiconfraternità della Carità*. The minutes of this organization, which date only from after the 1527 sack of Rome, include the names of influential Spaniards who can be linked to Baeza's elder son, Juan Rodríguez de Baeza. I therefore find this evidence entirely credible and not necessarily contradictory regarding Baeza's possible status as a resident of Granada in 1508–10.[26] Returning to Rome in 1510–11, he would have found himself in the midst of a critical international incident – his protector Cardinal Carvajal's rebellion against Julius II in the 'Schism of Pisa'.[27]

In his last surviving letter from Italy (24 December 1506), Hernando tells the Marquis that he was suffering from a recurrence of a serious illness he had had two years' previously, imploring him to help make provision for his son and his daughters:

> [...] the truth is that two years ago I suffered a very serious illness and when I thought I was cured I tried to find what started it and now I find that I am in it and my life is even more in doubt. I hope our Lord and his blessed mother will give me health.[28]

It is possible that Baeza was exaggerating his poor state of health if he was well enough to return to Spain, spend some time at court and attend to various family and business arrangements, and then return to Italy. It is also possible that, since that both Priego and Baeza knew that the king was in a position to intercept their letters, and the odd way in which Baeza describes his 'illness', the exchange was not about his physical health at all, but a coded reference to something more controversial. Whatever his state of health, we must conclude that Baeza wrote his memoir before his final visit to Rome, which means we can now date it with more certainty to between 1508 and 1511.

The manuscripts

When I began my research into Hernando de Baeza in 2012, only two manuscripts of his work were known to exist, neither of them originals. One is kept in the library of the Monastery of El Escorial (Y-111-6) and the other, which we can reliably regard as an eighteenth-century copy of this, forms part of the family archive of the Dukes of Osuna, now in the Biblioteca Nacional in Madrid (MSS/11267/21). The Escorial manuscript forms part of a bound volume which also contains a version of Fernando del Pulgar's *Crónica de los Reyes Católicos* and an introduction dedicated to Felipe II's heir Prince Carlos. This dedication refers to a serious accident suffered by the prince during its composition, by which I have dated it to around 1562 (the catalogue entry gives only 'sixteenth century').[29] Baeza's text is incomplete, breaking off in the middle of an emotionally charged dialogue between Boabdil and his mother. These two manuscripts formed the basis of the two mid-nineteenth-century editions which frame the work nostalgically in titles which refer to the 'last times' of the Kingdom of Granada.[30]

Since 2012, three further manuscripts have been identified which contain the end section dealing with the negotiations and arrangements for the ceremonial surrender of the city of Granada. It is this section which contains the explicit statement of Baeza's approach to the faith status of the *elches*: that they should not be forced to reconvert to Christianity against their will. The first was discovered in a private collection of the Escalante family in Cantabria and, although not available to the public, has been the subject of a doctoral thesis and journal publications which provide a detailed paleographic and codicological description, together with a transcript of the sections which are missing from the El Escorial and Osuna manuscripts and 'an English adapted translation' of these passages.[31] Titled '*Historia de los Reyes Moros de Granada*', the manuscript forms part of a codex put together by the first Bishop of Michoacán, Mexico, Vasco de Quiroga, in the mid-sixteenth century with two other texts – one by the royal chronicler Doctor Lorenzo Galíndez de Carvajal and the other by Quiroga himself. Galíndez was a jurist and member of the Royal Council, appointed by King Fernando in 1509 – after Isabel's death – to sift through all the various sources available and write a history of their reign.[32] His *Anales Breves del Reinado de los Reyes Católicos*, which appears in the codex between the texts of Baeza and Quiroga, has been published elsewhere and is comparatively well known.[33] Quiroga's text, meanwhile, is thought to be a treatise referred to as *De debellandis indis*, previously believed lost, which seems to have argued for a peaceful, assimilatory approach to the conversion of the indigenous people based on early Christian values.[34]

Another manuscript containing the ending of Baeza's work was identified in Yale University's rare book and manuscript library (Beinecke MS 633) and forms the basis of a new published edition to which I have contributed.[35] This version has been dated to the last quarter of the sixteenth century and, although it includes the ending, it lacks the first few pages and an explicit attribution to Baeza. It has a makeshift title squeezed on to the first sheet, which reads 'Linea de Los Reyes Moros de Granada y de su deçendencia hasta que aquella çiudad fue entregada a los reyes catholicos' ('Line of the Moorish Kings of Granada and their succession until the city was surrendered to the Catholic Monarchs').[36]

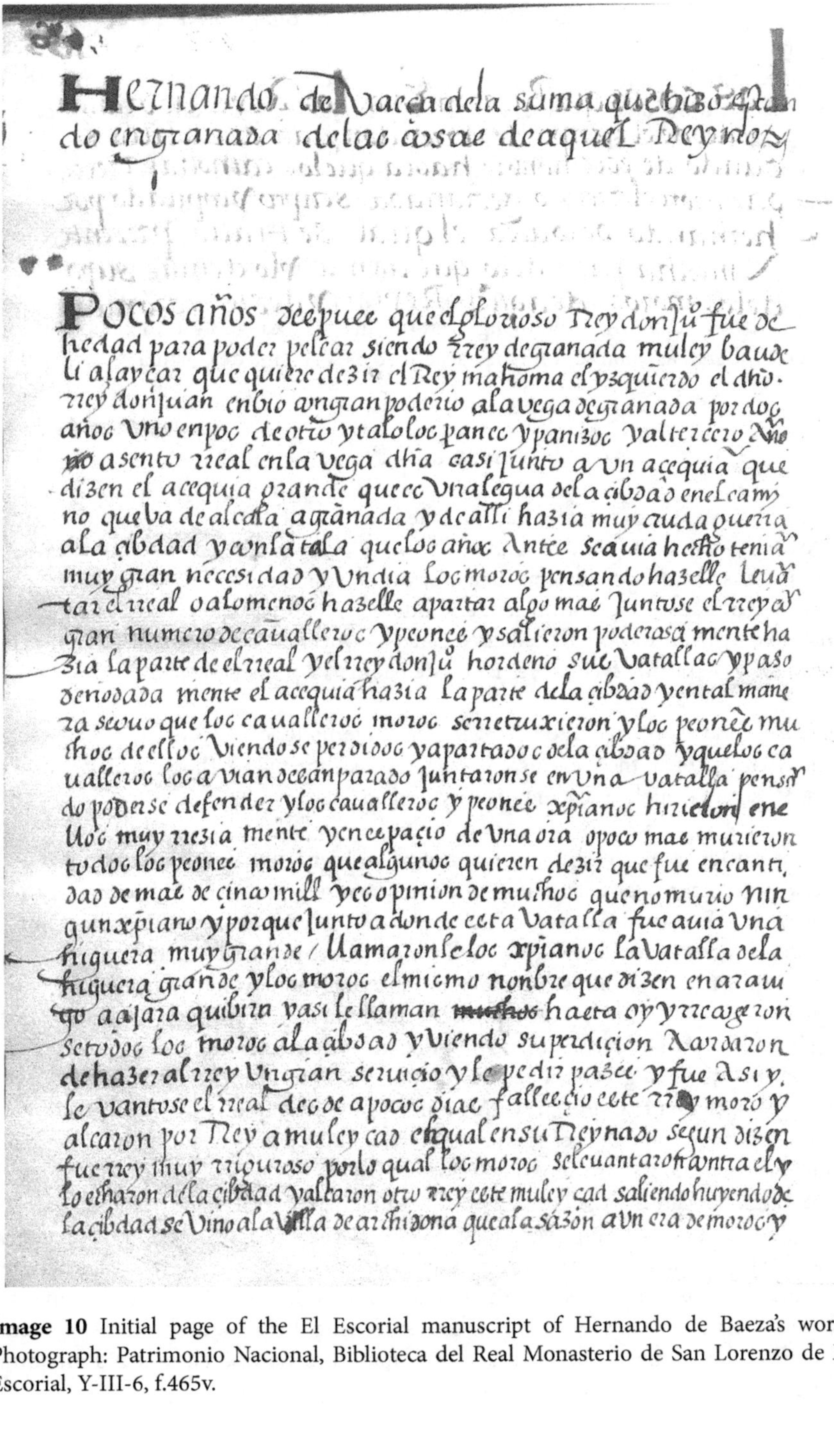

Hernando de Vaca de la suma que hizo estando en granada de las cosas de aquel Reyno

Pocos años despues que el glorioso Rey don Ju[an] fue de hedad para poder pelear siendo Rey de granada muley baua li alayzar que quiere dezir el Rey mahoma el yzquierdo el dicho Rey don Juan enbio vn gran poderio ala vega de granada por dos años, vno en pos de otro y talo los panes y panizos. al tercero año asento real en la vega dha casi junto a vn acequia que dizen el acequia grande que es vna legua dela cibdad en el camino que va de alcala a granada y de alli hazia muy auda guerra a la cibdad y en la tala que los años antes se auia hecho tenia muy gran necesidad y vn dia los moros pensando hazelle leuantar el real o a lo menos hazelle apartar algo mas juntose el rey a g[r]an numero de caualleros y peones y salieron poderosamente hazia la parte de el real y el Rey don Ju[an] hordeno sus batallas y paso osadamente el acequia hazia la parte dela cibdad y en tal manera se ovo que los caualleros moros se retruxieron y los peones muchos dellos viendose perdidos y apartados dela cibdad y que los caualleros los avian desanparado juntaronse en vna batalla pensando poderse defender y los caualleros y peones xpianos hizieron en ellos muy rezia mente y en espacio de vna ora o pocos mas murieron todos los peones moros que algunos quieren dezir que fue encantidad de mas de cinco mill y es opinion de muchos que no murio ningun xpiano y porque junto a donde esta batalla fue auia vna higuera muy grande/ llamaronle los xpianos la batalla dela higuera grande y los moros el mismo nonbre que dizen en arauigo aaçara quibira y asi le llaman ~~muchos~~ hasta oy y recogeron se todos los moros ala cibdad y viendo su perdicion andaron de hazer al rey vn gran servicio y le pedir pases y fue asi y levantose el real de ay a pocos dias fallecio este Rey moro y alcaron por Rey a muley çad el qual en su Reynado segun dizen fue Rey muy riguroso por lo qual los moros se leuantaron ayrria [con] el y lo echaron dela cibdad y alçaron otro Rey este muley çad saliendo huyendo de la cibdad se vino a la villa de archidona que a la sazon avn era de moros y

Image 10 Initial page of the El Escorial manuscript of Hernando de Baeza's work. Photograph: Patrimonio Nacional, Biblioteca del Real Monasterio de San Lorenzo de El Escorial, Y-III-6, f.465v.

The third complete manuscript is held in the Real Biblioteca de Madrid in which, like the Escalante version, Baeza's text stands alongside that of the royal chronicler Galíndez de Carvajal. The catalogue entry for this manuscript dates it only as 'sixteenth-century' and describes it as a 'fragment' of Fernando del Pulgar's chronicle of the Catholic Monarchs.[37]

A close examination of all the texts/parts of texts which are accessible shows that, while all four sixteenth-century manuscripts are closely related, none is an apograph of another – each contains unique errors or phrasings. The Escalante and Real Biblioteca manuscripts are probably both descended from a common source, which may itself share parentage with the Escorial manuscript. The Beinecke manuscript diverges more and bears distinctive signs of having been produced in Aragon – for example, Prince Juan is rendered as 'Joan' and further described as 'Príncipe de Castilla'.[38]

Baeza and Pulgar

Although Baeza's existing text can be dated to around 1510, there is evidence that an earlier version, or at least a book of notes, was in existence before then. The manuscripts themselves say that Baeza wrote it 'from the report ("suma") he made whilst in Granada'.[39] The chronicler Fernando del Pulgar who, soon after 1492, wrote a *Tratado* on the history of Granada dedicated to Queen Isabel, also refers to an earlier version, and explicitly credits Hernando de Baeza as a source for this:

> [I have drawn on] Hernando de Baeza, paid interpreter of the Moorish kings, and eye-witness of all these events, of which he has a manuscript book, which I have seen, a very complete account of everything in octavo.[40]

The existence of an earlier version appears highly likely not just because both Baeza and Pulgar refer to it, but because the material quoted by Pulgar did not find its way into the extant versions of Baeza's text. Pulgar's reference to a 'very complete account' suggests that there was originally much more material which Baeza chose not to include. Pulgar was himself a *judeoconverso* and moreover, one who had publicly expressed a critical view on the way the Inquisition was operating.[41] The indications that Baeza collaborated with him on a work of historiography, and that one manuscript is regarded as having been a section of Pulgar's chronicle, suggest that the juxtapositioning of their manuscripts within a single bound volume in the Escorial library is more than mere coincidence. The material which Pulgar says he took from Baeza, but which did not find its way into the versions of Baeza's text written after 1505, concerns observations regarding the ethnicity of the inhabitants of Granada at the time of the Christian takeover (he says very few were of 'African' origin), on asylum given in Granada to Castilian political dissenters and vice-versa, and on intermarriage between prominent Christian nobles and the Granadan royal family: all highly controversial points. Their omission sheds light on the underlying themes and messages of Baeza's original, which I suggest he reworked in a more discreet fashion to avoid inflaming contemporary sensibilities on these topics.

Pulgar is regarded as one of the great chroniclers of the Catholic Monarchs' reign, although commentary on his work has focussed largely on the material produced in the earlier part of his career.[42] Pulgar had been a court secretary and carried out foreign embassies both for Enrique IV and for Fernando and Isabel in the early days of their reign. He is believed to have been estranged from court after his public intervention criticizing the Inquisition (1480-2). His appointment as chronicler appears to have coincided with the start of the Granada War (1482) and lasted until around 1490, when his chronicle tails off.[43] It is known that he was frequently in Cordoba during the course of the war and there is an exchange of letters with the Count of Cabra discussing ways of portraying him in his work.[44] It is believed that he died soon after the end of the war, so it is reasonable to suppose that he and Baeza were in contact very soon afterwards in relation to the *Tratado*, which Pulgar himself indicates was a commission from the queen.[45] That work is believed to have been published in Granada in 1518 in the same volume as an edition of Pulgar's earlier *Claros varones* but the book is no longer extant.[46] Despite a dedication to the queen in which Pulgar explicitly identifies himself, authorship of the *Tratado* has been questioned on the basis that it cites Hernando de Baeza as a source.[47] According to Juan de Mata Carriazo, Pulgar would have already been dead by the time Baeza wrote his account, after the death of Isabel. This seems to be flawed reasoning since it does not allow for the existence of an earlier book of notes; however, in deference to Carriazo, the suggestion has had some degree of acceptance.[48] One study contested Pulgar's authorship on the basis of variations in content in relation to the *Crónica*, the fact that he was unlikely to have been alive in 1492, and the general observation that the *Tratado* is an inferior work.[49] However, other commentators – both early and more recent – have not questioned the veracity of the author's identification of himself as Pulgar.[50] In compiling the *Tratado*, Pulgar was undertaking a different commission and using different sources from those he used for his chronicle. The inferior quality may be due to infirmity and possible age-related mental decline, since he complained about suffering from problems of old age in a letter dated as early as 1481 or 1482.[51]

According to the El Escorial librarians, the juxtaposition of Baeza's manuscript in the same volume as Pulgar's chronicle is not significant: the manuscripts were bound by the library in the early days of its existence, without any particular concern for their content.[52] The Baeza manuscript has been cut to size, at the loss of some marginal annotations, whereas the Pulgar manuscript does not bear any marginal notes or evidence of trimming; this suggests some disparity of origin. But both works, and the dedication which accompanies them, appear to have been written by the same team of scribes. The hand that wrote the dedication also appears to have been responsible for parts of Baeza's manuscript. The heading that has been given to this version of Baeza's manuscript, 'the things that happened', resembles a common formulation for chapter headings in Pulgar's *Crónica* even, for example, 'De las cosas que pasaron en Granada'.[53] This formulation is very particular to Pulgar. We can assume that it is his own, since it is used in his preface to the earliest version of his chronicle: 'we will write, with the Lord God's help, the truth of the things that happened'.[54] It is strikingly simple and straightforward, promising a fresh and factual account of recently lived and witnessed events. The fact that the title given to Baeza's text echoes this heading (albeit without the Latinism 'de'), that they seem to have collaborated on a longer work about the 'kings' of Granada and that manuscripts of their works found their way into the same bound volume in the Escorial library all generate the impression that Baeza's work was intended to complete or complement Pulgar's chronicle. Though too long for a chapter, it could have been produced as a section to fit into a major work continuing Pulgar's unfinished chronicle which was in hand around the time that Baeza was writing.[55]

Baeza's connection with other chroniclers

It is known that other chroniclers, as well as Pulgar, used Baeza's text as a source. In 1948, Juan de Mata Carriazo showed that Francisco de Medina y Mendoza (1516–77) and Alonso de Santa Cruz (1505–67), both writing about the conquest of Granada in the mid-sixteenth century, used parts of the manuscript which had disappeared.[56] Santa Cruz was a cosmographer who worked in a semi-official capacity as a royal chronicler, while Medina y Mendoza drew on documents from the Mendoza family library in Guadalajara.[57] Carriazo showed that, while Medina y Mendoza cited Baeza as a source for details which are not in the Escorial/Osuna manuscripts, Alonso de Santa Cruz actually used whole sections of Baeza's text verbatim, though without crediting him.

The Beinecke manuscript with its makeshift heading provides evidence that the Aragonese historian Jerónimo Zurita (1512–80) also had access to Baeza's work. Zurita is known to have drawn on a very wide range of documentary sources for his extensive *Anales de Aragón* (written between 1562 and 1580) and, in 1664 or thereabouts, an inventory was made of them which includes a document with this same title.[58] The Beinecke manuscript adds that the work is by 'a very reliable author who took part in those events and is very well informed about things to do with the Moors'. The inventory repeats these very words, prefacing them with 'Zurita notes that … ', which suggests that it was Zurita himself who had considered Baeza's account reputable.[59]

It is evident then, that Hernando de Baeza's manuscript was known to some of the most prominent historians and royal chroniclers of the sixteenth century, that it was also circulating in aristocratic households and was available in the intellectual circles of those involved in the Christianization of the New World.[60] Despite this, it is absent from inventories of the contents of noble libraries made during the sixteenth century.[61] One explanation for this, in the context of increasingly fierce censorship, would be that its contents may have been perceived as deviant or in some way subversive.[62]

Baeza is aware that he is one of several authors producing accounts of the Granada War. At one point he says he wants to avoid being long-winded and will not go into details because 'they will be written in many other places'.[63] Among the historiographers cultivated by the Catholic Monarchs to boost their prestige and that of the nascent nation, the Sicilian Lucio Marineo Sículo (1460–1530) was at court as a chronicler from 1496.[64] Apart from Pulgar, Sículo is the only contemporary of Baeza's believed to have drawn on his work. He had studied in Palermo and Rome and had arrived in Spain in 1484 with the Enríquez family. He became a professor at Salamanca where the Marquis of Priego was his student and he later dedicated a monograph (*De Parcis*) to him.⁶⁵ He accompanied the king throughout his time in Italy (1506–7) and returned to Spain with him via Savona.⁶⁶ It is very likely therefore that he and Hernando de Baeza had direct contact with each other, probably in both Naples and Savona. However, Sículo's approach is very different from Baeza's. Sículo wanted to present the history of Spain in the context of classical history and his explicit purpose was to glorify the Catholic Monarchs, especially Fernando. In contrast to Baeza's ostensibly straightforward account of 'the things that happened', Sículo's style is sycophantic and pompous: as his biographer comments, 'he never feared lest he had no adjective left for the day of judgement.'⁶⁷ Baeza however is sparing in his use of adjectives. Sículo said he was disinclined to cover the war with Granada in any detail, since others who had been personally involved were in a better position to do so.⁶⁸ His early work, *De laudibus hispaniae*, was first published in 1496 and indeed contains no detail: the section on the Catholic Monarchs merely rehearses their virtues.⁶⁹ It was not until 1530 that his more complete *De rebus hispaniae* was published, in which he names a number of sources including Pulgar, Alonso de Palencia, Pedro Mártir de Anglería, Gonzalo de Ayora, Tristán de Silva and others whose names he said he did not wish to divulge, dismissing them as unknowns.⁷⁰ It is possible that Baeza might have been one of these men regarded as lesser contributors, but equally possible that Sículo accessed Baeza's work indirectly through one of his other sources.

In order to collect, sort and edit reports arriving from various sources on noteworthy events, the monarchs established a dedicated unit within the royal chancellery which has been described as a 'historiography workshop'.⁷¹ From 1509 – around the date that Baeza's work would have been composed – the person in charge of organizing and filtering this material was Doctor Lorenzo Galíndez de Carvajal (1472–1528), the man whose work appears alongside Baeza's in two of the extant manuscripts.⁷² He is associated with a hard line in relation to compulsory Christianity, having taken part in a Commission which in 1524–5 looked into the alleged forced baptisms of Valencian *moriscos* who were reverting to Islam – finding them valid. In 1526 he contributed an assimilation plan for Granadan *moriscos* redolent of Scotus, which involved removing children from their parents.⁷³ Galíndez was intending to compile a history of Castile, drawing on earlier chronicles and legal documents, but this never seems to have progressed beyond a collection of source texts and notes.⁷⁴ He had access to similar material to Sículo, naming Pulgar, Palencia, Tristán de Silva, and Gonzalo de Ayora as his principal sources.⁷⁵ His work, published in the nineteenth century as *Memorial de los Reyes Católicos*, contains only the briefest of notes on major events, organized chronologically by year from 1468 to Fernando's death in 1516. However, it includes a long preface in which Galíndez devotes a large portion to criticizing Pulgar's work, which he claimed was 'thin and sterile' and contained value judgements deriving from a misunderstanding of people's intentions. He says that Pulgar was too lavish in his praise for Cardinal Mendoza, while being 'hateful and even damaging' towards others.⁷⁶ Galíndez's complaint that Pulgar's chronicle was too thin seems misplaced, given that it ran into more than a hundred chapters, and his suggestion that Pulgar was not sufficiently adulatory of either the monarchs or leading nobles (other than Cardinal Mendoza) runs counter to some modern day assessments of him as no more than a propagandist for the Catholic Monarchs.⁷⁷ His critique shows how carefully

Baeza would have had to tread to make his account acceptable to gatekeepers of historical narrative such as Galíndez.

There is a notable consistency between the sources used by Sículo and Galíndez and those named by Alonso de Santa Cruz (1505–67), who also set himself the objective of completing Pulgar's unfinished chronicle and who used whole sections of Baeza's text in doing so.[78] The link between them and, I contend, the most likely channel by which Baeza's account reached Santa Cruz and the royal historiography unit, is Gonzalo de Ayora (1466–1538), who had played a leading role in the lobbying against the excesses of Lucero and had received a commission as royal chronicler as early as April 1501.[79]

Ayora, and his father before him, were *veinticuatros* of Cordoba Council and his family had served for many years as officials in the Customs House there.[80] Given that Hernando de Baeza's uncle had enjoyed the tenancy of the Customs House in Cordoba since the time of Enrique IV, they would have had at least some knowledge of each other through this connection. Either Ayora or his father (also Gonzalo), was a *veinticuatro* in Cordoba in 1480 – at the same time as Hernando's father, Juan de Baeza.[81] Ayora would certainly have been in contact with the Marquis of Priego over the Lucero affair (see previous chapter) and it has been argued that Ayora also knew the *Gran Capitán* and shared ideas with him concerning military innovations.[82] The Ayoras were *criados* of the Count of Cabra, whom Baeza portrays very favourably, calling the Count of Cabra 'saintly' in a depiction of him ordering mass to be said before the battle of Lucena.[83] Ayora's first priority was arms rather than letters, and he seems to have enjoyed 'making history' in both senses. He was captain of Fernando's guard against the French in the Pyrenean campaigns of 1503 and in 1505 fought with the *Alcaide de los Donceles* in North Africa, producing an account of the conquest of Mazalquivir.[84] He also took part in Cardinal Cisneros' military expedition to Oran in 1509, returning to court in early 1510 as a paid chronicler. This would fit well with the date of Baeza's work and Ayora is credited by both Sículo and Garibay with having written about the war of Granada, though there is nothing extant.[85] Given that Sículo and Santa Cruz are thought to have drawn on Hernando de Baeza, and indeed Santa Cruz used whole chunks of Baeza's text, I think it very likely that Baeza had provided Ayora with his Granada memoir, and that these authors took it from there.

Ayora was notably politically engaged and unafraid to speak his mind, and his career was marked by periods of banishment from court.[86] During the succession crisis unleashed by Isabel's death, he is alleged to have taken the side of Felipe I against Fernando, although understandably he later denied this.[87] We saw in the last chapter how he played an active role in lobbying both Queen Juana and Fernando in the campaign against Lucero. In the *comunero* uprising of 1520, like Bishop Antonio de Acuña, who is also linked to Baeza, Ayora supported the rebels. He made an elegant and powerful speech to the Royal Council in Valladolid calling on the Emperor and his Council to convene the *Cortes* so that all parties could come together to resolve their differences.[88] The political philosophy he articulated would have resonated strongly with Baeza, the *Gran Capitán*, and the Marquis, had any of them still been alive at the time. Ayora described the relationship between the monarch and his subjects as a 'mystic union' in which the former must take care of them, listen to their grievances and act with clemency. His vision of his society was as a 'cord of three strands': the grandees (by which I understand he meant the higher nobility) and church dignitaries, the *hidalgos* and *caballeros*, and the common people. When the rebels were crushed, Ayora was condemned and Don Francisco Pacheco, the Marquis's brother, went to plead with Charles V to pardon him. However, this was not successful and Ayora was forced to flee the country.[89] The Marquis's rebellion in 1508 has long been seen as a precursor to the *comunero* uprising, driven by a similar political principle as Cardinal Carvajal's rebellion against the Pope: that power-sharing rather than authoritarianism is the way to achieve justice.[90]

There is strong evidence then, to support the proposition that Hernando de Baeza wrote his narrative to feed into Gonzalo de Ayora's royal commission and that it was through Ayora that the account reached Galíndez and Santa Cruz, and eventually the library of El Escorial – it is known also that some of Santa Cruz's work was confiscated by the future Felipe II and placed in the royal archives.[91] This provenance would also explain its juxtaposition with Pulgar's chronicle – the manuscripts pre-date the establishment of the monastery (which was completed 1584) and the listing of its library acquisitions starts in 1571.[92]

Baeza's work in its historiographical context

The fourteenth and fifteenth centuries saw a movement towards the writing of recent history based on the first-hand experience of either the historiographer or his informants, linked to the growth of humanism and vernacular science.[93] In Spain, this approach had been exemplified by the Castilian royal chancellor and chronicler Pero (Pedro) López de Ayala (1332–1407) and his nephew Fernán Pérez de Guzmán (c. 1378–1460), who provided an important model for Fernando del Pulgar.[94] Pérez de Guzmán asserted that historians should be impartial, irreproachable, well-versed in rhetoric and if possible, witness events themselves.[95] Similarly, Alonso de Palencia (1423–92) defined history as 'what is seen and known' and remarked that the ancients only wrote history that they had themselves lived through.[96] Like Baeza, Palencia wrote from a privileged viewpoint at the centre of political events and, in his chronicle of Enrique IV, presents himself as an actor in his own narrative. In one example, which would have been significant for Baeza, he describes his efforts to reconcile warring factions in Cordoba in 1474.[97] Like Palencia's chronicle, Baeza's work contains personal reflections, judgements on character and insights based on the author's feelings about the people he knew and heard about. But Baeza avoids the stridency of Palencia's overt polemical stance and presents his opinions humbly.

The conquest of Granada has been seen as a turning point in a trend towards universalist, providentialist approaches to the writing of history as the fulfilment of a divine plan, since the triumph of Christianity over Islam was seen as proof that this interpretation was correct.[98] This was opposed to the tradition exemplified by López de Ayala, which emphasized individual agency and the principle that the power of the monarch was tempered by the wisdom of the nobility.[99] Baeza's account follows older humanist practice, emphasizing the particular and the role of the individual as a free agent – with all their virtues and frailties – whose views and experiences are valid. It does not look to the 'authorities' for essential patterns or guidelines: it is an empirical account rather than one written to match a theory.

To understand the discreet dissidence of Baeza's work, we must set it beside other contemporary sources which deal with the war of Granada and the Catholic Monarchs. We have already seen how Cardinal Carvajal framed Fernando and Isabel's campaign as fulfilling a divine mission to bring Christian dominion not just to the Iberian Peninsula, but to the whole world, ushering in a new age of Spanish hegemony.[100] Later, around the same time as he composed his epistle on the death of Prince Juan, Carvajal was involved in promoting another work highlighting the monarchs' illustrious lineage which presented Spain as even more preeminent in the history of the world. This was in the form of a collection of ancient texts – soon revealed as a forgery – put together by a man appointed by Alexander VI as his official papal theologian, Annio da Viterbo (c. 1432–1502).[101] It is clear that Annio's original intention had more to do with his own preoccupations with his home town than with Spain, but it was Carvajal and the monarchs' ambassador in Rome at that time, García Lasso de la Vega, who arranged for it to be published and they, it appears, were responsible for the last-minute inclusion of a chapter on the ancient history of the Spanish monarchy.[102] This claimed that, according to antiquarian sources, there was culture and learning in Spain even before the Greeks and presented a list of twenty-four ancient kings of Spain starting with Noah's grandson Tubal. Tubal was the legendary founder of Spain according to Gothic histories, but this account brought him out of mythology into what professed to be a properly sourced historical account.[103] The magnificently bound volume, the *Commentaria super opera diversorum auctorum de antiquitatibus loquentium*, known as the *Antiquitates*, appeared in 1498, prefaced by an overblown panegyric to the Spanish monarchs incorporating fulsome tributes to Carvajal and García Lasso de la Vega.[104] It is impossible to say whether Carvajal was himself aware that the sources used by Annio were forgeries – it seems likely that he was excited by the bigger picture rather than the detail – though it is reported that he kept the original manuscript and took it to Spain after Annio's death in 1502.[105] Although Annio's work was debunked as fake in the mid-sixteenth century, his narrative of the twenty-four kings found its way into historiography in works by Antonio Nebrija, Sículo, Florián de Ocampo and others.[106] The *Antiquitates* has been seen, on the one hand, as an odious example of the 'falsification of history' and on the other as an important step forward in the development of critical theory in the choice and evaluation of historical texts.[107]

Carvajal's role in Annio's publication shows how conscious he was of the use of history for political purposes and its potential for manipulation in the service of some 'greater good'. Given Hernando de Baeza's close association with Carvajal – it has been suggested that Annio, like Baeza, lodged in Carvajal's house – his own approach to writing history seems far from neutral.[108] His decision to write history in a way which reflected actual experience, using reliable witnesses and with a conspicuously more modest timeframe, must be set against the soaring conceit of Annio and Carvajal's constructions. Clearly Baeza was writing for a different purpose and using contemporary rather than ancient sources. But by resetting the temporal frame and quietly resisting an overly bombastic or triumphalist interpretation of the recent past, he explained processes and change in a way which played to a different agenda and did not seek justifications for the present in the ancient past.

The one Spanish chronicler whose work is exactly contemporaneous with Baeza's is Andrés Bernáldez, a parish priest from a village outside Seville, who presents a vision of the world deriving from the exclusionist current of thought which Baeza's must surely be intended to rebut. Bernáldez's account was never intended to be an official one – he himself states that it was intended for ordinary people ('gentes comunes').[109] Bernáldez was chaplain to a man strongly associated with the hard-line Fernandist tendency: the Archbishop of Seville, Diego de Deza, who was Inquisitor General during the Lucero affair and was removed from that role because of his protection for the man Baeza described as 'Satan'. Deza had also been responsible for the expulsion of *conversos* from the town of Guadalupe in 1500 and it was he who had urged the monarchs to set up an Inquisition tribunal in Naples.[110] However, he was nevertheless seen as open to persuasion, since he was included in the first confederation formed in Andalusia in support of Queen Juana after the death of Felipe I, and lobbied by the Lucero protestors. The Marquis of Priego continued to be in contact with him after the Lucero affair, and what remains of his personal correspondence contains seventeen letters written by the Archbishop – one of which even mentions a Juan de Baeza acting as an intermediary.[111] Baeza had a personal interest in influencing Deza in relation to his son's appointment as a member of Seville cathedral chapter. This background is important in understanding how Baeza's account of the conquest of Granada might have been designed to counterbalance the version being written by Bernáldez, and influence clearly intelligent men such as Deza who might be open to considering a different interpretation of the changes society was undergoing. In fact, Deza's position did appear to soften. After Fernando's death in 1516, which had resulted in some unrest in Seville, he wrote to the Marquis saying that he thought too hard a line was being taken against the perpetrators.[112] Deza was still Archbishop when Hernando's son finally won his legal battle in Rome relating to his appointment in Seville, and it has been claimed that he supported him in taking up a post of canon, despite the *limpieza de sangre* statute which Deza himself had put in operation by that time.[113] This may also indicate some softening of his position, though the papal instruction emanating from the legal hearing would clearly have weighed heavily.

Deza's chaplain Andrés Bernáldez was, like Baeza, writing at least twelve years after the conquest of Granada but his interpretation of what it meant for his country is very different from Baeza's.[114] The conquest of Granada was, for him, a miraculous confirmation of the political theology that blurred the distinction between secular and divine authority, attributed a messianic role to the Spanish monarchs and not only justified, but welcomed violence in pursuit of their aims.[115] Bernáldez was a supporter of the harshest approaches in dealing with heresy and conversion, following Duns Scotus in believing that children should be removed from parents whose Christian faith was in doubt.[116] He presents the reign of Fernando and Isabel as fulfilling a prophecy to rid the country of evil and, following Alonso de Espina, goes on to describe this evil as 'bad Christians', 'heretics' and 'Moors'.[117] He hails the triumph of good over evil and says that it was the conquest of Granada itself that had acted as a spur to write his chronicle: an historic milestone that from childhood he had always hoped to witness.[118]

Bernáldez presents the conquest of Granada, the work of the Inquisition and the Edict of Expulsion as all part of the same programme of action to stamp out evil. He vigorously defends the monarchs' 'lighting of the fire' against the heretics and makes a terrifying call for the burning to continue until there is no-one left.[119] His analysis of the 'beginnings of heresy', which he traces back to 1390 and the mass baptisms of Jews which allowed *conversos* to attain positions of power and influence in society, could well be a description of Baeza's own family history. Bernáldez portrays these events as the growth of all evil, with hate-ridden descriptions of 'stinking Jews' and *conversos* 'who were neither Jewish nor Christian', who did not fear excommunication, took sedentary jobs that did not involve much work and amassed great fortunes through usury.[120]

It is not known whether Bernáldez knew, or knew of, Baeza, who for him must have represented the embodiment of the 'leprosy' he said that heretics had passed on to their children.[121] Similarly, although we know that Baeza was aware of others writing accounts of the Granada War at the same time as he was, we do not know whether he knew of Bernáldez's work. But he was aware of the ideology which underpinned it: exclusionary, intransigent and backed up by violence. Bernáldez recounts in sadistic detail the horrendous torture and execution of the man who attempted to assassinate Fernando in Barcelona: a grim warning to would-be rebels which shows all too clearly why Baeza called for discretion rather than defiance in dissenting from royal authority.[122] Bernáldez's simplistic, baleful sermonizing contrasts strongly with Baeza's wry self-awareness in referring to one of his own letters as a 'sermon'.[123]

7

Castile in the mirror: A resistance narrative of the conquest of Granada

'There was so much mixing between the two nations on account of marriages'[1]

Hernando de Baeza's work has been widely appreciated for its authenticity and mined for snippets of information about the later years of the Nasrid regime.[2] However, the 'social logic' of the text has been ignored or misunderstood because of a lack of information about the identity and later activity of its author, and because the final crucial passages were believed lost until very recently. These gaps have been explained away by suggestions that Baeza emigrated to Fez with Boabdil, or that he died suddenly without finishing his tale.[3] In the light of the circumstances set out in the previous chapters, we are now able to understand the work as a discreetly dissident account of the fall of Muslim Granada. Studies exploring the rich array of sources on the mental landscape surrounding the conquest – including not only sermons and historiographical material, but letters, poetry, ballads and the visual arts – have tended to paint the ideological context as somewhat monolithic and static, whereas Baeza's work shows it as dynamic and contested.[4] This chapter will examine the ways in which Baeza resists key elements of the absolutizing ideology which was being projected on to the conquest – the glorification of the Catholic Monarchs, tendentious rhetoric concerning the Muslim heritage, exclusion of new Christian voices – and shows how Baeza uses the history of Granada to hold up a mirror to the prevailing circumstances in Castile.[5]

Representations of the Catholic Monarchs

Much has been written about the messianism attaching to the Catholic Monarchs, and Fernando in particular.[6] While commentary surrounding the conquest of Granada identified Fernando and Isabel as 'superhuman beings', 'fallen from the sky' to bring God's kingdom to the earth, Baeza is distinctive not only in avoiding hyperbole but in delivering discreet criticism.[7] His references to the monarchs are sparing in the use of honorifics or epithets. When he first introduces Fernando, he refers to him simply as 'the Catholic King'; yet in the same sentence he describes the already defunct Prince Juan as 'most excellent'.[8]

Image 11 *The Catholic Monarchs with Saint Helena and Saint Barbara*, Maestro de Manzanillo (*c.* 1500), detail. Painting/Alamy Stock Photo.

Baeza associates the discontent and divisions within the Granadan kingdom with the way that the emirs appropriated income and property belonging to the nobility. He explains that the men who carried out these seizures – the *alharriques* – were similar to the *ballesteros de maza* of Castilian monarchs – a sort of praetorian guard.[9] Thus, under the guise of a simple linguistic and cultural explanation, he subtly draws readers towards a parallel in their own society, highlighting disrespect for property rights as a fundamental marker of despotism.[10] On returning to Spain, the 'King of Aragon' (as he was pointedly called) had acted with similar tyranny against the Fernández de Córdobas in seizing and demolishing Montilla castle. He had also undertaken reprisals against their allies in the House of Medina Sidonia, seizing fortresses under their command and, when the town of Niebla resisted, in November 1508, exacted draconian punishment on their leaders.[11] Contemporary readers would have been well able to equate the 'rigour' of the latter-day Nasrid monarchs – which Baeza describes as leading to their extinction – with the intransigence of Fernando and inquisitors in the mould of Lucero snatching property from alleged heretics. Baeza gives voice to a position about the extent of royal power over property which would be at the heart of the *comunero* movement and would later be expressed in radical form by Bartolomé de Las Casas in relation to the *encomiendas* in the New World.[12]

It is also possible to read Baeza's portrayal of the Granadan emir as an allegory about Fernando of Aragon and his new French wife, Germaine de Foix. Baeza says Abū al-Ḥasan had ruled unchallenged and respected for twenty years with his first wife, but then descended into tyranny and vice after marrying a younger foreign bride – a child captive from Aguilar who he portrays rather unsympathetically.[13] At the time he was writing, there were still many in Andalusia who regarded Fernando's regency as illegitimate and recognized only Juana.[14] There was certainly rancour and ill-feeling against the new queen in the *Gran Capitán*'s household and among his allies, the anonymous chronicler who has provided so many insights into the *Gran Capitán*'s intimate circle depicts her as snobbish and spiteful.[15] Baeza's low opinion of the woman he says was known as 'La Romia' can perhaps therefore be read as mirroring an equally poor opinion of Fernando's new queen – and delivering sly criticism of Fernando's autocratic and unseemly behaviour after the death of Isabel.

Towards the end of his piece, he narrates an incident which subtly compares Fernando unfavourably to Boabdil and implies that he is morally inferior. With Granada under siege, Boabdil found out through his informants that Fernando had hatched a devious plan to break into the city.[16] Baeza records that Boabdil reacted with indignation on hearing about the plot and resolved to go out with his men and fight to the last.[17] He thus paints Fernando as treacherous in contrast to Boabdil as an upholder of chivalric values. Indeed, Baeza's assessment of Fernando's role in the conquest of Granada is not so far from Niccòlo Machiavelli's, with which it is roughly contemporaneous: 'Always using religion as a plea, so as to undertake greater schemes, he devoted himself with pious cruelty to driving out and clearing his kingdom of the Moors.'[18] Baeza, like Machiavelli, had observed Fernando's actions from the perspective of Italy and understood the difference between representation and reality, but he is condemnatory of the unscrupulous pursuit of power. His comment that Abū al-Ḥasan had subjugated the kingdom 'admirably' after having killed his rivals to the throne must surely be understood as sarcasm.[19]

There is further evidence of Baeza's partiality in his report that the *Alcaide de los Donceles* was given the honour of displaying Boabdil's bottom half on his coat of arms. The *Alcaide* was practically the only member of the Andalusian nobility who had given wholehearted support to Fernando during the interregnum and the Lucero affair. It is not difficult to imagine the guffaws of readers who disliked the *Alcaide* for his support of Fernando – and alignment with the Inquisitor Lucero – as they visualized this outlandish image. In writing up his narrative of the battle, Baeza was all too aware of how the issue of who had first captured Boabdil, the Count of Cabra or the *Alcaide de los Donceles*, had become entangled with latter-day rivalries and politics.

Given what we now know about Baeza's experience of Fernando's intransigence in the period 1505–10, his intervention depriving Baeza's son of his benefice in Seville, his support for Lucero, the punishment meted out to the Marquis, and his unhappy relationship with the *Gran Capitán*, Baeza had ample motivation for weaving an implicit criticism of Fernando into his tale. If his early readers picked up on this message, it is not surprising that they did not feel able to use or publish the whole narrative but merely took from it the key passages which interested them.

Baeza says very little about Queen Isabel, an omission which, in the context of the adulatory rhetoric of the time, is perhaps as telling as the subtle disapprobation he expresses for Fernando. However, he portrays Boabdil's mother as a dignified, politically able woman, and uses inclusive language, making a point of saying that his sources included both men and women, and that the large number of captives that Abū al-Ḥasan brought back to Granada included both men and women, boys and girls.[20] This too can be read as a political statement in the context of Juana I's right to the throne. Castilian law allowed women to inherit whereas this was not the case in Aragon, and Baeza perhaps saw Castilian practice as a better reflection of Pauline inclusivity.[21] The Marquis of Priego had no sons and was in fact ably succeeded by his daughter.[22]

Moors and Christians

While there were many harsh depictions of Moors/Muslims in the world in which Hernando de Baeza grew up, it has been argued that these sat side by side with more favourable, even romanticized accounts in which they appeared as 'valorous opponents and idealized paragons of chivalry'.[23] Certainly, medieval Spanish literature was able to distinguish between 'good' and 'bad' Muslims: the former generally being those who were willing to cooperate with Christians.[24] But, coinciding with the growth of anti-*converso* attitudes in the mid-fifteenth century, there was hardening of rhetoric against Muslims after the fall of Constantinople in 1453, led especially by Alonso de Espina.[25] It would be hard to argue that positive images of Muslims were particularly widespread in Hernando de Baeza's world. The key evidence put forward for positive depictions of Moors in the fifteenth century is the Islamophilia in the court of Enrique IV, echoed in Miguel Lucas de Iranzo's court in Jaén, frontier ballads and Hernando de Baeza himself, whom we must surely regard as an interested party making a deliberate point rather than an unwitting exemplar of rosy *convivencia*.[26] Enrique IV's alleged Islamophilia, far from being an example of a positive representation, was used to discredit him and Thomas Devaney argues that the representation of Muslims in the public spectacles organized by Lucas de Iranzo was intended to reassure the populace that it would be 'safe' to make war on them.[27] Devaney discusses the 'ideological dissonance' experienced by those whose personal experiences of friendship and intermingling clashed with an increasingly intolerant public rhetoric.[28] As a member of the Fernández de Córdoba household, where people of all backgrounds who would contribute to the growth of their domains had been welcome, Baeza would have felt this tension particularly strongly.

Wartime propaganda and the desire to display the righteousness of the divinely inspired mission against Granada involved a ratcheting up of rhetoric which emphasized the Moors' supposed iniquity and savagery.[29] Even Archbishop Hernando de Talavera, although generally regarded as the epitome of peaceful Christianization, thought it appropriate to exaggerate the extreme brutality of the 'Arabs' – a word which emphasizes their foreignness – in his mass to celebrate the conquest of Granada:

The Arabs came in like savage wild boars, devastating and exterminating Spain and like wild beasts never before seen they grazed on its lands. They profaned the holy temples. They left the bodies of Christians to be eaten by the birds of the air; the flesh of saints for the beasts of the earth. They spilt innocent blood throughout Spain as if it were water. They humiliated Christian people and made a mockery of the inheritance of Christ. They murdered widows and pilgrims. They killed children. They humiliated women and raped girls. They strung up princes by their hands. They had no shame in front of old people. They abused young men in shameful ways.[30]

Bernáldez's account reflects a certain grudging respect for the enemy with the admission that those defending Malaga conducted themselves 'like people from Spain' and he describes a Moor who 'behaved virtuously, like an *hidalgo*'.[31] But while Bernáldez interprets any virtue displayed by the Moors as 'Spanish' values, Baeza insists on the virtues and honourability of Muslims who are his 'great friends'. Among these are Abrahén de Mora, 'a good man and a clever strategist in war', Boabdil's mizwar Alhaje, 'a very great friend of mine', and 'a very honourable merchant named Abrahen Alcaici, who was a very great friend of mine'.[32] The use of the word 'amigo' as Baeza introduces these Muslim characters into his narrative seems deliberately chosen to disrupt the ideologically charged 'moro enemigo' repeated in so many official documents of the time.[33] Baeza declares that Boabdil, had he become a Christian, 'would have been one of the best that ever lived'.[34] It is clear that he is in no way making a general observation about all Granadans or all Muslims. He depicts Abū al-Ḥasan and his brother as cruel, tyrannical and vicious. Abū al-Ḥasan's 'vices' – which I understand as abandoning himself to pleasure with his new queen instead of attending to his kingly duties – summon up stereotypical images of Muslims in Christian chronicles as sexual predators, but in Baeza's account they are directly linked to the putsch which removed him from power.[35] Unlike Bernáldez, or Palencia, who describes Islam as a 'repugnant sect', he never resorts to essentialist bigotry towards Muslims, but rather stresses individual agency and human potential for vice or virtue, irrespective of background.[36]

Baeza uses the word 'moro' very frequently in his text, a word which presents some difficulties in translating. In his descriptions of battles and the war, the word is generally used to mean 'the side opposed to the Christians', and this leads towards understanding 'moro' as 'Muslim'. But this is not always an accurate reflection of what I think Baeza means. When, after the violent death of Don Alonso de Aguilar, Hernando de Baeza issued documents awarding lifetime grants of money to Luis de Nicuesa, the man who had recovered his lord's body from the Sierra Bermeja, he included the expression – straight out of the rhetoric emanating from the Castilian chancellery – 'moros enemigos de nuestra santa fe católica'.[37] I have pondered Baeza's use of this expression and wondered whether, in repeating a formula, he felt it jar with his own experience of friendships and respect. But if we focus on the word 'enemigos', as the first definition of what a 'moro' is, we can read it as an expression of political rather than religious difference. Baeza uses 'moro' and 'cristiano' as an means of identifying the two opposed sides, highlighting groups of people who live within different polities (e.g. 'the town of Archidona which at that time still belonged to the Moors').[38] His frequent use of 'rey moro' also highlights the political dimension of a royal family of a different lineage. The political sense of the word 'moro' is revealed strongly in Baeza's description of one of Boabdil's supporters as 'moro mudéjar', where I take 'moro' to mean 'fighting on Boabdil's side' and 'mudéjar' to mean 'Muslim subject of Christian monarchs'. Any idea of a rigid demarcation along religious grounds is further disrupted by this man's name, 'Santa Cruz', which suggests a fluid religious identity. While the Castilian/Aragonese side is strongly identified by its religion, the opposing side's religion is only one aspect of their identity, and Baeza, along with the *Gran Capitán*, was moving towards a more political understanding of the conflict following their experiences in Italy fighting against a Christian enemy. Religion is, of course, part of the picture but translating 'moro' as 'Muslim' gives undue weight to religious rather than political divisions and may lead us towards a 'clash of civilisations' narrative that has more to do with our own times than Baeza's own understanding of the historical juncture he was describing. We must also remember that the grain of truth underlying the fabled incident of the *Gran Capitan*'s accounts was ridicule of the idea that battles were won through religious devotion.

Baeza never makes religious differences central but rather describes aspects of Granadan religious and cultural life in a way which draws readers in; indeed, his insights into the Nasrid court have been one of the most highly valued aspects of his work.[39] For example, he describes the custom of the emir not speaking directly to his subjects, but rather through his visir, and the practice of bathing and perfuming the body before going into a situation of mortal danger.[40] Throughout the piece, he identifies parallels between Castilian and Granadan cultures, explaining that *alfaquis* 'are to the Moors like clergymen are to Christians', while their customary law and sharia were 'almost like canon and civil law' and the *alfaqui mayor* 'was like an Archbishop or even like a Pope for them' and spoke to the crowd from a 'pulpit'.[41] There is an echo here of Alfonso X's *Estoria de España* which explains the role of the caliph in a similar way and observes that emirs wear a 'cloth hat' rather than a crown (so that they can cast it to the ground when they are angry!)[42] Baeza does not comment at all on the custom of Friday prayers, using the word 'zala' with no explanation.[43] This may have been an aspect of the culture which was assumed to be familiar to readers, since Cisneros also uses it in a letter without explaining its meaning.[44] However, Baeza refers to Muslim evening prayers as the 'hour of vespers', using Christian monachal language in order to make an aspect of Islamic culture more understandable and less alien to his readers.[45] He also refers to Muslim celebrations in Granada for 'the feast of St John' – an example of shared culture dating from as early as the ninth century when Muslims, as conquerors, adopted the non-Islamic midsummer festival of their conquered subjects as *al-'ansara*.[46] While Baeza shows 'Moors' and 'Christians' as opposed in war, he also shows them as partners. He stresses the history of alliances between Granada and Castile, the pleasure Juan II and the future Enrique IV took in hosting Abū al-Ḥasan and his followers in Arévalo and their admiration for their skills on horseback.[47] In depicting Granadans and Castilians taking part in tournaments together and exchanging embassies and gifts, he shows that both sides shared a chivalric culture not only on the frontier, but in the Castilian heartland of Arévalo.[48] Both Moors and Christians can be described as *caballeros* and honourable people, with all that implies.[49] In his descriptions of the battles of La Higueruela (1431) and Lucena (1483) he breaks down barriers by alternating between the perspectives of each side, presenting even war as a shared experience. Baeza needs the language of 'Moors' and 'Christians' to describe the battles and cross-border politics which feature in his narrative, but he pulls towards using the words as a linked pair rather than antithetical categories: more like 'king/queen' than Bernáldez's 'good/bad' opposition.

When Baeza describes the Granadan knights in Enrique IV's court, he quotes from a ballad which references Juan II's admiration for the legendary beauty of Granada.[50] In doing so, he reminds his readers that some positive images of the Granadans had existed, both at courtly and popular levels. When, in 1508 or thereabouts, he arrived back in Granada, now officially an exclusively Christian city, Baeza realized that the challenge was not now to unify Christians against a common enemy, but to integrate Boabdil's former subjects, now superficially converted to Christianity, into a new polity. They were now '*compatriotas*', a term which Fernán Pérez de Guzmán (1376–1458) – a writer greatly admired by Pulgar – had previously used to include both Muslims and Jews.[51] He does not dwell on the issue of the *Capitulaciones* – in fact, he does not even tell us how the thorny issue of the *elches* was resolved – but rather offers a pragmatic history, looking towards the future. Baeza understood that narratives of the conquest of the city which were couched in the discourse of the past, which divided the population into victors and vanquished, would hinder, not help, reconciliation and social harmony.[52] Archbishop Talavera's good will, patience and well-meaning cultural advice had been doomed to failure because he had not recognized that, once Granada was being re-envisioned as a new Christian society, the conceptual framework inherited from thirteenth-century *reconquista* ideology also had to change.[53] Baeza provides a narrative which, instead of defining 'Moors' in opposition to Christians, starts to explain who the new *moriscos* were in terms of their own political and cultural history and how this related to experiences on the Christian side of the frontier. His is a 'resistance narrative' which depicts them as victims of circumstances rather than as romantic exotic others to be assimilated.[54] Although Baeza appears to welcome the Christianization of Granada, he never refers to it as a 'victory', a 'triumph' or even a 'conquest', rejecting any suggestion of a 'clash of civilisations', but rather feeling his way towards the concept of an Islamo-(Judeo?)-Christian civilization.[55] He sees the conquest of Granada not as the triumph of one group over another, but as the inevitable merging of neighbours, guided by God's will. Baeza was the first Christian writer to capture and memorialize the cultural and historical legacy of Nasrid Granada, explaining aspects of history and culture, how this related to experiences on the Christian side of the frontier. His contribution to historiography therefore tackles a question which has returned to exercise scholarly minds today: how to represent the history of 'al-Ándalus' within the history of 'Spain'.[56]

Conversos 'under erasure'

Baeza's deliberate blurring of the polarities inherent in dominant narratives of the defeat of the Muslims must surely owe much to his '*converso* condition'.[57] We can understand what lies behind his interpretation of history much better once we appreciate his own status as a *judeoconverso* and the experiences of exclusion and persecution that he and his family suffered. We have already seen how his stance reflects the egalitarian values of *converso* humanists such as Diego de Valera and Alonso de Cartagena.[58] Baeza gives his account status and cultural depth by quoting from Juan de Mena (1414–56), Spain's first 'national' poet, who in a 300-verse poem dedicated to Juan II – *Laberinto de Fortuna* – urged him to take forward the fight against the Muslims and set out a glorious vision for national renewal and unity if he would do so.[59] In the wake of the conquest of Granada, the *Laberinto* – known popularly as 'Las Trescientas' – had become extremely popular as a result of a new edition with extensive commentary by Hernán Núñez de Toledo (c. 1478–1553), a humanist and man of letters associated with the Mendoza family.[60] A copy of this commented version is listed in the inventory of the Marquis de Priego's books.[61] Mena was identified with the generation of strongly monarchist, patriotic *converso* intellectuals, like Cartagena, who boosted national prestige (primarily, but not exclusively, Castilian) and were seen as having helped create the climate for Fernando and Isabel's future success.[62] He was also a significant figure for Baeza, being not only a *converso*, but a *converso* from Cordoba, a member of its urban oligarchy, and a *veinticuatro* at a similar time to Baeza's father.[63] His prestige was extremely high at the time Baeza was writing, and Baeza's reference to him, the only literary figure named in his chronicle, draws attention to the role that *conversos* like himself had played in literary endeavour, in strengthening the monarchy, and boosting Spain's international status and prestige, making space for the *converso* voice. He describes how, just before the battle of Lucena (1483), the Count of Cabra had his men call on Santiago (St James, the patron saint of the war against Muslims in Spain) to come to their aid: 'all shouting with one voice, as the great Juan de Mena says, in the name of the good son of Zebedee'.[64] Baeza picks up on Mena's indirect way of referring to St James which emphasizes the saint's Jewish lineage. The quote is therefore rich in layers of cultural allusion and a subtle assertion of *converso* identity.[65]

It has been observed that *converso* authors – whose contribution to understanding the cultural world of Spain's Golden Age has been so fundamental – made use of *morisco* characters as a way of writing about their own predicament.[66] So it is reasonable to expect that the work of a *converso* author in relation to Granada should contain meanings relevant to his own situation. There are a number of instances where, although Baeza appears to be drawing a simple parallel between Muslim and Christian cultures, he can be understood as referring also to Judaism. One of these is in his explanation of the *taheli* which he describes as 'a small leather box with silk tassels hanging from it in which the Moors generally carry a Qur'an and from them Christian knights took to taking these *tahelís* to war, carrying relics and good prayers in them'.[67] As Inquisition records make all too clear, carrying scraps of biblical text in a 'tafeli' was also a Jewish tradition and Baeza, as a linguist with roots in Jewish culture, would surely have been aware of this.[68] Baeza also mentions on two occasions the Muslim belief in the Day of Judgement – an idea which Islam shares with both the other Abrahamic religions.[69]

Baeza is concerned with shared culture and shared history – he is engaged in 'de-othering'. He sees – perhaps deliberately depicts – events in Granada as a mirror image of what is happening in his own society. His sympathy for the *elches* must be understood in the light of the persecution being suffered by members of his own family at the hands of the Inquisition. He says, on behalf of the *elches*: 'They were truly people of very good intentions and very good to talk to, and those who were able to understand at the time they were taken captive had a wholesome belief in their hearts, almost as innocent as babes and they wanted to be Christians if they could.'[70] In stressing their interior spirituality, Baeza leaves his readers to make their own connection as to how else the *elches* might have been judged. The unspoken implication is that assumptions about their inner beliefs might be drawn from the sort of criteria being used by Inquisition such as fasting, penance, adoration of images, not only against the *elches* but against *conversos* like himself. Commentators have noted how Fernando del Pulgar was able to 'say without saying' in relation to his criticisms of the Inquisition.[71] We can see here Baeza also doing this, leaving the reader to fill in the gaps he leaves and, in doing so, delivering a discreet rebuke in relation to Inquisition practices.

There are other references too by means of which Baeza creates space for *judeoconversos* within his text without mentioning them directly, where they are present as it were 'under erasure'. Baeza has a particular sympathy for the Abencerrajes who, he says, were not of noble lineage but had emigrated to Granada from Africa. Like Baeza's own family, they had risen through their own merits to high-ranking positions, becoming 'almost the greatest lords of the kingdom'.[72] But, says Baeza: 'even so, they never changed the surname of their forefathers, who were saddlers, because the Moors are not given to despising good and noble people because they come from humble origins'.[73] Although Baeza presents his observation as praise for the meritocratic nature of Granadan society, it barely hides a criticism of exclusionist tendencies in his own.[74] With an understanding of Baeza's background, it emerges as a clear reference to anti-*converso* attitudes and practices in Castile which had forced many new Christians to change not only their names, but their occupations and places of residence in order to escape persecution.[75] Here Baeza's reference to the *converso* condition is so barely disguised; it is surprising that it has not already been commented on.

We can also detect a more profound message about identity and religious conversion. When Muslims or Jews were baptized as Christians, they changed their names. Baeza himself refers to the two sons Abū al-Ḥasan had with *La Romia* who were later baptized as Don Fernando and Don Juan.[76] But, in describing what is the mirror image of her sons' adoption of Christianity – *La Romia*'s integration into Islamic society – he notes that the former identity of such women was not erased, but continued to be acknowledged: 'This name *Romia* is what the Moors call Christian women who become Islamized, because they don't give them Moorish names but different ones to them and almost as a nickname they call them *Romia* all their lives, which means a person who was subject to Roman rule.'[77] In a context where the children and grandchildren of those condemned for heresy were forced to erase all trace of past identity and culture, the observation that the backgrounds of such women were publicly recognized seems an almost wistful reflection on Baeza's own circumstances.[78] It is perhaps significant also that the explanation Baeza gives of the name 'Romía' reflects not the individuals' ethnicity or religious origin, but their former civic status – again highlighting the political rather than categories of blood and faith with the baleful power to divide.

Ryan Szpiech has used the example of Baeza's *La Romía* in his discussion of conversion as a historiographical problem, pointing out that the word 'conversion' tends to be used uncritically in describing different circumstances in which individuals or groups change their religious affiliation.[79] He notes that the term carries a conceptual load derived from Pauline Christianity – that of transformative revelation – which gives a misleading impression of the way, for example, that individuals embraced Islam in the period under consideration. Baeza's piece includes examples of 'conversion' in both directions, but he avoids using the word 'converso' or any of its derivatives, no doubt because of the sense of insincerity and suspicion carried. Bernáldez, in contrast, uses it freely and is explicit about its negative connotations: 'Those that were baptised Christians stayed and were called "conversos" and that is how the name came about because they were converts converted to the Holy Faith, which they kept very badly and [...] most of them were secretly Jews.'[80]

In describing the Islamicization of Christians such as *La Romía*, Baeza uses the common frontier expression 'tornar' which carries a sense of both political and religious defection, as in the word 'tornadizo', generally translated as 'renegade'. Baeza uses it to denote an almost naturalistic process, such as leaves 'turning brown' in the autumn, which I have rendered in my translation as 'to become'. He avoids saying directly that the Christian captives he met in Granada had converted to Islam, twice noting that they had 'departed from' or perhaps 'been separated from' the Christian faith.[81] He seems to hint that there were two categories of *elche*, those who were 'as innocent as babes' and 'wanted to be Christians if they could', and on the other a more actively Islamicized group who made up Abū al-Ḥasan's personal guard, described as 'perverted Christians'.[82] In describing their reversion to Christianity, he talks of the first group 'leaving their error' and 'returning' to the Catholic faith, while he mentions his own efforts with the second group in trying to make them understand the 'error they were in' and the 'truth they had left'.[83] Although he gives the impression that he was perhaps not successful with this second group, he contributes powerfully to his own credibility in portraying himself 'admonishing sinners' in this way – an act of spiritual mercy which, according to Catholic teaching, required a high level of authority.[84] When expressing a certain disappointment that Boabdil did not espouse Christianity – and in the reference to *La Romía*'s sons quoted above – he simply uses the verb to be – 'si alcanzara a ser cristiano' – which we might translate as 'if he had made it to being a Christian'. Here he gently reveals an underlying hope that Boabdil might convert to Christianity in the manner of a Constantine or a Clovis – the dream of the conversion of opponents into allies identified in literature surrounding the crusades, as well as in one of Alfonso X's *Cantigas de Santa María*.[85] His point is to minimize religious differences, stressing moral qualities and the importance of free will – a principle which he subscribes to explicitly in describing his role in the *Capitulaciones*. In advocating patience and tolerance for those who had had little access to Christian teaching, he would have been aware not only of the plight of the *elches* and newly converted *moriscos*, but of the new generation of *judeoconversos* formed by Jews who remained in Spain following the Edict of Expulsion or returned after a short period of exile. It is no accident either that in portraying the Count of Cabra as the man capable of creating spiritual communion among his troops before the battle of Lucena, he is drawing attention to a family well known for its protection of *conversos* and activism on behalf of the victims of the Inquisitor Lucero.

Conclusion

Baeza yearns not just for spiritual inclusion but, as his comment on the Abencerrajes shows, for access to social and material status. This mirrors the advice which Pulgar gives to the monarchs in his *Tratado*, in which he argues explicitly for the integration of the defeated population of Granada – and, by analogy, other 'New Christians'– by giving them access to honours and positions. He uses the example of the Roman Empire as a precedent:

> It is very well established, not only in Spain but in all nations in antiquity, that valiant men [*valerosos*] should be let in and, even if they had been on the opposing side, given recompense for their deeds with noble titles; as Livy wrote the Romans did [...] this was the main reason why Rome became great.[86]

Pulgar goes on to say that this is the way to avoid the sort of division which had brought down the Nasrid kingdom of Granada – exactly the message contained in Baeza's text:

> [...] and I wish the same greatness on Your Highness's happy monarchy, which will be achieved through worship of God and by rewarding virtuous and strong men with honours and punishing the wicked and not allowing divisions which, as the Holy Spirit says, give rise to strife, just as we have seen in the Kingdom of Granada, that the division between them and the desire to rule brought about their end, dividing their lineages.[87]

I am in no doubt therefore that Baeza's call for integration and his focus on essential similarities rather than superficial differences were motivated as much by a concern for his own status as by a particular sympathy for the *elches* or, indeed, the *moriscos*. Pulgar's reference to Baeza's earlier observations about intermarriage between Granadans and Castilians clearly indicates a rejection of the notion of ethnic purity, a matter of pressing interest to *conversos* and one on which Pulgar had clear views. By the time Baeza was writing, and after his own family's experiences at the hands of the Inquisition, 'limpieza de sangre' had become an even more charged concept and it is likely to be for this reason that, in the later iteration of his account, Baeza collapses the message about ethnicity into a less sensitive one about cultural similarity – even hybridity – and shared history. The autobiographical elements in the work – many of which are only now becoming clear once we have an account of his life history – for example, the references to the 'lands of Aguilar' in relation to the exile of the Abencerrajes, the capture of *La Romia* and the attack on Cañete – bear witness to Baeza's desire not only to write about the history of Granada, but to tell his own story. We can therefore understand the piece not only as an effort to interpret the meaning of the conquest of Granada, but as an attempt to make sense of his own story in a context where it was impossible to refer openly to his own family history. The *converso* cleric Francisco Delicado, a near-contemporary of Baeza, said in the preface to his *La Lozana Andaluza* (a satirical work about *conversa* prostitutes in Rome which must surely be a take on circumstances that Baeza knew well) that, like Pulgar, he was 'writing to forget my grief'.[88] In a similar vein, a compelling case has been made for Cervantes reliving the trauma of his captivity through his writing.[89] It must be more than likely that Baeza too was writing, in part, as a kind of 'therapy'.

There is no scarcity of literature from the early years of the sixteenth-century warning of the dangers of tyranny.[90] However, advice on resisting it is, of its very nature, harder to find, lying hidden in texts such as Hernando de Baeza's. Baeza's carefully judged account of Abū al-Ḥasan's dissident courtier and his unhappy fate balances a tale of the fall of kings with a consideration of the role of lesser individuals – like himself – when facing implacable rulers. His humanistic ideals, advocation of a new Christianity and preference for mediation over violence echo the themes of much greater writers of his day such as Erasmus and Thomas More as well as those arguing for more humane treatment of the indigenous population of the New World – Baeza's work was written almost exactly contemporaneously with Antonio de Montesinos' seminal sermon on the topic.[91] With an understanding of Baeza's life history, and the milieux he inhabited, the social logic of the text becomes clear. It is in this wider intellectual context that we must situate Hernando de Baeza, one of those 'courtly middle-men', whose proximity to political power enabled him to play a role in history as well as to reflect on it, and a discreet dissident balancing opposing impulses to resist and be reconciled.[92]

Hernando de Baeza's history of Granada

This first English translation of Baeza's text is intended to reflect the original as closely as possible, so that it can be used by scholars who are not fluent readers of Spanish. Although none of the extant manuscripts are a copy of another, there are very few differences between them such as would impact on the translation. I have therefore used a composite of the manuscript texts which are in the public domain, eliminating corruptions and obvious scribal errors. It is unfortunate that the only complete text which is accessible – that in the Real Biblioteca de Madrid – is riddled with these, including omissions of words, phrases and some whole sections which interrupt both the syntax and the sense. In contrast, the Beinecke manuscript appears copied by someone who was deeply engaged in the content and its variations appear designed to aid understanding by readers. I have only been able to use extracts from the Escalante manuscript as published by Mercedes Delgado since the original is not available publicly. For these reasons, I have tended to favour the Escorial manuscript as a base though where significant variations do occur between manuscripts, I have signalled this in the notes and justified the choices I have made.

I have not included the various headings to the manuscripts which I take not to be part of Baeza's original text.[1] To improve readability of long sections of text with many embedded relative clauses, I have added punctuation, shortened sentences and, as a result of this, deleted some connectives. To aid referencing, I have created numbered sections according to the paragraph breaks in the three available manuscripts, with any discrepancies between them (which are minimal) once again noted where relevant. Where the original language contains a special or potentially ambiguous meaning, this has been given in the notes. Where the characters named are known as historical figures, I have used the current standard spelling or transliteration of their names. Where they are not known, I have maintained the spelling/transliteration from Arabic given in the original.

Hernando de Baeza, from the report[2] he made while in Granada of things relating to that kingdom.

1. A few years after the glorious King Don Juan was of an age to fight,[3] while Muley Baudeli al-Aysar, which means Muhammad the Left-handed, was King of Granada,[4] King Juan sent a great force of troops, two years running, into the

Vega of Granada and destroyed their crops of wheat and maize; and the third year he set up camp in the *Vega* next to an irrigation channel which is called the Great Watercourse, which is a league from the city on the road which goes from Alcalá to Granada,[5] and from there he made harsh war on the city, and with the destruction of crops the previous years they suffered great shortages. One day the Moors,[6] hoping to make him lift the siege, or at least to push him back a little, came out towards the camp with a great force of men on horse and on foot which their king had gathered. And King Don Juan gathered up his troops and valiantly crossed the watercourse towards the city, forcing the Moorish horsemen to retreat.[7] Many of the foot-soldiers, finding themselves abandoned and cut off from the city, and unprotected by the cavalry, formed ranks to defend themselves and the Christian horsemen and foot-soldiers attacked them violently and within little more than an hour all the Moorish foot-soldiers were killed, some people say more than five thousand, and many people are of the opinion that no Christian died. And because next to the site of this battle there was a very big fig tree, the Christians called this the Battle of the Great Fig Tree[8] and the Moors used the same name which they call in Arabic *acijara quibira*, and they still call it that today. All the Moors withdrew to the city and, in the light of their defeat, agreed to do the king a great service and sue for peace; this is what happened, and the siege was lifted. A few days later, this Moorish king died and they made Muley Sa'ad[9] king in his place whose rule, according to what they say, was very severe[10] and for this reason the Moors rose up against him and threw him out of the city and put another king in his place.[11] This Muley Sa'ad fled the city and went to the town of Archidona which at that time still belonged to the Moors, and from there he got a safe conduct from the captains of the frontier to send the Prince, his son Abū al-Ḥasan,[12] to King Juan; and he went with one hundred and fifty men which were his father's very best cavalrymen, and among them was a great *caballero*[13] named Abenámar, the one who, in the ballad, King Juan asked 'what castles are those?'[14] This Prince Abū al-Ḥasan, with his *caballeros* and many other people accompanying him, both Christians and Moors, went to the town of Olmedo, where King Juan was, and gave him his embassy, which was this:

'That the king his father kissed his Lordship's hands and feet and the earth under his feet, and informed him that, because the king his father had been reprimanding and punishing the many excesses and maladies that he found in the city and kingdom of Granada at the time he had been king, and because he wanted to govern and hold them in justice, they had risen up against him and had thrown him out of the city and had chosen another king and, according to the uses and customs of their law and sharia and sunnah[15] – which is almost like canon and civil law – he was the king and not the other one. He appealed to his Lordship as a powerful king and lord to help him recover his position and his kingdom, and as well as doing what kings and lords usually do when people come into their kingdoms in this way and ask for favour, he would take an oath and promise to be his loyal servant and put at his service all the parts of the kingdom which returned to his obedience and not wage war against his kingdom or any part of his realms but to treat him as his lord and very true friend.'[16]

When the king heard this embassy, he ordered lodgings to be given to the prince and his followers in the Moorish quarter of Arévalo where he stayed for some days. And the king enjoyed his company and seeing him and his men ride in the Moorish style[17] because they were very good horsemen, very skilled in the saddle jousting with canes[18] as well as doing other things.

2. A few days later the king ordered letters to be sent to all the *caballeros* on the frontier, telling them to favour and assist the said king and respond to his letters and appeals. And he ordered it to be promulgated across the whole frontier that there should be peace with all the places that returned to the service of King Muley Sa'ad, and he gave a number of letters signed with his name and translated by his interpreters for certain people of the city of Granada and the Albaicín, as requested by the Moorish king. With the herald and the help that King Don Juan had given, the Moorish king sent his servants secretly to the city, and when the people in Granada saw the letters they rose up in favour of King Sa'ad and threw out the other king, who went to the Alpujarra, which forms a great part of the Kingdom of Granada and is practically impregnable because it is such rough territory. When the Moorish King Sa'ad heard about this, he entered the city and told King Don Juan what had happened and gave him many thanks and, sending him the best present he could provide, he asked for the prince his son to be given permission to return. This was a very serious thing for King Don Juan and especially for Prince Don Enrique,[19] his son, because he was enjoying himself with him and his *caballeros*. But he could do no more except give him many things of cloth and silk and many other favours and he asked him to leave a number of *caballeros*, I think about thirty, there with him, among whom I think Abenámar remained as their leader, and so the prince returned to his own country to be with his father.

3. A few days later, the Moors of the city of Granada who supported the other king who had left exchanged letters to bring him back into the city. And the arrangement was that he should come back through the Sierra Nevada in order not to be noticed. King Sa'ad, who was in the city, was told about this and, in great secrecy, he sent his son to ambush the road the king who was coming had to pass through, and there was a fight there.[20] And the Prince Muley Abū al-Ḥasan captured the Moorish king and brought[21] him to the Alhambra and his father ordered him to be killed and his two young sons to be strangled with a towel.[22] And because, at the time they were killed, which was in a room which is on the right of the *Cuarto de los Leones*, a spot of blood fell on a white marble fountain there, and the sign of the blood stayed there for many years; Moors and Christians right up to the present call this fountain the fountain where the kings were murdered.[23] With this victory and justice, father and son subjected the city admirably.

4. Not much time passed before this king was short of funds, because previous kings had long dissipated the royal crown, selling a great part or almost all the possessions that were royal patrimony. And he started to stretch out his hand to take some of the property back, which the Moors took great objection to and,

believing that the son would treat them better, they agreed to proclaim him king and so they did. And when they told him, he arrested his father and sent him riding on a mule with fifty horsemen to the fortress of Salobreña, which is a castle on a very high rock beside the sea, which breaks on the rock itself. And it is a very sick place of murderous divisions where the Moorish kings used to put people that they did not want to put to death straightaway but kill them a short time later. And the king was there a very short time because then he died and three or four of his servants who were there guarding him brought his body to the city of Granada and took it up to the Alhambra without any dignity or respect and buried it there in the place where they used to inter their kings.

5. And when this prince was made king, he married a woman who I think was the daughter of that king that his father had previously murdered, and he was peacefully married to her for about twenty years and she gave him three sons and a daughter, who were all very notable and valiant people. Thus married, he was the most loved and feared king there had been for many years. And it happened that some Moorish troops[24] wanted to go and raid Christian territory and the guide that took them was from Aguilar, which is a place seven leagues from Cordoba.[25] And he agreed that, on a Saturday night – because the next day, Sunday, people would not be going out to work and the fields would be safe – he would take them to a place near Aguilar where there is a spring. So, this is what he did, and when some children came out to water their animals, they captured them. Among them they took a girl of ten or twelve who, when she was taken to be sold with the other children in Granada, was put in the fifth share which went to the king, who gave her to his daughter with the duty of sweeping her room. And in fact, I knew her many years later and, in my opinion, she had not been a beauty.[26] As she was part of the king's household and since as a general rule all the Moorish kings were given over to lust, and especially this one, whose idea was to make a clean sweep of all the young women in his house,[27] he got involved with her using one of his young pages as a go-between. And one of the nights when he sent for her, all the queen's maids were told about it and knew that the page had taken her through into a room where the king was, and they laid in wait for her to come back and when she did they gave her a beating with their slippers and left her half dead. The king was very upset about this and thought it had been done on the queen's orders so next morning he sent the page to fetch her and had her taken across his garden to a place to stay in another house next to this garden, all of which is now the Monastery of Santa Isabel la Real. And he sent for his *mizwar*, who was his chief justice and bodyguard and told him to pass with his guards to the other door of the house, because that was the sign that wherever he was, you knew that the royal person was present. And then in the morning he went there too without saying a word to the queen or to anyone else, and he sent for tailors and silversmiths and silk-workers and ordered them to make clothes and jewels for this woman such as befitted a royal person and it was thought that no queen in Granada had ever had anything like it. A few days later it was a festival for the Moors and what usually happens is that everyone, great and small, men and women, go up to pay their respects and kiss the king's

foot and the women the queen's hand. And when his grandees asked the king who the women had to go and speak to and pay them the compliments of the season, he said to the *Romia*. This name 'Romia' is what the Moors call Christian women who become Moorish, because they do not give them Moorish names but different ones to them and almost as a nickname they call them 'Romia' all their lives, which means a person who was subject to Roman rule. So, people did what the king ordered and from then on he lived with her and she was treated as his queen and he never again spoke to or saw the queen who was his wife, but rather she had her household with her children and people in the *Cuarto de los Leones* and the king lived in the *Torre de Comares* with the other queen. And they had two sons who were afterwards Christians, the elder was called Don Fernando after the Catholic King who was his godfather and the younger was called Don Juan after the most excellent Prince Don Juan,[28] who took part in his baptism in the same way.

6. With this king absorbed in his vices and presenting a shambolic figure, certain *caballeros*, servants both of the queen and of her father the king, rose up against the king and made war on him. Among them were those called 'Abencerrajes' which means 'sons of the saddler', who were originally from Barbary,[29] and they had passed into this country in order to die fighting Christians. And it is true to say they were the best men in the saddle and with the lance that it is believed there ever were in the Kingdom of Granada. And although they were almost the greatest lords of the kingdom, they never changed the surname of their forefathers the saddlers, because the Moors are not given to despising good and noble people because they come from humble origins. So the king made war against them and captured and put to death many of them, and among them one day he executed seven of the Abencerrajes, and after they had had their throats cut he ordered them to be laid on the floor one next to the other and said that anyone who wished should come in and see them. In this way he created so much fear in the kingdom that many of the Abencerrajes who were left crossed into Castile, and some went to the house of the Duke of Medina Sidonia and others to the House of Aguilar, and they treated them and their people there with great honour[30] until such time as the young king,[31] in whose time Granada was won,[32] became king and they returned to their houses and property. The others who stayed in the kingdom were gradually arrested by the king and they say that he put to death fourteen just of the Abencerraje family and, they say, one hundred and twenty-eight other *caballeros* and brave and notable people. Among these he killed a very brave man from the Albaicín, and although he was not one of the lineage he was very capable and respected.[33] And I think it is good to write here about the manner and cause of his death. This man had been from childhood a servant of the king, the father of the queen, and after the father died he stayed with the young daughter until she married the king. After that he always lived with the king and fought with him in many wars so that the king saw how brave and good he was, and for this reason he gave a huge amount to him and favoured him so much that he almost ruled the whole Albaicín. He was in favour and service with the king right up to when he separated from the

queen and started to live with the *Romia*. Then he stopped seeing and following the king but rather followed the queen and served her. And not only did he not follow the king, but he even spoke out against him,[34] and this was noted many times by some high-ranking people in his house and especially because he was such a valiant man and such a long-standing servant to the house. And even though many people reprimanded him and warned him to be quiet, he never did, until the king himself sent word to tell him to stop criticizing him,[35] because he did not want to have to punish him. This was not enough to silence him and there were mutterings about it in front of the king by some powerful nobles who even almost blamed the king for not doing anything about it. One day the king ordered him to come to one of his gardens and ordered him to stand by a door which led from the garden to the king's rooms, and the king set himself behind the door, so he could hear with his own ears what was happening.[36] And the man knew very well that he had been brought there so that the king could hear what he was saying, and the chief visir[37] – which was almost the same person as the king because the Moorish kings when speaking to people generally or to a particular person, whether present themselves or not, always channelled what they wanted to say through their chief visir and the replies were received in the same way – the chief visir said: 'Our Lord the King, may God exalt his honour and increase his estate, makes it known to you that he has heard from many people on different occasions what unpleasant words you have used about his Highness and even that you wanted to lay hands on his most fortunate person, and for many reasons he has not ordered you to be punished, but instead he sent to say that you must cease this language and return to his service as you were before, and he will grant you favours, but you have not wanted to do this and instead replied with hateful words. And because his royal person believes that people very often exaggerate, he wanted me to speak to you here where his royal person can be certain of the reply from your own mouth. In the name of God and that of his highness the king I tell you to abandon and depart from what you are saying and rid yourself of the bad feelings that you have for him and bear him only good will because he loved you well and would not want to hurt you.' And after the visir had spoken these words and many others, and the man knew that the king was there listening to him, he said: 'My Lord, has your honourable person any more to say?' The visir replied that he had not, and so he then said: 'You have said that I bear ill will towards the king, but how can I have good will? Aside from having killed my Lord the king – that was a question of government and he took him in a battle, and rightly so, so I will not question that. I saw that he was right when he married my lady the queen, his daughter and I put myself in his service and I was at the forefront of all the attacks he made on Christian lands and I did everything in his service that a good servant should and the same with the other differences I had with him, and his fortunate person is the best witness I have to all this. And they say that I would lay my hands on him if I could, but this, please God, has never entered my head: I know his Highness is here on earth in the place of God. You say that I should stop saying those unpleasant things and bear him good will but truly I will not be able to do that because he has left my lady the queen, when she was queen and daughter of a king, and such a noble person and the mother of so many, so noble children, and to take away her status and put her own slave in her place, there is no patience which can suffer this, or would be sufficient for me. And his Highness should know that if I knew that in my body there was any small part which still loved him, even if it was my right eye, I would tear it out with the point of this dagger."

7. When the king heard these words, he said, 'kill the unbeliever then' and he was killed.[38] And this king went so far in his cruelty that there was no-one left in his kingdom who could be called a man,[39] whether warrior or advisor, and he had almost as a watchword, 'kill him, because dead people never did anyone any harm',[40] and he had the whole kingdom in such subjection to him that almost everyone trembled when they heard his command.[41]

8. Once, he gathered an army and made a raid into the kingdom of Murcia on two places called Cieza and Villacarrillo,[42] taking prisoner everyone there and bringing them back to Granada tied to a rope. I think they would have numbered more than two thousand men and women, boys and girls, of which almost all gave up their Christian faith. And I met many of them, men and women, and they were truly people of very worthy intentions and very good to talk to and those who were able to understand at the time they were taken captive fully believed in their hearts, almost as innocent as babes[43] and they wanted to be Christians if they could. And I smuggled two of them out to the town of Motrin[44] and from there the commander Martín de Alarcón[45] sent them to Villacarrillo and to Cieza, where they were from, and when Granada was won, many others departed from the error in which they had been living and returned to our Holy Catholic faith.

9. Shortly after King Abū al-Ḥasan made this raid, he drew up his troops and went out into the vicinity of Alcalá la Real and Alcaudete, because he had made peace treaties with them, and he entered the lands of the Order of Calatrava and took the villages of Santiago and La Higuera,[46] snatching all the people and livestock, killing many people along the roads and on the farms and I think that he must have taken more than one thousand people captive. Almost all these too departed from our Holy Catholic faith and became apostates, although what I said above about those people I say about these too, because I also spoke to many of these who, when Granada was won, returned to the faith. A short time later, when the king found out that the town of Cieza had been repopulated, he went back there a second time and took everyone prisoner and set it on fire.

10. He made these and other raids into Christian lands, in particular one which went as far as the village of Cañete[47] – deliberately, because he took a great force of horsemen and foot soldiers, they say four thousand on horses and twenty thousand on foot – with the intention of killing anyone they found and devastating all the villages, and he would have carried it out had not our Lord in his providence afforded the opposite, because as in that region there was no fresh water they had marched all night since dawn [sic], they needed water but what they found was all salty. They agreed to turn back causing as little damage as possible, partly lest their people took longer and died of thirst and partly so

as not to attack people who might give chase. But, hurry as they might, a great number of men and beasts died before they reached fresh water and the Moors called that raid 'Thirst Road' and they still call it that today.

11. With this king reigning so well and powerfully over temporal matters, with such peace in the land and on the seas as had never been seen before, because of his huge expenses in paying for his people and other expenses, he found himself short and set out to continue what his father had begun in taking back the property which had belonged to the Crown which his predecessors had sold. And so he took it all back, a huge number of properties, which brought in very valuable income. And the people complained saying that this was causing them great hardship, and one of the reasons was because at the time they had bought the property, they had not done so by choice or at a price they set, but rather while they had been peacefully in their houses some servants of the king called *alharriques* – like the crossbow guards of the kings of Castile[48] – were sent with sales documents of the things that the king wanted to sell and the prices that the king wanted for them, and they were given to the people they had been ordered to take them to and they were required to give them the money that was specified, or pay with their lives. And because of this there was unrest in the kingdom, so there was an agreement that the king should take half the properties and rents as a contribution to his costs and expenses and the Moors agreed and so that was done.

12. In the midst of this discontent, some *caballeros* who were servants of the queen's father and opposed to the king made a deal with his brother, the one who later became the king called Zagal[49] – the one who surrendered Baza and Guadix and Almería and a great part of the Kingdom of Granada to the Catholic King and the Queen – of glorious memory[50] – and they made an agreement with certain *caballeros* from the city of Malaga and that prince stole away from his brother one night and went to the city of Malaga where they hailed him as king.[51] When the king his brother found out, he sent an army after him and when they had made camp and had him surrounded, he and his brother exchanged letters and one night he escaped from the fortress on a rope and went to where the army was camped and from there to Granada. Then, as soon as the prince arrived in the city, the king sent his *mizwar*, who was his chief executor of justice, and announced in the camp that the king pardoned those who had done or said anything against him, all except certain people, I think about ten or twelve. When they heard the announcement, immediately the city of Malaga rose up in favour of the king and those that knew very well that they would be in the number of those excepted from the pardon fled to the fortress and that same night they escaped over the walls. In this way they raised the king's standards in the fortress of Malaga after two or three days and they executed certain people. In this way, the kingdom was pacified and calm restored.

13. Not much later a comet appeared in the southern sky, trailing to the east, and as wide and as long as a two-handed sword, appearing from two hours before sunrise and lasting until the brilliance of the sun hid it. It was amazingly brilliant, and they say that it appeared for more than thirty days and people marvelled at

it. And some astrologers who were consulted by the king said that it meant a very great war leading to great destruction.

14. The king wanted to review the men he had for cavalry in his kingdom and he ordered letters to be sent so that everyone should come to a parade on certain days, distributed so that they would not get in the way of each other. And he spread it over thirty days and left the last day, which was the feast of St John, for his own household, where it was found that there were more than 700 horsemen, almost all Christians who had been taken captive. And, in truth, I knew almost one hundred of them, great men both in the saddle and in their bravery and they were held in high esteem by the king and by everyone in the kingdom both great and small, and almost all were officials of the royal household and commanders and captains of it. While the parade was going on, the king was in a small room which is opposite the door of the king's garden which is known as the *Generalife*, which means the most noble and most high of all the gardens,[52] and the horsemen passed between the king's room, which is two storeys' high, and the entrance to the garden by means of a path there, so that each one could see the king and pay homage to him, and the king could see and recognize each one of them. In this way, twenty-nine days passed, during which time they say that four thousand horsemen went by, and after them seven hundred lancers of the king's household started their parade. I saw many of those who were there, and they said it was a wonderful sight to see the horses and the caparisons displayed by the people of the kingdom and their king. And while, as I was saying, the men of the king's household were going past, almost half-way through, a little after midday, a mass of clouds rose up above the Sierra Nevada and started to spread all around to the east. Within the space of half an hour,[53] the whole sky grew very dark and very heavy rain started to fall with a lot of hail and stones and with great thunderclaps and lightening as if, some said, the Day of Judgement was coming, and it lasted four hours. The rivers rose so much, especially the Darro, that it overflowed its banks and uprooted many trees including a great walnut tree. When it was swept downstream, it was too big to fit under the bridge which is known today as Santa Ana, but went partly through and got stuck there. And all the other trees and grasses[54] and debris that the river was bringing down backed up and made a sort of dam. And as the water could not pass through, it rose up over the bridge and down the street where the Chancery is and right down to where the entrance to the city jail now is. The river swept away the whole street of the Zacatín[55] and all the leatherworkers' stalls and the silk bazaar,[56] and a great part of the city besides, where the damage was so great that it carried away and destroyed all the city's merchandise, because that used to be, and is, the place where almost all the trade is done, or at least the main place.

15. The whole city was in upheaval as a result of this, both because of the destruction and losses and because of the property that the king had appropriated and, because they were very tired of his royal person, and discontented, some servants of the queen's father tried to procure his downfall and got discussing how they could smuggle the king's eldest son, who was already over twenty years old, out of the Alhambra. And since he was in the *Cuarto de los Leones*, which was

next to where the king was, they were unable to find a way to do it. But divine providence, wanting to achieve something which it had ordained, permitted the youngest of the king's three sons to be struck with plague and die, so the queen asked if she could go and live in another nearby house with her sons and her people. And a *mudéjar* from the town of Mora, which is in the kingdom of Toledo, who at that time was living in Granada, who was called Abrahén de Mora,[57] was able to get into that house under the pretext of selling copperware and was able to give letters to the prince. In this way and with others, they made an arrangement with certain *caballeros* from the city of Guadix, especially two very brave men, Aben Adi and Aben Zeyd, who Abrahén de Mora[58] dealt with. And I knew Abrahén de Mora and considered him a friend and he was a good man and a clever strategist in war. He sent letters to Guadix to these *caballeros* hidden in some pans which he sent there with a young man from Guadalajara called Abrahén Robledo,[59] who was a metalworker's boy and his job was to take pans to be sold throughout the kingdom. And this was the Moor who later fought in the *Vega* with Fernando de El Pulgar.[60] And the arrangement was that, on the night they agreed, at about ten o'clock, six people should go with nine horses and wait by a watercourse next to the *Generalife* gardens, about two hundred paces from where the prince was. And then they went on foot, and Abrahén de Mora with them, to the bottom of the castle wall below where the prince lived, where he would be waiting for them and recognize them by an agreed signal. So, when they arrived and gave the signal, the prince, as if he was not able to sleep, went and threw down a small piece of string which he had in his hand, as had been agreed. And they tied a thick woollen rope to this string, which he was able to attach to a marble pillar and let himself down, along with his brother. And both were received by the *caballeros* with the homage and deference they deserved. And they were each given a sword and a dagger, and they say that the prince and his brother, although they were both so young, spoke brave words to the *caballeros* as if they were grown men.[61] In this way, they reached the place where they had left the horses and got up on them and they found the people waiting there for them on foot and they all went to the city of Guadix, arriving near there at dawn. When the prince arrived in the city, the same men who had taken him there sent some other *caballeros* from the city with the prince's young brother to the city of Almería, where they already had an arrangement. And when the young prince[62] arrived in Almería, they acclaimed his brother as king, and he received their homage and obedience on behalf of his brother.

16. They were there for about six months, during which time there never ceased to be contact between *caballeros* in Granada and the prince, and the men who had taken him to set him up as king in the city of Granada, and the discussions between them lasted until they had their intended aim. And after about six months they made him king and drove his father out of the city, and so the prince came to Granada and was there as king for six months reigning without any trouble; and meanwhile his father had retreated to the Alpujarras and the young prince was still in Almería enjoying great prosperity and good will.

17. At this time, the new king wed and celebrated a solemn marriage with a daughter of the king that his father had killed.[63] And after that some *caballeros* thought that, in order to satisfy the people, the king ought to make a raid on Christian territory, and he went out with a powerful force and raided the area of Luque and Baena part of the lands belonging to the Order of Calatrava, and he took a lot of people and livestock and went back to the city of Granada where he was received with great joy.

18. But as it is something almost natural that things do not stay the same for long, the grandees of the kingdom thought that, as there were so many troops gathered together, horseman and foot soldiers, before they dispersed, they should attempt another raid. This was almost against the will of the king but, following the view of his *caballeros*, he did what they said and went out towards Lucena, where the *Alcaide de los Donceles*,[64] whose town it was, was living at the time. And he [the *Alcaide*] went to defend it, only with very few people, not thought to be even one hundred and fifty horsemen, and he put out a call using smoke signals, which were the signs to warn and call for help against the Moors. In response to this call, the Count of Cabra came with only a very few men and he came in a way that the Moors did not see him coming, so they would not realize he had so few men.[65] Before he went up the hill where the *Alcaide de los Donceles* was, he sent word to say that he should send his standard and his drums and trumpets and that is what he did. And they used another flag instead of the standard and the Count ordered his drums and trumpets to be sounded and those of the *Alcaide* and with the two standards he positioned his troops so that one side of them could be seen from the Moors' camp. And when they saw the different standards and heard the different drums and trumpets, they thought that there was a great host of cavalry there. The Count had ordered the people when they arrived on the hill to spread out on one wing, one next to the other on the hill, so that from the Moors' camp it looked like a great number of people. And when they got up there, by agreement with the Count and the *Alcaide*, more than half of them slipped away and the rest spread out on the wing as they had been before. And with one of the standards, or with both, and with the same trumpets and drums they went down the hill again without being seen by the Moors and came up again on the other side sounding the drums and trumpets and displaying their troops and playing in a different way from the first and the second ones and they went up the hill joining the others on the wing where they were greeted with great shouts of joy, crying out, as the great Juan de Mena says, 'in the name of the son of good Zebedee'.[66] And this put great alarm among the Moors and they thought that they had been spotted there for several days and that the whole of Andalusia had been called up and that they were starting to arrive. And so they agreed what to do. Some thought that the king should go home before any more people arrived. Others said that the king should cross the stream, the little watercourse known as Martín González which had always been a barrier for the Christians, because they had not been able to cross it sometimes when the Moors had come out on raiding parties. They said that, as the king was coming with such a large number of troops, he should cross to the other side and put all his troops together there before the Christians arrived, because if they turned their

backs, the Christians who had already spotted them would give chase and as the whole country had been summoned there would be a great disaster.[67]

19. The al-'Attar of Loja,[68] a very old man, said to be more than eighty, a shrewd man and very wise when it came to warfare, said to the king, 'Sire, your Highness should not do either of these things, remain where you are, because you have so many men in the field and between now and this afternoon it is not possible for so many of them to come that they will outnumber us. And when we see how many come during the day, the night will give us cover and your royal person can decide what to do. And in addition, we have the stream between us and them and that gives us an advantage.' There was one *caballero* there who was not very experienced in warfare who said to the al-'Attar, 'For someone who has lived so long and with so little time left, you love life a lot.' And he turned to the king and said, 'Your Highness should cross, you have enough people here to do what you want.' And the al-'Attar said, 'Our Lord King should consider what he is doing and the advice that he takes, and he should take my advice. I say that whoever crosses the stream – whether it is the Christians coming over to us, however many they are, they will be lost and if we Moors cross over to them, we will all be lost.' And as Our Lord had already determined that the Moors should be lost, and that they and their king should be captured, he put in their hearts that they should cross the stream. So, they drew up their troops and agreed that, as the crossing would be damaged by so many people going over, the king should go in the second squadron. When this had been agreed, they raised the royal standard and sounding their drums and kettledrums and trumpets, they crossed the stream making a great noise.

20. While the Moors were deciding this, and discussing these different pieces of advice, the saintly Count took another tack. I say saintly, because I knew him and spoke with him a lot, and for many years I confessed to a friar of the Order of St Jerome who was his confessor[69] and I can say truly that from what I came to know, I think he was the most excellent member of the laity there has been in Castile in our time. And there are many accounts of it in his life, and not the least of these was this day because, while the Moors were deciding what to do, he ordered mass to be said because it was morning. And when mass was said, and before it was said and while it was being said, the Count and the *Alcaide* and all the others confessed. And when they saw the consecrated host in the hands of the priest, they all communed with it spiritually.

21. Then, when the mass was over, the Count made a speech and said to everyone that they should be brave and should not fear and that the truth of the Holy Catholic faith which guided them would give them victory and they should call on the Apostle Santiago and he would help them to win. They should not fear nor pay heed that there were many Moors and few of them, because that is why the Holy Mother Church says that the Lord God of Battles is holy, because he appears miraculously in them so that the few can conquer the many. And he said to them, 'See how sure I am that today the Moorish king with be captured and all his troops will be lost if we act bravely and know how to engage with them. And that must be by attacking them before any more of his men cross the stream.

We have an advantage over them in many things and they will have over us if we let them cross the stream, and not one of us will escape.⁷⁰ Let everyone put their hand in their saddlebag, and the foot soldiers in their rucksacks and have breakfast if you have something to eat. The Lord *Alcaide* and I will not break our fast until the battle is won.'

22. With these words he pulled his right arm out of the sleeve of his shirt and his jerkin, and with his bare arm he took his lance in his hand. And some say that he took off his helmet or *cervellera*⁷¹ and raised his dagger shouting 'Santiago! Santiago! Attack! Today is our day!' and he and the *Alcaide de los Donceles* galloped off side-by-side down the hill against the Moors with such great cries that it seemed that the air itself was alive with shouting. By this time, the first squadron and almost the second one had crossed the stream, so they were four or even five times more Moors than Christians but then almost all the Moors turned and fled back across the stream.

23. By this time, the al-'Attar had crossed the stream to where the Christians were and when he saw the disarray of his troops he went back towards the stream. Because so many horses had gone across, the crossing had become impassable so that the king's horse got stuck in the middle and could not go forward. And they say that, when the al-'Attar saw the king in this predicament, and the troops turning tail, he said, 'God forbid that I should die at my time of life at the hands of Christians or be captured by them.' And he said to the king, 'My Lord, may God help you and give you strength', and saying these words he went downstream to where there was a deep pool and he got off his horse and stretching out his head over his dagger he threw himself into the water. They say that his body was never found. It is thought that, as he was so old and skinny, the weapons he was carrying weighed him down and the water could not bring him to the surface.

24. And with the king in this agony and anguish, a Christian soldier arrived at the bank and lifted up his lance to strike the king with the iron, but a Moorish *mudéjar caballero* from Toledo called Santa Cruz who was also stuck on his horse next to the king, said 'Hold on! Hold on, you dog! Don't kill him, he's the king!'⁷² And when the soldier heard this he stopped, and at that moment another soldier, who was from Baena like the other one, came along on a pack animal and the first one said, 'This is the Moorish king.' And together they got him out of his saddle and set him on the mule and one of them got on with him and the other one led the animal by the halter and took him off down the road to Baena. And when the *Alcaide de los Donceles* and some of his men were told about this, four or five of them went after them and took the king from them and, putting him on a horse, they carried him off to Lucena, the *Alcaide de los Donceles'* town. As a result of this, the Count, as the one who first captured the king, was given the upper half of the Moorish king's body to put on his coat of arms and for his arms the *Alcaide de los Donceles* was given the king's body from the waist down.⁷³

25. After that, the Catholic Monarchs Don Fernando and Doña Isabel ordered the king to be taken from Lucena to Porcuna, which belongs to the Order of Calatrava, where he was held and treated very honourably, accompanied by many Moorish servants and followers of his, until the Catholic Monarchs favoured him

with his freedom under certain terms of an agreement which they ordered to be made, which we will not recount here to avoid being long-winded and because they will be written in many other places.

26. One of these terms, and the main one, was that their highnesses would favour him with help to return to his former status and for this purpose the grandees of Andalusia were ordered to respond to his calls for support. They issued him with a document signed with their royal names and, as a result of this treaty, he was released in the city of Cordoba. He went to kiss their Highnesses' hands and from there to the town of Alcaudete and, with the document he had been given, he called on certain grandees for their support. When they arrived, he consulted with them on how they could support him and he went to the places known as Vélez Blanco and Vélez Rubio which are on the frontier with the city of Lorca. And it had already been agreed that the commander there, and a visir who was a son-in-law of Abenámar, and one of his brothers who were known as the Aduladanes, would receive him there as king, and this is what happened as agreed.

27. We will leave this story here and return to King Muley Abū al-Ḥasan his father who, as we said, had taken refuge in the Alpujarras. When he heard about the capture and imprisonment of his son, he sent messengers to Granada and had it proclaimed that he would grant a general pardon to anyone who had done or said anything against his service in the recent revolts if they now gave him their support. Many people were therefore moved to come under his banner, and they sent messengers to tell him to come to Granada. This he did, bringing with him his brother the prince,[74] his wife *La Romia* and his two children. But when his first wife heard about her son's capture, she went to Almería with her other son and took her daughter and servants there.

28. When the king returned to Granada he assembled a strong army, put his brother the prince in charge of it, who went with his troops to Almeria and laid siege to it for almost six months. Seeing that he could not take it by force, he sent out a proclamation that he would offer a general pardon to all those who had done or said anything against his service, except eight or ten people. And they say that as King Abū al-Ḥasan was writing in his own hand the note of people who would be excepted from the pardon, and he was writing it in front of his wife the *Romia* queen, she intervened and forced and importuned him to put his son on the list of those not included in the pardon. Some say that he crossed it out[75] twice and twice she made him put it back and that when he had written it, he said, 'Although I am putting his name, it is my brother who has to go and carry it out and he will not order the execution of his nephew and the *mizwar* who has to go and carry it out will not cut the throat of his master.' Some people say maliciously that the queen did this in the belief that the king would never be released from captivity and that if the other one were dead, then her son would be king. Be that as it may, when the proclamation was made the siege of Almería was lifted and all the leaders who thought they were guilty fled to the fortress and that night escaped over the walls and some saved themselves by sea and others by land. Only the unhappy prince remained, because he thought that his tender age would save him from blame, especially as it was his own father who had to sentence him.

29. Two days later the *mizwar*, who was the chief justice of the king, arrived. The *mizwar* normally had to be a black freed slave because black people from Guinea normally do not have relatives that they can talk to about the king's justice, and no-one to be hurt by it. When the *mizwar* arrived at the fortress of Almería, he took the prince almost out of his mother's arms and throwing him down on a carpet he cut his head off. And it is said that when the *mizwar* arrived, the prince said, 'What? My father the king has sent you to cut my throat?' And the *mizwar* said, 'Yes, my Lord', and he replied, 'I have never heard nor read of a father doing such a thing to his son,[76] you should consider my young age. But, after all, you must fulfil his command. I need to wash my body to receive death.' And with these words he started to undo his clothes and went up to a patio and got into a pool where he washed himself. Then he asked for clean clothes and they gave them to him and so he passed out of this life with great courage and without any distress.

30. Some of those who knew him say that he was one of the most beautiful, benevolent and wise of the Moors, for his age. They all say that the *mizwar* consulted with the king's brother, the prince's uncle, and agreed his death with him, because he had come on his orders and he gave him, in the letter he brought with him, the list of those who had to die. And they even say that the *mizwar* gave his advice to the uncle, saying that although the king had been annoyed and he was coerced and forced to make the order, in his opinion his Lordship should not do it, and that he thought it was a bad thing to do. When the king told him to go and carry out this act of justice and he said that he and his brother should consider what they were doing, he told him to do it as if he had lost his senses. And the *mizwar* reasoned with him and argued that he should not put his nephew the prince to death, that they should hide him and say to the king that they had fulfilled his orders and that his son was dead. And some even say that this was the reason why the king did not order this *mizwar* to be arrested and cut to pieces when seven or eight months later he found out that his son had been killed, as will be explained later.[77]

31. When this had been carried out and the prince was dead, the *mizwar* returned to Granada and the prince, the brother of the king, struck camp and also returned to the city of Granada.

32. After about six months King Abū al-Ḥasan said to one of his pages, 'Go to my brother and tell him that I say to bring me my son here, I have a great desire to see him.' The page went to the prince and gave him this message. The prince replied, 'Tell his Highness that I do not understand what he is asking', and the page returned to the king with the reply and the king sent the message again with one of his commandants: 'Tell my brother to bring me my son, that six months is enough time for him to have hidden him from me'. When the prince heard these words, he went to the house of the visir, who as I said was almost the chief of the whole kingdom, and told him what had happened and asked him to go and speak to the king and tell him that his son was dead as he himself had written in his letter in the list of people who had to die, signed in his name. The visir did not want to go with this message but forced by the prince and seeing there was no alternative, he went and slipped into the room where the king was. A little while

later, the commandant who the king had sent to the prince arrived and gave his reply: 'Sire, I gave the prince your Highness's order and he gave the reply to the visir.' Then the visir said to the King, 'Your honourable person sent to the prince to tell him to send you your son the lord prince. He says that he is shocked that your Highness should ask him to do that, because he knows that you sent him a letter signed with your royal name ordering him to execute him, and he sent his *mizwar* to do this who had a list signed with your royal name with the names of certain people he had to kill and the first of those was the prince, and this is what was done. Have patience my lord.' Then the king replied: 'My brother wants me to thank him because he saved my son from death, bring him to me and I will repay him.' Then the visir repeated what he had said and swore that it was true that his son was dead and that he would not see him until the great Day of Judgement.[78]

33. When the king heard this, he started crying and shouting, 'Never has there been seen such great evil! No uncle has killed his nephew neither do I believe that such a thought could occur to him, he had to consider that I ordered it in anger, not for it to be carried out.' The king spoke with passion and pain, as a father, and started to howl out and wail, 'My son Yusaf, where is your beauty? Never did a father order this against a son, never did an uncle do such a thing against his nephew!', and as he said this, they say he beat his head against the walls with great blows through pure grief and passion.

34. A few days later, the king went blind, and they say that they gave him many medicines to return him his sight. One day, when they were treating him in a bath, they say that a spirit entered into his body and, in truth, this was so because it banged him on the floor many times and out of his mouth it said some of those things which those who are in the grip of that passion tend to say.

35. When his brother the prince saw this, he set himself up as king in the city and took the king his brother and set him on a mule with the two princes his sons on another two, and sent them to the fortress of Salobreña. Some say that when they told the older son, who was afterwards called Don Fernando, to get on the mule, he refused to do it and told them to bring him a horse and he would ride that. When his father heard that he said, 'Ride, you bastard dog. Your father is going on a mule; you can too.' He left his wife, that is *La Romia*, there and the new king had her there with him so that, with flattery and telling her that she had to marry him, she would show him where the treasures were and tell him where her jewels and those of the king were hidden.

36. King Abū al-Ḥasan, blind and maddened by demons, soon died there in Salobreña, I think in less than six months. His body was brought back on a mule by three or four of his servants who were guarding him, and it was put in the place which is now called the *Campo del Principe*.[79] His body was there alone from early morning, almost from dawn to the end of the day with only those servants who had brought it. Neither the king nor anyone else came until the hour of vespers, when some *alfaquis* arrived – these are to the Moors like clergymen are to Christians – and they conducted a ceremony and took him up to the Alhambra to bury him where the other kings were usually buried. Oh,

wonderful justice of God! For him to be treated by his brother in the same way that he treated his father, to be given the same death and burial!

37. With King Abū al-Ḥasan in prison, his brother the prince set himself up as king and, since there was no-one left of royal blood save the children who he was holding prisoner, he lorded it over the whole country and held it in his sway for a time. While the king was in the city of Granada, his nephew was in the towns of Vélez exchanging letters with certain *caballeros* from the Albaicín, who promised to obey him and raise him up as their king and lord. On the basis of this, with great bravery and daring, and with only twelve horsemen and almost the same number on foot, he dared to come at night with men who guided him from the towns of Vélez to the city of Granada, which is more than twenty leagues, and he came to within half a league from the Albaicín, as had been agreed. Almost forty men came out on foot to meet him and he dismounted there, and gently and bravely spoke words of great friendship to them thanking these *caballeros* for the danger they had put themselves in. Promising them his favour, he took a sword in one hand and a dagger in the other, and with half the people in front of him and the other half behind and by his sides, he went and entered the Albaicín via a secret entrance, which is where the others had left from. When he arrived, they put him in a house where there were already a lot of armed men. These, and those who had come with the king, started shouting, 'Almighty God, may our Lord King Muley Boabdil[80], son of Muley Abū al-Ḥasan, be exalted!' Then they all came one after the other to kiss his hand and foot and left him there with ten or twelve men to accompany him, and all the others went out into the Albaicín, calling out his name and letting the people know that their natural king was there with them. Then they took care to close all the gates between the Albaicín and the city and barricaded the wooden gates with stone and earth and planks of wood so that the people from the city could not get in.

38. The king was in the Albaicín for about a year, fighting with his uncle the king, who was in the city, and the Catholic Monarchs favoured him because, on the basis of their treaty, he sent heralds to declare peace all along the frontier. A *mudéjar caballero* called Bobadilla[81] went to the town of Alcaudete to do this and Abrahén de Mora[82] – the one who, as we said earlier, took this king to Guadix, and who had already acted as his interpreter and his chief standard-bearer – gave him a letter for me on the orders of the king to tell me some of the things that had happened and saying that, as he needed a person who would come to the Catholic Monarchs on his behalf, he would be pleased if I would be willing to do that. I did not accept at that time, because it was dangerous to go into the Albaicín. The king knew about me from the time that his royal person was released from captivity and came to the town of Alcaudete from where, as I said before, he issued a call to the grandees of Andalusia. I was living there at the time, and through the good offices of a *mizwar* of his called Alhaje,[83] a very great friend of mine, his royal person had talked to me in a very friendly way. A short time after that, as I shall describe below, the city rose up in his favour and set him up as king and then, via this same Bobadilla, the king wrote to me again and I went there, where I had long conversations with his royal person, and his

mother and wife and children, servants and maids. Everything I wrote about that day when the king was taken prisoner, I heard from the king's own mouth. And he spoke to me only in the language of Castile, although with quite a strong accent, so one day I asked him why he did not use Castilian because he knew it so well, and he said something quite significant: 'Yes, I speak it, but as I am not very fluent, I am afraid of making a mistake, and mistakes in the mouth of a king are very ugly.' And I took this to be the word of a great person and, as God is my witness, over the three or four years that I knew him, because that is how long I knew him for, that is what he was. I really believe that if he had ever become a Christian, he would have been one of the best people that ever lived. And all the other stories which I have recounted, I heard from the many perverted Christians there, both in the city of Granada and in the king's household, and I spoke to them a lot and made efforts to get them to recognize the truth which they had abandoned, and the error they were living in. As I considered them my friends and I knew that they – both men and women – knew a lot about what had happened, I always asked questions to be certain and, depending on the quality of their persons and the manner of their conversation, I certainly believe the things that I have related in part, as if I had seen them myself.

39. The king was in the Albaicín, and his uncle set up as king in the city, until the Catholic King Don Fernando marched out in force and set his army around the town of Vélez Malaga.[84] At that time the Moors who lived there sent letters to the king who was in the Albaicín and to the *alfaquis* and elders of the city of Granada, informing them that the Christian king was marching on them with a huge army, and if they sent help they would be serving God and they would be saved, and if not then they had no choice but to surrender the town. When they saw this, the Moors sent to the king who was in the Alhambra asking him to come to the Great Mosque to Friday prayers[85] because they wanted to speak to him there. And the king went and the chief *alfaqui* made a speech and read the letters, to which the visir responded in the name of the person of the king and said to the people in his presence, that his Highness would go to try to lift the siege of Vélez or else die there with all his followers, but as his nephew was in the Albaicín, how could he leave the city? As soon as he left by one gate, his nephew would come in by another. And the leading Moors and the chief *alfaqui* in their name replied that if he wanted to go, they would all swear to keep the city in peace and tranquillity and free of trouble until he returned and they would not allow his nephew nor any other person do anything against his service or against his estate but they would rather die along with their wives and children. The king responded through his visir that if they swore this on oath, then he would go. With these words of the chief visir to the people, the chief *alfaqui*, who was like an Archbishop or even like a Pope for them, got up in the pulpit, or that high spot where he generally spoke to the people. With the agreement of the king, he took in his hands what is called a *taheli,* which is a small leather box[86] with silk tassels hanging from it in which the Moors generally carry a Qur'an and from them Christian knights took to taking these *tahelís* to war, carrying relics and good prayers in them. And he raised it high and said: 'The King and Our Lord

demand that you all swear by the words written here that none of you present, nor those of you absent, will, while he is away providing this support, say or do or advise anything contrary to the service of his royal person or in favour of his nephew.' And everyone replied, 'Yes, we swear.'

40. Then the king said to the people, 'Let's go then, so that tomorrow we will be ready for the fight.' Soon after that, the king with as many troops as he could find left and went to the city of Vélez and set up on the high ground called the Sierra de Aventomiz. But no sooner had he left Granada, almost before he reached Vélez, a scrofulous old Moor more than sixty years old appeared, with his throat covered in lumps. His job was selling things for women going to bathe at the entrance to the baths which was demolished to make the foundations for the cathedral. He climbed up the tower by the gate known as Biba Mazdal,[87] which is below the cathedral, and shut the gate of the tower after him and, taking off the headdress he was wearing, he tied it to a lance he was carrying and started shouting saying, 'Long Live King Muley Boabdil, son of Muley Abū al-Ḥasan!' He kept shouting this, and the cry was taken up from the other towers and when the king who was in the Albaicín heard it he rode out with his followers and his royal standard and drums and kettledrums and trumpets and made a great noise in the town and in the Albaicín. The king went down towards the Puerta Elvira and his *mizwar* went into the town with heralds declaring a general pardon for anything anyone had done or said. Then the whole city rose up for this king, who set himself up in the Alcazaba[88] in the houses which now belong to the Marquis of Zenete,[89] and all the *alfaquis* and elders of the city went to swear obedience to him in the name of the people and kiss his feet.

41. This news reached the king his uncle when he was in the camp at Vélez and, at almost two in the morning, he packed up, thinking that he would arrive in the city in time to reverse some of what had been done. As he was coming back along the road, some other messengers arrived telling him exactly what had happened. When the king heard that, he turned back and went to the Alpujarras and from there to the cities of Baza and Guadix, where he stayed for two or three years until the Catholic King laid siege to Baza, which was the longest and hardest fought siege there had ever been in the Kingdom of Granada.[90] In the end, he surrendered and made terms with the Catholic King, in which he handed over the towns of Baza and Guadix and Almería and the whole of the Alpujarras and many other places which were under his control, because only the city of Granada and a few hamlets near it were in the hands of the young king.[91] After they had surrendered in this way, the king and his followers left for Africa.

42. After King Don Fernando had brought Baza to a conclusion, he sent as ambassadors to the King of Granada: Gonzalo Fernández, commander of Illora, who afterwards rightly achieved fame as the *Gran Capitán* because of the great excellence and nobility of his person and the great deeds he accomplished, through the will of God, and Martín de Alarcón, commander of Moclín.[92] When he heard what they had to say, the Moorish king thought that there was a change in what had been agreed and he told them that he would send his own messengers to his Highness. These were a *caballero* of his household

called Abul Cacín,[93] who spoke to the king and to the queen in Cordoba and was with them for several days. And when he returned with the reply, the king was very frightened and amazed and would have wanted to go back to war, but some grandees[94] advised him not to do so, but to send messengers again. So this is what the king did, and when the king and queen were in Seville, he sent the chief visir of the city of Granada, who at that time was a *caballero* named Yusaf Aben Comixa,[95] who took with him a very honourable merchant named Abrahén Alcaiçi,[96] who was a very great friend of mine. These also returned very discontented, saying that the terms which had been agreed twice with the king were not being adhered to. This caused uproar in the city and, from then on, there was war between Christians and Moors and it lasted for about two years. The Catholic King sallied forth with an army and set up his camp in the middle of the *Vega* outside Granada, where he stayed for eight months attacking the city. And the war was so intense that of 2,250 cavalrymen in the city at the time the king laid siege to it, no more than 150 were left at the time it was surrendered.[97]

43. While, as we said, the king was besieging Granada, almost two leagues away, he agreed to create a fortified town there which is called Santa Fe, so that he could leave some military units there to make war on the city and lift camp until summer. Some of his leading men said that, rather than striking camp, he should sally forth and the Christians should engage the Moors in skirmishing and gradually draw them away from the city, and when they were away from the gates, they should turn on them, not to rob or kill, but to get into the city, even though Christians would be intermingled with the Moors and some might die. The king decided to take this advice and agreed to do it, but the plan was discovered by a *mudejar* who had left the Albaicín with Abul Caçiçi Abencerraje[98] to go to the camp. That evening just before sunset, when the troops were returning to the camp, he secretly stayed behind and told a Moor everything that had happened in the camp for him to tell the king so that they would be warned. When the Moor told him, the king agreed with his *caballeros* to go out and give battle with as many people as they could, and for them all to die rather than to suffer the affront of such a great city being taken in this way.

44. Having agreed this, the next day the king got up and perfumed his body in the way that the Moors do when they put themselves at risk of death, and he asked for his arms. At the door of the room in the *Torre de Comares*, with his mother, wife and sister present, and many ladies and maids in waiting, and fully armed, he asked for his mother's hand and asked her to give him her blessing. He hugged his sister and kissed her on the neck and embraced his wife and kissed her on the face and did the same to a little son of his, in the same way as he did ordinarily when he went out to battle. And that day he added a little speech, asking his mother and everyone else to forgive him anything he had done to upset them. The queen his mother was shocked at this new behaviour and asked him in distress, 'What has happened, my son?' The king replied, 'Nothing my lady, but there are reasons why I must do this.' And when she heard these words the mother took hold of her son and said, 'My son, swear to God and by the obedience you owe to me as your mother that you will tell me what you are

going to do and where you are going to go.' And as she said this, she started to cry and when all the other women saw that the mother of the king was in tears, a huge cry went up through the whole building as if he were already dead. And still the mother held on to her son and would not let him go until he told her what had happened and what had been planned in the Christian camp. At this, his mother replied, 'But son, who will look after your poor mother, and wife and children and sister and relatives and servants and this whole city, and the other places you are responsible for? What account will you give to God leaving them in such a predicament, giving the order that we should all die by the sword or be taken captive? Take care what you are doing: serious tribulation requires serious council.' The king replied: 'My lady, it is much better to die once than to remain alive and die many times.' The mother said, 'What you say is true, son, if only you were to die, and everyone were to be saved and the city freed, but such great loss is wrong.' The king replied, 'Leave me[99] my lady, my men are waiting for me.' His mother said, 'May God forbid that the king should go beyond the gardens[100] of this city and until he has promised me to hold back his troops and not put himself into danger today.' And she did not let go of his hands until he had sworn to do so on the *tahelí* which he carried, for this was the way that the king and Moorish grandees swore their oaths.

45. So the king went out into the field of battle and ordered his men to hold back so that what had been agreed in the Christian camp could not be put into practice. And from then on, some say that his mother advised the king to find a way with the Catholic Monarchs for them and the city and the villages to be free to leave for Africa.[101] And that certainly seems to have been the case because, a few days later, talks started and Gonzalo Fernández de Córdoba, afterwards known as the *Gran Capitán*, together with Hernando de Zafra, secretly came into the Alhambra one night, at the request of the Moorish king, with a Moorish gentleman[102] who had already been secretly to the [Christian] camp twice or even three times. And it was in order to stop this man deceiving the Moorish king, as he had already tried to do on another occasion, that I advised the king.[103]

46. With the agreement and command of their Highnesses, sent to me secretly with a captive who I had released, who lived in Marbella,[104] they asked me to give the order for these men to enter safely, so that the business could be brought to a conclusion more certainly and more quickly. This was both because of the great cost of maintaining the camp and because winter was coming, and people were tired. When these men came into the Alhambra, they stayed that night in the house of the man who brought them in, the one I mentioned earlier called Abū al-Qāsim *el Muleh*.[105] They stayed there all the next day and part of the following night, and at ten o'clock on the second night, while the king was alone with me between the two doors of the patio of the *Cuarto de Comares* and the other door which goes out into the patio where the large water trough is set on the ground, a Moorish *caballero* came in bringing with him Gonzalo Fernández de Córdoba and Hernando de Zafra. These men talked for a long time and discussed some points which were preventing an agreement being reached, although they had been discussed at length in the camp. And I remember two of them: one was in

relation to the apostates or *elches* who are Christians who become Moors, that they should not be forced to return to our Holy Catholic faith against their will, and the other was that the Moorish king in no way wanted to dismount from his horse and kiss the hands of the Catholic Monarchs when the time came for him to come out of the city to hand it over. He said that he would rather allow himself to be cut into a thousand pieces. And, in the discussions about this it seemed to me, although I was nothing there, that the first should not rightfully be done,[106] and the other was a matter of vanity. And they agreed as a solution that the king, when he came to pay homage to the Catholic Monarchs, should put his hands on the pummel of his saddle and make a move to dismount from his horse, and that the king and queen should say to the interpreter to tell the king not to dismount and that he should not do so, and that he should arrive on horseback with his hat in his hand and show his intention to take their Highnesses' hands and they should hide their hands when he came near and he should kiss them on the shoulder. With this, the differences were agreed, and the men signed the agreement there in the name of the Catholic Monarchs, and in the same way, Abū al-Qāsim signed on behalf of the Moorish king, in his presence and at his command. The arrangement was that on the tenth of January 1491,[107] the city should be handed over accordingly. Then the men left the palace on their horses and the Moorish gentleman[108] who had brought them went with them.

Notes

Dedication

1 From *De las cosas memorables de España* (1539) online at: https://books.google.co.uk/books?id=ycuPOOMZ2usC&printsec=frontcover&hl=es#v=onepage&q&f=false

Abbreviations

2 Where capitalized, this follows referencing practice in the archive concerned.

Introduction

1 Following Hernando de Baeza, who knew and respected him, and for the sake of clarity in a work steeped in Castilian rather than Arabic sources, I refer to him as 'Boabdil'.
2 Baeza: 46. 'de derecho could also be translated as 'legally' – an even stronger statement. Quotes from Baeza's work refer to the numbered sections in my translation which appears on pp. 125–46.
3 Miguel Ángel Ladero, *Los mudéjares de Castilla*, (Granada, 1989), pp. 151–6.
4 Miguel Ángel Ladero (ed.), *La incorporación de Granada a la Corona de Castilla*, (Granada, 1993).
5 José Rodríguez Molina, 'Libre determinación religiosa en la frontera de Granada', *Estudios de Frontera 2*, (Alcalá la Real, 1998), pp. 693–708; Diego Melo Carrasco, 'Algunas consideraciones en torno a la frontera, la tregua y libre determinación en la frontera castellano-granadina S. XIII–XV', *Estudios de Historia de España*, 14 (2012), 114–18.
6 Isabelle Poutrin, 'The Jewish Precedent in the Spanish Politics of Conversion of Muslims and Moriscos', *Journal of Levantine Studies*, 6 (2016), 71–87.
7 Marcel Bataillon, *Erasmo y España*, (Mexico, 1966); Stefania Pastore, *Una herejía española, conversos alumbrados e Inquisición (1449–1559)*, (Madrid, 2010); Bruce Rosenstock, 'Against the Pagans: Alonso de Cartagena, Francisco de Vitoria and converso political theology', in Amy Aronson-Friedman and Gregory Kaplan (eds.), *Marginal Voices*, (Leiden, 2012), pp. 117–40; Gregory Kaplan, 'Towards the establishment of Christian identity: the conversos and early Castilian humanism', *La Corónica*, 25 (1996), 53–68.
8 Alain Milhou detects the same combination of humility and pride in Christopher Columbus: *Colón y su mentalidad mesiánica en el ambiente franciscanista español*, (Valladolid, 1983), pp. 91–2.

9 Concepción Villanueva Morte and Álvaro Fernández de Córdova Miralles, *El Embajador Claver: diplomacia y conflicto en las 'Guerras de Italia' (1495-1504)*, (Madrid, 2020).

10 Manuel Fernández Álvarez, 'La crisis del nuevo estado', *HEMP*, 17, 2, (Madrid, 1969), pp. 643-729; José Szmolka Clares, 'Nobleza y autoritarismo en Andalucía. La contribución de Granada a la sumisión del estamento nobiliario andaluz, 1504-1510', *Cuadernos de Estudios Medievales*, 6-7 (1981), 293; Antonio Álvarez-Ossorio, 'Razón de linaje y lesa majestad. El Gran Capitán, Venecia y la corte de Fernando el Católico (1507-1509)', in Ernest Berlenguer (ed.), *De la unión de las coronas al Imperio de Carlos V*, 3, (Madrid, 2001), pp. 385-451.

11 The identification of the author with this individual is compelling, though not completely conclusive. The plentiful evidence on which I have based my judgement is set out in 'Esbozo biográfico', Juan Pablo Rodríguez Argente del Castillo, Teresa Tinsley and José Rodríguez Molina (eds.), *La Relación de Hernando de Baeza sobre el Reino de Granada*, (Alcalá la Real, 2018), pp. 31-40. However, Mercedes Delgado, having first proposed a similar hypothesis in her 2012 doctoral thesis, has since rejected it, although at time of writing she has not brought forward any credible alternative: 'La *Historia de los Reyes Moros de Granada*, de Hernando de Baeza. Una crónica entre el romance de frontera, la autobiografía y la leyenda', *Philología Hispalensis*, 31, 2 (2017), 15-36. Should evidence emerge in future that suggests that our author is not who we think he is, we can be sure that it was someone very like him, and the insights provided into the times in which he lived will remain valid.

12 Maureen Flynn, 'Mimesis of the last judgement, the Spanish *auto de fe*', *Sixteenth Century Journal*, 22, 2 (1991), 281-97.

13 Rafael Gracia Boix, 'Los autos de fe de la Inquisición', *BRAC*, 105 (1983), 75-6.

14 Henry Kamen, *The Spanish Inquisition. An Historical Revision*, (London, 1997), pp. 200-1.

15 Luis Suarez Fernández, *Los Reyes Católicos. Fundamentos de la monarquía*, (Madrid, 1989), p. 28.

16 Manuel Peña Díaz, *Las Españas que (no) pudieron ser. Herejías, exilios y otras conciencias (s.XVI-XX)*, (Huelva, 2009), p. 14; Peter Burke, *Exiles and expatriates in the history of knowledge, 1500-2000*, (Lebanon, NH, 2017).

17 Baeza: 6-7.

18 'por matar los Bencerrajes que eran la flor de Granada/acogiste a los judíos de Córdoba la nombrada/degollaste un caballero persona muy estimada': quoted by Eugenia Fosalba Vela, 'Sobre la verdad de los Abencerrajes', *Butlletí de la Reial Acadèmia de les Bones Lletres de Barcelona*, 48 (2001), 330.

19 Alain Milhou, *Pouvoir royal et absolutisme dans l'Espagne du XVIième siècle*, (Toulouse, 1999), especially chapter titled 'Propaganda mesiánica y opinión pública', pp. 33-44.

20 For example, the remonstrations of the official ordered to execute the emir's own son and later, the contrivances of courtiers having to tell the emir that it had been carried out: Baeza: 30, 32.

21 María Concepción Quintanilla, *Nobleza y señoríos en el Reino de Córdoba: la casa de Aguilar (siglos IV-XV)*, (Córdoba, 1979).

22 Pilar Rábade Obradó, *Una élite de poder en la corte de los Reyes Católicos. Los judeoconversos*, (Madrid, 1993)and 'La élite judeoconversa de la Corte de los Reyes Católicos y el negocio fiscal', *En la España medieval*, 37, (2014), 205-22; Miguel

Ángel Ladero, 'Fray Hernando de Talavera en 1492: de la corte a la misión', *Chronica Nova*, 34 (2008), 249–75.
23 Baeza: 18.
24 Although Baeza's letters contain a few set phrases in Latin, there is no indication that he had received instruction in the language and documents issued by the *Gran Capitán* in Latin are written in a different hand.
25 Domínguez Ortiz, *La clase social de los conversos en Castilla en la edad moderna*, (Madrid, 1955), p. 61; Tarsicio Azcona, La elección y reforma del episcopado español en tiempo de los Reyes Católicos, (Madrid, 1960); Fernando Villaseñor, 'Los códices iluminados de Arias Dávila', in Carlos Hernando Sánchez (ed.), *Roma y España un crisol de la cultura europea en la Edad Moderna*, (Madrid, 2007), pp. 155–72.
26 Carlos Hernando Sánchez, 'Un tratado español sobre la corte de Roma en 1504: Baltasar del Río y la sátira anticortesana' in *Roma y España*, pp. 189–238.
27 Juan Gil, *Los conversos y la Inquisición sevillana*, 2, (Seville, 2000), pp. 118–20.
28 Felipe Fernández Armesto, *1492. El nacimiento de la modernidad* (Barcelona, 2010), is a case in point.
29 Miguel Ángel Ladero, Los últimos años de Fernando el Católico, 1505–1517, segunda edición, (Madrid, 2019); Andrew Devereux, *The Other Side of Empire. Just War in the Mediterranean and the Rise of Early Modern Spain*, (Ithaca, 2020).
30 For example, Henry Kamen, 'Fernando el Católico, el absolutismo y la Inquisición', in Aurora Egido and José Enrique Laplana (eds.), *La imagen de Fernando el Católico en la Historia, la Literatura y el Arte*, (Zaragoza, 2014), pp. 15–28, also Ladero, *Los últimos años*.
31 José Enrique López de Coca Castañer, 'La conquista de Granada. El testimonio de los vencidos', *Norba*, 18 (2005), 33–50.
32 Stephen Gilman, *The Spain of Fernando de Rojas: the intellectual landscape of 'La Celestina'*, (Princeton, 1972).
33 Gerónimo Zurita, 'Historia del Rey D. Fernando el Católico de las empresas y ligas de Italia', *Las Glorias Nacionales*, V, (Madrid, 1853), pp. 992; 'Crónica Manuscrita' in Antonio Rodríguez Villa, *Crónicas del Gran Capitán*, (Sevilla, 1908), p. 389.

Chapter 1

1 ACS. ELS. A-8, 1588.f. 27r.
2 Pedro Barrantes Maldonado, *Crónica del Rey Don Enrique III*, (Madrid, 1868), pp. 15–16.
3 Ibid., p. 27.
4 Quotation from David Nirenberg, *Anti-Judaism. The Western Tradition* (New York, 2014), p. 227. See also John Edwards, 'Religious Belief and Social Conformity: the "converso" Problem in Late-Medieval Cordoba', *Transactions of the Royal Historical Society*, 31 (1981), 115–28; Philip Daileader, *Saint Vincent Ferrer. His World and Life. Religion and Society in Late Medieval Europe*, (New York, 2016), pp. 111–28. For a fuller bibliography: Isabel Montes Romero-Camacho, 'El problema converso. Una aproximación historiográfica (1998–2008)', *Medievalismo*, 18 (2008), 109–247.
5 John Edwards, *Religion and Society in Spain c. 1492*, (Aldershot, 1996), chapter titled 'The Beginnings of a Scientific Theory of Race? Spain, 1450–1600', pp. 625–36; David

Nirenberg, 'Mass Conversion and Genealogical Mentalities: Jews and Christians in Fifteenth-Century Spain', *Past and Present*, 174 (2002), 1–39.

6 Ana Echevarría, *The Fortress of Faith. The Attitude Towards Muslims in Fifteenth-Century Spain* (Leiden, 1999); Rosa Vidal Doval, *Misera Hispania: Jews and Conversos in Alonso de Espina's Fortalitium Fidei*, (Oxford, 2013).

7 Bruce Rosenstock, *New Men: 'Conversos', Christian Theology and Society in Fifteenth-Century Spain*, (London, 2002) and 'Against the Pagans'; John Edwards, 'New light on the *converso* debate? The Jewish Christianity of Alfonso de Cartagena and Juan de Torquemada', in Simon Barton and Peter Linehan (eds.), *Cross, Crescent and Conversion. Studies on Medieval Spain and Christendom in Memory of Richard Fletcher* (Leiden, 2008), pp. 311–26; María Laura Giordano, '"La ciudad de nuestra conciencia". Los conversos y la construcción de la identidad judeocristiana (1449–1556)', *Hispania Sacra*, 125 (2010), 43–91; Pastore, *Una herejía*, pp. 43–8.

8 Albert Sicroff, 'El "Lumen ad revelationem gentium" de Alonso de Oropesa', *Actas del cuarto Congreso Internacional de Hispanistas*, 2 (Salamanca, 1982), pp. 655–65.

9 Sicroff, 'El "Lumen"', pp. 660–1.

10 Ibid., p. 654; Bataillon, *Erasmo*, pp. 60–1; Pastore, *Una herejía*.

11 Edwards, 'New light', p. 322; 'Juan de Torquemada', *DBE*. He was uncle of the future Inquisitor General, Tomás.

12 Kaplan, 'Toward the establishment'.

13 Manuel Parada López de Corselas and Jesús R. Folgado García, 'Jan van Eyck, Alonso de Cartagena, y *La Fuente de la Gracia*', *Boletín del Museo del Prado*, 53 (2017), 16–31.

14 José Manuel Escobar Camacho, 'La Córdoba de Los Reyes Católicos', *Arte, arqueología e historia*, 2012, 83–96.

15 Pedro Ramírez de Baeza: AGS.MP, Leg 41, f.25; AGA.Priego,1115/152-160; AGS. RGS.LEG.147504.419; Gonzalo Rodríguez de Baeza: AGS.RGS.LEG,147711.295: AGS.EMR.MER.2.F.153-154; see also Manuel González Jimenez, Ricardo Córdoba de la Llave et al., *Libro Primero de las Ordenanzas de Cordoba*, (Cordoba, 2016), pp. 64, 203, 275, 336, 549; Juan de Baeza: AGS.RGS.LEG.147711.299; Javier López Rider, 'Aportación al estudio de la hacienda del concejo de Córdoba a fines de la Edad Media', *HID*, 41 (2014), 312.

16 Alonso de Palencia, *Crónica de Enrique IV*, (Madrid, 1905), p. 108; Diego de Valera, 'Memorial de diversas hazañas: crónica de Enrique IV', in Cayetano Rosell (ed.), *Crónicas de los Reyes de Castilla*, (Madrid, 1878), p. 78; Andrés Bernáldez, *Historia de los Reyes Católicos*, (Granada, 1856), p. 99.

17 ACS. ELS. A-8, 1588.f. 27r.

18 Margarita Cabrera Sánchez, *Nobleza, oligarquía y poder en Córdoba a final de la Edad Media*, (Cordoba, 1998), p. 354.

19 For example, Juan de Baeza: AGS. ERM.41,25; RAH. M-48, ff.224 and 227; AGS.RGS. LEG.148901.253, 363 and 379; AGA. Priego, 1132/154.

20 Emilio Cabrera Muñoz, 'Los conversos de Baena en el siglo XV', *Meridies*, V–VI (2002), 245. Various members of the Baeza family are recorded in regular attendance at council meetings: AMC. Actas capitulares, 1479, SF/L 00001.

21 AGS.RGS.LEG.147711.299 and 295; AGS.EMR.MER.2.F.153-154; Priego,1062/535-536; Manuel Nieto Cumplido, 'Miembros del concejo de Córdoba, 1300–1475', *Archivo de La Catedral de Córdoba. Inventarios y Estudios*, (Cordoba, 2012), p. 37.

22   Nicholas Round, 'La rebelión toledana de 1449', *Archivum*, 16 (1966), 385–446; Eloy Benito Ruano, *Los orígenes del problema converso*, (Madrid, 2001), pp. 41–71.
23   Albert Sicroff, *Los estatutos de limpieza de sangre. Controversías entre los siglos XV y XVII* (Newark, 2010).
24   Albert Sicroff, 'The Jeronymite Monastery of Guadalupe in Fourteenth and Fifteenth-Century Spain', in Marcel Hornick (ed.), *Collected Studies in Honour of Américo Castro's Eightieth Year*, (Oxford, 1965), pp. 397–422.
25   Albert Sicroff, 'Clandestine Judaism in the Hieronymite monastery of Nuestra Señora de Guadalupe', in Izaak Langnas (ed.), *Studies in Honor of M. J. Benardete*, (New York, 1965), pp. 89–125; Gretchen Starr-Le Beau, *In the Shadow of the Virgin. Inquisitors, friars and conversos in Guadalupe*, (Princeton, 2003).
26   Baeza: 20.
27   Manuel Nieto Cumplido, *Infancia y juventud del Gran Capitán (1453–1481)*, (Cordoba, 2015), p. 68.
28   Ibid., pp. 120–1.
29   Soledad Gómez Navarro, *Mirando al cielo sin dejar el suelo: Los jerónimos cordobeses de Valparíso en el Antiguo Régimen*, (Madrid, 2014), p. 404.
30   AHPC.10295P, ff.1-26.
31   José de Sigüenza, *Historia de la Orden de San Jerónimo*, 2, (Madrid, 1907), p. 263.
32   John Edwards, *Christian Córdoba: The City and Its Region in the late Middle Ages*, (Cambridge, 1982); Manuel Nieto Cumplido, *Historia de Córdoba: Islam y Christianismo*, (Cordoba, 1984).
33   Brian Tate, 'La historiografía del reinado de los Reyes Católicos', in Juan Antonio González Iglesias and Carmen Codoñer Merino (ed.), *Antonio de Nebrija, Edad Media y Renacimiento*, (Salamanca, 1994), p. 288.
34   Isabel del Val Valdivieso, 'Los bandos nobiliarios durante el reinado de Enrique IV', *Hispania*, 35 (1975), (249–94); Margarita Cabrera Sánchez, 'Los regidores de Córdoba en 1480. Aproximación prosopográfica' *Meridies*, 3 (1996), 61–88.
35   Quintanilla, *Nobleza*, p. 116.
36   Juan Gómez Bravo, *Catálogo de los Obispos de Córdoba*, (Cordoba, 1778), p. 351.
37   Nieto Cumplido, *Infancia y juventud*, p. 80; Cabrera Sánchez, *Nobleza*, p. 37. María Concepción Quintanilla, 'El dominio de las ciudades por la nobleza. El caso de Cordoba', *En la España Medieval*, 10 (1987), 109–24.
38   Quintanilla, *Nobleza*, p. 116, quoting from a document in the Archivo Ducal de Medinaceli which I have been unable to track down.
39   'Catálogo de los documentos del Monasterio de San Jerónimo de Valparaíso', *Inventarios y estudios*, (Biblioteca de la Catedral de Córdoba, 2006). The document, dated 1 July 1472, excommunicates Juan de Baeza, Fernando de Baeza, Gonzalo Rodríguez de Baeza and his son Alfonso.
40   Ibid.
41   'Mandato de los Inquisidores' dated 2 January 1481: Fidel Fita Colomé, 'Nuevas fuentes para escribir la historia de los judíos españoles', *BRAH*, 15 (1889), 447–9.
42   Palencia, *Crónica*, p. 108; De Valera, *Memorial*, p. 78; Bernáldez, *Historia*, p. 99. See also: Miguel Angel Ladero, *La hacienda real de Castilla en el siglo XV*, (La Laguna, 1973); Edwards, *Christian Córdoba*, pp. 58–92.
43   AHN. Inquisición, 1515, Exp. 2, f. 603v. I am grateful to the late Joaquín Zejalbo for drawing my attention to this file, which has been invaluable for exploring Hernando de Baeza's geneaology; Ana Echevarría, *Knights on the Frontier*, (Leiden, 2009), p. 128.

44 José Damián González Arce, 'La evolución del almojarifazgo de Córdoba entre los siglos XIII y XV', *En la España medieval*, 37 (2014), 165–204; López Rider, 'Aportación', p. 281; AGA.Priego. 1115/152-160. Sancho Sánchez also collected tax in Jaén: AGS. RGS. 147705,191,2. González Arce (192) refers to Gonzalo Fernández de Baeza, someone whose name does not appear elsewhere in connection with this. However, I believe that the surname 'Fernández' is either a mistake in the original document or a transcription error since there is evidence elsewhere that Gonzalo 'Rodríguez' de Baeza and Sancho Sánchez de Córdoba were collaborating at this time over tax collecting: AHNOB. Luque.C.116.D.65.
45 González Arce, 'La evolución', 192–3.
46 López Rider, 'Aportación', 281.
47 José Enrique Ruiz Domènec, *El Gran Capitán. Retrato de una época*, (Barcelona, 2001), pp. 46–60.
48 Rafael Ramírez de Arrellano, *Historia de Córdoba desde su fundación hasta la muerte de Isabel la católica*, 3–4, (Ciudad Real, 1917), p. 237
49 John Edwards, 'The "Massacre" of Jewish Christians in Cordoba, 1473–1474', in Mark Leven and Penny Roberts (eds.), *The Massacre in History*, (New York, 1999), pp. 55–68; Manuel Nieto Cumplido, 'La revuelta contra los conversos de Córdoba de 1473', in *Homenaje a Antón de Montoro en el V centenario de su muerte* (Montoro, 1977), pp. 41–9; Margarita Cabrera Sánchez, 'El problema converso en Córdoba. El incidente de la Cruz del Rastro', in Manuel González Jiménez (ed.), *La Península Ibérica en la Era de los Descubrimientos* (1391–1492), (Sevilla, 1997), pp. 331–9; Norman Roth, 'Anti-converso riots of the fifteenth century, Pulgar and the Inquisition', *En la España Medieval*, 15 (1992), 367–94.
50 Palencia, *Crónica*, p. 112.
51 RGS.LEG.147711.295 and 299.
52 ACS. ELS. A-8, 1588.f. 23r.
53 Francisco Fernández de Béthencourt, *Historia genealógica y heráldica de la monarquía española*, 6 (Madrid, 1905), p. 99.
54 Palencia, *Crónica*, p. 114; Antón de Montoro, *A Don Alonso de Aguilar cuando la destrucción de los conversos de Córdoba*, (Madrid, 1989); Francisco Fernández de Córdoba, 'Historia y descripción de la antigüedad y descendencia de la Casa de Córdova', *Boletín de la Real Academia de Córdoba* (*BRAC*), 74 (1956), 142.
55 John Edwards, 'Nobleza y religión. Don Alonso de Aguilar (1447–1501)', *Ambitos*, 3 (2000), 16–17.
56 José Amador de Los Ríos, *Historia social, política y religiosa de los judíos*, (Madrid, 1876), p. 639; Luis Maraver y Alfaro, *Historia de Córdoba*, 12, p. 195: online at https://biblioteca.cordoba.es/index.php/biblio-digital/manuscritos/503-manuscrito-maraver-alfaro.html (accessed 2 March 2021).
57 José Rodríguez Molina, 'Tendencia integradora del Gran Capitán con moros y judíos', in Francisco Toro Ceballos (ed.), *Los Fernández de Córdoba*, (Alcalá la Real, 2018), pp. 497–522.
58 'Catálogo de la exposición de recuerdos de la vida del Gran Capitán', *BRAC*, 69 (1953), p. 215; L. de Torre and R. Rodríguez Pascual, 'Cartas y documentos relativos al Gran Capitán', *RABM*, 34 (1916), p. 312.
59 AGA. Priego.1132/154-157.
60 'Catálogo Monasterio de San Jerónimo de Valparaíso', document dated 1 August 1472.

61　APNC.14120P. cuaderno 8, f.12v; Ibid., 14111P, cuaderno 4 (1473–4), f.29v. cited by Nieto Cumplido, *Infancia y juventud*, p. 177.
62　AHN. Baena. C. 158.D 60–68, digital image 42.
63　Ibid., image 47.
64　Ibid., image 28; Baeza: 20
65　Ruiz Domènec, *El Gran Capitán*, pp. 89–90.
66　Paulina Rufo Ysern, 'Los Reyes Católicos y la pacificación de Andalucía (1475–1480)', *HID*, 15 (1988), 217–50; Suárez Fernández, *Fundamentos*, p. 75.
67　RGS.LEG.1477 and 1478 passim.
68　AGS. RGS.LEG.147801,65; AGS.RGS.LEG.147711.299; AGS.RGS.LEG.147711.295; AGS.RGS.LEG.147801.4; ibid., 85; AGS.RSG.LEG.147712.398; 1115/152-160.
69　AGS.RGS.LEG.147809.1.
70　AGS.CCA.PUE.6.2.D.227.
71　Pilar Ostos-Salcedo, *Notariado, documentos notariales y Pedro Gonzalez de Hoces, veinticuatro de Córdoba*, (Sevilla, 2005).
72　AGA. Priego. 1115/162; AHN. CLERO-SECULAR/REGULAR, 483.
73　Kamen, *The Spanish Inquisition*, p. 43.
74　Pastore, *Una herejía*, pp. 75–7.
75　Francisco de Medina y Mendoza, 'Vida del Cardenal D. Pedro Gonzalez De Mendoça', in *Memorial Histórico Español*, 6, (Madrid, 1853)
76　Juan Antonio Llorente, *Historia critica de la Inquisición*, 1, (Barcelona, 1870); Henry Charles Lea, *A History of the Inquisition in Spain*, 1, (London, 1906), pp. 89–94; Ángel Alcalá, *Judios. Sefarditas. Conversos. La expulsión de 1492 y su consecuencia*, (Valladolid, 1995); Francisco Márquez Villanueva, 'Conversos y cargos concejiles en el siglo XV', *Revista de Archivos, Bibliotecas y Museos*, 63 (1957), 504–40.
77　Gómez Navarro, *Mirando el cielo*, p. 407.
78　Rafael Gracia Boix, *Autos de Fe y causas de la Inquisición en Córdoba*, (Cordoba, 1982), pp. 1–4. See also Luis Maraver y Alfaro, who believes his conviction was revenge for one of his servants having killed the Inquisition's constable. *Historia de Córdoba: desde los más remotos tiempos hasta nuestros días*, 12, pp. 351–62. Digitalised manuscript available online at https://biblioteca.cordoba.es/index.php/biblio-digital/manuscritos/503-manuscrito-maraver-alfaro/1891-maraver-alfaro-t12.html (last accessed 3 January 22).
79　AGS.RGS.LEG.148410.206
80　AGS.ERM.MER.116.
81　AGS.RGS.LEG.148504.41; AGS.RGS.LEG.148507.45; Gómez Navarro, *Mirando al cielo*, p. 407.
82　AGS.RGS.LEG.148507.45.
83　AGS.RGS.LEG.149102.233.
84　John Edwards, *Inquisition*, (Slough, 2009), pp. 98–9.
85　AGS.RGS.LEG.148803.6 and 148901.253.
86　AGS.RGS.LEG.148901.379.
87　AGA.Priego.1116/613-619.
88　Ibid.
89　ADM. Leg. 199, 23 August 1504.
90　AGS. RGS.LEG.149102.233.
91　Stephen Gilman, 'A generation of "conversos"', *Romance Philology*, 33, 1 (1979), 87–101.
92　Ruiz Domènec, *El Gran Capitán*, p. 126.

93 Michael Agnew, 'The Silences of Fernando de Pulgar in his "Crónica de los Reyes Católicos"', *Revista de estudios hispánicos*, 36 (2002), 477–99.
94 Nicholas Henshall, *The Myth of Absolutism*, (London, 1992), pp. 123–5.
95 Antonio Domínguez Ortiz, *La clase social de los conversos en Castilla en la edad moderna*, (Madrid, 1955); Julio Caro Baroja, *Los judíos en la España moderna y contemporánea, 1* (Madrid, 1986); John Edwards, 'Religious faith and doubt in Late Medieval Spain: Soria circa 1450–1500', *Past and Present*, 120, (1988), 3–35.
96 Miguel Ángel Ladero, 'Sociedad y poder real en tiempos de Isabel la Católica', *Medievalismo*, 13–14 (2004), 11–28.
97 Francisco Cantera Burgos, 'Fernando del Pulgar and the conversos', in Roger Highfield (ed.), *Spain in the Fifteenth Century, 1369–1516*, (London, 1972); Norman Roth, *Conversos, Inquisition and the Expulsion of the Jews from Spain*, (Wisconsin, 2002), pp. 108–14.
98 Ibid.; Juan de Mata Carriazo, 'Estudio preliminar', in Fernando del Pulgar (ed.), *Crónica de los Reyes Católicos*, (Madrid, 1943), pp. xlix–lviii.
99 Pastore, *Una herejía*, pp. 98–113; 'Juan de Lucena', *DBE;* Juan Antonio Llorente, *Anales de la Inquisición de España*, (Madrid, 1812), pp. 288–97.
100 Fernández de Córdoba, 'Historia y descripción', 74, 140. 'As a dog returneth to his vomit, so a fool returneth to his folly', *Proverbs*, 26:11.
101 AHN, Inquisición, 1515, Exp.2, f.603r.
102 Fernández de Córdoba, 'Historia y descripción', 74, 140.
103 Juan de Mata Carriazo, *En la Frontera de Granada*, (Granada, 1971); Manuel García Fernández, 'La alteridad en la frontera de Granada (siglo XIII al XV), 'in Manuel García Fernández and Carlos Alberto González Sánchez (eds.), *Andalucía y Granada en tiempos de los Reyes Católicos*, (Seville, 2006), pp. 87–110; José Rodríguez Molina, *La vida de moros y cristianos en la frontera*, (Alcalá la Real, 2007).
104 Fernández de Córdoba, 'Historia y descripción', *BRAC*, 73, (1955), 120.
105 Carriazo, *En la frontera*, pp. 85–142.
106 Roser Salicrú i Lluch, *El sultanat de Granada i la Corona d'Aragó, 1410–1458*, (Barcelona, 1998), pp. 399, 410, and 444.
107 Baeza: 6.
108 Echevarría, *Knights*, p. 192.
109 Rodríguez Molina, *Vida de moros*, p. 342.
110 Juan de Mata Carriazo, *Hechos del Condestable Don Miguel Lucas de Iranzo*, (Madrid, 1940), p. 443, and 'Las últimas treguas con Granada', *Boletín del Instituto de Estudios Giennenses*, 3 (1953), 11–43. For this reason, I reject Mercedes Delgado's suggestion that Baeza may have been a *criado* of the Count of Cabra: 'Historia de los Reyes Moros', p. 24.
111 Emilio Lafuente y Alcantara (in the same volume as Hernando de Baeza's memoir), *Relaciones de algunos sucesos de los últimos tiempos del Reino de Granada* (Madrid, 1868), pp. 71–152.
112 Ibid., p. 83.
113 Baeza: 10.
114 Ibid., p. 9.
115 Joaquín Durán y Lerchundi, *La toma de Granada, y caballeros que concurrieron a ella*, 1, (Madrid, 1893), pp. 329–41; Francisco Fernández de Béthencourt, *Historia genealógica y heráldica de la monarquía española*, 6, pp. 82–101.

116 José Enrique López de Coca, 'Notas y comentarios a unas cartas del secretario Francisco de Madrid sobre la revuelta de Sierra Bermeja (1500–1501)', *CEHGR*, 18 (2006), 189–208.
117 Ibid., p. 207.

Chapter 2

1 Baeza: 46.
2 Miguel Ángel Ladero, *La Guerra de Granada (1482–1491)*, (Granada, 2007), pp. 45–7.
3 Baeza: 15.
4 Baeza: 38.
5 ADM. AH.Leg. 198: letter from the monarchs to Don Alonso de Aguilar, February 1485.
6 José Rodríguez Molina, 'Relaciones pacíficas en la frontera con el Reino de Granada', in Pedro Segura Artero (ed.), *Actas del Congreso la Frontera Oriental Nazarí como Sujeto Histórico (S. XIII-XVI)*, (1997), p. 270; José María Ruiz Povedano, 'Alcaudete, una villa señorial de frontera al final de la edad media', in *Colección de documentos para la historia de Alcaudete (1240–1516)*, (Jaén, 2009), pp. 95–116.
7 Juan Antonio López Cordero, 'Alcaudete (Jaén), refugio de la mujer transgresora en época bajomedieval', in Manuel Cabrera Espinosa and Juan Antonio López Cordero (eds.), *IV Congreso virtual sobre historia de las mujeres*, (Jaén, 2012), pp. 1–9.
8 Ruiz Povedano, *Colección de documentos*, especially documents 152, 166, 172, 197, and 208.
9 Gracia Boix, *Autos*, p. 1.
10 AGS.RGS.LEG.148411.80.
11 RGS.LEG.148504.328: published in Ruiz Povedano, *Colección de documentos*, pp. 371–5. Alonso de Palencia, *Guerra de Granada* (ed. Rafael Peinado Santaella, Granada, 1998), pp. 62–8.
12 Manuel Colmeiro, *Cortes de los antiguos reinos de León y de Castilla*, Madrid, 1883, ch. XXI. http://www.cervantesvirtual.com/obra-visor/cortes-de-los-antiguos-reinos-de-leon-y-de-castilla-2/html/fefc50d0-82b1-11df-acc7-002185ce6064_102.html#I_37_ (accessed 2 March 2021).
13 Lorenzo Padilla Mellado, 'Determinación de las dubdas de las cuentas que tenían presentes los alhaqueques en la frontera de la cuidad de Jahén y el Reino de Granada (1488)', in Toro Ceballos and Rodríguez Molina (eds.), *Estudios de Frontera 9*, p. 524; Carriazo, *En la frontera*, p. 253; AGS.RGS.LEG.149404,80.
14 Miguel Ángel Ladero, *Granada. Historia de un país islámico (1232–1571)*, (2nd edn. Madrid, 1979), p. 159; Ana Echevarria, 'Trujamanes and Scribes: Interpreting Mediation in Iberian Royal Courts', in van der Höh, Marc et al. (eds.), *Cultural brokers at Mediterranean courts in the Middle Ages*, (Munich, 2013), p. 90.
15 José García Antón, 'La tolerancia religiosa en la frontera de Murcia y Granada en los últimos tiempos del Reino Nazarí', *Revista Murgetana*, 57 (1980), 133–43; Rodríguez Molina, 'Libre determinación'.
16 Melo Carrasco, 'Algunas consideraciones'.
17 Robert Burns (ed.), *Las Siete Partidas, Volume 5: Underworlds: The Dead, the Criminal, and the Marginalized (Partidas VI and VII)*, (Pennsylvania, 2001); see also Partida VII, título XXV, ley II quoted in Poutrin, 'Los derechos de los vencidos', p. 21.

18 Palencia, *Crónica*, p. 112; Valera, *Memorial*, p. 78.
19 Maraver, Historia de Córdoba, 12, p. 190.
20 Tariq Barkawi, 'Connection and Constitution: Locating War and Culture in Globalisation Studies', *Globalizations*, 1, 2 (2004), 155–70.
21 Ladero, *Guerra*, pp. 50–1.
22 Baeza: 26. The document itself is not extant but there is a certificate referring to it dated 5 July 1483: AGS.PTR.LEG.11.DOC.8. See also Ruiz Domenec, *El Gran Capitán*, pp. 151–2.
23 Baeza: 1; L. P. Harvey, *Islamic Spain 1250–1500*, (Chicago, 1992), pp. 26–8.
24 Rodríguez Molina, 'Tendencia integradora', p. 516.
25 Ladero, *Guerra*, p. 104.
26 Juan de Mata Carriazo, 'Historia de la guerra de Granada', *HEMP*, 17 (Madrid, 1968), p. 515.
27 Mariano Gaspar y Remiro, 'Ultimos pactos y correspondencia íntima entre los Reyes Católicos y Boabdil', (Granada, 1905), p. 105; 'Capitulación de la toma e entrega de Granada', *CODOIN* 8, 435.The document states 'su hijo de Alhadramín' – a double possessive which has frequently been misread to mean Boabdil's son.
28 Fernando de la Granja, 'Condena de Boabdil por los alfaquíes de Granada', *Al-Andalus*, 36 (1971), 145–76.
29 Baeza: 38.
30 María Concepción Quintanilla, *Títulos, grandes del reino y grandeza en la sociedad política. Fundamentos en la Castilla medieval*, (Madrid, 2006), pp. 63–95.
31 Baeza: 29.
32 Hernando del Pulgar, *Crónica de los Señores Reyes Católicos*, (Valencia, 1780), p. 236.
33 Ladero, *Guerra*, p. 54; Rodríguez Molina, 'Tendencia integradora', p. 516.
34 Baeza: 15; Hernán Pérez Del Pulgar, 'Breve parte de las hazañas del Gran Capitán', in Antonio Rodríguez Villa (ed.), *Crónicas del Gran Capitán*, (Madrid, 1908), pp. 56, 573. This individual is not to be confused with the royal chronicler: see Hernán Pérez del Pulgar, *DBE*.
35 Mariano Gaspar Remiro, *Documentos árabes de la corte nazarí de Granada*, (Madrid, 1911), pp. 32–5; Ladero, *Guerra*, p. 58.
36 Ladero, *Guerra*, p. 109.
37 Pérez del Pulgar, 'Breve parte', p. 573. This account conflicts with the royal chronicler's, who says that the Marquis of Cadiz and Don Alonso de Aguilar negotiated on behalf of Fernando with men representing Boabdil, who was injured: Pulgar, *Crónica*, pp. 275–6.
38 Salar, 30 May 1486; Íllora, 9 June, Moclín 16 June, and Colomera 19 June: Miguel Ángel Ladero, *Castilla y la conquista del Reino de Granada*, (Valladolid, 1969), p. 44.
39 Francisco Toro Ceballos, *El discurso genealógico de Sancho de Aranda*, (Alcalá la Real, 1993), pp. 147–8.
40 Pulgar, *Crónica*, p. 289; Palencia, *Guerra*, p. 272; AGS. RGS. LEG.149008,8.
41 Pérez del Pulgar, 'Breve parte', p. 563; Gaspar y Remiro, 'Últimos tratos', p. 23; Carriazo, 'Historia de la guerra', pp. 727–33; Ladero, *Castilla y la conquista*, p. 48.; Toro Ceballos, *El discurso genealógico*, p. 149.
42 Bernáldez ignores it altogether; although Palencia mentions it, he presents it as a short-term task and finish assignment commissioned by Fernando: *Guerra*, p. 297. Pulgar only mentions Fernán Alvarez (*Crónica*, p. 289); however, the anonymous chronicler who continued his narrative does refer to Fernández de Córdoba and Alarcón's activity in the Albaicín: *Crónicas de los Reyes de Castilla*, (Madrid, 1878), p. 514.

43 Gaspar Remiro, *Documentos árabes*, p. 38; Ladero, *Castilla y la conquista*, p. 46.
44 Pérez del Pulgar, 'Breve parte', pp. 562–5.
45 Baeza: 38.
46 Ibid.
47 Pérez del Pulgar, 'Breve parte', p. 577.
48 Ibid.
49 Miguel Garrido Atienza, *Las Capitulaciones para la entrega de Granada*, (Granada, 1910), pp. 71–2.
50 Ladero, *Guerra*, p. 64.
51 Baeza: 38.
52 See, for example, Julio Quesada Cañaveral y Piedrola, *Boabdil: Granada y la Alhambra hasta el Siglo XVI*, (Granada, 1925), who pictures Baeza reading and translating Castilian stories to him, p. 63.
53 Pulgar, *Crónica*, p. 349; Ladero, *Castilla y la conquista*, pp. 31 and 46; Baeza: 15.
54 AGA. Priego 1001/368-390.
55 Ladero, *Castilla y la conquista*, p. 54.
56 Baeza: 42.
57 Ibid.; Ladero, *Castilla y la conquista*, p. 62.
58 Ángel González Palencia, 'Adición a los documentos árabes del Cenete', *Al-Andalus*, 6 (1941), 477–80, p. 480. His family lived in Toledo and he acted as Boabdil's translator and go-between in the period between the handover of Granada and his departure from Spain in 1493: 'Capitulación de los Reyes Católicos con Muley Babdali' and associated documents: *CODOIN*, 8, pp. 439, 451, 455, 456, 460, 463.
59 Baeza: 42.
60 Gaspar y Remiro, 'Últimos pactos', p. 15.
61 Ladero, *Castilla y la conquista*, p. 63–5.
62 See, for example, Washington Irving, *Chronicle of the conquest of Granada*, (Teddington, 2007).
63 Ladero, *Castilla y la conquista*, p. 67.
64 Baeza: 44.
65 The two embassies to Fernando in Cordoba: AGS.CMC.L. 108, quoted in Ladero, *Castilla y la conquista*, p. 54; letter to the queen, in Arabic, acknowledging receipt of 'mercedes y beneficios' which she had sent with a man named Guzmán: Gaspar Remiro, *Documentos árabes*, p. 46; gifts sent in the spring of 1489, plus 50 Christian captives: Ibid., *Últimos pactos*, p. 411; letter to the monarchs dated 22 January 1490: p. 419.
66 Ibid., p. 28.
67 Baeza: 42. Further details and disambiguation regarding Aben Comixa: José Enrique López de Coca, 'Converso, hidalgo, fraile y renegado: don Juan de Granada Abencomixa', *HID*, 39, (2012), 129–51.
68 Baeza: 46.
69 Gaspar y Remiro, 'Últimos pactos', p. 10; Suárez Fernández, *El tiempo de la guerra*, pp. 241–2.
70 Baeza: 45.
71 Delgado, 'A newly-discovered manuscript', p. 562.
72 Baeza: 15; Ladero, *Castilla y la conquista*, p. 31.
73 Ibid., p. 46.
74 Palencia, *Guerra*, p. 240.
75 Baeza: 15.

76 Gaspar y Remiro, 'Últimos pactos', pp. 18, 33, 76; Padilla, 'Determinación'; José Enrique López de Coca, 'La emigración mudéjar al Reino de Granada en tiempo de los Reyes Católicos', *En la España Medieval*, 26 (2003), 208.

77 Raúl González Arévalo, 'Un molino en Deifontes (Granada). De Yuça de Mora a Ambrosio de Espíndola (1494)', *CEHGR*, 26 (2014), 459–72; María Amparo Moreno Trujillo, *La memoria de la ciudad. El primer libro de actas del cabildo de Granada (1497–1502)*, (Granada, 2005), p. 118.

78 Gaspar y Remiro, 'Últimos pactos'. On Zafra: Miguel Ángel Ladero, *Hernando de Zafra. Secretario de los Reyes Católicos*, (Madrid, 2005); Enrique Pérez Boyero, 'Hernando de Zafra: secretario real, oligarca granadino y señor de vasallos', *Miscelánea Medieval Murciana*, 18 (1993–4), 175–208.

79 Letter from Zafra to the Marquis of Villena, dated August 1490 in José Antonio García Luján, *Treguas, guerra y capitulaciones de Granada (1457–1491). Documentos del archivo de los Duques de Frías*, (Granada, 1998), p. 141; Pérez del Pulgar, 'Breve parte', p. 577.

80 Ibid.

81 Gaspar y Remiro, 'Últimos pactos', pp. 19–20.

82 Baeza: 46.

83 Mercedes Delgado Pérez, 'De Granada a Michoacán: Vasco de Quiroga y la génesis de un códice fronterizo', in Francisco Toro Ceballos y José Rodríguez Molina (eds.), *Estudios de Frontera*, 9, (Alcalá la Real, 2014), p. 179.

84 Pérez del Pulgar, 'Breve parte', pp. 561, 569.

85 van der Höh et al., *Cultural brokers*.

86 Medina y Mendoza, 'Vida del Cardenal', p. 290.

87 Gaspar y Remiro, 'Últimos pactos', pp. 79–80.

88 Baeza: 8.

89 Antonio de la Torre, *Cuentas de Gonzalo de Baeza, tesorero de Isabel la Católica*, (Madrid, 1955), p. 309. See also record in AGS.ERM.41.30. Fernán de Baeza seeking dispensation to marry Leonor de Molina, daughter of Gonzalo Gómez de Molina of Úbeda, because of blood ties: AHPC 14105, f.310r.

90 Baeza: 46.

91 Pérez del Pulgar, 'Breve parte', p. 577. There is no indication as to the date of this.

92 Emilio Cabrera Muñoz, 'Cautivos cristianos en el Reino de Granada durante la segunda mitad del siglo XV', in Segura Graíño (ed.), *Relaciones exteriores del Reino de Granada*, pp. 227–36.

93 See especially: Jerónimo Münzer, 'Viaje por España y Portugal en los años 1494 y 1495', *BRAH*, 84 (1924), pp. 100 & 117; Lucio Marineo Sículo, *Vida y hechos de los Reyes Católicos*, (Madrid, 1943), p. 119; Jerónimo Zurita, *Anales de Aragón*, 8, (Zaragoza, 1967), p. 603.

94 José María Ruiz Povedano, 'Exaltación y propaganda de la nueva monarquía hispánica con motivo de la conquista de Málaga (1487)', in *Andalucía Medieval: Actas del III Congreso de Historia de Andalucía*, 6, (Cordoba, 2003), pp. 475–6.

95 María Julieta Vega García-Ferrer, *Fray Hernando de Talavera y Granada*, (Granada, 2007), p. 287.

96 Baeza: 8.

97 Miguel Ángel Ladero, 'Limosnas, dádivas y liberaciones en torno a la toma de Granada (1490–1492)', *CEHGR*, 24 (2012), 3–31.

98 Ibid., 9.

99 Ibid., 22–3.

100 Ibid., 29.
101 Ibid., 25, 30.
102 Juan de Mata Carriazo, 'Continuación inédita de la "Relación" de Hernando de Baeza', *Al-Andalus*, 13, 2 (1948), 431–42; María del Carmen Pescador del Hoyo, 'Cómo fue de verdad la toma de Granada, a la luz de un documento inédito', *Al-Andalus*, 20, 2 (1955), 283–344.
103 Baeza: 46.
104 Garrido Atienza, *Las capitulaciones*. Gaspar Remiro, *Documentos árabes*; *Ultimos pactos*; Carriazo, 'Historia de la guerra de Granada'; Ladero, *Castilla y la conquista*; López de Coca, 'La conquista de Granada' and 'El reverso del Reino de Granada. La visión de los vencidos', in Luis Antonio Ribot and Julio Valdeón (eds.), *Isabel la Católica y su época*, 2, (Valladolid, 2007), pp. 955–83; Alfredo Bustani et al., *Fragmento de la época sobre noticias de los Reyes Nazaritas; o capitulacion de Granada y emigración de los andaluces a Marruecos*, (Morocco, 1940); Yolanda Moreno Koch, 'La conquista de Granada y la expulsión de Sefarad según las crónicas hispanohebreas', in *I Congreso de Historia de Andalucía. Andalucía Medieval*, 2, (Cordoba, 1978), pp. 329–37; Fernando Velázquez Basanta, 'La relación histórica sobre las postrimerías del Reino de Granada, según Ahmad al-Maqqarí (siglo XVII)', in Celia del Moral (ed.), *En el epílogo del islam andalusí. La Granada del siglo XV*, (Granada, 2002), pp. 481–554.
105 Ladero, *Granada. Historia de un país islámico* and *Granada después de la conquista. Repobladores y Mudéjares*, (Granada, 1988); José Enrique López de Coca Castañer, 'Las capitulaciones y la Granada mudéjar' in Ladero (ed.), *Incorporación*, pp. 263–305; José López Nevot, *La organización del municipio de Granada durante el siglo XVI (1492-1598)*, (Granada, 1994); David Coleman, *Creating Christian Granada: Society and Religious Culture in an Old-World Frontier City, 1492–1600*, (New York, 2003); Rafael Peinado Santaella, *Aristócratas Nazaríes y principales castellanos*, (Málaga, 2008).
106 Leopoldo Eguilaz Yanguas, *Reseña histórica de la conquista del Reino de Granada por los Reyes Católicos, según los cronistas árabes*, (Granada, 1894); Gaspar Remiro, Documentos árabes and Últimos pactos; Garrido Atienza, Las capitulaciones; L. P. Harvey, 'Chronicling the fall of Nasrid Granada', in Alan Deyermond (ed.), *Historical Literature in Medieval Iberia*, (London, 1996), p. 105.
107 Carriazo, 'Historia de la guerra', p. 727.
108 Baeza: 25.
109 Ruiz Domènec, *El Gran Capitán*, pp. 507 and 543.
110 Gaspar Remiro, *Documentos árabes*.
111 Diego Clemencín, *Elogio a la Reina Isabel la Católica*, (Madrid, 1820), pp. 377–8; Carriazo, 'Historia de la guerra', p. 733. I discuss this in my 'Esbozo Biográfico'.
112 Fernando del Pulgar, 'Tratado de los Reyes de Granada y su origen', in Antonio Valladares de Sotomayor (ed.), *Semanario erudito*, 11-2, (Madrid, 1788), p. 59. See chapter 7 for further discussion of Baeza's relationship with Pulgar.
113 Gaspar Remiro, *Documentos árabes*, p. 46.
114 Palencia, *Guerra*. Letter to Bishop of Astorga, pp. LXXV–XCVII.
115 Baeza: 45.
116 Ladero, 'Limosnas'.
117 Ibid., 16–22.
118 Ladero, 'Limosnas'. The 27 July entry says the cloth was given to Baeza ('<a Baeça>') while on 5 August the gift was 'Para <Baeça>'.

119 Ibid., 7.
120 On 3 November 1491 and again on the 18th: AHNOB. Luque. C. 145. D. 10; and C.498. D. 15-18.
121 Echevarría, 'Trujamanes', p. 79; Hilary Footitt and Mike Kelly, *Languages at War: Policies and Practices of Language Contacts in Conflict*, (Basingstoke, 2012).
122 Mike Kelly and Catherine Baker, *Interpreting the Peace: Peace Operations, Conflict and Language in Bosnia-Herzegovina*, (Basingstoke, 2013). No page numbers.
123 Mona Baker, *Translation and Conflict, a Narrative Account*, (Abingdon, 2006).
124 Carriazo, 'Historia de la guerra', pp. 849-71; López de Coca, 'Las capitulaciones'; Miguel Ángel Ladero, Granada después de la conquista: repobladores y mudéjares (Granada, 1993).
125 Juan Meseguer Fernández, 'Fernando de Talavera, Cisneros y la Inquisición en Granada', in Joaquín Pérez Villanueva (ed.), *La Inquisición Española. Nueva Visión, Nuevos Horizontes*, (Madrid, 1980), pp. 371-400; Antonio Cortes Peña, 'Mudéjares y moriscos granadinos, una visión dialéctica tolerancia-intolerancia', in *Granada 1492-1992: Del reino de Granada al futuro del mundo mediterráneo*, (Granada, 1995), pp. 87-114; Manuel Barrios Aguilera, *Granada Morisca: la convivencia negada*, (Granada, 2002); Harvey, *Islamic Spain*, pp. 307-23; Isabelle Poutrin, 'Los derechos de los vencidos: las capitulaciones de Granada (1491)', *Sharq al-Ándalus*, 19 (2008-9), 11-34.
126 Celia del Moral, 'La última misiva diplomática de al-Andalus: la risala de al-'Uqayli, enviada por Boabdil al sultán de Fez en demanda de asilo', in *En el epílogo del islam andalusí. La Granada del siglo XV*, (Granada, 2002), 201-59.
127 Discussed in detail in my article 'El Gran Capitán en las capitulaciones de Granada', *II Congreso Los Fernández de Córdoba*, (Alcalá la Real, 2021), 803-12.
128 Carriazo, 'Historia de la guerra', pp. 849-68; Poutrin, 'Los derechos', pp. 230-5.
129 Baeza: 46.
130 Palencia, *Guerra*, p. XCV; Baeza: 46.
131 Fernández de Córdoba, 'Historia y descripción', pp. 74, 146.
132 Baeza: 46.
133 Pérez del Pulgar, 'Breve parte', p. 572; Pulgar, *Crónica*, p. 217.
134 Palencia, *Guerra*, p. XCVI.
135 Raúl González Arévalo, 'Ecos de la toma de Granada', in *Homenaje al profesor Eloy Benito Ruano*, 1, (Murcia, 2010), p. 348; Carriazo, *En la frontera*, pp. 311-90.
136 Baeza: 46.
137 Pastore, *Una herejía*; Rosenstock, 'Against the Pagans'; Isabelle Poutrin, 'The Jewish Precedent'.
138 Baeza: 8.
139 José Goñi Gaztambide, 'La polémica sobre el bautismo de los moriscos a principios del siglo XVI', *Anuario de la Historia de la Iglesia*, 16 (2007), 209-15.
140 Francisco Martín Hernández (ed.), *Hernando de Talavera, Católica Impugnación*, (Barcelona, 1961), p. 106; Isabella Iannuzzi, *El poder de la palabra en el siglo XV: Fray Hernando de Talavera*, (Valladolid, 2009), pp. 337-52.
141 Goñi Gaztambide, 'La polemica'; José Gil Sanjuán, 'El parecer de Galíndez sobre los moriscos andaluces (año 1526)', *Baetica*, 11 (1988), 385-401.
142 Poutrin, 'The Jewish precedent', 77.
143 Poutrin's article, 'Los derechos', reviews the provisions of the *Capitulaciones* against canon law and argues that they were always designed to bring about conversion to Christianity.

144 Goñi Gaztambide, 'La polémica'.
145 Baeza: 1.
146 Giordano, 'La ciudad'.
147 See Chapter 6 for further discussion of Baeza´s manuscripts.
148 Poutrin, 'The Jewish precedent', 78-9.
149 Garrido Atienza, *Las Capitulaciones*, pp. 234 and 280; Meseguer Fernández, 'Fernando de Talavera'; Poutrin, 'Los derechos'.
150 Miguel Ángel Ladero, 'Mudéjares y repobladores en el Reino de Granada (1485-1501)', *Cuadernos de Historia Moderna*, 13 (1992), 47-71.
151 Pérez del Pulgar, 'Breve parte', p. 577.
152 Ruiz Domènec, *El Gran Capitán*, pp. 206-7.
153 Rafael Peinado Santaella,'"Cristo pelea por sus castellanos". El imaginario cristiano de la guerra de Granada', in Manuel Barrios Aguilera and José Antonio González Alcantud (eds.), *Las Tomas: Antropología histórica de la ocupación territorial del Reino de Granada*, (Granada, 2000), pp. 453-524.
154 Álvaro Fernández de Córdova Miralles, Alejandro VI y los Reyes Católicos: relaciones político-eclesiásticas, 1492-1503, (Rome, 2005), p. 146.
155 Rosana de Andrés, 'Las "entradas reales" castellanas en los siglos XIV y XV, según las crónicas de la época', *En la España Medieval*, 4 (1984), 47; Thomas Devaney, *Enemies in the Plaza. Urban spectacle and the end of Spanish Frontier culture, 1460-1492*, (Philadelphia, 2015).
156 See for example, the exterior walls of the Monastery of San Juan de los Reyes in Toledo, founded by the monarchs around this time.
157 Latin original and Castilian translation: Vega García, *Fray Hernando de Talavera*, pp. 257-97.
158 José Manuel Nieto Soria, *Propaganda y opinión pública en la historia*, (Valladolid, 2007).
159 Nicasio Salvador Miguel, 'La conquista de Málaga (1487). Repercusiones festivas y literarias en Roma', in Daniel Baloup and Raúl González Arévalo (eds.), *La Guerra de Granada en su contexto internacional*, (Toulouse, 2017), pp. 161-282; Carlos de Miguel Mora, *Bernardino de Carvajal, La conquista de Baza*, (Granada, 1995).
160 Fernández de Córdova Miralles, *Alejandro VI*, pp. 145.
161 Ruiz Povedano, 'Exaltación y propaganda' and 'Roma y los sermones de la Guerra de Granada (1486-1492): de la propaganda a la política de imagen de los Reyes Católicos', in Javier García Benítez (ed.), *El valor del documento. Estudios en homenaje al profesor José Rodríguez Molina*, (Almería, 2018), pp. 225-83; Salvador Miguel, 'La conquista de Málaga', pp. 161-282; Peinado Santaella, 'Cristo pelea'; Devereux, *The other side*.
162 Fabrizio Cruciani, *Teatro nel Rinascimento. Roma 1450-1550*, (Roma, 1983), pp. 228-40; Caroli Verardi, *Historia Baetica: la caduta di Granata del 1492* (ed. Maria Chiabò et al., Rome, 1993) and within this, Paola Farenga, 'Circostanze e modi della diffusione della Historia Baetica', pp. XV-XXXV; María Dolores Rincón González, 'La divulgación de la toma de Granada: objetivos, mecanismos y agentes', *Anuario de Estudios Medievales*, 40/2 (2010), 603-15; González Arévalo, 'Ecos'.
163 Farenga, 'Circostanze e modi'.
164 Cristina Potz, '*Historia Baetica*: Dramatic Play or Historical Document?' *Journal of Historical and European Studies*, 1, (2008), 71-6; Álvaro Fernández de Córdova Miralles, 'La emergencia de Fernando el Católico en la Curia papal: identidad y propaganda de un príncipe aragonés en el espacio italiano (1462-1492)', in Aurora

Egido Martínez and José Enrique Laplana, *La imagen de Fernando el Católico en la Historia, la Literatura y el Arte*, (Zaragoza, 2014), p. 70.

165 Discussed further in Teresa Tinsley, 'Reframing the Reconquista' *(forthcoming)*. For the notion of *Reconquista* in sixteenth to nineteenth century historiography, see Martín Ríos Saloma, *La Reconquista: una construcción historiográfica (siglos XVI-XIX)*, (Madrid, 2011).

166 Discussed in my article, 'España sin frontera. La (re)visión historiográfica de Hernando de Baeza, c. 1510', in Manuel García Fernández et al. (eds.), *Las fronteras en la Edad Media hispánica, Siglos XIII-XVI*, (Seville, 2019), pp. 101–114.

167 Pastore, *Una herejía*, pp. 112–13.

168 Ibid., pp. 154–63.

169 Luis Suárez Fernández, 'La conversion de los musulmanes', HEMP, 17, 2, pp. 285–308.

170 'El parecer de Fray Hernando de Talavera, para los moriscos del Albaicín' in Antonio Gallego Burín and Alfonso Gámir Sandoval, *Los moriscos del reino de Granada según el Sínodo de Guadix de 1554 de 1554*, (facsimile edition of 1968 original, Granada, 1996), p. 161.

171 López de Coca, 'Las capitulaciones', p. 304.

172 Harvey, *Islamic Spain 1250-1500*, pp. 330–1.

173 'Such a condition is distinguished by a dynamic interplay of variables among an increased number of new, small and scattered, multiple-origin, transnationally connected, socio-economically differentiated and legally stratified immigrants': Steven Vertovec, 'Superdiversity and its Implications', *Ethnic and Racial Studies*, 30, 6 (2007), 1024–54.

174 Coleman, *Creating Christian Granada*, pp. 62–72; Gallego Burín and Gámir Sandoval, *Los moriscos*.

Chapter 3

1 ADM.AH. Leg.199, 26 December 1504.

2 M. Kriegel, 'La prise d'une decisión: l'expulsion des juifs d'Espagne en 1492', *Revue Historique*, 240 (1978), 87; Haim Beinart, *The Expulsion of the Jews from Spain*, (Oxford, 2005).

3 'Chronicón de Valladolid', *CODOIN*, 13, (Madrid, 1848), p. 187.

4 Torre and Rodríguez, 'Cartas y documentos', 300–1.

5 AGS.RGS.LEG,149212,161.

6 AHN. Inquisición, 1515, Exp.2. f. 102r.

7 Pedro Martir d'Anglería, *Epistolario*, 2 (Madrid, 1955), p. 218.

8 AHN. Inquisición, 1515, Exp.2. f.604r.

9 Miguel Ángel Ladero, 'Los conversos de Córdoba en 1997', *El Olivo*, 29–30 (1989), 187–205.

10 AGS. CMC. 100.

11 Ladero, 'Los conversos de Córdoba'.

12 AGA.Priego.1115/152-160.

13 ACS. Actas Capitulares.0758 (L.10) 0002, discussed in Gil, *Los conversos*, 2, p. 110, and noted by Joaquín Hazañas, *Maese Rodrigo, 1444–1509*, (Seville, 1909), p. 327.

14 Ibid.

15 Llorente, *Historia crítica*, pp. 142–51.
16 Shlomo Simonsohn, *The Apostolic See and the Jews: Documents 1464–1521*, (Toronto, 1990), document dated 29 August 1497.
17 Sicroff, *Los estatutos*.
18 Gil, *Los conversos*, p. 110.
19 Juan Gil, 'Conversos al servicio del Gran Capitán', in Ana Leal de Faria et al. (eds.), *Problematizar a História. Estudos de História moderna em homagem a Maria do Rosario Themudo Barata*, (Lisbon, 2007), pp. 491–8; María Amparo Moreno Trujillo, 'Las actuaciones de la Inquisición y los escribanos judeoconversos del entorno del Conde de Tendilla', *HID*, 37 (2010), 181–210.
20 For example, Pedro de Baeza: AHNOB, Luque, C.144, D.41; AHN. Diversos-Colecciones, 18, N.1613; 'Catálogo de la exposición de recuerdos de la vida del Gran Capitán', p. 211, and Pedro and Diego de Baeza, p. 215; Torre and Rodríguez, 'Cartas y documentos', 306, and Pedro and Diego de Baeza, p. 316. Diego de Baeza: Rodríguez Villa, *Crónicas*, p. XX; Alvaro de Baeza: AGS. RGS, LEG,150106,34; AGA. Priego, 1010, 317–37 and 350–9.
21 ADM. AH. Leg.199.
22 AGA.Priego.1010/255-315.
23 AGA.Priego.1010/381-385; AGA. Alcala. 1195/524-533; Béthencourt, *Historia genealógica*, pp. 120–1; Toro Ceballos, *Discurso genealógico*, p. 116; Asociación Albariza, 'Don Fadrique Enríquez de Ribera. Un puente al Renacimiento' (2012), online: http://asociacionalbariza.com/web/index.php/trabajos/ver/36 (accessed 27 February 2018).
24 AGA. Priego.1010/246-251.
25 Their wives were sisters: Cabrera Sánchez, *Nobleza*, p. 49.
26 AGA. Priego 1010/244-337.
27 AGA. Priego.1010/341.
28 AGA, Alcalá. 1195/524-533.
29 Ibid.
30 AGA.Priego.1002/8-17.
31 ADM. AH. Leg.200, 25.
32 Carmen Álvarez Márquez, 'La biblioteca de Don Fadrique Enríquez de Ribera, Marqués de Tarifa', *HID*, 13 (1986), 1–40.
33 Pedro García Martín, 'La Odisea al Paraíso. La peregrinación a Jerusalén de Don Fadrique Enríquez de Ribera', *Arbor*, 180 (2005), 559–80.
34 Vicent Lleó Cañal, *La Casa de Pilatos*, (Madrid, 1998); Barbara Fuchs, *Exotic Nation, Maurophilia and the Construction of Early Modern Spain*, (Philadelphia, 2009), pp. 52–7.
35 AGA.Priego 1010/386-394; ADM. AH. Leg. 199, 24 December 1506.
36 Fidel Fita Colomé, 'La Inquisición en Guadalupe', *BRAH*, 23 (1893), 283–343.
37 Starr-Le Beau, *In the Shadow*, pp. 237–56.
38 Santa Cruz, *Crónica*, pp. 243–4; Ginés Pérez de Hita, *Historia de los Vandos de los Cegríes y Abencerrages*, (Barcelona, 1757), pp. 549–57; Fuchs, *Exotic Nation*, pp. 113–14.
39 Bethencourt, *Historia genealógica*, 6, p. 104; 'Crónica General del Gran Capitán', in Antonio Rodríguez Villa, *Crónicas del Gran Capitán*, (Madrid, 1908), p. 71; Paolo Giovio, 'Crónica del Gran Capitán', in ibid., p. 491.
40 Bethencourt, *Historia genealógica*, 6, p. 104; AHPM. Escribanías siglo XVI, Leg.7, will of Gonzalo de Córdoba, 1533.

41 AHN. Inquisición, 1515, Exp. 2. f.122v.
42 Further discussion of this type of subterfuge in Enrique Soria Mesa, *El cambio inmóvil. Transformaciones y permanencias en una élite de poder*, (Córdoba, ss.XVI–XIX) (Cordoba, 2000); Pilar Rábade Obradó, 'La invención como necesidad: genealogía y judeoconversos', *En la España medieval*, 1 (2006), 183–202; Gregorio Salinero and Isabel Testón, *Un juego de engaños: movilidad, nombres y apellidos en los siglos XV a XVIII*, (Madrid, 2010).
43 Mártir, *Epístolario*, p. 248; Caro Lynn, *A College Professor of the Renaissance. Lucio Marineo Sículo*, (Chicago, 1937), p. 167.
44 Carriazo, 'Estudio preliminar', p. cxvii.
45 RAH, Salazar, M46, F175v.
46 ADM. AH. Leg. 271. 1-2. Antonio Paz y Melia, who recorded the first of these documents in his *Series de los más importantes documentos del Archivo del excelentísimo señor Duque de Medinaceli*, (Madrid, 1915), dates it wrongly as 1505. The grant was confirmed by The Marquis's successor, Catalina Fernández de Córdoba, in 1517, citing Hernando de Baeza as the counter signatory: ADM. AH. Leg. 277.35.
47 AGA. Alcalá.1195/524-533.
48 Douglas Blow, *Doctors, Ambassadors, Secretaries. Humanism and Professions in Renaissance Italy*, (Chicago, 2002), cover blurb. See also Catherine Fletcher, *Diplomacy in Renaissance Rome. The Rise of the Resident Ambassador*, (Cambridge, 2015).
49 ADM. AH. Leg. 199, 23 August 1504.
50 Ibid.
51 Ibid., 26 December 1504.
52 E.g., in relation to arrangements for Baeza's daughters: ADM. AH. Leg. 199, 25 September 1504.
53 Ibid.
54 ADM. AH. Leg. 199, 26 December 1504.
55 Ibid.
56 ADM.AH. Leg. 200.25.
57 Ibid.
58 ADM. AH. Leg. 199, 24 December 1506.
59 Ibid.
60 Enrique Otte, *Sevilla y sus mercaderes a fines de la Edad Media*, (Seville, 1996), p. 40.
61 Nieto Cumplido, *Infancia y juventud*; Cabrera Sánchez, *Nobleza*, pp. 395–426; Jesús Rodríguez Velasco, *La caballería castellana en la baja edad media: textos y contextos*, (Montpellier, 2000).
62 María Concepción Quintanilla, 'La biblioteca del Marqués de Priego', *En la España Medieval*, 1 (1980), 352.
63 Benedetto Croce, *España en la vida italiana durante el Renacimiento*, (Madrid, 1925); Manuel Peña Díaz, 'Las relaciones culturales entre España e Italia en la época del Gran Capitán', in *I Jornadas Cátedra Gran Capitán*, (Montilla, 2003), pp. 55–79; Devid Paolini, 'Los Reyes Católicos e Italia: los humanistas italianos y su relación con España', in Nicasio Salvador Miguel and Cristina Moya García (eds.), *La literatura en la época de los Reyes Católicos*, (Madrid/Frankfurt, 2008), pp. 189–205; Nicasio Salvador Miguel, 'Intelectuales españoles en Roma durante el gobierno de los Reyes Católicos', in Patrizia Botta (ed.), *Rumbos del hispanismo en el umbral de Cincuentenario de la AIH, 1*, (Rome, 2012), pp. 47–64.

64	ADM.AH. Leg. 199, 25 September 1504.
65	ADM. AH. Leg. 201.90; 'Rodrigo Ponce de León, 1490–1530', DBE.
66	Fernández de Córdoba, 'Historia y descripción', 74, 158.
67	ADM.201 docs 53-61; Gracia Boix, Autos, p. 94, Ibid. La historia de la Inquisición en Córdoba. Colección de documentos, (Cordoba, 1982), p. 86; AGA. Priego, 1002/212-251; 390–443.
68	Antonio Díaz Rodríguez, El Clero Catedralicio en la España moderna: los miembros del Cabildo de la Catedral de Córdoba (1475–1808), (Cordoba, 2012), p. 223. Velasco Romero is mentioned in Catalina Pacheco's will: RAH, Salazar, M46,175v-195. See also: AHN. Universidades. 745. N6, f. 39.
69	ADM. AH. Leg. 199, 26 December 1504 and 24 December 1506.
70	AGA. Priego, 1010/361-364; 396-402; 662-695; Ibid., 1002/212-251; AGA. Alcalá 1195/524-533.
71	AGA. Priego, 1001/501-655; Ibid., 1010/255-293; 435-441. See also various mentions in AGS. RGS. between 1492 and 1500.
72	Béthencourt, Historia genealógica, 7, pp. 71–2.
73	Antonio Díaz Rodríguez, El Clero Catedralicio, p. 437.
74	Julian Weiss, 'Flavius Josephus, 1492', International Journal of the Classical Tradition (2016).
75	BL. Add.MS.28500. Corregidor: RGS.LEG.148002,211.
76	John Laursen and Cary Nederman, Beyond the Persecuting Society. Religious toleration before the Enlightenment, (Philadelphia, 1997), p. 84.
77	He became Duke of Terranova in 1497 and Duke of Sessa in 1507: Ruiz Domènec, El Gran Capitán, pp. 281, 419; Peinado Santaella, Aristócratas nazaríes, pp. 213–30; Ladero, 'Mudéjares', p. 59; María Amparo Moreno Trujillo, 'El nuevo fisco castellano y el Gran Capitán: la carta de privilegio de los Reyes Católicos sobre las mercedes de Orgiva (Granada)', in Homenaje a Antonio Domínguez Ortiz, 1 (Granada, 2008), 669–88.
78	Moreno Trujillo, La memoria de la ciudad. El primer libro de actas del cabildo de Granada (1497–1502), p. 422; Torre and Rodríguez Pascual, 'Cartas y documentos', 306, 312.
79	Ruiz Domènec, El Gran Capitán, pp. 85–101; Diego de Valera, Doctrinal de príncipes, (Madrid, 1995); Juan de Mata Carriazo (ed.), Crónica de Don Alvaro de Luna, (Madrid, 1940). Neither of these works are recorded in his nephew's library, though other similar works are.
80	ASV.REG.LAT.1199.287r-289r; Thomas Frenz, Die Kanzlei der Päpste der Hochrenaissance (1471–1527), (Tübingen,1986), p. 363. See also my article 'Networks of influence between the Vatican and Andalusia at the beginning of the sixteenth century', Pedro A. Galera Andreu and Amparo López Arandia (eds.), Un humanista giennense en Roma. Gutierre González Doncel (Jaén, in press). Further discussion and references on the crucial figure of Cardinal Carvajal follow in Chapter 4.
81	ADM. AH. Leg. 199, 24 September 1504. The Marquis and his wife had six daughters in total, born between 1495 and 1512. Diego de Baeza is Hernando's brother – see genealogical chart p. 12.
82	Asociación Albariza, 'Don Fadrique Enríquez', p. 9.
83	Quintanilla, 'Biblioteca', 366 and 379.
84	ADM. AH. Leg.201.90
85	ADM. AH. Leg. 199, 25 September 1504.

86 Antonio Díaz Rodríguez, 'La instrumentalización de los cabildos catedrales', in Enrique Soria Mesa and Antonio Díaz Rodríguez (eds.), *Iglesia, poder y fortuna. Clero y movilidad social en la España moderna*, (Granada, 2012), pp. 124-5.
87 Diaz calls clergy who fell into this gap between theory and practice 'phantom prebendaries': 'Purity of Blood and the Curial Market in Iberian cathedrals', *eHumanista*, 4 (2016), p. 52. Online at: www.ehumanista.ucsb.edu/sites/secure.lsit. ucsb ... /5%20ehumconv.4.gam.Díaz.pdf (accessed 7 August 2018).
88 ADM. AH. Leg. 199, 26 December 1504; Ricardo San Martín Vadillo, *Documentos para la historia de Alcalá la Real (1427-1501)*, (Alcalá la Real, 2016), pp. 107-9, 118-19.
89 ADM.AH. Leg.199, 26 December 1504.
90 Fernando de Pulgar, *Claros varones de Castilla*, (Madrid, 2007), p. 119; Brian Tate, 'Introduction', in Fernando Del Pulgar (ed.), *Claros varones de Castilla*, (Oxford, 1971), p. xlvii.
91 Sicroff, *The Jeronymite Monastery*, p. 422.
92 RGS.Leg.148811.237 and 148801.254.
93 José Enrique López de Coca, 'Tenencias de fortalezas en el Reino de Granada', in *Homenaje al profesor Juan Torres Fontes*, 2 (Murcia, 1987), p. 932.
94 Padilla, 'Determinación de dubdas', p. 521.

Chapter 4

1 ADM. Leg.199. Letter from Hernando de Baeza to the Marquis of Priego, Naples, 24 December 1506.
2 Thomas Dandelet, *Spanish Rome, 1500-1700*, (New Haven, 2008), p. 6.
3 Enrique Soria Mesa and Antonio Díaz Rodríguez, *Iglesia, poder y fortuna. Clero y movilidad social en la España moderna*, (Granada, 2012); Manuel Vaquero Piñeiro, 'La presencia de los españoles en la economía romana (1500-1527)', *En la España Medieval*, 16 (1993), 287-305 and *La renta y las casas. El patrimonio inmobiliario de Santiago de los Españoles en Roma entre los siglos XV y XVII*, (Rome, 1999).
4 Álvaro Fernández de Córdova Miralles, 'Reyes Católicos: mutaciones y permanencias de un paradigma político en la Roma del Renacimiento', in Carlos Hernando Sánchez (ed.), *Roma y España: un crisol de la cultura europea en la Edad Moderna*, (Madrid, 2007), pp. 133-54; Maria A. Visceglia, 'Roma e la monarchia cattolica nell'eta dell'egemonia spagnola in Italia', in ibid., pp. 49-78.
5 Michael Mallett and Christine Shaw, *The Italian Wars 1494-1559*, (Harlow, 2012), pp. 1, 14.
6 Fernández de Córdova Miralles, 'La emergencia de Fernando'.
7 Mallett and Shaw, *The Italian Wars*, pp. 19-34.
8 The treaty was signed in Chambord on 10 October 1500 and in Granada on 11 November: Mallett and Shaw, p. 58.
9 Gonzalo Fernández de Oviedo, in Rodríguez Villa, *Crónicas*, p. LXI.
10 Desiderius Erasmus, *Education of a Christian prince*, (trans. Lester Born), New York, 1963, p. 238.
11 L. Serrano y Pineda, 'Correspondencia de los Reyes Católicos con el Gran Capitán durante las campañas de Italia', *RABM*, 29, (1913), p. 275.
12 ACS. ELS. A-8, 1588, f. 12v.

13 AZ. Altamira, 17, D75.
14 Rosana de Andrés Díaz, *El último decenio del reinado de Isabel I a través de la tesorería de Alonso de Morales*, (Valladolid, 2004), doc. 1959.
15 ADM. AH. LEG.199.
16 José Manuel Nieto Soria, 'Relaciones con el Pontificado. Iglesia y poder real en torno a 1500. Su proyección en los comienzos del reinado de Carlos I', *Studia Historica. Historia Moderna*, 21, (1999), 19–48 and 'Política eclesiástica de los Reyes Católicos durante el pontificado de Alejandro VI', in Paulino Iradiel et al. (eds.), *De València a Roma a través dels Borja*, (Valencia, 2006), 91–112; Amparo López Arandia, 'Castellanos y curia romana a inicios del siglo XVI: Gutierre González', *Dimensioni e problemi della ricerca storica*, 2 (2005), 55–87; José Goñi Gaztambide, 'Bernardino López de Carvajal y las bulas alejandrinas', *Anuario de Historia de Iglesia*, 1, (1992), 93–112; Fernández de Córdova Miralles, *Alejandro VI y los Reyes*.
17 Antonio Rodríguez Villa, 'D. Francisco de Rojas. Embajador de los Reyes Católicos. Documentos justificativos', *BRAH*, 28 (1896), 323–5.
18 Álvaro Fernández de Córdova Miralles, 'Cesar Borja en el seu context historic: entre el pontificat i la monarquia hispànica', in Idem, Fernández de Córdova Miralles, Jon Arrizabalaga, and María Toldrà (eds.), *Cesar Borja, cinc-cents anys després (1507–2007)*, (Valencia, 2009), pp. 11–98; Mallett and Shaw, *The Italian wars*, pp. 77–9.
19 Francesco Guicciardini, *The History of Italy*, 3, (trans. Austin Parke Goddard), London, 1753, p. 231.
20 Álvaro Fernández de Córdova Miralles, 'Los Reyes Católicos ante la elección pontificia de Pío III: la acción negociadora hispana en sede vacante (1503)', in Alejandra Guzmán Almagro et al. (eds.), *Pere Miquel Carbonell i el seu temps (1434–1517)*, (Barcelona, 2014), p. 2.
21 Nunzio Faraglia, 'Gli Orsini ai soldi di spagna', *Archivio Storico per le Province Napoletane*, 6 (1881), 551–62.
22 'Crónica manuscrita', p. 389.
23 Jerónimo Zurita, *Historia del rey Don Fernando el Católico. De las empresas, y ligas de Italia*, José Javier Iso, Pilar Rivero and Julián Pelegrín (eds.) V, LXXIII. Online edition: https://ifc.dpz.es/publicaciones/ebooks/id/2423 (accessed 18 March 2022). Later, in the same section, Zurita erroneously calls him 'Gonzalo de Baeza', possibly confusing him with the royal treasurero de that name.
24 'Crónica manuscrita', p. 389.
25 Fernández de Córdova Miralles, 'Pio III'.
26 Ibid.
27 Álvaro Fernández de Córdova Miralles, 'El cardinal Giuliano della Rovere y los reinos ibéricos. Rivalidades y convergencias en el Mediterráneo occidental', in Flavia Cantatore et al. (eds.), Metafore di un pontificato. Giulio II e Savona, (Rome, 2009), pp. 119–63; Christine Shaw, *Julius II, the Warrior Pope*, (Oxford, 1996).
28 *Dispacci di Antonio Giustinian, ambasciatore veneto a Roma dal 1502 al 1505* (ed. Pascuale Villari, Vol II, Florence, 1876), p. 267.
29 Alessandro Capata, 'L'immagine machiavelliana di Giulio II nella Legazione presso la corte papale del 1503', in Paolo Procaccioli (ed.), *Giulio II: La cultura non classicista*, (Rome, 2010), pp. 65–80.
30 Zurita, *Historia del Rey don Fernando*, V, LXXIII; Fernández de Córdova Miralles, 'Pio III'.
31 Beltrando Costabili, Ferrarese Envoy, in Ludwig Pastor (ed.), *History of the Popes*, 6, (Wilmington, 1906), p. 208.

32 Ibid., p. 211.
33 José Doussinague, *Fernando el Católico y el cisma de Pisa*, (Madrid, 1946).
34 Fernández de Córdova Miralles, 'Pio III', p. 14.
35 Doussinague, *Cisma de Pisa*.
36 Fernández de Córdova Miralles, 'Giuliano della Rovere'.
37 Rafael Gutiérrez Cruz, *Los presidios españoles del Norte de Africa*, (Melilla, 1997), pp. 249–50.
38 Christine Shaw, 'The Motivation for the Patronage of Julius II' in Martin Gosman et al. (eds.), *Princes and Princely Culture, 1450–1650*, (Leiden, 2005), pp. 43–62.
39 Shaw, *The Warrior Pope*.
40 Desiderius Erasmus, *Against War*, (Boston, 1907), p. xi; Bernard Schmidt, 'Julius II, the Papal Monarch' in Jochen Sander (ed.), *Raphael and the Portrait of Julius II*, (Petersberg, 2013), p. 24.
41 AZ. Altamira, 18, D34.
42 Capata, 'L'immagine machiavelliana'.
43 'Crónica Manuscrita', p. 389. This was Tomasso Regolano: Giustinian, *Dispacci*, p. 275.
44 Enrique Garramiola Priego, 'El autor de la "Crónica manuscrita" del Gran Capitán', *Crónica de Córdoba y sus Pueblos*, 8 (2002), 207–14.
45 ASV.REG.LAT.1199.287r-289r; Frenz, *Die Kanzlei der Päpste*, p. 363. On the importance of 'familiae' as social institutions: John D'Amico, *Renaissance Humanism in Papal Rome*, (New York, 1983), p. 36.
46 APNM. Escribanías S.XVI. Legajo 32: will of *Licenciado* Juan Rodríguez de Baeza, his cousin and namesake. AHPS. Pedro Castellanos 1555. Libro 4.3390: will of Hernando de Baeza, who was Juan Rodríguez de Baeza's son from an early relationship with a woman from Montilla named Leonor Fernández.
47 ADM. AH. Leg.199, 26 December 1504.
48 ACS. Expediente A-8, 1588. f.12v.
49 Fernández de Córdova Miralles et al., *Cèsar Borja*; Sarah Bradford, *Cesare Borgia, his life and times*, (London, 2011).
50 Capata, 'L'immagine machiavelliana, p. 65.
51 Rodríguez Villa, 'Francisco de Rojas', p. 396.
52 Among many accounts: Zurita, *Historia del Rey don Fernando*, V, LXXIII; 'Crónica manuscrita', p. 434.
53 Giustinian, *Dispacci*, 3, p. 29.
54 Ibid., 2, p. 510.
55 Ibid., p. 511.
56 Ibid., 3, p. 77.
57 Paolo Giovio, 'Crónica del Gran Capitán', in Rodríguez Villa, *Crónicas*, p. 539.
58 Ruiz Domènec, *El Gran Capitán*, p. 365.
59 Rodríguez Villa, 'Francisco de Rojas', pp. 391–2.
60 Ibid., p. 390.
61 Giustinian, *Dispacci*, 3, pp. 518–19.
62 Treaty document between Gonzalo Fernández de Córdoba and Cesare Borgia, 6 July 1504: AZ. Altamira, 16, D.155A, transcribed in Serrano y Pineda, 'Correspondencia', *RABM*, 26, (1912), pp. 302–3.
63 Giovio, 'Crónica del Gran Capitán', p. 539.
64 Fernández de Córdova Miralles, 'Cesar Borja', p. 66.

65 Teodoro Fernández Sánchez, *El discutido extremeño Cardenal Carvajal* (*D. Bernardino Lòpez de Carvajal y Sande*), (Cáceres, 1981); Bernardino de Carvajal, *La conquista de Baza* (ed. Carlos de Miguel Mora, Granada, 1995); Tomás González Rolán, 'Diplomacia y humanismo a finales del siglo XV: el cardenal extremeño Bernardino López de Carvajal', in César Chaparro Gómez, Manuel Mañas Gómez, and Delfín Ortega Sánchez (eds.), *Nulla dies sine linea. Humanistas extremeños: de la fama al olvido*, (Cáceres, 2009), pp. 143–56; 'Bernardino López de Carvajal y Sande', DBE.
66 AZ. Altamira, 18, D34; ADM. AH. Leg. 199, letter of 25 September 1504.
67 Goñi Gaztambide, 'Bernardino López de Carvajal y las bulas'.
68 Flavia Cantatore, 'Un committente spagnolo della Roma de Alessandro VI: Bernardino de Carvajal', in Maria Chiabò and Silvia Maddalo (eds.), *Roma di fronte all'Europa al tempo di Alessandro VI*, (Roma, 2001), pp. 861–72; Isabella Iannuzzi, 'Bernardino de Carvajal: teoria e propaganda di uno spagnolo all'interno della Curia romana', *Rivista di storia della Chiesa in Italia*, 2 (2008), 25–46; Marta Albalá Pelegrín, 'Humanism and Spanish Literary Patronage at the Roman Curia: The Role of the Cardinal of Santa Croce, Bernardino López de Carvajal (1456–1523)', *Royal Studies Journal*, 4, 2, (2017), 11–37.
69 Iannuzzi, 'Bernardino de Carvajal'.
70 Bernhard Schirg, 'Betting on the anti-Pope. Giovanbattista Cantalicio and his cycle of poems dedicated to the schismatic Cardinal Bernardino de Carvajal in 1511', *Spoliam*, 12 (2015), 1–38.
71 Manuel Vaquero Piñeiro, 'I funerali romani del Principe Giovanni e dalla Regina Isabella di Castiglia', in Chiabó et al. (eds.), *Roma di fronte all'Europa*, pp. 641–56; Nelson Minnich, 'The Role of Prophecy in the Career of the Enigmatic Bernardino López de Carvajal', in Marjorie Reeves (ed.), *Prophetic Rome in the High Renaissance Period*, (Oxford, 1992), pp. 111–20; in the same volume: Anna Morisi-Guerra, 'The "Apocalypsis Nova". A Plan for Reform', pp. 27–50.
72 Vicente Calvo Fernández, 'El cardenal Bernardino de Carvajal y la traducción latina del "Itinerario" de Ludovico Vartema', *Cuadernos de Filología Clásica*, 18 (2000), 303–21; John Edwards, 'Conversion in Córdoba and Rome: Francisco Delicado's 'La Lozana Andaluza', in Roger Collins and Anthony Goodman (eds.), *Medieval Spain: Culture, Conflict and Coexistence*, (Basingstoke, 2002), pp. 202–24; José Antonio Ollero Pina, 'La Historia Parthenopea de Alfonso Fernández Benadeva, la Inquisición y otras cosas de familias', in León Carlos Alvarez Santaló (ed.), *Estudios de Historia Moderna en Homenaje al profesor Antonio García-Barquero*, (Seville, 2009), pp. 549–83. In April 1504, coinciding with Baeza's time in Rome, there were theatrical performances in the Vatican and in the house of Cardinal San Severino: Cruciani, *Teatro nel Rinascimento*, p. 307.
73 Kathleen Weil-Harris and John D'Amico, 'The Renaissance Cardinal's Ideal Palace: A Chapter from Cortesi's 'De Cardinalatu', *Memoirs of the American Academy in Rome*, 3 (1980), 45–119; Bernhard Schirg, 'Cortese's Ideal Cardinal? Praising Art, Splendour and Magnificence in Bernardino de Carvajal's Roman Residence', *Journal of the Warburg and Courtauld Institutes*, 22 (2017), 61–83; Albalá, 'Humanism'.
74 Ibid. (Albalá).
75 Carvajal, *La conquista de Baza*.
76 Andrew Devereux provides a detailed study of the arguments used to justify Fernando's expansionist agenda: *The Other Side of Empire. Just War in the*

Mediterranean and the Rise of Early Modern Spain, (Ithaca, 2020), with discussion of Hostiensis on p. 106.
77 Tinsley, 'Reframing the reconquista'
78 Goñi Gaztambide, 'Bernardino López de Carvajal'.
79 Alessandro Scafi, 'The African Paradise of Cardinal Carvajal', *Renaissance and Reformation*, 31, 2 (2008), 7–28.
80 Tomás González Rolán and Pilar Saquero Suárez-Somonte, 'Un importante texto político-literario: La epístola consolatoria a los Reyes Católicos', *Cuadernos de Filología Clásica, Estudios Latinos*, 16 (1999), 247–77.
81 Minnich, 'The role of prophecy', p. 113.
82 Carlos Hernando Sánchez, 'El Gran Capitán y los inicios del Virreinato de Nápoles', *El Tratado de Tordesillas y su época*, 3, (Valladolid, 1995), p. 1825.
83 Ibid., p. 1826.
84 Garrett Mattingly, *Renaissance Diplomacy*, (Boston, 1971); Ochoa Brun, *Historia de la Diplomacia*, 4; Christine Shaw, 'The Papal Court as a Centre of Diplomacy: From the Peace of Lodi to the Council of Trent', in Florence Alazard et al. (eds.), *La papauté à la Renaissance*, (Paris, 2007), pp. 621–38.
85 Rodríguez Villa, 'Francisco de Rojas', p. 386.
86 Giustinian, *Dispacci*, 3, p. 98.
87 Shaw, *The Warrior Pope*.
88 Rodríguez Villa, 'Francisco de Rojas', p. 393.
89 Ibid., pp. 428–31; Friedrich Edelmayer, '¿Descubrimiento o encuentro? Maximiliano I y los Reyes Católicos', *El Tratado de Tordesillas y su época*, 1, 217–226.
90 Manuel Fernández Álvarez, *Juana la Loca. La cautiva de Tordesillas*, (Madrid, 2008), Gillian Fleming, *Juana I. Legitimacy and conflict in sixteenth century Castile*, (London, 2018).
91 Alessandro Serio, 'Una representación de la crisis de la unión dinástica: los cargos diplomáticos en Roma de Francisco de Rojas y Antonio de Acuña (1501–1507)', *Cuadernos de Historia Moderna*, 32 (2007), 13–29; Álvaro Fernández de Córdova Miralles, 'Antonio de Acuña antes de las Comunidades, su embajada en Roma al servicio de Felipe el Hermoso', in István Szászdi León-Borja and Joseph Pérez (eds.), *Iglesia, eclesiásticos y la revolución comunera*, (2017), pp. 71–121; José Martínez Millán, 'De la muerte del príncipe Juan al fallecimiento de Felipe el Hermoso (1497–1506)', in José Martínez Millán (ed.), *La Corte de Carlos V*, 1 (Madrid, 2000), pp. 45–72.
92 Alonso de Santa Cruz, *Crónica de los Reyes Católicos* (ed. Juan de Mata Carriazo, 2, Sevilla, 1951), p. 10.
93 IVDJ. GC.T11.1, 57, 98, 107 and 109.
94 Rodríguez Villa, 'Francisco de Rojas', pp. 399–400.
95 Serrano y Pineda, 'Correspondencia' *RABM*, 25, (1911), p. 429.
96 Carlos Hernando Sánchez, 'El Gran Capitán y la agregación del Reino de Nápoles', in Giuseppe Galasso and Carlos Hernando Sánchez (eds.), *El Reino de Nápoles y la monarquía de España. Entre agregación y conquista*, (Rome, 2004), p. 188.
97 Mártir, *Epistolario*, p. 89.
98 John Edwards, 'Trial of an Inquisitor: The Dismissal of Diego Rodríguez Lucero, Inquisitor of Cordoba in 1508', *Journal of Ecclesiastical History*, 37, 2, (1986), 240–57.
99 For a detailed and nuanced account of the *Gran Capitán*'s position at this juncture, see: Álvaro Fernández de Córdova Miralles, 'El Gran Capitán y los Hapsburgo: conflict y mediación en los inicios de la crisis sucesoria', in Francisco Toro Ceballos (ed.), *Congreso Fernández de Córdoba II*, (Alcalá, 2021), pp. 203–16.

100 Hernando Sánchez, 'El Gran Capitán y la agregación', p. 191.
101 Ibid.
102 Manuel Rivero Rodríguez, *De la separación a la reunión dinástica: la Corona de Aragón entre 1504–1516*, (Madrid, 2000), p. 90.
103 Dispatches of Philibert Naturel, one of Felipe I's ambassadors in Rome from Archives Départementales du Nord (Lille): Fernández de Córdova Miralles, 'Antonio de Acuña'. I am very grateful to Dr Fernández de Córdova for alerting me to this document and allowing me access to his notes.
104 Alonso de Santa Cruz provides a roll call of these, *Crónica*, 2, p. 42.
105 John Edwards, 'La révolte du Marquis de Priego', *Mélanges de la Casa de Velázquez*, 12 (1976), 165–72.
106 Gil González Davila, *Teatro eclesiástico de las iglesias metropolitanas y catedrales de los reynos de las dos Castillas*, 2, (Madrid, 1647), pp. 409–11; 'Antonio de Osorio de Acuña', *DBE*; Augustín Redondo, 'Luther et l'Espagne 1520–1536', *Mélanges de la Casa Velásquez*, 1 (1965), 124.
107 Serio, 'Una representación de la crisis'; 'Cartas de Felipe el Hermoso', *CODOIN*, 8, (Madrid, 1846), pp. 306–8.
108 Ibid., pp. 271–2.
109 Fernando's orders in code, with contemporaneous transcription: IVDJ.GC.TII, 30; Fernández de Córdova Miralles, 'Antonio de Acuña', pp. 13–15.
110 Ruiz Doménec, *El Gran Capitán*, pp. 398–9; Zurita, *Historia del Rey don Fernando*, VI, VI.
111 Ruiz Domènec, *El Gran Capitán*.
112 Hernando Sánchez, 'El Gran Capitán y los inicios'.
113 Serrano y Pineda, 'Correspondencia', *RABM*, 25–9; Rodríguez Villa, 'Francisco de Rojas'; Giustinian, *Dispacci*, 2.
114 Hernando Sánchez, 'El Gran Capitán y la agregación', pp. 184–6.
115 Quoted in Serio, 'Una representación de la crisis', p. 19, from Marino Sanuto, *Diarii*, (Bologna, 1969), 6. c. 37.
116 Zurita, *Historia del Rey don Fernando*, V, LXXI.
117 Ruiz Domènec, *El Gran Capitán*, pp. 365–7; Hernando Sánchez, 'El Gran Capitán y los inicios', pp. 1834–5.
118 Serrano y Pineda, 'Correspondencia', *RABM*, 23, p. 500.
119 Ibid., 24, pp. 566–8; British Library, Add MS 28698, ff.8-9.
120 Filippo Tamburini, *Ebrei, saraceni, cristiani, vita sociale e vita religiosa dai registri della Penitenzieria apostolica: secoli 14-16*, (Milan, 1996), p. 24.
121 Armando Cotarelo, *Fray Diego de Deza: ensayo biográfico*, (Madrid, 1902), p. 143.
122 Hernando Sánchez, 'El Gran Capitán y los inicios', p. 1831.
123 RAH. A8, f.220-221 (the part of the letter which deals with his reasons is missing, but the sense has been captured by Zurita, *Historia del Rey don Fernando*, V, LXX). See also Felipe Ruiz Martín, 'La expulsión de los judíos del Reino de Nápoles', *Hispania*, 34 (1948), 28–76 and 179–240.
124 Ruiz Domènec, *El Gran Capitán*, pp. 365–7.
125 Felisa Bermejo, 'La diaspora sefardi en Italia a raiz de la explusion de Espana en 1492 de los judios', *Artifara*, 1 (2002), Addenda; Fernando Suárez Bilbao, 'El triste epilogo de los judios espanoles: el exilio italiano', in José Martínez Millán and Manuel Rivero Rodríguez (eds.), *Centros de poder italianos en la monarquía hispánica (siglos XV-XVIII)*, 1, (Madrid, 2010), pp. 99–162.
126 IVDJ. E52.C68/4.
127 Serrano y Pineda, 'Correspondencia', *RABM*, 24, pp. 566–8.

128 Daniel Eisenberg, *Spanish Writers on Gay and Lesbian Themes. A Bio-Critical Sourcebook*, (Westport, 1999), p. 11.
129 Hernando Sánchez, 'El Gran Capitán y los inicios', p. 1834.
130 Torre and Rodríguez, 'Cartas y documentos', *RABM*, 35, (1916), 436–8.
131 ADM. AH. Leg.199, 23 August 1504. Transcription and detailed discussion in Teresa Tinsley, 'La desilusión del Gran Capitán', in Francisco Toro Ceballos (ed.), *Los Fernández de Córdoba*, (Alcalá la Real, 2018), pp. 625–33.
132 Serrano y Pineda, 'Correspondencia', RABM, 25, pp. 308 and 427–428. See also Zurita, *Historia del Rey don Fernando*, V, LXXIII.
133 BNE, MSS. 20211/16.
134 Serio, 'Una representación de la crisis', p. 21; Zurita, *Historia del Rey don Fernando*, V, LXXIII; Serrano y Pineda, 'Correspondencia', *RABM*, 26, p. 310.
135 RAH, Salazar, A-11, F.424; Cotarelo, *Fray Diego*, p. 29; Zurita, Historia del Rey don Fernando, V, LXXI.
136 ADM. AH. Leg.199, 23 August 1504.
137 Rojas is known to have come from a relatively humble background, see Rodríguez Villa, 'Francisco de Rojas'.
138 'ni yo digo que ellos yerran en su oficio, ni la Reina en su comisión, aunque posible sería su alteza hauer errado en ge lo cometer, y aun ellos en el proceder, e lo uno ni lo otro no por malas intinciones, mas por dañadas informaciones agenas': Carriazo, 'Estudio preliminar', p. lvii.
139 Poutrin, 'The Jewish precedent', p. 78.
140 Zurita, *Historia del Rey don Fernando*, VI, VII–XIV.
141 ADM. AH. Leg.199, 24 December 1506.
142 Fernández Alvarez, *Juana la Loca*, pp. 130–8; Fleming, *Juana I*.
143 Santa Cruz, *Crónica*, 2, pp. 72–4.
144 'Crónica general', p. 245; 'Crónica manuscrita', p. 443; Giovio, *Crónica*, p. 543.
145 Tribunal de Cuentas, *Las cuentas del Gran Capitán*, (Madrid, 1983), p. 6.
146 Real Academia Española, *Diccionario de la Lengua Española*, online edition: http://dle.rae.es/?id=BaAYElz (accessed 16 March 2021).
147 Tribunal de Cuentas, *Las Cuentas*, p. 22; AGS. CMC.1EP.Leg.147.
148 Juan Granados, *El Gran Capitán*, (Barcelona, 2006), pp. 604–7.
149 Lyndal Roper, *Martin Luther. Renegade and Prophet*, (London, 2017).
150 RAH. Salazar A-11.430, published in Torre and Rodríguez, 'Cartas y documentos', *RABM*, 35, p. 435. José Rodríguez Molina, 'Tendencia integradora', p. 521.
151 Niccolò Machiavelli, *The Prince*, (trans. W. K Marriott), Project Gutenberg EBook: https://www.gutenberg.org/files/1232/1232-h/1232-h.htm#link2HCH0017 (accessed 16 March 2021), Chapter 21.

Chapter 5

1 Hernando de Baeza: letter dated 23 August 1504, ADM. AH. Leg.199.
2 Tarsicio Herrero del Collado, 'El proceso inquisitorial por delito de herejía contra Hernando de Talavera', *Anuario de Historia del Derecho Español*, 39 (1969), 689; Lea, *History*, pp. 191–3; Gracia Boix, *Autos de Fe*, p. 7.
3 Gracia Boix, *Colección de documentos*, (Cordoba, 1982), p. 86.

4   Mártir, *Epistolario*, 2, pp. 175–9, p. 193.
5   Lea, *History*, 1, p. 199.
6   Azcona, *Elección y Reforma;* 'La Inquisición española, procesada por la Congregación General', in Joaquín Pérez Villanueva (ed.), *La Inquisición Española. Nueva visión, nuevos horizontes,* (Madrid, 1980), pp. 89–163; Edwards, 'La révolte'; 'Trial of an Inquisitor'; 'Elijah and the Inquisition: messianic prophecy among conversos in Spain c.1500', *Nottingham Medieval Studies*, 28 (1984), 79–94; Bartolomé Yun, *Crisis de subsistencia y conflictividad social en Córdoba a principios del siglo XVI*, (Cordoba, 1980); Ana Cristina Cuadro García, 'Acción inquisitorial contra los judaizantes en Córdoba y crisis eclesiástica (1482–1508)', *Revista de Historia Moderna. Anales de la Universidad de Alicante*, 21 (2003), 11–28; Pastore, *Una herejía,* pp. 113–24.
7   Gracia Boix, *Colección de documentos,* pp. 96–107.
8   Cuadro García, 'Acción', pp. 33–4.
9   Edwards, 'Elijah'.
10 Gracia Boix, *Colección de documentos,* p. 101.
11 Edwards, 'Trial of an Inquisitor'.
12 ADM.AH. Leg.199, 24 December 1506.
13 ADM, AH. Leg.200.30. Transcribed in Paz y Melia, *Series,* p. 113.
14 AGA. Priego. 1002, 396–440.
15 AGA. Priego.1065, 35–40.
16 ADM. AH. Leg. 199, 24 December 1506.
17 Margarita Cabrera Sánchez, 'Cristianos nuevos y cargos concejiles. Jurados conversos en Córdoba a finales de medievo', *Espacio, Tiempo y Forma*, III, 29 (2016), 159.
18 Mártir, *Epistolario*, 2, p. 175.
19 AHN. Inquisición,1515, Exp.2. f.101v.
20 Ibid.
21 José Szmolka Clares, *Epistolario del Conde de Tendilla (1504–1506)*, 2, (Granada, 1996), pp. 717–18.
22 Lea, *History*, p. 568; Gil, *Los conversos*, 2, p. 296.
23 Lea, *History*, 1, p. 202.
24 See, for example, ADM, AH. 200, 78, a letter to the Marquis referring to others arrested by Lucero, including a Sancho de Córdoba on whose behalf the Marquis is intervening, and a Gonzalo de Baeza linked to the Marquis of Villena (not Hernando's brother).
25 Szmolka, *Epistolario*, 2, passim; Moreno Trujillo, 'Las actuaciones'.
26 Yuen-Gen Liang, *Family and empire. The Fernández de Córdoba and the Spanish Realm*, (Philadelphia, 2011), p. 71; Pastore, *Una herejía,* pp. 117–24; Martínez Millán, 'De la muerte', pp. 56–9.
27 Henry Charles Lea, 'Lucero the Inquisitor', *The American Historical Review*, 2, (1897), 611.
28 Gracia Boix, *Colección de documentos,* pp. 96–107; Lea, *History,* pp. 191–204.
29 AZ. Altamira.18, D34.
30 ADM. AH. Leg. 199, 24 December 1506.
31 Azcona, *Elección y Reforma,* p. 220. Pastore, *Una herejía,* pp. 98–111; Fernández de Córdova Miralles, 'La emergencia de Fernando', pp. 73–6.
32 Clemencín, *Elogio*, p. 384.
33 Lorenzo de Padilla, 'Crónica de Felipe I', *CODOIN*, 8, (Madrid, 1846), p. 129. These were: Rodrigo de Pimentel, Count of Benavente; Juan de Guzmán, Duke of Medina

Sidonia; Diego Hurtado de Mendoza, Duke of Infantazgo; Diego Pacheco, Marquis of Villena; Pedro Manrique, Duke of Nájera, and Juan Girón, Count of Ureña.
34 'Cartas de Felipe el Hermoso', *CODOIN*, 8, pp. 336–42.
35 Cotarelo, *Fray Diego*, p. 220; *CODOIN* 8, pp. 336–7.
36 Rodríguez Villa, 'Francisco de Rojas', 448;
37 Lea, *History*, p. 196.
38 Herrero del Collado, 'El proceso inquisitorial'; Lea, 'Lucero', p. 618; Luis Ramírez de Las Casas Deza, 'Anales de Córdoba', *CODOIN*, 112 (Madrid, 1895), p. 282.
39 Mártir, *Epistolario*, 2, pp. 193–4.
40 Lea, *History*, 1, p. 197.
41 Cotarelo, *Fray Diego*, pp. 150, 214; María Concepción Quintanilla, 'El dominio de las ciudades por la nobleza. El caso de Córdoba', *En la España Medieval*, 10 (1987), p. 123.
42 Pedro Aranda Quintanilla de Mendoza, *Archetypo de virtudes. Espexo de prelados*, (Palermo, 1653), pp. 166–8.
43 Béthencourt, *Historia genealógica*, 6, p. 107.
44 Edwards, 'La révolte', p. 168.
45 Szmolka, *Epistolario*, 2, p. 717.
46 Ibid., p. 718.
47 'Diego Fernández de Córdoba y Arrellano', *DBE*.
48 Szmolka, *Epistolario*, 2, p. 718.
49 Ibid., pp. 719–20.
50 Padilla, 'Crónica', p. 153.
51 ADM. AH. Leg.199, 24 December 1506. I am grateful to Teresa Witcombe for providing me with this insight.
52 Azcona, *Elección y Reforma*, pp. 364–7; AHNOB. Luque.C.442.D.88. On Torres: Rafael Marín López, *El Cabildo de la Catedral de Granada en el Siglo XVI*, (Granada, 1998), passim.
53 Cesáreo Fernández Duro, 'Noticias de la vida y obra de Gonzalo de Ayora y fragmentos de su crónica inédita' *BRAH*, 17, (1890), 433–75.
54 Gracia Boix, *Colección de documentos*, p. 103.
55 Ibid., p. 448.
56 Iannuzzi, *El poder de la palabra*, p. 479.
57 Azcona, 'La Inquisición española', p. 127.
58 Kamen, 'Fernando el Católico', p. 18.
59 Cotarelo, *Fray Diego*, p. 143.
60 ADM. AH. Leg. 199, 24 December 1506.
61 Padilla, 'Crónica', p. 152; Zurita, *Historia del Rey don Fernando*, VII, XXIIII.
62 Gracia Boix, *Colección de Documentos*, pp. 97–8.
63 ADM. AH. Leg.201,44. This is a letter to the Marquis of Priego from an unknown intermediary who had been negotiating with Pedro Ponce over 'el propósito de Baeça'.
64 Gómez Bravo, *Catálogo de los Obispos*, p. 399.
65 Zurita, *Historia del Rey don Fernando*, VII, XXIX. See also Llorente, *Historia crítica*, p. 203.
66 Gómez Bravo, *Catálogo de los Obispos*, p. 399; Béthencourt, *Historia genealógica*, 6, pp. 107–8.
67 Gracia Boix, *Colección de Documentos*, p. 91.

68 Ibid., pp. 102–6.
69 ADM. AH. Leg. 199, 24 December 1506.
70 Lea, *History*, p. 203, transcript, p. 582.
71 AHN. Inquisición,1515, Exp.2. f.101v.
72 Szmolka, *Epistolario*, 2, pp. 451, 452, 458, 463, 466, 473, 486.
73 Ibid., p. 751.
74 Ibid., 1, pp. CXII–CXVIII.
75 María Concepción Quintanilla, 'Facciones, clientelas y partidos en España en el tránsito de la edad media a la modernidad', in Javier Alvarado Planas (ed.), *Poder, economía, clientelismo*, (Madrid, 1997), p. 41; Liang, *Family and Empire*, pp. 70–2.
76 Cotarelo, *Fray Diego*, p. 351.
77 Liang, *Family and Empire*, pp. 55–72.
78 Baeza: 24.
79 ADM. AH. Leg. 199, 24 September 1504.
80 Díaz, 'Instrumentalización'; 'El precio del nepotismo. Coadjutoría y resigna en las catedrales andaluzas (ss. XVI-XVIII)', *Chronica Nova*, 35 (2009), 288–309.
81 ADM.AH.Leg.199, 24 December 1506.
82 ADM. AH. Leg. 199, 24 December 1506.
83 *Cruden's Complete Concordance*, (London, 1930), p. 494.
84 ADM. AH. Leg. 199, 24 December 1506.
85 ACS. Actas Capitulares, 07053 (L5). Noted by Hazañas, *Maese Rodrigo*, p. 300.
86 On 18 April Fernando wrote to the *Gran Capitán* and to Carvajal demanding that the position be given to Morales, not Baeza's son: Torre and Rodríguez, 'Correspondencia', *RABM*, 28 (1913), 376; AZ, Altamira,18, D76. Immediately on receiving it, late at night on 2 May, Carvajal wrote to the *Gran Capitán* explaining the predicament and suggesting that they find a good alternative for Baeza's son because they could not go against the will of the King: AZ. Altamira, 18, D34. On 18 July, Fernando wrote to the *Gran Capitán* and to Hernando de Baeza thanking them for according with his wishes: *RABM*, 29 (1913), 276; AZ, Altamira, 17, D75. On 22 August the *Gran Capitán* wrote apologetic letters to Fernando and Morales, mentioning that Baeza had also written to Morales: IVDJ, E52,68.27; GC, TII, 62.
87 Diaz, 'El precio del nepotismo', 297.
88 Szmolka, *Epistolario*, 2, p. 673; ADM. AH. Leg. 199, 24 December 1506.
89 'aquel yntenso', ibid.
90 Hazañas, *Maese Rodrigo*, pp. 307–10; http://www.fundacionmedinaceli.org/monumentos/hospital/index.aspx (accessed 2 February 2022).
91 ADM. AH. Leg. 199, 24 December 1506.
92 Bataillon, *Erasmo*, p. 86; Hélène Rabaey, 'Un inquisiteur humaniste. Diego López de Cortegana (1455–1524)', *Cahiers du CRIAR*, 18–9 (2000), 79–114; Francisco Escobar Borrego, Samuel Díez Reboso and Luis Rivero García (eds.), *La Metamorfosis de un inquisidor: el humanista Diego López de Cortegana (1455–1524)*, (Sevilla, 2012).
93 Quintanilla, 'Biblioteca', p. 373; Juan Gil, 'Apuleyo en la Sevilla renacentista', *HABIS*, 23 (1992), 297–306.
94 Rafael Pérez García, 'El mundo editorial de la Sevilla de Diego López de Cortegana' in Escobar Borrego et al., *Metamorfosis*, pp. 77–8.

95 AHPS. Castellanos, 1555/4/3390. This document, which contains Hernando de Baeza II's will, is referenced in Gil, *Los conversos*, 2, p. 254.
96 Tinsley, 'Networks of influence'.
97 Lea, *History*, p. 205.
98 Boix, *Colección de documentos*, p. 94.
99 Paz y Melia, *Series*, pp. 87–8.
100 Lea, *History*, pp. 207–8.
101 Ibid., pp. 208–9.
102 Ibid., p. 568; Gil, *Los conversos*, 2, p. 296; José Solís, 'El humanismo en Sevilla en la época de Diego López de Cortegana' in Escobar et al, *La Metamorfosis de un Inquisidor*, p. 43; Rabaey, 'Un inquisiteur humaniste'.
103 Lea, *History*, p. 369.
104 ADM.AH. Leg 278.11: the document mentions Diego de Baeza. Fernández Álvarez, 'La crisis', p. 691.
105 'Crónica manuscrita', p. 457.
106 Andrés Bernáldez, 'Historia de los Reyes Católicos' in *Crónicas de los Reyes de Castilla*, (Madrid, 1878), pp. 734–5; Zurita, *Historia del Rey don Fernando*, VIII, XX.
107 Among the many accounts of this incident: Ibid.; Martir, *Epistolario*, 2, pp. 248–67; Fernández de Córdoba, 'Historia y descripción', 74, pp. 164–70; Pedro Barrantes Maldonado, 'Illustraciones de la Casa de Niebla', 1-II, Memorial Histórico Español, 9–10, (Madrid, 1857), pp. 439–40; Padilla, 'Crónica', pp. 166–8; Edwards, 'La révolte'; Quintanilla, 'Facciones'; Antonio Espejo Galiani, 'Don Pedro Fernández de Córdoba: otra muestra de nobleza díscola desde el señorío de Aguilar de la Frontera', *Arte, Arqueología e Historia*, 19, (2012), 291–6.
108 Bernáldez, 'Historia', pp. 734–5.
109 Béthencourt, *Historia genealógica*, 6, pp. 108–9.
110 'Temo que sobre su cabeza se muela tal haba', Mártir, *Epistolario*, 2, p. 248.
111 Fernández de Córdoba, *Historia y descripción*, pp. 164–70.
112 Bernáldez, 'Historia', p. 735.
113 RAH. Salazar. A-12.275-276, with names reported in Yun, *Crisis*, Appendix III, pp. 281–3. Fernando de Alarcón as the Marquis's *contador*: AHMA. Protocolos notariales L412.f.609r.
114 Béthencourt, *Historia genealógica*, 6, p. 110; Pedro de Alcocer, *Relación de algunas cosas que pasaron estos reinos desde que murió la reina católica Dona Isabel, hasta que se acabaron las comunidades en la ciudad de Toledo*, (Seville, 1872), p. 27.
115 RAH. Salazar. A-12.275-276; Yun, *Crisis*, Appendix III, pp. 281–3; Teodomiro Ramírez de Arrellano, *Colección de documentos inéditos ó raros y curiosos para la historia de Córdoba*, 1, (Cordoba, 1909), pp. 232–5; Maraver, *Historia de Córdoba*, 14, p. 59; ADM. AH. 3, 5–1.
116 Rodríguez Villa, *Crónicas*, p. LV.
117 Ibid.; 'Crónica general', p. 249; 'Crónica manuscrita', pp. 458–9.
118 Ibid.
119 Ruiz Domènec, *El Gran Capitán*, p. 441; Antonio Álvarez-Ossorio, 'Razón de linaje y lesa majestad. El Gran Capitán, Venecia y la corte de Fernando el Católico (1507-1509)', in Ernest Berlenguer (ed.), *De la unión de las coronas al Imperio de Carlos V*, 3, (Madrid, 2001), pp. 385–451.
120 ADM. AH. Leg.199, 23 August 1504.

121　Antonio Rodríguez Villa, 'Un cedulario del Rey Católico, 1508–1509', *BRAH*, 55, (1909), 205, 220–1.
122　AHNob, Villena, C12, D154; transcribed almost in full in Fernández de Córdoba, 'Historia y descripción', 74, pp. 164–70.
123　Béthencourt, *Historia genealógica*, 6, p. 109.
124　'Crónica general', p. 249.
125　Ibid.
126　Ruiz Domènec, *El Gran Capitán*, pp. 438–42.
127　Rosenstock, 'Against the Pagans'; Luis Suárez Fernández, 'El máximo religioso', *HEMP*, 17, 2, (Madrid, 1969), pp. 205–301. *Fundamentos*, p. 28.
128　Szmolka, *Epistolario*, 2, p. 717.
129　Ibid.
130　Pérez del Pulgar, 'Breve parte', p. 564.
131　Ibid., p. 565.
132　Ibid., p. 574.
133　Ruiz Domènec *El Gran Capitán*, p. 480.
134　Alvarez-Ossorio, 'Razón de linaje', lists names on p. 401.
135　Szmolka, *Epistolario*, 2, p. 463.
136　Helen Nader, *The Mendoza family in the Spanish Renaissance*, (Berkeley, 1972), pp. 150–79.
137　Ibid., pp. 25–6.
138　ADM.Leg.199, Baeza, 23 August 1504. This appears to be a reference to a hadith narrated by Abdullah ibn Amr, which Baeza may have become aware of through his close association with Muslims, referring to sectarianism and heterodoxy: 'And if the people of Israel were fragmented into seventy-two sects, my Ummah will be fragmented into seventy-three sects. All of them will be in Hell Fire except one sect'. Al-Tirmidhi Hadith 171. Along similar lines, Sunan Abu Dawood Hadith 4579 says 'The Jews were divided into 71 or 72 sects as were the Christians.' I am grateful to Roger Boase of Queen Mary University of London for drawing my attention to this.

Chapter 6

1　Beinecke MS 633, f.1.
2　Baeza: 5.
3　Ibid.: 14.
4　Baeza: 40; Zenete spent time in Italy at the same time as Baeza and frequented the literary circles of Cardinal Carvajal: Miguel Falomir Faus, 'El primer viaje a Italia del Marqués de Zenete', *Anuario del Departamento de Historia y Teoría del Arte*, 6 (1994), 101–20; Mercedes Gómez Ferrer, 'Las almonedas de libros del Marqués de Zenete en 1529 y 1535 en Valencia', *Lemir*, 14 (2010), 231–46; DBE: Rodrigo Díaz de Vivar y Mendoza.
5　David Coleman, *Creating Christian Granada*.
6　José Pita Andrade, *El libro de la Capilla Real de Granada*, (Granada, 1994).
7　José Doussinague, 'Fernando V en las vistas de Savona de 1507', *BRAH*, 108, (1936), 99–146.
8　RAH. Salazar A-12,151. Letter dated 6 July 1507.
9　Álvarez-Ossorio, 'Razón de linaje', p. 409.

10 ADM. AH. Leg.199, 25 September 1504 and 24 December 1506.
11 ADM.AH Leg. 200.25.
12 'Crónica Manuscrita', p. 454; Antonio Alvarez-Ossorio, 'Razón de linaje y lesa majestad. El Gran Capitán, Venecia y la Corte de Fernando el Católico (1507–1509)', in Ernest Berlenguer (ed.), *De la unión de las coronas al Imperio de Carlos V*, 3, (Madrid, 2001), pp. 385–451.
13 AGA.Priego.1063.408 and 305. However, he is not named as a witness to the vow of loyalty the *Gran Capitán* made to Fernando and Queen Juana on 14 May 1508: AGS. PTR. Leg. 7. D 246.
14 AHN.Villena.C.12, D.154. This document is a later (undated) copy.
15 Rodrigo Álvarez de Córdoba called a meeting of the Corregidor and those involved to hear Queen Juana's pardon read out: ADM. AH.3, 5-1; Gonzalo de Córdoba witnessed the Marquis empowering *Licenciado* Pedro Valles to retake possession of the office of *alcalde* on his behalf: ADM.Leg.271.41.
16 BNE.20211/27-52 (Cartas de Gonzalo Fernández de Córdoba); RAH. Salazar. A-14.13; AZ. 271.88-102 and 130-134.
17 IVDJ, E39, C51, 1.
18 APNG.G2.f.150r and G4.f.429v, the latter transcribed in Juan Obra Sierra, *Mercaderes Italianos en Granada*, (Granada, 1992), pp. 91–2.
19 Carriazo, 'Continuación inédita', p. 527; Benito Sánchez Alonso, *Historia de la historiografía española*, 1 (Madrid, 1941), p. 372.
20 Lafuente y Alcántara, *Relaciones*, p. 16.
21 RB.II/2503.f.6r; RBME.Y-111-6, f. 470r; Beinecke MS.633, f. 3r; Mercedes Delgado, 'Certezas e hipótesis sobre el final de la "crónica granadina" de Hernando de Baeza', *Anaquel de Estudios Arabes*, 29 (2018), 52.
22 Baeza: 5.
23 AHN. Inquisición.1515. f. 604r.
24 AGA. Priego.1002.390-443.
25 ACS. Expedientes de Limpieza de Sangre. A-8. f. 4r.
26 AASGC, T220.
27 Doussinague, *Cisma de Pisa*.
28 ADM.AH. Leg.199, 24 December 1506.
29 RBME.Y-111-6. f.12v. Catalogue entry online: http://rbme.patrimonionacional.es (accessed 20 July 2018).
30 Marc J Müller, *Die letzten Zeiten von Granada*, (Munich, 1863), pp. 57–95; Lafuente y Alcántara, *Relaciones*.
31 Mercedes Delgado Pérez, 'A newly-discovered manuscript of the *Historia de los Reyes Moros de Granada* by Hernando de Baeza', *Manuscript Studies*, 2, 2 (2017), 540–67, and 'Certezas'. The English translation is unsatisfactory in many places.
32 Richard Kagan, *Clio and the Crown. The Politics of History in Medieval and Early Modern Spain*, (Baltimore, 2009), pp. 53–4.
33 'Anales breves […] que dejo manuscritos el Dr. D. Lorenzo Galíndez Carvajal', *CODOIN 18*, (Madrid, 1851), pp. 227–536; *Crónicas de los Reyes de Castilla*, (Madrid, 1878), pp. 533–65.
34 Delgado, 'De Granada a Michoacán.'
35 Juan Pablo Rodríguez Argente del Castillo, Teresa Tinsley and José Rodríguez Molina, *La Relación de Hernando de Baeza sobre el Reino de Granada*, (Alcalá la Real, 2018).
36 Beinecke MS 633, f.1r.

37   IBIS Base de datos del patrimonio bibliográfico de Patrimonio Nacional. Papeles varios. https://realbiblioteca.patrimonionacional.es/cgi-bin/koha/opac-detail.pl?biblionumber=83500&query_desc=kw%2Cwrdl%3A%20II%2F2503 (2 February 2022).
38   Beinecke MS 633, f.1v.
39   RB.II/2503, f. 1; RBME. Y-111-6, f.465v; Delgado, 'A newly discovered manuscript', p. 553.
40   Pulgar, 'Tratado', pp. 59–60; Delgado notes that the manuscript versions of the *Tratado* vary slightly and that one seventeenth-century copy states that Baeza was a paid interpreter of the *Catholic Monarchs*: 'Certezas', p. 52.
41   E. Michael Gerli, 'Social crisis and conversion. Apostacy and Inquisition in the chronicles of Fernando del Pulgar and Andrés Bernáldez', *Hispanic Review*, 70 (2002), 147–67.
42   Carriazo, 'Estudio preliminar'; Brian Tate, 'Introduction', Fernando del Pulgar, *Claros varones de Castilla*, (Oxford, 1971)and 'Poles Apart. Two official historians of the Catholic Monarchs: Alfonso de Palencia and Fernando del Pulgar', in José María Soto Rábanos (ed.), *Pensamiento medieval hispano: homenaje a Horacio Santiago-Otero*, 1, (Madrid, 1998), pp. 439–63; Miguel Ángel Pérez Priego, 'Introducción', in Fernando de Pulgar, *Claros varones de Castilla*, (Madrid, 2007), pp. 11–68; Miguel Ángel Pallares Jiménez, 'Un pliego de las letras de Hernando del Pulgar', *Aragón en la Edad Media*, 12 (1995), 319–36; Ignacio Navarrete, 'Rhetorical and narrative paradigms in Fernando del Pulgar's Crónica de los Reyes Católicos', *Hispanic Review*, 2 (2004), 261–86; Silvia Iriso, 'Una *fablilla* de Fernando de Pulgar', *Revista de Literatura Medieval*, 13, 2 (2001), 63–76; Devid Paolini, 'Fernando del Pulgar. "Glosa a las Coplas de Mingo Revulgo". Addenda et corrigenda', *Revisita de Literatura Medieval*, 20 (2008), 247–54.
43   Carriazo, 'Estudio preliminar', pp. xvii–xviii.
44   Ibid.
45   Nicasio Salvador Miguel, *Isabel la Católica. Educación, mecenazgo y entorno literario*, (Alcalá de Henares, 2008), pp. 227–8; Pérez Priego, 'Introducción', p. 18; Pulgar, 'Tratado', p. 57.
46   Tate, 'Introduction', p. lvii.
47   Carriazo, 'Historia de la guerra', p. 394; see also Cabrera Muñoz, 'La guerra de Granada a través de las crónicas', p. 450; Lafuente Alcántara, *Relaciones*, p. VII. Carriazo said he would do a study on the *Tratado* but never did: 'Estudio preliminar', p. cvi.
48   José Enrique López de Coca, 'The Making of Isabel de Solís', in Roger Collins and Anthony Goodman (eds.), *Medieval Spain: Culture, Conflict and Coexistence*, (Basingstoke, 2002), p. 241.
49   John McKenna, *El 'Tratado de los Reyes de Granada y su origen'*, (MA dissertation, University of Kansas, 1963).
50   Esteban de Garibay, *Compendio Historial de España*, 4, (Barcelona, 1628), p. 324; Tate, 'Poles apart', p. 451.
51   Iñaki Bazán Díaz, 'Fernando del Pulgar y la vejez', *Miscelánea Medieval Murciana*, 16 (1990), 149–62.
52   As discussed in person 28 May 2016.
53   Pulgar, *Crónica*, 'Tabla de los capítulos', pp. 377–84.
54   Fernando del Pulgar, *Crónica de los Reyes Católicos* (ed. Juan de Mata Carriazo, Madrid, 1943), p. 3; Agnew, 'Silences', p. 478.

55 Pedro Hernández Martínez, 'Crónicas y cronistas en la España de los Reyes Católicos', *Revista EPCCM*, 15 (2013), 235–68.
56 Francisco de Medina y Mendoza, 'Vida del Cardenal D. Pedro González de Mendoça', in *Memorial Histórico Español*, 6, (Madrid, 1853), p. 305; Alonso de Santa Cruz, *Crónica de los Reyes Católicos*, (Seville, 1951); Juan de Mata Carriazo, 'Continuación inédita de la "Relación" de Hernando de Baeza', *Al-Andalus*, 13, 2 (1948), 431–42.
57 Antonio Herrera Casado, 'El historiador D. Francisco de Medina y Mendoza (1516–1577)', *Wad-al-Hayara*, 8 (1981), 445–51; 'Alonso de Santa Cruz', *DBE*.
58 Xavier Salas, 'Los inventarios de *La Alacena de Zurita*', *Butlletí de la Reial Academia de Bones Lletres de Barcelona*, 17, (1944), 80–177.
59 Ibid., p. 125.
60 See Pescador, 'Como fue de verdad'; Delgado, 'Certezas', 48; Gonzalo Argote de Molina, *Nobleza de Andalucía*, (Jaén, 1866), p. 52; *Epitome de las historias de la gran Casa de Guzmán*, BNE, Mss/2256-Mss/2258; José Gallardo, *Ensayo de una Biblioteca de libros raros y curiosos*, 3, (Madrid, 1888), p. 666; Barrantes Maldonado, 'Illustraciones', p. 397.
61 José María Rocamora, *Catálogo abreviado de los manuscritos de la biblioteca del excelentísimo señor Duque de Osuna*, (Madrid, 1882); Trevor Dadson, *Libros, lectores y lecturas: estudios sobre bibliotecas particulares españolas del Siglo de Oro*, (Madrid, 1998); Isabel Beceiro, *Libros, lecturas y bibliotecas en la España Medieval*, (Murcia, 2007).
62 See dedicated section in Joaquín Pérez Villanueva (ed.), *La Inquisición Española. Nueva visión, nuevos horizontes*, Joaquín, (Madrid, 1980), pp. 513–692.
63 Baeza: 25.
64 Lynn, *A College Professor*, p. 108. See also 'Lucio Marineo Sículo', *DBE*.
65 Ibid., pp. 146, 167.
66 Ibid., p. 177.
67 Ibid., p. 73.
68 Lynn, *A College Professor*, p. 200.
69 BNE, Biblioteca Digital Hispánica, INC/922; Georges Cirot, *Etudes sur l'historiographie espagnole. Les histoires générales d'Espagne entre Alphonse X et Philippe II (1284–1556)*, (Bordeaux/Paris, 1905), pp. 78–80.
70 Marineo Sículo, *Vida y hechos*, p. 93.
71 Kagan, *Clio and the Crown*, pp. 53–6.
72 Juan Torres Fontes, *Estudio sobre la Crónica de Enrique IV del Dr. Galíndez de Carvajal*, (Murcia, 1945); José María Ruiz Povedano, 'El doctor Lorenzo Galíndez de Carvajal, hombre de negocios en el Reino de Granada', *Baetica*, 3 (1980), 167–84; José Soto Vázquez and Ramón Pérez Parejo, 'Testimonios inéditos y perdidos del doctor Galíndez de Carvajal', *Lemir*, 13 (2009), 33–41; Delgado, 'Un manuscrito inédito', p. 3.
73 Gil Sanjuán, 'El parecer de Galíndez'; Goñi Gaztambide, 'La polemica'; Poutrin, 'The Jewish precedent', 78.
74 Soto Vazquez, 'Testimonios ineditos'.
75 'Anales breves', *Crónicas de los Reyes de Castilla*, (Madrid, 1878), p. 537. Although the work was not published until the nineteenth century, there are many surviving manuscript versions but, as yet, no overarching critical edition: José Soto Vázquez, 'Problemas de transmisión del "Memorial de los Reyes Catolicos" de Lorenzo Galíndez de Carvajal', Jesús Cañas Murillo et al. (eds.), *Medievalismo en Extremadura*, (Caceres, 2009), pp. 963–78.

76 'Anales breves', p. 536.
77 Michael Agnew, 'Crafting past and present: the figure of the historian in fifteenth-century Castile', (2000). *Dissertations available from ProQuest. AAI9976394.* https://repository.upenn.edu/dissertations/AAI9976394
78 Carriazo, 'Estudio preliminar', p. cxxvii; and in Santa Cruz, *Crónica*, pp. clxxxvii–cxciii.
79 Rafael Ramírez de Arrellano, 'Estudios biográficos', *BRAH*, 41 (1902), 304.
80 AGS.REG.LEG,147907,14; AGS,CCA,CED,9,91,4.
81 AGS.CCA-PUE-6.2.227.
82 Miguel Angel Orti Belmonte, 'La biografía de Gonzalo de Ayora', *BRAC*, 74 (1956), 14; Marcelino Cardalliaguet, 'Cronistas, apologistas y biógrafos de la Reina Isabel de Castilla', Revista de Extremadura (2004), p. 1024.
83 Baeza: 20. This is the second count of Cabra, who died in 1487. The relationship between the Ayoras and the Cabras: AGS. RGS.LEG.147511,533.2, and Cabrera Sánchez, *Nobleza*, p. 369.
84 Eugenio de Ochoa, 'Cartas de Gonzalo de Ayora', *Epistolario español*, 1, (Madrid, 1850), pp. 61–74.
85 Fernández Duro, 'Noticias', p. 434.
86 Ibid., p. 439.
87 Ibid., p. 451.
88 Reproduced by Prudencio de Sandoval, *Historia de la vida y hechos del Emperador Carlos V*, (Madrid, 1955–56), 5.36.
89 Orti Belmonte, 'Biografia de Gonzalo de Ayora', 5; ADM. AH. Leg.199, 24 December 1506; Manuel Danvila, 'Un manuscrito de la biblioteca nacional de Madrid acerca de las comunidades atribuido a Gonzalo de Ayora', *BRAH*, 28 (1896), 97–135; Ramírez de Arellano, 'Estudios biográficos', pp. 316–18; I have explored elsewhere the Baeza family's links to the revolutionary *Santa Junta* which operated from 1520 to 1521: 'Conversos y comuneros. The trial of Juan Rodríguez de Baeza, Salamanca, 1520', *Historia y Genealogía*, 9 (2020), 79–92.
90 A sixteenth-century account, wrongly attributed to Ayora, makes a specific connection between the Marquis's 'rebellion' and the events of 1520: Manuel Danvila, 'Un manuscrito', p. 105; Stephen Haliczer, *The Comuneros of Castile: the forging of a revolution, 1475–1521*, (Madison, 1981); John Edwards, 'La noblesse de Cordoue et la révolte des "comunidades" de Castille', in *Bandos y querellas dinásticas en España al final de la Edad Media*, (Paris, 1991), pp. 135–55; Julio Valdeón, 'La conflictividad social en Castilla', in *El Tratado de Tordesillas y su época*, (Junta de Castilla y León, Valladolid, 1995), pp. 315–24. See also Alcocer, *Relación*.
91 Kagan, *Clio and the Crown*, p. 73.
92 RBME, online: http://rbme.patrimonionacional.es/home/Sobre-la-Biblioteca/Historia/Procedencias-principales.aspx (2 February 2022).
93 Brian Tate, *Ensayos sobre la historiografía peninsular del siglo XV*, (Madrid, 1970). Alan Deyermond, 'Learned prose and the rise of fiction, 1300–1500', *A Literary History of Spain. The Middle Ages*, (London, 1971), pp. 136–77; B. L. Ullman, 'Leonardo Bruni and Humanist Historiography', in *Studies in the Italian Renaissance*, (Rome, 1973), pp. 321–43; William Crossgrove, 'The vernacularisation of Science, Medicine and Technology in Late Medieval Europe', *Early Science and Medicine*, 5, 1 (2000), 47–63; Christian Bratu, 'De la grande histoire à l'histoire personelle. L'émergence de l'écriture autobiographique chez les historiens français du Moyen Age', *Mediaevistik*, 25 (2012), 85–117.

94 Tate, *Ensayos,* pp. 33–54; 'Pero López de Ayala' and 'Fernán Pérez de Guzmán', *DBE.*
95 James Fogelquist, 'Introduction', *Pedro del Corral, Crónica del rey Don Rodrigo,* (Madrid, 2001), p. 53, quoting from Pérez de Guzman's *Generaciones y semblanzas.*
96 Weiss, 'Flavius Josephus'; Tate, 'Poles Apart'.
97 Palencia, *Crónica,* pp. 263–7.
98 José Cepada Adan, 'El providencialismo en los cronistas de los Reyes Católicos', *Arbor,* 17 (1950), 177–90; Nader, *The Mendoza family,* pp. 19–34 (chapter entitled 'Political propaganda and the writing of history in fifteenth-century Castile'); Juan Carlos Conde, 'La historiografía en verso: precisiones sobre las características de un (sub)género literario', *Medioevo y Literatura,* II (1995), 47–59; Kagan, *Clio and the crown,* pp. 16–56.
99 Nader, *The Mendoza family,* pp. 25–6.
100 Carvajal, *La conquista de Baza*; Peinado Santaella, 'Cristo pelea', pp. 467–72; Fernández de Córdova Miralles, 'La emergencia de Fernando', pp. 60–1.
101 Eugene Tigerstedt, 'Johannes Annius and "Graecia mendax"', in Charles Henderson (ed.), *Classical, Medieval and Renaissance Studies in honour of B. L. Ullman,* II, (Rome, 1964), pp. 293–310; Walter Stephens, 'From Berossos to Berosus Chaldaeus: the forgeries of Annius of Viterbo and their fortune', *The World of Berossos,* (Weisbaden, 2013), pp. 277–89.
102 Caballero López, 'Annio de Viterbo'.
103 Brian Tate, 'Mitología en la historiografía española de la Edad Media y del Renacimiento', *Ensayos,* pp. 13–32.
104 Marc Mayer i Olivé, 'El prefacio de las *Antiquitates* de Juan Annio de Viterbo: oportunidad e intención política', in José María Maestre Maestre et al. (eds.), *Humanismo y pervivencia del mundo clásico. Homenaje al profesor Juan Gil,* (Instituto de Estudios Humanísticos, 2015), pp. 117–8.
105 Tigerstedt, 'Johannes Annius', p. 299.
106 José Antonio Caballero López, 'Annio de Viterbo y la historiografía española del siglo XVI', in *Humanismo y tradición clásica en España y América,* (León, 2002), pp. 117–18; Tate, *Ensayos,* p. 190.
107 Julio Caro Baroja, *Las falsificaciones de la historia,* (Barcelona, 1992), pp. 49–78; Anthony Grafton, *Defenders of the text. The traditions of scholarship in an age of science 1450–1800,* (Cambridge, 1994), pp. 76–103, and *Forgers and critics: creativity and duplicity in Western scholarship,* (Princeton, 1990), pp. 48–64 and 104–7.
108 Tate, (*Ensayos,* p. 25) references Tigerstedt in relation to this assertion; however, Tigerstedt only says that Carvajal took the manuscript to Spain.
109 Bernáldez, *Historia,* p. 30.
110 Starr-Lebeau, *In the shadow,* pp. 237–9; Cotarelo, *Fray Diego,* p. 143.
111 ADM.AH. Leg. 271. 103-118 (106).
112 Ibid.
113 Ruth Pike, *Aristocrats and Traders. Sevillian society in the 16th century,* (Ithaca, NY, 1972), p. 54; Juan Gil, *Los conversos,* 2, pp. 103–7. Neither author appears aware of Juan Rodríguez de Baeza's link with Hernando.
114 Bernáldez, *Historia,* p. 28; José Enrique López de Coca, 'El otro en la crónica de Andrés Bernáldez', in Ricardo Córdoba de La Llave et al. (eds.), *Estudios en homenaje a Emilio Cabrera Muñoz,* (Córdoba, 2015), pp. 293–306.
115 Rosenstock, 'Against the Pagans'. Rosenstock does not mention Bernáldez specifically.
116 López de Coca, 'El otro', pp. 305–6.
117 Bernáldez, *Historia,* pp. 27–8.

118 Ibid., p. 29.
119 Ibid., p. 28.
120 Ibid., pp. 98; 97; 99.
121 Ibid., p. 104.
122 Ibid., p. 267.
123 ADM. AH. Leg.199, 23 August 1504.

Chapter 7

1 Pulgar, 'Tratado', pp. 59–60, claiming that this observation came from Hernando de Baeza's book of notes.
2 For example, Rafaela Castrillo, 'Salobreña, prisión real de la dinastía Nasrí', *Al-Ándalus*, 2 (1963), 463–72; Fernando de la Granja, 'Condena de Boabdil por los alfaquíes de Granada', *Ál-Andalus*, 36 (1971), 145–76; Luis Seco de Lucena, 'La Administración Central de Los Nazaríes', *Cuadernos de La Alhambra*, 10–11 (1974–5), 21–6; Harvey, *Islamic Spain*, pp. 262, 265 and 283; Catherine Gaignard, *Maures et Chrétiens à Grenade: 1492–1570* (Paris, 1997), pp. 15–18.
3 Ruiz Domènec, *El Gran Capitán*, p. 206; Lafuente Alcántara, *Relaciones*, p. x.
4 Conde, 'La historiografía en verso'; Peinado Santaella, 'Cristo pelea' and 'El final de la Reconquista: elegía de la derrota, exaltación del triunfo', in Manuel García Fernández and Carlos Alberto González Sánchez (eds.), *Andalucía y Granada en tiempos de los Reyes Católicos* (Sevilla, 2006); Ruiz Povedano, 'Exaltación y propaganda'; Salvador Miguel, 'La conquista de Málaga'.
5 See also: Tinsley, 'Granada como espejo de Castilla en la "Relación" de Hernando de Baeza', in Francisco Toro Ceballos (ed.), *Estudios de Frontera*, 11 (Alcalá la Real, 2020), pp. 467–74 and 'Reframing the reconquista'.
6 Ana Isabel Carrasco Manchado, 'Propaganda política en los panegíricos de los Reyes Católicos. Una aproximación', *Anuario de Estudios Medievales*, 25, 2 (1995), 517–44; Ruiz Povedano, 'Exaltación'; Peinado Santaella, 'Cristo pelea'; Devereux, *The other side of empire*.
7 Peinado Santaella, 'Cristo pelea', p. 504, quoting letters of Pedro Mártir de Anglería.
8 Baeza: 5.
9 Ibid.: 11.
10 Henshall, *Absolutism*, pp. 123–5.
11 Szmolka, 'Nobleza y autoritarismo'; Fernández Álvarez, 'La crisis', pp. 696–9.
12 Milhou, *Pouvoir royal et absolutisme*, pp. 45–55.
13 Known as Ṯurayya (Zorayda) in Arabic sources, she has passed into legend as Isabel de Solís: López de Coca, 'The making of Isabel de Solís'.
14 Quintanilla, 'Facciones'.
15 Rodríguez Villa, *Crónicas del Gran Capitán*, pp. LV and 456.
16 Baeza: 43.
17 Ibid.
18 Machiavelli, *The Prince*, 21. Machiavelli was writing in 1513.
19 Baeza: 3.
20 Baeza: 38; 8.
21 Galatians, 3.28.

22 Elena Bellido Vela describes her as the 'cornerstone' of the history of Montilla: 'Ana Ponce de León, Condesa de Feria', *Montillanos en la Memoria*, (Montilla, 2013), pp. 172–5. I am grateful to Antonio Luis Jiménez Barranco for additional material on Catalina Fernández de Córdoba, not yet in the public domain.

23 Derek Lomax, *The Reconquest of Spain* (London, 1978), p. 39 and see also María Soledad Carrasco Urgoiti, *The Moorish Novel* (Boston, 1976); John Tolan, *Sons of Ishmael. Muslims through European Eyes in the Middle Ages*, (Florida, 2008).

24 Ron Barkai, *Cristianos y musulmanes en la España medieval (El enemigo en el espejo)* (Madrid, 1984), pp. 237–46 and 288.

25 Echevarría, *Fortress of faith*, especially, pp. 18–19.

26 Carriazo (ed.) *Hechos del Condestable*; María Soledad Carrasco Urgoiti, *El moro de Granada en la Literatura (del siglo XV al XX)* (Madrid, 1956), p. 28.

27 Devaney, *Enemies in the Plaza*, p. 92.

28 Ibid., pp. 14–15.

29 Peinado Santaella, 'Cristo pelea', p. 512; Ruiz Povedano, 'Exaltación y propaganda', p. 493.

30 Vega García, *Fray Hernando de Talavera*, pp. 284–5.

31 López de Coca, 'El otro', pp. 297–8.

32 Baeza: 15; 38; 42.

33 ADM, AH. 277.1 and 2.

34 Baeza: 38.

35 Barkai, Cristianos y musulmanes, p. 287; Simon Barton, *Conquerors, Brides, and Concubines. Interfaith Relations and Social Power in Medieval Iberia* (Philadelphia, 2015).

36 Palencia, *Guerra*, p. 108.

37 ADM, AH. 277.1 and 2.

38 Baeza: 1.

39 For example: Seco de Lucena, 'La Administración Central', pp. 21–6; Barbara Boloix, *Las sultanas de la Alhambra*, (Granada, 2013).

40 Baeza: 6; 44.

41 Ibid.: 36; 39; 1.

42 Barkai, *Cristianos y musulmanes*, p. 238.

43 Baeza: 39. In referring to the rooms in the Alhambra, he uses the Spanish names still used today: 'Torre de Comares' and 'Cuarto de Leones'.

44 Poutrin, 'Los derechos', p. 18.

45 Baeza: 36.

46 Ibid.: 14; Fernando de la Granja, 'Fiestas cristianas en Al-Andalus', *Al-Andalus*, 34 (1969), 1–53 and 35 (1970), 119–42.

47 Baeza: 1.

48 Carrasco Urgoiti, *El moro de Granada en la Literatura*, p. 26.

49 Baeza: 1.

50 Ibid., p. 3. The ballad is the *Romance de Abenámar*: Juan Torres Fontes, 'La historicidad del Romance Abenámar, Abenámar', *Anuario de Estudios Medievales*, 8 (1972), 225–56.

51 Tate, 'Introduction', p. xxx.

52 Tinsley, 'La "nueva convivencia" de Hernando de Baeza', in Javier García Benítez (ed.), *El valor del documento. Estudios en homenaje al profesor José Rodríguez Molina*, (Almería, 2018), pp. 199–212.

53 Tinsley, 'Reframing the *Reconquista*'.

54 Baker, *Translation and Conflict*, p. 33.
55 Samuel Huntington, 'The Clash of Civilizations?', *Foreign Affairs*, 72, 3 (1993), 22–49; Richard Bulliet, *The Case for Islamo-Christian Civilisation*, (New York, 2006); Adam Kosto, 'Reconquest, Renaissance and the Histories of Iberia', in Thomas F. X. Noble and John Van Engen (eds.), *European Transformations. The Long Twelfth Century* (Notre Dame, 2012).
56 María Rosa Menocal, 'Why Iberia?', *Diacritics*, 36, 3–4 (2006), 7–11; María Isabel Fierro Bello, '¿Qué hacer con al-Ándalus?' and other articles in José Torrecilla and Antonio Cortijo Ocaña, 'Al-Ándalus y la identidad española: historia y mito', *eHumanista*, 37 (2017), http://www.ehumanista.ucsb.edu/volumes/37 (accessed 20 March 2021).
57 E. Michael Gerli, 'The *converso* Condition: New Approaches to an Old Question', in Ivy A. Corfis and Ray Harris-Northall (eds.), *Medieval Iberia. Changing Societies and Cultures in Contact and Transition* (Woodbridge, 2007), pp. 3–15.
58 Kaplan, 'Toward the establishment'.
59 Teresa Jiménez Calvente, 'Los comentarios a *Las Trescientas* de Juan de Mena', *Revista de Filología Española*, 82 (2002), 25; María Rosa Lida de Malkiel, *Juan de Mena, poeta del prerrenacimiento español* (Mexico, 1950); Juan de Mena, *Laberinto de Fortuna*, (ed. Louise Vasvari Fainberg), (Madrid, 1982). Baeza's quote, p. 156.
60 Hernán Núñez de Toledo, *Glosa sobre las 'Trezientas' del famoso poeta Juan de Mena* (eds. Julian Weiss and Antonio Cortijo Ocaña, Madrid, 2015); Cristina Moya García, 'El "Laberinto de Fortuna" y la frontera de Granada', in Francisco Toro Ceballos and José Rodríguez Molina (eds.), *Estudios de Frontera 9* (Alcalá la Real, 2014), pp. 491–8; Helen Nader, '"The Greek Commander" Hernán Núñez de Toledo, Spanish Humanist and Civil Leader', *Renaissance Quarterly*, 31, 4 (1978), 463–85; Jiménez Calvente, 'Los comentarios', p. 36.
61 Quintanilla, 'Biblioteca', 371.
62 Gilman, 'A generation of "conversos"'; Gregory Hutcheson, 'Cracks in the Labyrinth: Juan de Mena, "Converso" Experience, and the Rise of the Spanish Nation', *La Corónica*, 25, 1 (1996), 37–52.
63 Adeline Rucquoi, 'Las oligarquías urbanas y las primeras burguesías en Castilla', in *Tratado de Tordesillas*, 1, p. 345.
64 That is, St James/Santiago: Baeza: 18.
65 Gilman, 'A Generation of *conversos*?', pp. 89, 95.
66 Francisco Márquez Villanueva, 'La criptohistoria morisca (los otros conversos)', in Augustín Redondo (ed.), *Les problèmes de l'exclusion en Espagne (XVIe-XVIIe siècles). Idéologie et discours*, (Paris, 1983), pp. 77–94; Fuchs, *Exotic Nation*, p. 36.
67 Baeza: 39.
68 José María Chamorro, 'El léxico de los judeoconversos según los procesos Inquisitoriales', *MEAH*, 55 (2006), 124.
69 Baeza: 14; 32.
70 Baeza: 8.
71 Carriazo, 'Estudio Preliminar', p.lvii; Gerli, 'Social Crisis and Conversion'.
72 Baeza: 6.
73 Ibid.
74 Julio Caro Baroja has commented on this, but not in relation to *judeoconversos*: *Los moriscos del Reino de Granada* (Madrid, 1991), p. 218.
75 Enrique Soria Mesa, 'Tomando nombres ajenos. La usurpación de apellidos como estrategia de ascenso social en el seno de la élite granadina durante la época

moderna', in Soria Mesa et al. (eds.), *Las élites en la época moderna: la monarquía española*, I (Cordoba, 2009), pp. 9–27.
76   Baeza: 5.
77   Ibid.
78   Rábade Obradó, 'La invención como necesidad'.
79   Ryan Szpiech, 'Conversion as a historiographical problem: the case of Zoraya/Isabel de Solís', in Yaniv Fox and Yosi Yisraeli (eds.), *Contesting Inter-Religious Conversion in the Medieval World* (New York, 2017), pp. 24–38.
80   Bernáldez, *Historia*, pp. 96–7.
81   Baeza: 8; 9.
82   Ibid.: 38.
83   Ibid.
84   Charles Herberman (ed.), *The Catholic Encyclopaedia*, 10 (New York, 1913), p. 199.
85   Tolan, *Sons of Ismael*, pp. 66–78.
86   Pulgar, *Tratado*, pp. 63–4.
87   Ibid.
88   Francisco Delicado, *Retrato de la Lozana Andaluza* (Madrid, 1871), p. 1.
89   María Antonia Garcés, *Cervantes in Algiers. The Captive's Tale* (Nashville, 2005).
90   For example, Erasmus's *Education of a Christian Prince* (1516) or Thomas More's *History of King Richard III* (1512–19). Erasmus approaches the topic in his elaboration of the fable of the scarab and the eagle but seems to conclude that resistance leads only to everlasting conflict and slaughter: Denis L Drysdall, 'Erasmus on Tyranny and Terrorism: Scarabaeus aquilam quaerit and the Institutio pricipis christiani', *Erasmus of Rotterdam Society Yearbook*, 29 (2009), 89–102.
91   Silke Jansen and Irene Weiss (eds.), *Fray Antonio de Montesino y su tiempo*, (Madrid/Frankfurt, 2017), especially Bernat Hernández, 'Un sermón dominico en La Española de 1511 y sus contextos medievales y atlánticos', pp. 55–69.
92   Michael Jones, 'Philippe de Commynes – a courtly middle-man', *History Today*, 39, 3 (1989), 34–41.

Hernando de Baeza's history of Granada

1   The Escorial manuscript contains a separate page as a preface which translates as: 'The things that happened between the kings of Granada from the time of King Juan of Castile, second of that name, till the Catholic Monarchs won the kingdom of Granada, written and compiled by Hernando de Baeza, who was present for most of what he recounts, and the rest he learnt from the Moors of that kingdom and from their chronicles.' See p. 102 for headings used in the other manuscripts.
2   'suma'.
3   Juan II (1405–54) inherited the throne aged one and came of age in 1419.
4   'Alayçar'. Reigned 1419–27, 1430–1, 1432–45, 1447–53: 'Muhammad IX', *DBE*.
5   The author's perspective is as from Castile.
6   Recognizing the negative connotations the word 'Moor' now carries, I was initially inclined to translate it as 'Muslim'. However, as I became more familiar with the text, I felt that to do so would tend to frame the events Baeza describes as a 'clash of civilisations', which is exactly what he is trying to avoid. See Chapter 8 for discussion of this.

7	Juan II 'valiantly' crossing the watercourse in this scene contrasts later with the Moors' ill-advised decision to cross a stream at Lucena and their ignominious defeat – see below sections 18–24.
8	'la vatalla de la higuera grande'. This is the Battle of La Higueruela, 1 July 1431, Juan II's most important victory against Granada.
9	'Çad'. Reigned 1454–5, 1455–62, 1463–4: 'Sa'ad (Ciriza)', *DBE*.
10	'rriguroso'.
11	Here Baeza collapses the chronology: although Mohammed IX was deposed after La Higueruela, he later returned to the throne on several occasions, and it was not until 1454 that he was replaced by Sa'ad.
12	'Abulhacen'. Generally rendered in Spanish as Muley Hacén.
13	'Caballero' is a word which appears frequently in the text and is difficult to translate. In some contexts, it seems to come heavily laden with the overtones of chivalric culture; elsewhere it refers to a high-status or honourable individual (perhaps 'gentleman'), while in some contexts it simply means someone riding a horse. I have retained the original Spanish where this gives a better sense of the richness of meaning contained.
14	Torres Fontes, 'La historicidad del Romance Abenámar'.
15	'jara y çuna'. Baeza's German editor Müller suggests that 'jara' is a rendering of what he transliterates from Arabic as *schar'* (law), and gives 'çuna' as *sunna*: *Die letzten Zeiten*, p. 61.
16	This seems like a summary rather than an actual document transcribed by Baeza.
17	'a la gineta': with short stirrups.
18	The 'juego de cañas' was a typical sport played on both sides of the frontier.
19	The future Enrique IV.
20	The Beineke manuscript starts here with ' … su batalla y el prinçipe […]'.
21	'truxo': here Baeza writes as from the Alhambra.
22	'Ahogar con una touaja'.
23	This legend is still told to visitors to the Alhambra today.
24	'almogávares'.
25	In reality, about 50 kilometres. Baeza is very specific about the distance, suggesting that it is a location he knows well.
26	'no auia sido muger de buen gesto'. López de Coca translates this section, rendering this as 'she did not seem to me to be a woman with a good face': 'The making of Isabel de Solís', p. 227. Santa Cruz uses Baeza's words 'buen gesto' but, without the negative, powerfully contributing to the legend of Isabel de Solís (*Crónica*, p. 39).
27	'lleuar todas las donzellas de su casa por vn rasero'.
28	Isabel and Fernando's only son, who died in 1497 aged nineteen.
29	'allende': a common way of referring to North Africa at the time.
30	Baeza seems to be saying that the Abencerrajes treated the Castilian nobles and their households well, not the other way around.
31	'rey chiquito'. Boabdil was known in Castilian circles the 'Rey Chico' to distinguish him from his father. Here Baeza adds another diminutive, perhaps to express a certain affection.
32	'se ganó Granada'.
33	'Del linaje', according to the Escorial manuscript, though Beinecke gives 'de linaje', which would give the alternative translation 'not of noble birth', and Real Biblioteca is ambiguous, running the words together as 'delinaje'.
34	'aun ponia lengua en él'.

35 'que cesase su lengua'.
36 The way Baeza dramatizes this scene perhaps owes a debt to the theatrical performances he would have seen in Italy.
37 'alguacil mayor'.
38 The contrast between the servant's well-argued defence of his stance and the emir's brusque response serves to highlight the moral distance between the two.
39 'hombre'.
40 This seems to be a popular saying which the manuscripts render very slightly differently. Real Biblioteca and Escalante use the present tense here: 'don't do harm'.
41 The Beinecke manuscript does not make a paragraph break here.
42 Cieza is in Murcia, Villacarrillo is in Jaén, in fact, a long way from Murcia, but perhaps along the route they took. Juan Torres Fontes dates the assault on Cieza as 1477: 'Dualidad fronteriza: guerra y paz', in Pedro Segura Artero (ed.), *La Frontera Oriental Nazarí como sujeto histórico*, (Almería, 1997), p. 65.
43 'casi se estavan en la ynocencia del capillo': the *capillo* was a cloth headdress used at baptism and in penitential rites.
44 'villa de Motrin'. Presumably the frontier fortress-town of Moclín, captured in 1486 and held for the Crown by Martín de Alarcón. Delgado notes that the Escalante manuscript renders it as 'Motril': 'Certezas', p. 44.
45 Martín de Alarcón: Duran y Lerchundi, *La toma de Granada*, 2, pp. 441–7.
46 This took place on 29 September 1471 and was one of the most shocking raids of the period, particularly as it was seen to have been supported by Christians. It is recounted by a contemporary in: Carriazo (ed.), *Hechos del Condestable,* pp. 443 and 467.
47 One of the core possessions of the House of Aguilar.
48 'Ballesteros de maça'. These were court officials who formed a sort of praetorian guard for the Castilian kings: Francisco Martínez López, *Los oficios palatinos en la Castilla de los Reyes Católicos* (Madrid, 2004), p. 174.
49 Muhammad XII, 'al-Zagal', *DBE*.
50 Lafuente Alcantara renders this using the adjective 'católica', with the effect of making the 'glorious memory', refer only to the queen. However, the manuscripts clearly state 'católicos' and are ambiguous as to whether the king is also dead.
51 This was in 1470: Harvey, *Islamic Spain*, p. 265.
52 This phrase is not in the Real Biblioteca manuscript.
53 The Escorial manuscript varies from the other three here, citing one hour.
54 The Escorial version does not mention grasses (hierbas).
55 Then, as now, a main shopping street.
56 'alcaiceria'.
57 A close collaborator of Boabdil's, involved in cross-border exchanges for the ransoming of captives: Padilla, 'Determinación de dubdas', p. 521, and other references in note 248.
58 The Escorial and Real Biblioteca manuscripts show 'Alora', presumably in error since the previous mention clearly reads 'Mora'. The Beinecke version gives this correctly.
59 See discussion of this individual in Chapter 3.
60 This is Hernán Pérez del Pulgar, later the author of a biography of the *Gran Capitán* ('Breve Parte'), not the chronicler Fernando del Pulgar.
61 Readers are perhaps being reminded of Jesus speaking to the elders in the temple.
62 Baeza distinguishes between Boabdil, who is the 'príncipe', and his younger brother, the 'ynfante'.

63 Baeza contrasts the solemnity of Boabdil's marriage with the dissoluteness of Abū al-Ḥasan.
64 Don Diego Fernández de Córdoba, Lord of Lucena, Espejo and Chillón, *DBE*.
65 The Real Biblioteca version omits the first half of this sentence – presumably a case of eye skip.
66 That is, St James, Santiago. From the poem known as 'Las Trescientas', discussed in Chapter 8. The Real Biblioteca manuscript omits part of his sentence and the Beinecke manuscript omits 'good' in front of Zebedee.
67 There is no paragraph break here in the Real Biblioteca manuscript.
68 A well-known veteran of the frontier.
69 Each manuscript renders this slightly differently. The Real Biblioteca and Escalante versions indicate a friar or friars whom Baeza knew well, but not necessarily his own confessor (noted by Delgado, 'Certezas', pp. 45–6). I have favoured the Escorial version here, with the Beinecke version offering a similar sense.
70 The Real Biblioteca manuscript omits 'not' here, which makes no sense. In the next sentence the scribe duplicates a phrase, suggesting a lapse in concentration.
71 Type of helmet which covers the back of the neck illustrated at: http://armasyarmadurasenespaa.blogspot.com/2013/04/cascos.html (accessed 25 March 2021).
72 The first of a number of colourful idiomatic exchanges that Baeza includes which complement the more formal dialogues.
73 Baeza uses the word 'cinta': an archaic form of 'cintura': 'desusado: parte estrecha del cuerpo sobre las caderas', *Real Diccionario del Español, Edición del Tricentenario* (2017): https://dle.rae.es/cinta (accessed 26 March 2021).
74 'Ynfante', i.e. Zagal.
75 'lo testo'.
76 Baeza brings to mind the story of Abraham and Isaac – even perhaps the death of Jesus. His readers would indeed have heard and read of a father being ready to sacrifice his son.
77 Here Baeza depicts the challenge for court officials attempting to dissuade a monarch from following a bad policy. The Beinecke and Escalante manuscripts vary from the other two in suggesting that the *mizwar* was in fact put to death for his pains (Delgado, 'Certezas', p. 46). However, the build-up describing the *mizwar*'s efforts to prevent the execution, and the author's observation that 'this was the reason', suggest that it is the Escorial and Real Biblioteca manuscripts that correctly reflect the author's intention here.
78 Here Baeza presents the consternation of court officials having to speak truth to power.
79 So called after marriage celebrations there in 1497 for Prince Juan and Margaret of Austria.
80 'Baudeli'.
81 I have not been able to identify this individual, like Santa Cruz, another *mudéjar* with a Christian-sounding surname.
82 The Escorial, Real Biblioteca and Beinecke manuscripts all give Abrahén de Alora though, as the previous mention in section 15 makes clear, the reference is clearly to Baeza's *mudéjar* friend, the man from Mora, Toledo.
83 A Muslim resident of Granada by this name was involved in a court case in 1493: AGS. RGS, LEG.149305,210.
84 1487.

85	'zala'.
86	Alcántara Lafuente renders this in Spanish as 'capa'. The El Escorial manuscript is unclear; it could be read as 'caxa' or 'capa' and the Real Biblioteca manuscript definitely gives 'capa'. However, the Beineke manuscript is clear in giving 'caxa' = box and this is the more likely rendering.
87	See José and Manuel Oliver Hurtado, *Granada y sus monumentos árabes*, (Malaga, 1875), p. 198.
88	This is the Alcazaba Cadima (al-Qasba Qadima), the original eleventh-century fortress occupying the upper Albaicín.
89	'Rodrigo Díaz de Vivar y Mendoza', first Marquis of Zenete, *DBE*. The palace is now the Hospital de la Tiña: http://www.albaicin-granada.com/seccion.php?listEntrada=127 (26/3/2021).
90	The Christian troops set up camp outside Baza in June 1489 and the town surrendered at the end of that year: Carriazo, 'Historia de la guerra', pp. 749–72.
91	'rey pequeño'.
92	Here 'Moclín' is clear.
93	Abū al-Qāsim.
94	Presumably Granadans, but Baeza leaves open the possibility that it might have been advice from the Castilian side.
95	Otherwise known as Yusuf ibn Kumasha. See Chapter 2, note 67 in main text.
96	The Beinecke gives 'al caya'. See Chapter 2, note 58 in main text for further references to this individual.
97	The section used almost verbatim by the chronicler Alonso de Santa Cruz starts here.
98	This seems to be a new character.
99	The Escorial manuscript ends here.
100	'huertas' in each of the three manuscripts. The sense might suggest it should be 'puertas' (gates) – however the next section makes clear that they did go out beyond the gates of the city.
101	'pasar allende'.
102	'caballero'.
103	The Beinecke manuscript contains a blank space here, while the Real Biblioteca and Escalante manuscripts start a new paragraph.
104	The Escalante manuscript gives 'de ençima de Marbella' (Delgado, 'A newly-discovered manuscript', p. 560); however, both the Beinecke and Real Biblioteca manuscripts give the more probable 'veçino de Marbella'.
105	'Abulcaçin El Male'.
106	'de derecho': this can be understood also as a legal question – see discussion in Chapter 3.
107	This dating is anomalous, given that we know that the surrender document was signed at the end of November 1491 and the handover took place at the beginning of January 1492. Editors and copyists seem to have noted this anomaly since, in the Real Biblioteca manuscript, the date has been corrected from 1490 and the Beinecke manuscript, which also gives 1490, has been amended to 1492. The Escalante manuscript gives 1491 and Delgado suggests that Baeza may have been following a dating system based on Easter: 'Certezas', 562.
108	The Escalante manuscript inserts the word 'perro' (dog) here, ibid.

Selected bibliography

Published primary sources

Baeza, Hernando de, 'Las cosas que pasaron', in Lafuente y Alcántara, Emilio (ed.), *Relaciones de algunos sucesos de los últimos tiempos del Reino de Granada* (Madrid, 1868), pp. 1–45.
Baeza, Hernando de, 'Cosas de Granada', in Müller, Marc J. (ed.), *Die letzten Zeiten von Granada* (Munich, 1863), pp. 57–95.
Bernáldez, Andrés, 'Historia de los Reyes Católicos', in *Crónicas de los Reyes de Castilla* (Madrid, 1878), pp. 567–773.
Fernández de Córdoba, Francisco, 'Historia y descripción de la antigüedad y descendencia de la Casa de Córdova', *BRAC*, 70–92 (1954–72), paginated consecutively and separately from the rest of the journal.
Galíndez de Carvajal, Lorenzo, 'Anales breves [...] que dejo manuscritos el Dr. D. Lorenzo Galindez Carvajal', *CODOIN*, 18 (Madrid, 1851), pp. 227–536; also published in *Crónicas de los Reyes de Castilla* (Madrid, 1878), pp. 533–65.
Garrido Atienza, Miguel, *Las capitulaciones para la entrega de Granada* (Granada, 1910).
Gaspar y Remiro, Mariano, 'Documentos árabes de la Corte Nazarí de Granada, o primeros tratos y correspondencia íntima entre los Reyes Católicos y Boabdil sobre la entrega de Granada', *RABM*, 21 (1909), 330–9; 531–5; 22 (1910), 260–9; 421–31; 23 (1910), 137–48; 410–23.
Gaspar y Remiro, Mariano, *Últimos pactos y correspondencia íntima entre los Reyes Católicos y Boabdil* (Granada, 1910).
Gracia Boix, Rafael, *La historia de la Inquisición en Córdoba. Colección de documentos* (Cordoba, 1982).
Guicciardini, Francesco, *The History of Italy*, 3 (trans. Austin Parke Goddard), London, 1753.
Machiavelli, Niccòlo, The Prince, Project Gutenberg EBook: https://www.gutenberg.org/files/1232/1232-h/1232-h.htm#link2HCH0017 (last accessed 16 December 2017).
Marineo Sículo, Lucio, *Vida y hechos de los Reyes Católicos* (Madrid, 1943).
Mártir de Anglería, Pedro, *Epístolario*, 2 (Madrid, 1955).
Medina y Mendoza, Francisco de, 'Vida del Cardenal D. Pedro González de Mendoça', in *Memorial Histórico Nacional*, Colección de documentos, opúsculos y antigüedades, 6 (Madrid, 1853), pp. 153–310.
Miguel Mora, Carlos de, *Bernardino de Carvajal, La conquista de Baza* (Granada, 1995).
Moreno Trujillo, María Amparo, *La memoria de la ciudad. El primer libro de actas del cabildo de Granada (1497–1502)* (Granada, 2005).
Palencia, Alonso de, *Guerra de Granada. Edición de Rafael Peinado Santaella* (Granada, 1998).
Pulgar, Fernando del, 'Tratado de los Reyes de Granada y su orígen', in Valladares de Sotomayor, Antonio (ed.), *Semanario erudito*, 11–12 (Madrid, 1788), pp. 57–144.

Pulgar, Fernando del, *Crónica de los Reyes Católicos*, Edición y estudio por Juan de Mata Carriazo (Madrid, 1943).
Rodríguez Villa, Antonio, 'D. Francisco de Rojas. Embajador de los Reyes Católicos. Documentos justificativos', *BRAH*, 28 (1896), 295–402.
Rodríguez Villa, Antonio, *Crónicas del Gran Capitán* (Madrid, 1908).
Ruiz Povedano, José María, *Colección de documentos para la historia de Alcaudete (1240–1516)* (Jaén, 2009).
Salazar Mir, Adolfo de, *Los expedientes de limpieza de sangre de la Catedral de Sevilla*, 1–3 (Seville, 1995).
Santa Cruz, Alonso de, *Crónica de los Reyes Católicos*, ed. Carriazo, Juan de Mata (Seville, 1951).
Serrano y Pineda, L. Ildefonso, 'Correspondencia de los Reyes Católicos con el Gran Capitán durante las campañas de Italia', *RABM*, 25 (1911), 26 (1912), 28 (1913) and 29 (1913).
Szmolka Clares, José, *Epistolario del Conde de Tendilla (1504–1506)*, 1–2 (Granada, 1996).
Talavera, Hernando de, 'La misa y el oficio de la toma de Granada', in Vega García-Ferrer, María Julieta (ed.), *Fray Hernando de Talavera y Granada* (Granada, 2007), pp. 257–97.
Torre, L de and Rodríguez Pascual, R., 'Cartas y documentos relativos al Gran Capitán', *RABM*, 28 and 29 (1913), 34 (1916), 35 (1916), 39 (1918) and 44 (1923).
Valera, Diego de, 'Memorial de diversas hazañas: Crónica de Enrique IV', in *Crónicas de los Reyes de Castilla* (Madrid, 1878), pp. 1–95.
Zurita, Gerónimo de, 'Historia del Rey D. Fernando el Católico de las empresas y ligas de Italia', in *Las glorias nacionales*, V (Madrid–Barcelona, 1853), pp. 691–1290.

Secondary literature

Agnew, Michael, 'The silences of Fernando de Pulgar in his "Crónica de los Reyes Católicos"', *Revista de estudios hispánicos*, 36 (2002), 477–99.
Álvarez-Ossorio, Antonio, 'Razón de linaje y lesa majestad. El Gran Capitán, Venecia y la Corte de Fernando el Católico (1507–1509)', in Berlenguer, Ernest (ed.), *De la unión de las coronas al Imperio de Carlos V*, 3 (Madrid, 2001), pp. 385–451.
Azcona, Tarsicio, 'La Inquisición española, procesada por la Congregación General', in Joaquín Pérez, Villanueva (ed.), *La Inquisición Española. Nueva visión, nuevos horizontes* (Madrid, 1980), pp. 89–163.
Barkai, Ron, *Cristianos y musulmanes en la España medieval (El enemigo en el espejo)* (Madrid, 1984).
Bataillon, Marcel, *Erasmo y España, estudios sobre la historia espiritual del siglo XVI* (Mexico, 1966).
Beinart, Haim, *The Expulsion of the Jews from Spain* (Oxford, 2005).
Benito Ruano, Eloy, *Los orígenes del problema converso* (Madrid, 2001).
Béthencourt, see Fernández de Béthencourt.
Bratu, Christian, 'De la grande histoire à l'histoire personelle. L'emergence de l'écriture autobiographique chez les historiens français du Moyen Age', *Mediaevistik*, 25 (2012), 85–117.
Bulliet, Richard, *The Case for Islamo-Christian Civilisation* (New York, 2006).
Burke, Peter, *Exiles and Expatriates in the History of Knowledge, 1500–2000* (Lebanon, NH, 2017).

Caballero López, Jose Antonio, 'Annio de Viterbo y la historiografía española del siglo XVI', in *Humanismo y tradición clásica en España y América* (León, 2002).
Cabrera Sánchez, Margarita, *Nobleza, oligarquía y poder en Córdoba al final de la Edad Media* (Córdoba, 1998).
Carrasco Urgoiti, María Soledad, *The Moorish Novel* (Boston, 1976).
Carriazo, Juan de Mata, 'Continuación inédita de la "Relación" de Hernando de Baeza', *Al-Ándalus*, 13, 2 (1948), 431–42.
Carriazo, Juan de Mata, *En la frontera de Granada* (Granada, 1971).
Catlos, Brian, *Kingdoms of Faith: A New History of Islamic Spain* (London, 2018).
Coleman, David, *Creating Christian Granada: Society and Religious Culture in an Old-World Frontier City, 1492–1600* (New York, 2003).
Croce, Benedetto, *España en la vida italiana durante el Renacimiento* (Madrid, 1925).
Cuadro García, Ana Cristina, 'Acción inquisitorial contra los judaizantes en Córdoba y crisis eclesiástica (1482–1508)', *Revista de Historia Moderna. Anales de la Universidad de Alicante*, 21 (2003), 11–28.
D'Amico, John, *Renaissance Humanism in Papal Rome* (New York, 1983).
Dandelet, Thomas, *Spanish Rome, 1500–1700* (New Haven, 2008).
Delgado Pérez, Mercedes, 'A Newly-Discovered Manuscript of the Historia de los Reyes Moros de Granada by Hernando de Baeza', *Manuscript Studies*, 2, 2 (2017), 540–67.
Delgado Pérez, Mercedes, 'La Historia de los Reyes Moros de Granada, de Hernando de Baeza. Una crónica entre el romance de frontera, la autobiografía y la leyenda', *Philología Hispalensis*, 31, 2 (2017), 15–36.
Delgado Pérez, Mercedes, 'Certezas e hipótesis sobre el final de la "crónica granadina" de Hernando de Baeza', *Anaquel de Estudios Árabes*, 29 (2018), 33–62.
Devaney, Thomas, *Enemies in the Plaza. Urban Spectacle and the End of Spanish Frontier Culture, 1460–1492* (Philadelphia, 2015).
Devereux, Andrew, *The Other Side of Empire. Just War in the Mediterranean and the Rise of Early Modern Spain* (Ithaca, 2020).
Deyermond, Alan (ed.), *Historical Literature in Medieval Iberia* (London, 1996).
Díaz Rodríguez, Antonio, *El Clero Catedralicio en la España moderna: los miembros del Cabildo de la Catedral de Córdoba (1475–1808)* (Cordoba, 2012).
Díaz Rodríguez, Antonio, 'Purity of Blood and the Curial Market in Iberian Cathedrals', *eHumanista Conversos*, 4 (2016), 38–63. Online at: https://www.ehumanista.ucsb.edu/sites/secure.lsit.ucsb.edu.span.d7_eh/files/sitefiles/conversos/volume4/5%20ehumconv.4.gam.D%C3%ADaz.pdf (accessed 7 June 2021).
Echevarría, Ana, *The Fortress of Faith. The Attitude towards Muslims in Fifteenth-Century Spain* (Leiden, 1999).
Echevarría, Ana, *Knights on the Frontier. The Moorish Guard of the Kings of Castile (1410–1467)* (Leiden, 2009).
Edwards, John, 'La révolte du Marquis de Priego', *Mélanges de la Casa de Velázquez*, 12 (1976), 165–72.
Edwards, John, 'Religious Belief and Social Conformity: The "Converso" Problem in Late-Medieval Cordoba', *Transactions of the Royal Historical Society*, 31 (1981), 115–28.
Edwards, John, 'Elijah and the Inquisition: Messianic Prophecy among Conversos in Spain c.1500', *Nottingham Medieval Studies*, 28 (1984), 79–94.
Edwards, John, 'Trial of an Inquisitor: The Dismissal of Diego Rodríguez Lucero, Inquisitor of Cordoba in 1508', *Journal of Ecclesiastical History*, 37, 2 (1986), 240–57.
Edwards, John, 'Religious Faith and Doubt in Late Medieval Spain: Soria *circa* 1450–1500', *Past and Present*, 120 (1988), 3–35.

Edwards, John, *Religion and Society in Spain, c.* 1492 (Aldershot, 1996).
Edwards, John, 'New Light on the Converso Debate? The Jewish Christianity of Alfonso de Cartagena and Juan de Torquemada', in Barton, Simon and Linehan, Peter (eds.), *Cross, Crescent and Conversion. Studies on Medieval Spain and Christendom in Memory of Richard Fletcher* (Leiden, 2008), pp. 311–26.
Egido Martínez, Aurora and Laplana, José Enrique (eds.), *La imagen de Fernando el Católico en la Historia, la Literatura y el Arte* (Zaragoza, 2014).
Escobar Borrego, Francisco, Díez Reboso, Samuel and Rivero García, Luis (eds.), *La Metamorfosis de un inquisidor: el humanista Diego López de Cortegana (1455–1524)* (Seville, 2012).
Fernández de Béthencourt, Francisco, *Historia genealógica y heráldica de la monarquía española*, 6 (Madrid, 1905) and 7 (Madrid, 1907).
Fernández de Córdova Miralles, Álvaro, *Alejandro VI y los Reyes Católicos: relaciones político-eclesiásticas, 1492–1503* (Rome, 2005).
Fernández de Córdova Miralles, Álvaro, 'Los Reyes Católicos ante la elección pontificia de Pío III: la acción negociadora hispana en sede vacante (1503)', in Guzmán Almagro, Alejandra et al. (eds.), *Pere Miquel Carbonell i el seu temps (1434–1517)* (Barcelona, 2014).
Fernández de Córdova Miralles, Álvaro, 'Antonio de Acuña antes de las Comunidades, su embajada en Roma al servicio de Felipe el Hermoso', in Szászdi León-Borja, Istvánand Pérez, Joseph (eds.), *Iglesia, eclesiásticos y la revolución comunera* (Sahagún, 2017), pp. 71–121.
Fernández de Córdova Miralles, Álvaro, 'El Gran Capitán y los Hapsburgo: conflicto y mediación en los inicios de la crisis sucesoria (1504–1505)', in Toro Ceballos, Francisco (ed.), *II Congreso Fernández de Córdoba* (Alcalá la Real, 2021), 203–16.
Fernández de Córdova Miralles, Álvaro, Arrizabalaga, Jon and Toldrà, María (eds.), *Cesar Borja, cinc-cents anys després (1507–2007)* (Valencia, 2009), pp. 11–98.
Fernández Sánchez, Teodoro, *El discutido extremeño Cardenal Carvajal (D. Bernardino Lòpez de Carvajal y Sande)* (Cáceres, 1981).
Fleming, Gillian, *Juana I: Legitimacy and Conflict in Sixteenth-Century Castile* (London, 2018).
Fuchs, Barbara, *Exotic Nation: Maurophilia and the Construction of Early Modern Spain* (Philadelphia, 2009).
Galasso, Giuseppe and Hernando Sánchez, Carlos (eds.), *El Reino de Nápoles y la monarquía de España. Entre agregación y conquista* (Rome, 2004), pp. 169–211.
Gerli, E. Michael, 'Social Crisis and Conversion. Apostasy and Inquisition in the Chronicles of Fernando del Pulgar and Andrés Bernáldez', *Hispanic Review*, 70 (2002), 147–67.
Gerli, E. Michael, 'The Converso Condition: New Approaches to an Old Question', in Corfis, Ivy A. and Harris-Northall, Ray (eds.), *Medieval Iberia. Changing Societies and Cultures in Contact and Transition* (Woodbridge, 2007), pp. 3–15.
Gil, Juan, *Los conversos y la Inquisición sevillana*, 1–8 (Seville, 2000).
Gil, Juan, 'Conversos al servicio del Gran Capitán', in Leal de Faria, Ana et al. (eds.), *Problematizar a História. Estudos de História moderna em homagem a Maria do Rosario Themudo Barata* (Lisboa, 2007), pp. 491–8.
Gilman, Stephen, 'A Generation of "conversos"', *Romance Philology*, 33, 1 (1979), 87–101.
Giordano, María Laura, '"La ciudad de nuestra conciencia". Los conversos y la construcción de la identidad judeocristiana (1449–1556)', *Hispania Sacra*, 125 (2010), 43–91.

Goñi Gaztambide, José, 'La polémica sobre el bautismo de los moriscos a principios del siglo XVI', *Anuario de la Historia de la Iglesia*, 16 (2007), 209-15.
González Rolán, Tomás, 'Diplomacia y humanismo a finales del siglo XV: el cardenal extremeño Bernardino López de Carvajal', in Chaparro Gómez, César, Mañas Gómez, Manuel, and Ortega Sánchez, Delfín (eds.), *Nulla dies sine linea. Humanistas extremeños: de la fama al olvido* (Cáceres, 2009), pp. 143-56.
Gracia Boix, Rafael, *Autos de Fe y causas de la Inquisición en Córdoba* (Cordoba, 1982).
Grafton, Anthony, *Forgers and Critics: Creativity and Duplicity in Western Scholarship* (Princeton, 1990).
Haliczer, Stephen, *The Comuneros of Castile: The Forging of a Revolution, 1475-1521* (Madison, WI, 1981).
Harvey, L. P., *Islamic Spain 1250 to 1500* (Chicago, 1992).
Hernando Sánchez, Carlos, 'El Gran Capitán y los inicios del Virreinato de Nápoles', in Junta de Castilla y León (ed.), *El Tratado de Tordesillas y su época*, 3 (Valladolid, 1995), pp. 1817-54.
Hernando Sánchez, Carlos (ed.), *Roma y España un crisol de la cultura europea en la Edad Moderna* (Madrid, 2007).
van der Höh, Marc et al. (eds.), *Cultural Brokers at Mediterranean Courts in the Middle Ages* (Munich, 2013).
Iannuzzi, Isabella, *El poder de la palabra en el siglo XV: Fray Hernando de Talavera* (Valladolid, 2009).
Kagan, Richard, *Clio and the Crown. The Politics of History in Medieval and Early Modern Spain* (Baltimore, 2009).
Kamen, Henry, *The Spanish Inquisition. An Historical Revision* (London, 1997).
Kaplan, Gregory, 'Towards the Establishment of a Christian Identity: The Conversos and Early Castilian Humanism', *La Corónica*, 25 (1996), 53-68.
Ladero, Miguel Ángel, *Granada después de la conquista: repobladores y mudéjares* (Granada, 1993).
Ladero, Miguel Ángel (ed.), *La incorporación de Granada a la Corona de Castilla* (Granada, 1993).
Ladero, Miguel Ángel, *La Guerra de Granada (1482-1491)* (Granada, 2007).
Ladero, Miguel Ángel, 'Limosnas, dádivas y liberaciones en torno a la toma de Granada (1490-1492)', *CEHGR*, 24 (2012), 3-31.
Ladero, Miguel Ángel, *Los últimos años de Fernando el Católico (1505-1517)* (Madrid, 2019).
Lea, Henry Charles, 'Lucero the Inquisitor', *The American Historical Review*, 2 (1897), 611-26.
Lea, Henry Charles, *A History of the Inquisition in Spain*, 1 (London, 1906).
Liang, Yuen-Gen, *Family and Empire. The Fernández de Córdoba and the Spanish Realm* (Philadelphia, 2011).
López de Coca Castañer, José Enrique, 'The Making of Isabel de Solís', in Collins, Roger and Goodman, Anthony (eds.), *Medieval Spain: Culture, Conflict and Coexistence* (Basingstoke, 2002), pp. 225-41.
López de Coca Castañer, José Enrique, 'La conquista de Granada. El testimonio de los vencidos', *Norba*, 18 (2005), 33-50.
López de Coca Castañer, José Enrique, 'El reverso de la conquista del Reino de Granada. La visión de los vencidos', in Ribot, Luis Antonio and Valdeón, Julio (eds.), *Isabel la Católica y su época*, 2 (Valladolid, 2007), pp. 955-83.
Lynn, Caro, *A College Professor of the Renaissance. Lucio Marineo Sículo* (Chicago, 1937).

Mallett, Michael and Shaw, Christine, *The Italian Wars, 1494–1559* (Harlow, 2012).
Maraver y Alfaro, Luis, *Historia de Córdoba: desde los más remotos tiempos hasta nuestros días*, 12, pp. 351–62. Digitalised manuscript available online at https://biblioteca.cordoba.es/index.php/biblio-digital/manuscritos/503-manuscrito-maraver-alfaro/1891-maraver-alfaro-t12.html (last accessed 3 January 2022).
Martínez Millán, José, 'De la muerte del príncipe Juan al fallecimiento de Felipe el Hermoso (1497–1506)', in Martínez Millán, José (ed.), *La Corte de Carlos V*, 1 (Madrid, 2000), pp. 45–72.
Meseguer Fernández, Juan, 'Fernando de Talavera, Cisneros y la Inquisición en Granada', in Pérez Villanueva, Joaquín (ed.), *La Inquisición Española. Nueva Visión, Nuevos Horizontes* (Madrid, 1980), pp. 371–400.
Milhou, Alain, *Colón y su mentalidad mesiánica en el ambiente franciscanista español* (Valladolid, 1983).
Milhou, Alain, *Pouvoir royal et absolutisme dans l'Espagne du XVIième siècle* (Toulouse, 1999).
Moreno Koch, Yolanda, 'La conquista de Granada y la expulsión de Sefarad según las crónicas hispanohebreas', in *Andalucía medieval: actas del I Congreso de Historia de Andalucía*, 2 (Cordoba, 1978), pp. 329–37.
Moreno Trujillo, María Amparo, 'Las actuaciones de la Inquisición y los escribanos judeoconversos del entorno del Conde de Tendilla', *HID*, 37 (2010), 181–210.
Moya García, Cristina, 'El "Laberinto de Fortuna" y la frontera de Granada', in Toro Ceballos, Francisco and Rodríguez Molina, José (eds.), *Estudios de Frontera 9* (Alcalá, 2014), pp. 491–8.
Nader, Helen, *The Mendoza Family in the Spanish Renaissance* (Berkeley, 1972).
Nieto Cumplido, Manuel, *Infancia y juventud del Gran Capitán (1453–1481)* (Cordoba, 2015).
Nieto Soria, José Manuel, *Propaganda y opinión pública en la historia* (Valladolid, 2007).
Nirenberg, David, 'Mass Conversion and Genealogical Mentalities: Jews and Christians in Fifteenth-Century Spain', *Past and Present*, 174 (2002), 1–39.
Nirenberg, David, 'The Extinction of Spain's Jews and the Birth of its Inquisition', in *Anti-Judaism. The Western Tradition* (New York, 2014), pp. 217–45.
Ollero Pina, José Antonio, 'La Historia Parthenopea de Alfonso Fernández Benadeva, la Inquisición y otras cosas de familias', in Alvarez Santaló, León Carlos (ed.), *Estudios de Historia Moderna en Homenaje al profesor Antonio García-Barquero* (Seville, 2009), pp. 549–83.
Pastore, Stefania, *Il vangelo e la spada. L'Inquisizione di Castiglia e i suoi critici (1460–1598)* (Rome, 2003).
Pastore, Stefania, *Una herejía española, conversos alumbrados e Inquisición (1449–1559)* (Madrid, 2010).
Peinado Santaella, Rafael, '"Cristo pelea por sus castellanos". El imaginario cristiano de la guerra de Granada', in Barrios Aguilera, Manuel and González Alcantud, José Antonio (eds.), *Las Tomas: Antropología histórica de la ocupación territorial del Reino de Granada* (Granada, 2000), pp. 453–524.
Peinado Santaella, Rafael, 'El final de la Reconquista: elegía de la derrota, exaltación del triunfo', in García Fernández, Manuel and González Sánchez, Carlos Alberto (eds.), *Andalucía y Granada en tiempos de los Reyes Católicos* (Sevilla, 2006).
Peña Díaz, Manuel, *Las Españas que (no) pudieron ser. Herejías, exilios y otras conciencias (s. XVI-XX)* (Huelva, 2009).

Pescador del Hoyo, María del Carmen, 'Cómo fue de verdad la toma de Granada, a la luz de un documento inédito', *Al-Ándalus*, 20, 2 (1955), 283–344.
Poutrin, Isabelle, 'Los derechos de los vencidos: las capitulaciones de Granada (1491)', *Sharq al-Ándalus*, 19 (2008–9), 11–34.
Poutrin, Isabelle, 'The Jewish Precedent in the Spanish Politics of Conversion of Muslims and Moriscos', *Journal of Levantine Studies*, 6 (2016), 71–87.
Quintanilla, María Concepción, *Nobleza y señoríos en el Reino de Córdoba: la casa de Aguilar (siglos XIV y XV)* (Córdoba, 1979).
Quintanilla, María Concepción, 'La biblioteca del Marqués de Priego', *En la España Medieval*, 1 (1980), 347–84.
Quintanilla, María Concepción, 'Facciones, clientelas y partidos en España en el tránsito de la edad media a la modernidad', in Alvarado Planas, Javier (ed.), *Poder, economía, clientelismo* (Madrid, 1997).
Rábade Obradó, María del Pilar, *Una élite de poder en la corte de los Reyes Católicos. Los judeoconversos* (Madrid, 1993).
Rábade Obradó, María del Pilar, 'La invención como necesidad: genealogía y judeoconversos', *En la España medieval*, 1 (2006), 183–202.
Reeves, Marjorie (ed.), *Prophetic Rome in the High Renaissance Period* (Oxford, 1992).
Ríos Saloma, Martín, *La Reconquista: una construcción historiográfica (siglos XVI-XIX)* (Madrid, 2011).
Rivero Rodríguez, Manuel, *De la separación a la reunión dinástica: la Corona de Aragón entre 1504–1516* (Madrid, 2000).
Rodríguez Argente del Castillo, Juan Pablo, Tinsley, Teresa and Rodríguez Molina, José, *La Relación de Hernando de Baeza sobre el Reino de Granada* (Alcalá la Real, 2018).
Rodríguez Molina, José, 'Relaciones pacíficas en la frontera con el Reino de Granada', in Segura Artero, Pedro (ed.), *Actas del congreso La frontera oriental Nazarí como sujeto histórico (S. XIII-XVI)* (1997), pp. 253–88.
Rodríguez Molina, José, 'Libre determinación religiosa en la frontera de Granada', in *Estudios de Frontera 2* (Alcalá la Real, 1998), pp. 693–708.
Rodríguez Molina, José, *La vida de moros y cristianos en la frontera* (Alcalá la Real, 2007).
Rodríguez Molina, José, 'Tendencia integradora del Gran Capitán con moros y judíos', in Toro Ceballos, Francisco (ed.), *II Congreso Fernández de Córdoba* (Alcalá la Real, 2018), pp. 497–522.
Rodríguez Velasco, Jesús, *La caballería castellana en la baja edad media: textos y contextos* (Montpellier, 2000).
Rosenstock, Bruce, *New Men: 'Conversos', Christian Theology and Society in Fifteenth-Century Spain* (London, 2002).
Rosenstock, Bruce, 'Against the Pagans: Alonso de Cartagena, Francisco de Vitoria and Converso Political Theology', in Aronson-Friedman, Amy and Kaplan, Gregory (eds.), *Marginal voices: Studies in Converso Literature of Medieval and Golden Age Spain* (Leiden, 2012), pp. 117–40.
Roth, Norman, *Conversos, Inquisition and the Expulsion of the Jews from Spain* (Wisconsin, 2002).
Rufo Ysern, Paulina, 'Los Reyes Católicos y la pacificación de Andalucía (1475–1480)', *HID*, 15 (1988), 217–50.
Ruiz Domènec, José Enrique, *El Gran Capitán. Retrato de una época* (Barcelona, 2002).
Ruiz Povedano, José María, 'Exaltación y propaganda de la nueva monarquía hispánica con motivo de la conquista de Málaga (1487)', *Andalucía Medieval: Actas del III Congreso de Historia de Andalucía*, 6 (Cordoba, 2003), pp. 473–96.

Ruiz Povedano, José María, 'Roma y los sermones de la Guerra de Granada (1486–1492): de la propaganda a la política de imagen de los Reyes Católicos', in García Benítez, Javier (ed.), *El valor del documento. Estudios en homenaje al profesor José Rodríguez Molina* (Almería, 2018), pp. 225–83.

Salvador Miguel, Nicasio, *Isabel la Católica. Educación, mecenazgo y entorno literario* (Alcalá de Henares, 2008).

Salvador Miguel, Nicasio, 'Intelectuales españoles en Roma durante el gobierno de los Reyes Católicos', in Botta, Patrizia (ed.), *Rumbos del hispanismo en el umbral de Cincuentenario de la AIH*, 1 (Rome, 2012), pp. 47–64.

Salvador Miguel, Nicasio, 'La conquista de Málaga (1487). Repercusiones festivas y literarias en Roma', in Baloup, Daniel and González Arévalo, Raúl (eds.), *La Guerra de Granada en su contexto internacional* (Toulouse, 2017), pp. 161–282.

Serio, Alessandro, 'Una representación de la crisis de la unión dinástica: los cargos diplomáticos en Roma de Francisco de Rojas y Antonio de Acuña (1501–1507)', *Cuadernos de Historia Moderna*, 32 (2007), 13–29.

Shaw, Christine, *Julius II, the Warrior Pope* (Oxford, 1996).

Shaw, Christine, 'The Papal Court as a Centre of Diplomacy: From the Peace of Lodi to the Council of Trent', in Alazard, Florence and La Brasca, Frank (eds.), *La papauté à la Renaissance* (Paris, 2007), pp. 621–38.

Sicroff, Albert, 'El "Lumen ad revelationem gentium" de Alonso de Oropesa', in De Bustos Tóvar, Eugenio (ed.), *Actas del cuarto Congreso Internacional de Hispanistas*, 2 (Salamanca, 1982), pp. 655–65.

Sicroff, Albert, *Los estatutos de limpieza de sangre. Controversias entre los siglos XV y XVII* (Newark, 2010) (first published in French in 1960).

Soria Mesa, Enrique, *El Cambio inmóvil. Transformaciones y permanencias en una élite de poder* (Córdoba, ss. XVI-XIX) (Córdoba, 2000).

Soria Mesa, Enrique and Díaz Rodríguez, Antonio, *Iglesia, poder y fortuna. Clero y movilidad social en la España moderna* (Granada, 2012).

Starr-Le Beau, Gretchen, *In the Shadow of the Virgin. Inquisitors, friars and conversos in Guadalupe* (Princeton, 2003).

Szmolka Clares, José, 'Nobleza y autoritarismo en Andalucía. La contribución de Granada a la sumisión del estamento nobiliario andaluz, 1504–1510', *Cuadernos de Estudios Medievales*, 6–7 (1981), 277–96.

Szpiech, Ryan, 'Conversion as a Historiographical Problem: The Case of Zoraya/Isabel de Solís', in Fox, Yaniv and Yisraeli, Yosi (eds.), *Contesting Inter-Religious Conversion in the Medieval World* (New York, 2017), pp. 24–38.

Tate, Brian, *Ensayos sobre la historiografía peninsular del siglo XV* (Madrid, 1970).

Tate, Brian, 'Poles Apart. Two Official Historians of the Catholic Monarchs: Alfonso de Palencia and Fernando del Pulgar', in Soto Rábanos, José María (ed.), *Pensamiento medieval hispano: homenaje a Horacio Santiago-Otero*, 1 (Madrid, 1998), pp. 439–63.

Tinsley, Teresa, 'Esbozo biográfico', in Rodríguez Argente Del Castillo, Juan Pablo, Tinsley, Teresa and Rodríguez Molina, José (eds.), *La Relación de Hernando de Baeza sobre el Reino de Granada* (Alcalá la Real, 2018), pp. 31–40.

Tinsley, Teresa, 'La desilusión del Gran Capitán, según el testimonio de su secretario, Hernando de Baeza', in Toro Ceballos, Francisco (ed.), *I Congreso Fernández de Córdoba* (Alcalá la Real, 2018), pp. 625–3.

Tinsley, Teresa, 'La "nueva convivencia" de Hernando de Baeza', in García Benítez, Javier (ed.), *El valor del documento. Estudios en homenaje al profesor José Rodríguez Molina* (Almería, 2018), pp. 199–212.

Tinsley, Teresa, 'España sin frontera: La (re)visión historiográfica de Hernando de Baeza, c. 1510', in Manuel García, Fernández (ed.), *Las fronteras en la Edad Media hispánica* (Seville, 2019), pp. 101–14.

Tinsley, Teresa, 'Conversos and comuneros. The trial of Juan Rodríguez de Baeza, Salamanca, 1520', *Historia y Genealogía*, 9 (2020), 79–92.

Tinsley, Teresa, 'Granada como espejo de Castilla en la "Relación" de Hernando de Baeza', in Francisco Toro, Ceballos (ed.), *Estudios de Frontera* 11 (Alcalá la Real, 2020), pp. 467–74.

Tinsley, Teresa, 'El Gran Capitán en las Capitulaciones de Granada', in Francisco Toro Ceballos (ed.), *Los Fernández de Córdoba. Nobleza, hegemonía y fama* (Alcalá la Real, 2021), pp. 803–12.

Tinsley, Teresa, 'Reframing "Reconquista". Hernando de Baeza's Take on the Conquest of Granada', in Liuzzo Scorpo, Antonella (ed.), *A Plural Peninsula. Studies in Honour of Professor Simon Barton* (Leiden, forthcoming).

Tinsley, Teresa, 'Networks of Influence between the Vatican and Andalusia at the Beginning of the Sixteenth Century', in Galera Andreu, Pedro A. and López Arandia, Amparo (eds.), *Un humanista giennense en Roma. Gutierre González Doncel* (Jaén, forthcoming).

Tolan, John, *Sons of Ishmael. Muslims through European Eyes in the Middle Ages* (Florida, 2008).

Torrecilla, José and Cortijo Ocaña, Antonio (eds.), 'Al-Andalus y la identidad española: historia y mito', *eHumanista*, 37 (2017), http://www.ehumanista.ucsb.edu/volumes/37 (last accessed 22 June 2021).

Valdeón, Julio, 'Motivaciones socio-económicas de las fricciones entre viejo cristianos, judíos y conversos', in Alcalá, Angel (ed.), *Judíos. Sefarditas. Conversos. La expulsión de 1492 y sus consecuencias* (Valladolid, 1995), 69–88.

Vidal Doval, Rosa, *Misera Hispania: Jews and Conversos in Alonso de Espina's Fortalitium Fidei* (Oxford, 2013).

Yun, Bartolomé, *Crisis de subsistencia y conflictividad social en Córdoba a principios del siglo XVI* (Cordoba, 1980).

Index

A

Aben Comixa, *See* Comixa, Aben
Abenámar 126-7, 138
Abencerrajes 23-5, 29, 121, 123-4, 129, 144, 148, 187
Abramavel family 77
Abū 'Abd Allāh Muhammad, *See* Boabdil
Abū al-Ḥasan (Mohammed X) 5, 23, 25, 115-18, 121-2, 124
   in Hernando de Baeza's history 126-33, 138-41, 189
Abū al-Qāsim 32-4, 37-8, 41, 144-6
Acuña, Antonio de (1465-1526) 75, 108
Africa 29, 44, 72, 81, 104-5, 121, 143, 145
   See also North Africa
Aguayo, Pedro de 27-8
Aguilar (town) 31, 115, 124, 128
Aguilar, Alonso de (1447-1501)
   attitude to difference 22, 24
   and Baeza family 3, 12-13, 16, 18, 21, 38, 63
   and the Civil War 14-15, 23, 39
   and *conversos* 16-17, 22
   death 51-2, 56, 117
   and Granada 23, 25, 27, 29, 35
   and the Inquisition 20, 47-8, 87
   matrimonial strategies 49-50
Ahmed (son of Boabdil) 28
Alarcón, Fernando de 94-5, 176
Alarcón, Martín de 29-33, 36-7, 131, 143, 156, 188
al-'Attar 136-7, 189
Albaicín
   Alcazaba Cadima 190
   dissident courtier from 129
   morisco rebellion (1499-1500) 44
   support for Boabdil 29-30, 33, 36, 97, 141-4, 156
   support for Sa'ad 127
Albendín 38, 55
Albret, Carlota 71

Alcaiçi, Abrahén (el Cayci) 31-2, 117, 144
Alcaide de los Donceles, *See* Diego Fernández de Córdoba
Alcalá de Henares
Alcalá la Real 15-16, 24, 58, 126, 131
   See also Íñigo López de Tendilla, Fernán Álvarez
Alcaudete 24-7, 29-30, 50, 58, 131, 138, 141
Alexander VI (Pope) 42, 48-9, 61, 64-5, 68, 71, 110
Alfonso, Prince of Castile (1453-1468) 14-16
Alfonso II of Naples (r.1494-5) 61
Alfonso V of Aragon (1396-1458) 61
Alfonso X of Castile (1221-1284) 28, 40, 118, 122
Alhaje 29, 117, 141
Alhama 25
Alhambra
   architectural influence 51
   burials of deposed emirs 128, 140
   escape of Boabdil 25, 32-3, 37, 39, 133-4
   Generalife 133-4
   scene of murders 127, 129
   stronghold of Zagal 142
   surrender negotiations 1, 35, 145, 184
Alhaqueque 27, 58-9
Almería 132, 134, 138-9, 143
Alonso de Córdoba, Martín 92
Alonso de Montemayor, Martín (Lord of Alcaudete) 27
Álvarez, Alonso 48
Álvarez, Beatriz (daughter of Hernando de Baeza) 12
Álvarez, Beatriz (sister of Gonzalo de Córdoba) 12, 48
Álvarez, Fernán 29-30, 156
Álvarez, Teresa (daughter of Hernando de Baeza) 12, 14

Álvarez, Teresa (mother of Gonzalo de Córdoba) 85
Álvarez de Córdoba, Francisco 52
Álvarez de Córdoba, Licenciado Alonso 101
Álvarez de Toledo, Fernán 58
Anaya, Luis 92
Anjou, House of 61
Antequera 100
apostasy 1, 35, 39–40, 47, 49, 131, 146
Aquinas, Thomas 28
Aragon 2, 9, 19, 42, 45, 62, 66, 72, 74–5, 104, 116 *See also* Alonso V, Fernando II, Juan II
Aranda, Pedro de 6
Archbishop, *See* Cisneros, Deza, Talavera
Archidona 118, 126
Arcos, Duke of, *See* Rodrigo Ponce de León
Arévalo 16, 118, 127
Arias Dávila, Pedro 6, 86
Arriola, Juan 89
Auto de fe 4, 20, 27, 83, 87
Ayora, Gonzalo de 88, 107–9, 181

B
Baena 14, 87, 135, 137
Baeza, Álvaro de 12, 163
Baeza, Beatriz de 12, 52, 85
Baeza, Diego de 12, 48, 57, 85, 163, 165, 176
Baeza, Francisco Rodríguez de 12, 100
Baeza, Gonzalo de 12, 48, 55, 58, 95, 173
Baeza, Hernando de
  absence from historical record 35–8
  death 101
  family 12–14, 84–6, 90–2
  identity 148
  as intermediary 27, 30–5, 57–9
  links with chroniclers 104–9
  as narrator in his own work 99, 109, 117, 121–4, 128–9, 131, 136, 141–2, 145
  as secretary to Gran Capitán 63–81
  as servant to Alonso de Aguilar 27, 47–51, 56–7
  as servant to Marquis of Priego 51–6
Baeza, Juan de 111
Baeza, Juan de (escribano) 33
Baeza, Juan de (Hernando's father) 12–13, 17, 19–20, 150–1

Baeza, Pedro de 12, 48, 54–5, 85, 163
Baeza, Teresa de 34
Bailén 95, 100
Baptism
  of children 22, 35, 40, 129, 188
  coercive 22, 40–1, 44, 107
  of Jews 9–10, 112, 122
  of Muslims 1, 4, 24, 33, 99
Barcelona 48, 112
Basque Country 65
Baza 31–3, 42, 58, 72, 132, 143
Beinecke manuscript 102, 104, 106, 125, 187–90
Bernáldez, Andrés (chronicler) 36, 43, 94, 111–12, 117, 119, 122, 156
Black Legend 4
Blásquez, Rodrigo 84
Boabdil (Abū 'Abd Allāh Muhammad)
  capture at Lucena 27, 90, 135–7
  coup against father 25, 133–4, 141
  defence of Granada 145
  embassies, delegations 32–3, 58–9
  and Hernando de Baeza 29, 31, 33–4, 37, 55, 57, 99, 117, 147
  hope for his conversion to Christianity 122
  members of his family and court 118, 135, 156–7, 188
  representations of 26, 32, 77, 90–1, 102, 115, 187
  return to the Albaicín 141–3
  surrender of Granada 1, 38–41, 146
  as vassal of Catholic Monarchs 28–31, 36, 97, 138
Bobadilla 30, 141, 189
Bocanegra, Bernardino 95
Bocanegra, *Licenciado* Luis 63
Bologna 65, 89
Borgia, Cesare 62, 64–6, 68–71, 73, 75, 77
Borgia, Giovanni 68
Borgia, Rodrigo, *See* Alexander VI
Boscà, Pere 42
Burgos 94, 100

C
Caballería 49–50, 57, 81, 115–16, 119
Cabra, Counts of, *See* Diego Fernández de Córdoba
Cajetan, Thomas 79

Calabria 63, 77
Calatrava, Order of 23–4, 131, 135, 137
Cañete 17, 19, 23, 124, 131
Cantabria 102
Capitulaciones 35–6, 38–41, 43–4, 47, 66, 70, 119, 122, 145–6
captives
    adoption of Islam 1, 28, 40, 121–2, 131
    Christians taken to Granada 24, 116, 131, 133
    exchange of 5, 27
    liberation of 34–5, 42, 145, 157
    ransoming of 5, 23, 26, 33, 59
    See also La Romia
Cárcamo, Alonso de 95
Carlos of Austria (son of Felipe II) 102
Carriazo, Juan de Mata 105–6
Carrillo de Velasco, María 50
Cartagena, Alonso de 10–11, 13, 18, 45, 71, 97, 120
Carvajal, Cardinal of Santa Cruz, *See* Bernardino López de Carvajal
Castile
    and Aragon 2, 9, 72, 75
    Civil War 14–16, 23
    Fernando's governorship 83, 96, 98
    and Granada 27–8, 30, 113, 118
    monarchy 3, 6, 42–3, 45, 73–5, 81–2
    See also Felipe I, historiography, Isabel I, Inquisition, Juana I
Castilla, Sancho de 83
Castro del Río 88
Catherine of Aragon 69
Catholic Monarchs 18, 57
    alliance with Boabdil 25, 137–8
    and the Inquisition 4, 15, 19, 77
    and papal conclaves 64, 66, 70
    representations of 3, 5–6, 34, 39, 42–3, 71, 106–7, 110–11, 113–16
    title 61
    See also Fernando II, Isabel I
El Cayci, *See* Abrahén Alcaiçi
Cenete, Marquis of, *See* Rodrigo Díaz de Vivar y Mendoza
Cervantes, Miguel de 124
Chacón, Gonzalo 21, 57
Charles V, Emperor (1500–1558) 72, 86, 97, 109

Charles VIII of France (1479–1498) 61–3, 77
Chivalric ideas, *See caballería*
Christianity
    Christianization
        of Castile and Aragon 9–11, 24, 107
        of Granada 1–2, 40–1, 43–4, 102, 119, 120–2
        of the New World 106
    new conceptions of 4, 10, 14, 51, 97, 124
    triumph over Islam 38, 72, 81, 96, 109
    See also Baptism, *elches*
chronicles 12, 14–15, 19, 30, 36, 39, 51, 65, 80–1, 106–9
    See also Ayora, Bernáldez, Galíndez, Medina y Mendoza, Palencia, Pérez del Pulgar, Pulgar, Santa Cruz, Sículo, Silva, Valera, Zurita
Cieza 34, 131, 188
Cisneros, Francisco Jiménez de (Archbishop and Cardinal) 33, 43–4, 93, 96, 108, 118
Civil War 14–16, 21, 23
Colomera 29, 58, 156
Colonna (Italian barons) 65
Columbus, Christopher 72
Comixa, Aben 32–3, 37, 144, 157
Comunero(s) 75, 108–9, 114
Converso(s)
    avoidance of persecution 6, 30, 49
    the 'converso problem' 9
    Cordoban conversos 12–14
    and the monarchy 43, 58, 77, 87–9
    and the nobility 12–14, 17–18, 52–9, 74
    persecution 15, 19–22, 27–8, 51, 83–6, 111–12
    reconciliation and rehabilitation 47–8
    scholarship and literature 5, 10, 17, 45, 56, 86, 104, 120–4
    social status 5–6, 34, 49, 92–3
    See also limpieza de sangre
Convivencia 41, 116
Córdoba, Alfonso de 12, 20, 84
Córdoba, Gonzalo de 12, 20, 47–8, 52, 85, 88–9, 95, 163, 178
Cortegana, *See* Diego López de Cortegana
Cortesi, Paolo 71–2

D

Daza, Juan (Bishop of Cordoba) 94
Daza, Licenciado Diego 56, 85, 94
Delgadillo, Licenciado Diego 12
Delgado, Mercedes 125, 148, 154
Delicado, Francisco 124
della Rovere, Giulio, *See* Julius II
Devaney, Thomas 116
Deza, Alonso de 78
Deza, Diego de (Archbishop and Inquisitor) 43, 51, 77, 86, 88–90, 92–3, 111
Díaz de Vivar y Mendoza, Rodrigo (Marquis of Zenete) 99, 143, 177
diplomacy 52, 63, 66, 69, 72–6
dissidence 5–6, 110
Doña Mencia 18
Duns Scotus 10, 40, 43, 72, 79

E

Écija 51
Elche(s) 1, 5, 22, 34, 39–41, 44, 85, 102, 119, 121–3, 146
Emilia-Romagna 68
Emirs, *See* Abū al-Ḥasan, Boabdil, Muhammad IX, Sa'ad, Zagal
Encina, Juan del 72
Enrique IV of Castile (1425–1474) 10, 14–16, 18, 27, 48, 57
(alleged) Islamophilia 116, 118–19, 127
Enríquez, Alfonso (Bishop of Osma) 94
Enríquez, Elvira 50, 52, 55
Enríquez, Enrique 50, 52
Enríquez, Fadrique (Almirante de Castilla) 52, 94
Enríquez, Fadrique (Marquis of Tarifa) 51
Erasmus, Desiderius 2, 63, 67, 81, 93, 124, 186
Escalante manuscript 102, 104, 125, 188–90
Escorial manuscript 102–6, 109, 125, 186–90
Espina, Alonso de 10, 111, 116
Excommunication 15, 17, 22, 112, 151

F

Federigo I of Naples (1452–1504) 62–3
Felipe I of Castile/of Hapsburg (1478–1506) 72–6, 79–80, 82, 86–7, 95, 108

Felipe II of Spain (1527–1598) 102, 109
Fernández, Beatriz 12, 19–20
Fernández de Alcaudete, Pedro 19
Fernández de Córdoba, Alfonso (*contador*), *See* Alfonso de Córdoba
Fernández de Córdoba, Alonso (Lord of Aguilar), *See* Alonso de Aguilar
Fernández de Córdoba, Alonso (Lord of Alcaudete) 50
Fernández de Córdoba, Catalina 116, 184
Fernández de Córdoba, Diego (*Alcaide de los Donceles*) 87–8, 90, 94, 108, 115, 135–7, 189
Fernández de Córdoba, Diego (I Count of Cabra, 1410–1481) 14–15, 17, 23–4
Fernández de Córdoba, Diego (II Count of Cabra, 1445–1487) 29, 91, 105, 108, 115, 120, 123, 135–7, 181
Fernández de Córdoba, Diego (III Count of Cabra, 1460–1525) 38, 56, 74, 84–5, 87–90, 97
Fernández de Córdoba, Gonzalo (*Gran Capitán*)
  accounts episode (*cuentas*) 80–1, 118
  conflict with Fernando 74–9, 95, 100, 115
  during conquest of Naples 3, 62–7
  early life and family affairs 16–17, 21, 49–50, 57
  during Granada War 30, 33–4, 36
  political philosophy 93–4, 96–7, 108
  role in papal conclaves 64–8
  in surrender negotiations 41, 143, 145
  as viceroy 43, 68–81, 89, 92, 98
Fernández de Córdoba, María 50
Fernández de Córdoba, Pedro (Lord of Aguilar, 1425–1455,) 14, 23
Fernández de Córdoba, Pedro (Marquis of Priego) 20, 49–52, 55, 92, 106, 111
  conflict with Fernando 75–6, 82, 93–6
  opponent of the Inquisition 74, 85–90, 108–9
  relationship with Hernando de Baeza 52–9, 78–9, 84, 91–2, 100–1, 111
Fernández de Ulloa, Diego 58
Fernando (son of La Romia) 121, 129, 140

Fernando II of Aragon (Fernando el Católico)
  claim on Naples 61–3, 65–6, 69
  conflict with *Gran Capitán*, (*see* under Gonzalo Fernández de Córdoba)
  and *conversos* 87–9
  as Governor of Castile 6–7, 73–5, 108
  during the Granada War 29, 31–3, 142–4
  hawkishness 3, 43, 59, 74, 77, 81–2, 94–7, 114
  and Hernando de Baeza 92
  in Italy 79–81, 93, 100
  resistance to 52, 83, 90, 94–7, 99
  rivalry with Felipe I 75
  See also Catholic Monarchs
Ferrante I of Naples 61
Ferrante II of Naples 62
Florence 65–6, 69–70, 72
Foix, Germaine de 75, 115
Forlì 68–70
Fornovo 62
Fray Fernando 18
frontier 2–3, 5, 15, 22–5, 28–30, 40–1, 116, 127, 138, 141
Fuente, Juan de la 83

G
Gaeta 65, 76
Galíndez de Carvajal, Doctor Lorenzo 102, 104, 107–9
Geraldini, Antonio 42
Gilman, Stephen 7
Girón, Pedro (Master of the Order of Calatrava) 14, 24
Giustinian, Antonio 66, 69, 73
Golden Age 3, 120
Gómez de Medina, Fernán 56
González de Mendoza, Pedro (Cardinal) 19, 22, 71, 99, 107
Gran Capitán, *See* Gonzalo Fernández de Córdoba
Granada
  celebrations of its conquest 42–3, 72, 116–17
  conquest 2, 25–41
  factionalism 126–43 passim
  flood 99, 133

frontier 2, 15, 20, 22–8, 58, 125–8, 131
  post-conquest 44, 83, 86, 88, 90, 99–100
  Pulgar's *Tratado* 104–6
  siege 144–5
  war (1482–1492) 25–32, 81, 135–8
  See also Alhambra, Albaicín, *Capitulaciones*, Christianization, chronicles, emirs
Granados, Juan 80
Guadalajara 33, 106, 134
Guadalupe 13, 51, 111
Guadix 25

H
heresy 4, 6, 10, 19, 40, 43, 48–9, 71, 83, 111–12, 121
Hernando Sánchez, Carlos 76
Herrera, Elvira 49–50, 54–5
Herrera, Gonzalo 47
Hieronymites, *See* Jeronymites
Higuera de Calatrava 24, 131
historiography 43–5, 52, 104–13, 119 *See also* chronicles
Hojeda, Alonso de 19
Hosmín 29
humanism 2, 5, 10, 52, 56, 71, 109, 120, 124

I
Íllora 29, 35, 143, 156
Infantas, Pedro de las 94
Innocent VIII 42, 71
Inquisition
  attacks on Baezas 2–3, 19–21, 27, 47–8, 84–6
  beginnings 4, 12, 15–16, 19
  criticism of 21–2, 40, 44, 79, 97, 104–5, 121
  excesses 83–4
  resistance to 20–1, 77, 86–90
  See also Auto de fe, conversos, Inquisitors, *reconciliados*
Inquisitors, *See* Sancho de Castilla, Diego de Deza, Juan de la Fuente, Francisco Jiménez de Cisneros, Diego López de Cortegana, Diego Rodríguez de Lucero, Torquemada

interpreters 27, 33–4, 38–9, 104, 127, 141, 146
Isabel I of Castile (1451–1504)
  accession to throne 14–16, 18
  charitable gifts 34, 37–8
  converso courtiers 6, 43
  depiction by Hernando de Baeza 100–1, 116, 132
  glorification 3, 42, 110
  implications of her death 3, 6–7, 21, 49, 68, 73–4, 76, 83–4
  See also Catholic Monarchs, Juan, Prince of Castile
Islam 1–2, 34, 42, 56, 109, 117–18
  See also Baptism, *morisco(s),* Muslims
Islamicization/Islamization 40–1, 121–2
Islamophilia 116

J
Jaén 56, 58, 91–3, 116, 152
  Treaty of (1246) 28
Jerome, Saint 56, 83, 136
  Church of 101
Jeronymites 10, 13–14, 17, 19, 22, 51, 58, 136
Jews
  in Castile and Aragon 2, 4, 9–16, 28, 47, 51, 112, 119
  in Granada 5, 25, 44
  in Italy 70, 77
  See also conversos, Judaism
Jiménez de Cisneros, Francisco, *See* Cisneros
Josephus 56
Juan (son of La Romia) 121, 129
Juan II of Aragon 61
Juan II of Castile (1405–1454) 6, 18, 28, 118–20, 125–7
Juan, Prince of Castile and Aragon (1478–1497) 43, 72, 74, 104, 110, 187, 189
Juana of Aragon 62
Juana I of Castile (1479–1555) 72, 74–5, 79–80, 86–9, 93, 95, 108, 111, 115–16
Juana of Castile 'La Beltraneja' 18
Judaism 10, 19, 22, 44, 56, 120
Julius II, Pope 57, 64, 66–8, 71, 73, 77, 83, 89, 93, 101

K
Kumasa, Yusuf Ibn, *See* Aben Comixa

L
La Alcarria 93
La Axarquía 27
La Higueruela (battle, 1431) 119, 126, 187
La Rambla 18, 50
La Romia (wife of Abū al-Ḥasan) 115, 121–2, 124, 129–30, 138, 140, 183
  See also Isabel de Solís
Ladero Quesada, Miguel Ángel 35, 38
Lafuente y Alcántara, Emilio 100–1, 190
Las Casas, Bartolomé de 114
Lasso de la Vega, García 110
Lea, Charles Henry 89
Limpieza de sangre 3, 13, 49, 51, 93, 111, 123
  records 7, 12, 15, 19, 49, 52, 68, 101
Loja 29–30, 33, 58, 96, 136
López de Ayala, Pedro 109
López de Carvajal, Bernardino, Cardinal of Santa Cruz 66–7, 71–2, 87–8, 109
  as Baeza's protector in Rome 7, 57, 61, 67, 73–4, 82, 86, 91–2, 101
  overseer of Cesare Borgia 69–71
  as propagandist 42–3, 74, 110
  supporter of Felipe I 75
López de Cortegana, Diego 93–4
López de Mendoza, Íñigo (Count of Tendilla) 29, 33, 44, 86–8, 90, 97–8
Louis XII of France 62, 65, 70, 73; 75, 100
Lucas de Iranzo, Miguel 116
Lucena 25, 27–8, 36, 39, 88, 90–1, 108, 119–20, 123, 135, 137
Lucena, Juan de 22, 41, 86
Lucero, *See* Diego Rodríguez Lucero
Lumen ad revelationem gentilium 10
Luque 135
Luther, Martin 58, 75, 81

M
Machiavelli, Nicolò 66–8, 81, 115
Maestro del Toro, *See* Alonso de Toro
Málaga 27, 31, 39, 42, 51, 58, 117, 132
Manrique de Lara, Alfonso 94
Manuel, Juan 75
manuscripts, *See* Beinecke, Escalante, Escorial, Real Biblioteca

Marbella 24, 34, 145, 190
Marineo Sículo, Lucio, *See* Sículo
Martínez, Ferrán 9
Martínez de Osma, Pedro 71
Mártir de Anglería, Pedro 52, 56, 74, 83, 85, 87, 94, 107
Maximilian I of Hapsburg (1459–1519) 72–4
Mayorga, Francisco de 87
Medina del Campo 50, 56
Medina Sidonia, Duke of 29, 114, 129
Medina y Mendoza, Francisco 34, 106
Mena, Juan de 6, 18, 56, 71, 120, 135
Mendoza, Cardinal, *See* Pedro González de Mendoza
Mendoza, Francisco de 56, 89, 94
messianism 5, 111, 113
Messina 62
Mexico 102
Milan 62
Mizwar 29, 44, 117, 128, 132, 138–41, 189
Moclín 29, 58, 143, 156
Molina, Beatriz de 34
monasteries
    Calabazanos (Palencia) 51
    Écija 51
    Guadalupe 13, 51
    Santa Isabel la Real (Granada) 99, 128
    Valparaíso (Cordoba) 14, 22
Montejícar 58
Montesinos, Antonio de 124
Montilla 7, 17, 29, 37, 47, 51–2
    castle 94, 96, 114
    vicar, *See* Blásquez
Montoro, Antón de 17
Mora, Abrahén de 25, 27, 30, 33, 59, 117, 134, 141
Mora, Yusa de 33, 37
Morales, Alonso de 63, 92, 175
Morales, Doctor Antonio de 55
More, Sir Thomas 124
Morisco(s) 3, 41, 44, 93, 107, 119–20, 123
Moro(s) 117–18
Mudéjar(s) 1, 24, 30, 32, 44, 93, 118, 134, 137, 141, 144
Muhammad IX of Granada 125, 186
Muhammad XI of Granada, *See* Boabdil

Muhammad XII of Granada, *See* Zagal
Muslims 1, 13, 15, 23–4, 34, 41–2, 44, 116–21, 186
    See also Baptism, Christianization, Islam, *morisco(s)*, *mudejar(s)*

N
Naples, city 43, 69–70, 73, 81
    Baeza's letters from 52–5, 78, 99–100
Naples, kingdom
    Gran Capitán as Viceroy of 73–4, 76–9, 89
    Spanish conquest of 3, 61–7, 75, 98
Nasrids 2, 24, 28, 37, 40, 113–14, 118–19, 123
Naturel, Philibert 75, 87
Navarre 90
Nebrija, Antonio de 110
New World 1, 10, 41, 71–2, 106, 114, 124
    See also Mexico
Nicuesa, Luis de 52, 117
Niebla 93, 114
North Africa 44, 67, 86, 90, 108, 129, 187
    See also Africa
Núñez de Toledo, Hernán 120

O
Ocampo, Florián de 110
Olmedo 126
Oropesa, Alonso de 10, 13–14, 19, 45, 51, 97
Orsini (Italian barons) 65
Ostia 69

P
Pacheco, Catalina 52
Pacheco, Francisco 50, 54–5, 109
Pacheco, Juan 14–15
Palencia, Alonso de 33, 37, 39, 56, 107, 109, 117
Palermo 106
Palma del Río 50
Pandolfino, Francesco 69
Pedrosa, *Licenciado* Juan de 50, 78, 80
Peixo, Luis 78, 80
El Pequeñí 32
Pérez de Guzmán, Fernán 109, 119
Pérez del Pulgar, Hernán de 29–30, 33–4, 36, 41, 97, 134

Pisa 65, 72
    See also Schism of Pisa
Pius III 65–6
Pogroms 5, 9, 12, 16–17, 28
Ponce de León, Pedro 89
Ponce de León, Rodrigo (Duke of Arcos) 55, 58
Popes, *See* Alexander VI, Innocent VIII, Julius II, Pius III
Porcuna 29, 55, 137
Portocarrero, Luis 50
Portocarrero, María 50
Priego, I Marquis of, *See* Pedro Fernández de Córdoba
propaganda 39, 43, 71, 107, 116
prophecy 34, 42, 71, 84, 111, 132–3
    See also messianism, providentialism
providentialism 109
Pulgar, Fernando de 6, 21, 58, 109, 121, 156
    and Hernando de Baeza 37, 102, 104–6

Q
Queen
    first wife of Abū al-Ḥasan 128–31, 134, 138, 144–5
    See also Isabel I, Juana I
Quiroga, Vasco de (Bishop of Michoacán) 102

R
Ramírez de Baeza, Pedro 12
Ramírez de Guzmán, Diego (Bishop of Catania) 86, 94
Real Biblioteca de Madrid 104, 125, 187–90
Reconciliado(s) 4, 20–1, 48
Reconquista
    in historiography 43
    as ideology 3, 72, 119
Reggio-Calabria 77
Regolano, Tommasso 65, 67
religious self-determination 2, 28, 40
Riario, Raffaele 43
Río, Baltasar del 6
Robledo, Abrahén 31, 33, 134
Rodríguez, Aldonza 48
Rodríguez de Baeza, Alfonso (paymaster of Alcalá) 12, 15
Rodríguez de Baeza, Alonso/Alfón/Alfonso 12, 16, 151
Rodríguez de Baeza, Fernán 12, 14, 158
Rodríguez de Baeza, Francisco 12, 100
Rodríguez de Baeza, Gonzalo 12–13, 16, 18–20, 150
Rodríguez de Baeza, Juan (*corregidor* of Medina del Campo) 56
Rodríguez de Baeza, Juan (Hernando's son) 12, 48, 57, 67, 168
Rodríguez de Baeza, *Licenciado* Juan 168
Rodríguez de Lucero, Diego (Inquisitor) 44, 55, 74, 83–90, 92–4, 96–8, 114–15
    See also Gonzalo de Ayora, Diego de Deza
Rojas, Francisco de (Ambassador in Rome) 65–6, 69–70, 73–4, 78–9, 81, 83, 87
Rome 6–7, 42–3, 48–9, 51, 58, 61, 75, 91, 123–4
    Hernando de Baeza in 65–70, 73–4, 77, 93, 101
    See also Carvajal, Diplomacy, Vatican
Ronda 42
Roussillon 65
Rufo, Juan (Bishop of Bertinoro) 87
Ruiz Domènec, José Enrique 16, 21, 41, 57, 97

S
Sa'ad (emir 1454–1455 and 1455–1462) 126–8, 187
Salamanca 71, 106
Salar 29, 58, 156
Salobreña 128, 140
Sánchez de Córdoba, Mencia 12, 17, 48
Sánchez de Córdoba, Sancho 15–16, 19
Sannazaro, Jacopo 43
Santa Cruz, Alonso 106, 108–9
Santa Cruz, Cardinal, *See* Bernardino López de Carvajal
Santa Cruz, *mudéjar* 118, 137
Santa Fe 32, 144
Santa María de la Trassierra 94
Santaella 20, 50
Santiago (St James, patron of Spain) 120, 135–7
Santiago, Order of 96, 100
Santiago de Calatrava 24, 131

Sanuto, Mariano 76
Savona 100, 107
Schism of Pisa 71, 101
Seville 9, 19, 31–2, 40, 51, 144
    cathedral 6, 48–9, 58, 63, 67, 82, 92–3, 111
    See also Diego de Deza, Diego López de Cortegana
Sicily 61–2, 73, 75, 77, 106
Sículo, Lucio Marineo 36, 52, 106–8, 110
Sierra Bermeja 24, 51, 117
(Las) Siete Partidas 28, 40
Silva, Tristán de 38, 107
Simancas, Francisco de 94
Slaves 5, 29, 34, 39, 131, 139
Solier, Pedro (Bishop of Cordoba) 15
Solís, Alfonso (Bishop of Cadiz) 19
Solís, Isabel de 183, 187 *See also* La Romia
Szpiech, Ryan 122

T
Talavera, Fray Hernando de 6, 40
    accused by Inquisition 83, 87–8, 93, 98
    as Archbishop of Granada 19, 34, 42–4, 116, 119
Tarifa, Marquis of, *See* Fadrique Enríquez
tax collection 13, 15–22, 48, 152
Tendilla, Count of, *See* Íñigo López de Mendoza
Toledo 9, 13, 27, 88, 92, 134, 138
Toro 87
Toro, Alonso de (Maestro de Toro) 55, 83
Torquemada (Inquisitor) 85, 89
Torquemada, Juan de 10
Torre, Doctor de la 94
Torres, Jorge de 88
Torres Naharro, Bartolomé 72
(Las) Trescientas 56, 120
Tubal 110

U
Úbeda 34

V
Valencia 94, 100, 107
Valera, Diego de 21, 57, 120
Valladolid 90, 108
Valparaíso, *See* monasteries
Vatican 6, 57–9, 67–8, 71
    See also Popes
Velasco, Bernardino 94
Velasco, Diego 20
Velasco, Gaspar de 14
Velasco, Pedro 12
Velasco Romero, Gonzalo 55–6, 58, 165
Vélez Blanco 29, 138, 141
Vélez Málaga 58, 142–3
Vélez Rubio 29, 138, 141
Venice 62–3, 72
Verardi, Carlo 43
Villacarrillo 34, 131, 188
Villafáfila, Concord of 79
Viterbo, Annio di 110

W
Wills 7, 17, 34, 51, 55, 74, 84

Y
Yusaf (brother of Boabdil) 138–40

Z
Zafra, Bartolomé de 19
Zafra, Hernando de 6, 33–5, 37, 39, 41, 145, 158
Zag, Rabí 16
Zagal (Muhammad XII) 29–32, 100, 132, 138–43
Zahara 25
Zamora 58
Zenete, Marquis of, *See* Rodrigo Díaz de Vivar
Zorayda, *See La Romia*

www.ingramcontent.com/pod-product-compliance
Lightning Source LLC
Chambersburg PA
CBHW062220300426
44115CB00012BA/2150